Authoritarianism and Resistance in Turkey

Esra Özyürek · Gaye Özpınar
Emrah Altındiş
Editors

Authoritarianism and Resistance in Turkey

Conversations on Democratic and Social Challenges

 Springer

Editors
Esra Özyürek
European Institute
London School of Economics
London
UK

Emrah Altındiş
Harvard Medical School
Harvard University
Harvard, MA
USA

Gaye Özpınar
Law Office
Boston, MA
USA

ISBN 978-3-319-76704-8   ISBN 978-3-319-76705-5   (eBook)
https://doi.org/10.1007/978-3-319-76705-5

Library of Congress Control Number: 2018934378

Cover photo by Fatih Pinar

Printed on acid-free paper

This Springer imprint is published by the registered company Springer International Publishing AG
part of Springer Nature
The registered company address is: Gewerbestrasse 11, 6330 Cham, Switzerland

For those unnamed heroes who have dedicated their lives for a just and equal world.

Acknowledgements

This book would not have come to fruition if it were not for the Gezi Uprisings of 2013 or the ongoing resistance of the people of Turkey against a brutal state and political system. Despite the ever-increasing government authoritarianism and oppression, the democratic struggle in Turkey is very much alive. Every day thousands of people in Turkey including women, students, union workers, socialists, LBGTQ activists, Kurdish liberation movement activists, and Alevis hold meetings, organize panels and rallies, and take courageous steps as part of their democracy struggle. Therefore, it is essential to start acknowledging these people and their families who risk their lives to have a more democratic Turkey.

Furthermore, we would not be compelled to start an international dialogue at times of neoliberal authoritarianism among different social movements if it were not for the millions of people fighting against different faces of oppression within spaces including the Black Lives Matter, Occupy Wall Street, Tahrir Square, Syntagma Square, Indignados, the Kurdish Liberation movement, and many other unheard forms of resistance around the world.

We, as editors of this book, have been living abroad for a long time, and after getting so many questions about Turkey we came to realize that there is no book in English which directly gives the perspective of the individuals who struggle for freedom and democracy in Turkey every day. We chose a nontraditional format based on interviews with these brave individuals to reach out to a wider audience, including those readers who might be outside of the usually limited academic boundaries. Emrah and Gaye originally conceptualized and started the book and Esra joined the project toward the end and help it bring to completion.

Since we started the book project at the end of 2014, two contributors to this book were arrested for purely political reasons. Our friend and a prominent investigative journalist Ahmet Şık was arrested on December 29, 2016 and is still behind bars in Silivri Prison in Istanbul because of the illogical allegations and charges pressed against him. Professor Şebnem Korur Fincancı, a very important human rights defender and forensic doctor, was arrested in June 2016 and spent 10 days in prison for supporting a freedom of expression campaign, "Guest Editor-in-Chief Campaign for Özgur Gündem daily".

Furthermore, Prof. Yüksel Taşkın, Prof. Ahsen Deniz Morva, Prof. Bülent Şık, and Prof. İbrahim Kaboğlu lost their academic positions as part of a bigger purge of hundreds of academics for having signed a Peace Petition asking the government to stop the violence against Kurdish citizens. Most of the academics who took part in this project are signatories of the Peace Petition and are currently being prosecuted with 7.5-year prison charges. Some of the contributors are living in self-imposed exile. We are proud of their courage and for our names to be associated with theirs. It is important to note that in times of fear, it takes courage to talk in public and before an international audience about authoritarianism and resistance. The process for this book was a collective effort from the very first day with no expectation to have any financial gains, so we cannot thank enough to the authors of the book for their contributions, patience, and strong will.

We would also like to thank Zeynep Oğuz, Nesi Altaras, İstem Özen, Seda Saluk, and Ahu Sıla Bayer for translating some of the interviews originally given in Turkish. We thank Sofia Arias, Khury Petersen-Smith, Anand Vaidya, Alpana Mehta, and four anonymous readers for commenting on the manuscript and special thanks to Greg Bennetts for editing some of the text and Theresa Truax-Gischler for editing the entire manuscript. We'd also like to acknowledge journalist photographer Fatih Pınar for the cover picture.

The intellectuals have a strong role in both resistance to and reproduction of the power relations. In the course of Turkish history, intellectuals were specifically targeted by the government and never stopped the resistance. From Sabahattin Ali to Tahir Elçi to Hrant Dink, the history of Turkey can be written based on this resistance. We wanted to make an intellectual contribution to the democracy struggle of Turkey and the world to better understand today's Turkey. Thank you for being a part of our collective project, which we hope will continue with your feedback, thoughts, questions, and essays. Thank you for reading this work.

Emrah Altındiş
Gaye Özpınar
Esra Özyürek

Contents

About the Editors

Esra Özyürek is an Associate Professor and the Chair for Contemporary Turkish studies at the European Institute, London School of Economics. She received her B.A. in sociology and political science at Boğaziçi University, Istanbul and her M.A. and Ph.D. in anthropology at the University of Michigan, Ann Arbor. Before joining LSE, she taught in the anthropology department at the University of California, San Diego. As a political anthropologist, she seeks to understand how Islam, Christianity, secularism, and nationalism are dynamically positioned in relation to each other in Turkey and in Europe. She is the author of *Being German, Becoming Muslim: Race, Religion and Conversion in the New Europe* (Princeton University Press, 2014) and *Nostalgia for the Modern: State Secularism and Everyday Politics in Turkey* (Duke University Press, 2007). She is also the editor of *The Politics of Public Memory in Turkey* (Syracuse University Press, 2007) and *Unuttukları ve Hatırladıklarıyla Türkiye'nin Toplumsal Hafızası* (İletişim Yayınevi, 2002).

Gaye Özpınar is an immigration and human rights lawyer, born and raised in Turkey. She came to the US to study politics at Brandeis University and stayed on to continue her education in law at Suffolk University. While pursuing her studies, she was a student volunteer with the Suffolk Civil Rights Project and the Massachusetts American Civil Liberties Union. Through the Political Asylum and Immigration Reform Project, she worked with many torture survivors. She is the past president and a current board member of Bostonbul, a forum of activists that organically came together in Boston in June 2013 as the Gezi protests took place in Turkey. She has given interviews with Turkish dailies such as *Agos*, *T24*, and *BirGün* on human rights issues. She is also a member of the American Immigration Lawyers Association and the National Lawyers Guild. In 2015, she was selected as a Rising Star and a Top Female Attorney in Massachusetts by *Super Lawyers* magazine.

Emrah Altındiş is an award-winning Medical Scientist at Harvard Medical School (Boston, USA). He received his M.Sc. in Biotechnology from Middle East Technical University (Ankara, Turkey) and Ph.D. in Molecular and Cellular Biology from Bologna University (Bologna, Italy). He has published several scientific research articles in the fields of microbiology and diabetes. He has been also a human rights activist, and for over a decade wrote political opinion pieces to various Turkish newspapers (Radikal, BirGün, Cumhuriyet), journals (Birikim), and websites (Diken, Bianet), and has given interviews to several media outlets.

Abbreviations

AKP	Justice and Development Party (*Adalet ve Kalkınma Partisi*)
CHP	Republican People's Party (*Cumhuriyet Halk Partisi*)
DİSK	Confederation of Progressive Trade Unions (*Türkiye Devrimci İşçi Sendikaları Konfederasyonu*)
DP	Democratic Party (*Demokrat Parti*)
ECHR	European Court of Human Rights
HAK-İŞ	Confederation of Turkish Real Trade Unions (*Hak İşçi Sendikaları Konfederasyonu*)
HDP	People's Democratic Party (*Halkların Demokratik Partisi*)
ISIS	Islamic State of Iraq and Syria
KCK	Union of Kurdistan Communities (*Koma Civakên Kurdistan*)
KESK	Confederation of Public Employees' Trade Unions (*Kamu Emekçileri Sendikaları Konfederasyonu*)
Memur-Sen	Confederation of Civil Servant Trade Unions (*Memur Sendikaları Konfedarasyonu*)
MHP	Nationalist Movement Party (*Milliyetçi Hareket Partisi*)
NIA	National Intelligence Agency (*Milli Istihbarat Teskilati*)
PKK	Kurdistan Workers' Party (*Partiya Karkerên Kurdistanê*)
TİP	Workers Party of Turkey (*Türkiye İşçi Partisi*)
TİSK	Confederation of Turkish Employers Unions (*Türkiye İşveren Sendikaları Konfederasyonu*)
TÜRK-İŞ	Confederation of Turkish Trade Unions (*Türkiye İşçi Sendikaları Konfederasyonu*)
WEF	World Economic Forum

Introduction

Esra Özyürek

Abstract This book is an attempt to understand authoritarianism and resistance in Turkey by focusing on what is new and what is old in the country. However, instead of arguing for or against the thesis that Turkey changed since 2002, it shows, the root of the most recent transformations in Turkey is the 1980 military coup. Based on interviews with the country's leading progressive intellectuals, the book's themes follow the major changes that have occurred since the transformative 1980 military coup. By focusing on this pivotal moment, the book tries to unsettle the assumption that Erdoğan and his Islamic ideology are the sole actors of recent turn towards authoritarianism in contemporary Turkey. It draws attention to the simultaneous destruction of democracy and opening of the country to global flows of capital, goods, ideas, and technologies that continue to influence both mainstream and dissident politics. In so doing, it demonstrates that Erdoğan is not simply a new reactionary version of the revolutionary Mustafa Kemal Atatürk who is going to reverse time and send society back to 1922, before the birth of the Republic of Turkey. Rather, he is a talented leader who harvested seeds sown for less democracy and more capitalism in 1980.

Keywords Turkey · Authoritarianism · Resistance

There are two possible beginnings to this introduction:

The Turkey we used to know is not there anymore. Before reaching its 100th anniversary in 2023, the top-down, modernized, secularized republican regime we once knew, wherein a bureaucratic elite makes the decisions for its people, assimilates ethnic differences, and prioritizes its military, economic, and cultural alliances with the West over the East, will no longer exist. In 2002, pious Sunni Muslims whom the early republican regime marginalized and silenced, but always relied upon, took over the government. Fifteen years after their rise to power, they

E. Özyürek (✉)
European Institute, London School of Economics, London, UK
e-mail: e.g.ozyurek@lse.ac.uk

have entirely transformed the country. Under the strong and single-handed leadership of Recep Tayyip Erdoğan, Turkey now has an authoritarian regime based on Islamic principles and unregulated capitalism.

A European Union candidate whose membership was once a serious prospect, Turkey no longer has much of a relationship with the EU. Once NATO's biggest ally, it no longer allows member states to use its main air base. Its official doctrine, which once forcefully assimilated ethnic differences, now embraces sectarian language. A country that once had an albeit imperfect parliamentary democracy just rendered its parliament defunct, placing all judiciary, legislative, and executive powers in the hands of a single ruler who will also have the power to unilaterally control the economy and declare wars. A state that once strove to perform, if not enact, egalitarianism now unabashedly distinguishes between those citizens who support the regime and those who do not.

Or:

Close to celebrating its 100th anniversary, it looks like Turkey in 2023 will be quite similar to the single-party regime established in 1923. It is ruled top-down, economy, judiciary, and legislative are in the hands of the political elite, opposition is heavily stifled, and cult of leadership stands in place of democracy. Just like in the early of the early Republic, New Turkey is also quite isolated. It is not at the moment clear who its allies are.

Is this a "New Turkey" as the President Erdoğan and his cadres likes to call it? Or is it the Old Turkey in new garments? This New Turkey, they claim, is also the original old one. The "origin" invoked here is the Ottoman Empire with its caliphate still in place. Erdoğan sometimes says that he will take the country back 80 years to a time before the republic was declared and the caliphate abolished. Other times, he says he will take it back 200 years, to a time before the constitution and parliament were introduced.

This book is an attempt to understand what is new and what is old about Turkey. However, instead of arguing for or against the thesis that Turkey changed since 2002, it shows, the root of the most recent transformations in Turkey is the 1980 military coup. Based on interviews with the country's leading progressive intellectuals, the book's themes follow the major changes that have occurred since the transformative 1980 military coup. By focusing on this pivotal moment, the book tries to unsettle the assumption that Erdoğan and his Islamic ideology are the sole actors in contemporary Turkey. It draws attention to the simultaneous destruction of democracy and opening of the country to global flows of capital, goods, ideas, and technologies that continue to influence both mainstream and dissident politics. In so doing, it demonstrates that Erdoğan is not simply a new reactionary version of the revolutionary Mustafa Kemal Atatürk who is going to reverse time and send society back to 1922, before the birth of the Republic of Turkey. Rather, he is a talented leader who harvested seeds sown for less democracy and more capitalism in 1980.

Modern Turkey was born out of the ashes of the Ottoman Empire. The Late Ottomans fought against the Greek army and committed genocide against the

Armenians and Assyrians. Atatürk, the founding "father of the republic," brought together Turkish and Kurdish forces to reestablish a state. After the foundation of the republic in 1923, he pushed the Kurds to the sidelines and attempted to Westernize the country with the iron fist of an authoritarian leader. Under his rule, Turkey adopted the Latin script, changed the weekly day of rest from Friday to Sunday, made men take off their fezzes and wear hats with brims, gave women the right to vote and to be elected to government, and established a state-sponsored industry that would create a Turkish-Muslim bourgeoisie. This period was also marked by enormous pressure being brought to bear on Islamic groups and lifestyles.

During the first general elections of 1950, the conservative Democratic Party (*Demokrat Parti*, hereafter DP) won the elections. Promising the country more democracy, the party became increasingly authoritarian. During this period, Turkey became a member of NATO and benefited from Marshall Plan aid aimed at rebuilding war-torn Europe. The aid helped to industrialize agriculture and connect the country through the construction of a system of highways. In 1960, the military launched a coup d'état and forcefully introduced a more democratic constitution. The period between 1960 and 1980 saw an increase in industrialization, workers' rights, politicization, and polarization of citizens at the far left and far right ends of the political spectrum.

Although the military has always been a major political player in Turkish politics, it left its biggest mark on the country with the 1980 coup d'état. By taking workers' rights away and bringing an end to state protectionism in certain fields overnight, it turned the country into a cheap labor market and opened its doors to the circuit of global capitalism. Simultaneously, the generals put unbalanced pressure on the left, while the military junta worked to embolden right-wing movements, thereby mobilizing Turkish and Islamic identities as a sociopolitical glue—a "Turkish-Islamic synthesis" designed to hold the nation together and prevent political friction. Throughout the following decades, students were taught a Turkish-Islamic chauvinist ideology that envisioned Islam as a superior religion and Turks as superior Muslims.

As the 1980s brought new capital to Turkey, religiously conservative Anatolian businessmen benefited and in turn supported religiously conservative political parties. Kurds are among those who carried the heaviest burden of the 1980 military coup because the generals increased pressure on the already-marginalized group. The Kurdistan Workers' Party (*Partiya Karkerên Kurdistanê*, hereafter PKK) was established by a group of Kurdish students in the politicized atmosphere of 1978 and carried out its first attack in 1984 in the politically oppressive atmosphere of the post-junta regime. The PKK has proved to be one the longest surviving guerrilla organizations in the world and a party to the war that killed over 40,000 people over the course of some 30 years. In their fight against the insurgents, the Turkish state has penalized virtually all of its Kurdish citizens, forcefully removing them from their villages in security operations, creating terror in Kurdish-majority cities, and subjecting them to disappearances that still await justice. Forced migrations have added millions to cities without proper planning, and Kurds have become a source of cheap labor in mushrooming sweatshops.

While heavy war raged in the east of the country, the western regions saw an influx of new ideologies, communication technologies, and riches brought by new access to transnational capital. As Turkey gained access in the late 1980s to private TV and radio for the first time, new ideas and identities, including feminism, environmentalism, gay and minority rights, were first openly discussed. Turkey was slowly entering into the intellectual and artistic streams and networks of the world. Film festivals, an international art biennial, and high quality academic conferences were hosted in Istanbul. Istanbul became a new nexus of multiple flows of people, capital, ideas, and goods, including drugs and arms. At the same time the city itself was discovered as a new capital that could be sold to international investors.

The 1990s were also marked by deep economic crisis, high inflation rates, and an increasingly intensifying war against the Kurds. The neoliberal policies and primacy of investors over bureaucrats that the Justice and Development Party (*Adalet ve Kalkınma Partisi*, hereafter AKP) built itself on were first established by the right-wing governments of Turgut Özal and Tansu Çiller. The Turkish economy was finally stabilized when Kemal Derviş, former head of the United Nations Development Programme, was appointed as minister of economy by Bülent Ecevit. Derviş implemented major structural reforms and made sure that the state banks, and especially the central bank, would remain independent of political pressure. He also pushed for major structural reforms in agriculture, energy, and budget processes, releasing them from political control. Thanks to these policies, in 2001 he was able to secure 20 billion US dollars in new loans from the IMF and the World Bank, which helped bring down inflation regularly approaching three-digit numbers as low as 12% in one year. Economists concur that it was these policies that were behind the so-called Turkish economic miracle the AKP government benefited from through the first decade of the 2000s.

In the 1990s, Erdoğan, the then mayor of Istanbul, benefited the most from the new capital streaming especially into Istanbul. As the city witnessed an unprecedented level of urban transformation, a new class of builders was created. The city was transformed by massive building projects: several bridges and underground passages connected the Asian and European continents; new land masses were created by filling in the sea; and, ironically, the 1999 earthquake became the legitimating point for expropriation and demolition of old buildings and the construction of new ones. The new wealth and other transformations in the country carried Erdoğan and his party to national power in 2002, and he remained there while steadily increasing his power base. Erdoğan and the AKP utilized the new communication technologies available to Turkey to individually connect with citizens in need and to thereby receive votes from then in return. AKP officials boasted of figuring out "the sociology" of Turkey. Under the AKP, the state resources were distributed in return for votes.

The AKP government was in the beginning supported by Western powers who saw Erdoğan as the savior who would introduce a moderate Islamic democracy to the Middle East, thereby opening up the entire region to global capitalism. At the time, Turkey had embraced more democratic measures, had dramatically improved its economy, had successfully curtailed the power of the army, and had become a European Union accession candidate. However, as the AKP consolidated its power, it became less liberal. Or, to put it more pointedly, it became increasingly authoritarian in order to consolidate its power. As the government began to view parliament and the judiciary as impediments to economic growth driven by the construction sector, it took steps to weaken both. And as the Arab Spring failed and turned into the Arab Winter, the AKP's dreams of coming out of this historic moment as a regional leader were crushed. At the time, Turkey became involved in the Syrian civil war by supporting Islamist dissidents with the hope of toppling Bashar Assad, gaining control over parts of Syria, and staving off the rising Kurdish movement.

One could argue that the AKP has always been built on a reactionary ideology, and that the liberalizing promises were not possible to fulfill. The decades-old National Outlook (*Milli Görüş*) ideology within which Erdoğan and the AKP cadres had been socialized has been Islamist, nationalist, and anti-Semitic. When he was in high school, Erdoğan wrote, directed, and played the lead role in a play with the title "Mason, Communist, Jew." Even though Erdoğan distanced himself in the early 2000s from this movement, when he first introduced the idea of an executive presidency, he told foreign journalists that the ideal successful president in a unitary state he had in his mind was none other than Adolf Hitler (Spencer 2016). Even though his advisors later claimed this statement was taken out of context, the Nazi leader has been a figure of adoration among people close to him. Similarly, in an interview he gave when still the mayor of Istanbul, Erdoğan declared that democracy was a train he would ride and then debark from as soon as he reached his destination. We can never know how things would have turned out had the Arab Spring succeeded, but there is sufficient evidence to suggest that Erdoğan would allow democracy only as long as it benefitted him.

In 2017, Turkey looks dramatically different. Once the strongest ally of NATO, its American and German allies are now looking to establish new air bases as an alternative to Turkey's İncirlik. Once the darling of the EU, Erdoğan and his cabinet members have been prevented from giving speeches to Turkish citizens in several European countries. A frustrated Turkey tries to balance triangulated relations between the USA, Russia, and China, but has yet to gain an advantageous position. The Turkish economy is dramatically worsening, support for the AKP is plummeting, and the government is becoming increasingly authoritarian, as can be seen with the new measures passed in the suspiciously close 2017 constitutional referendum, condemned by international observers for irregularities including ballot-box stuffing. The Kurdish-Turkish peace process (2013–2015), initiated by the AKP together with the jailed PKK leader Abdullah Öcalan, has come to a halt, and the government has begun a major crackdown on its one-time allies, resulting in unprecedented human rights violations. Many of the democratic rights and freedoms gained in the early 2000s are now lost.

In the 2010s, the AKP radically altered the balance of power in Turkey. In 2014, it broke off relations with one of its closest allies, the US-based cleric Fethullah

Gülen, and accused him of masterminding the failed coup attempt of July 2016. When the AKP came to power in early 2000s, they had popular support but not the support of the military and bureaucratic cadres. And so they made an alliance with Fethullah Gülen, a former provincial charismatic imam who led a tight community, and who had become rich and powerful beginning in the 1980s by investing money in education. The Gülen movement provided the AKP with loyal military personnel, judges, teachers, police, and other bureaucratic personnel, and in return the AKP allowed Gülen members to take over these institutions. Gülenists were quick to return the favor by initiating major high-profile trials against all actors that could challenge the AKP. The Ergenekon and Balyoz trials targeted high-level military officers, journalists, and opposition lawyers for plotting a coup against the government. At the same time, the Union of Kurdistan Communities (Koma Civakên Kurdistan, hereafter KCK) trial targeted pro-Kurdish intellectuals and activists. Gülen-affiliated lawyers used fabricated evidence, and the trial procedure did not follow procedure. Yet, as from 2014, this alliance also broke down due to internal power struggles that are not yet completely clear to outside observers. Gülenists released voice recordings related to major AKP corruption scandals. In return, the AKP declared war on the Gülen movement. They took over their television stations, newspapers, universities, schools, and major holding companies and began to clear them from the military, police forces, and judiciary.

With the military coup attempt of July 2016, Turkey took a major turn. Because the power of the military had been curtailed over the preceding decade, the incidence took all observers by surprise. This diminishment in power likely led the military—heretofore notorious for being able to carry out successful coups—to attempt a surprisingly amateurish and poorly coordinated intervention. Within a few hours, Erdoğan had pointed the finger at Fethullah Gülen and had called upon citizens to descend into the streets and stop the coup. Erdoğan's followers blocked tanks with their bodies and lynched soldiers, many of whom seemed unaware that they were part of a coup. As soon as the threat had passed, Erdoğan declared that the coup attempt had been a gift from God, and under the state of emergency that ensued he forcefully purged anyone he viewed as being linked to the Gülen movement, along with other Kurdish and left-wing opposition members. The measures that followed the failed coup are not too far off from those enacted during its 1980 successful forerunner. In the post-coup-attempt purges, some 150,000 government personnel were dismissed, 100,000 individuals were detained and 50,000 arrested, 149 media outlets were shut down, 150 journalists jailed, 17 universities closed, 8,000 academic personnel were dismissed, vast quantities of property were confiscated, and close to 1,000 allegedly Gülen-affiliated businesses are taken over by the state (Srivastava 2017). During emergency measures, access to Twitter and YouTube was blocked. At the time of this writing, access to Wikipedia has been blocked indefinitely because the web site makes connections between the Turkish government and a terrorist organization, namely ISIS, the Islamic State of Iraq and Syria. The top echelon of Kurdish politicians has been jailed, and elected mayors in the southeast—and later in the west—have been replaced with interior ministry personnel. Those purged include the investigative journalist Ahmet Şık, previously jailed for one year in 2011–2012 for having outed the Gülenist movement. In December 2016, Şık is once again incarcerated, this time with the accusation that he himself is a Gülenist.

Under state of emergency measures, Turkey held the most significant referendum of its 93-year history. With a slim margin of only 2%, the Turkish people voted in favor of constitutional transition to an executive presidency. International agencies such as the Organization for Security and Co-operation in Europe, invited to observe the referendum, noted that the campaign took place on an unlevel playing field; the "No" campaign had next to no opportunity to make its case and a number of senior officials had equated "No" supporters with terrorist sympathizers (OSCE 2017). At the time of the election, nine MPs, including the two co-chairs of the pro-Kurdish Peoples' Democratic Party (*Halkların Demokratik Partisi*, hereafter HDP) were in jail. Significantly, the Republican People's Party (*Cumhuriyet Halk Partisi*, hereafter CHP) claimed that some 3 million votes did not have the official stamp or signature necessary to validate them. In other words, although Erdoğan held all powers in his hand and managed to make the opposition ineffective, he had much less support than he expected. Moreover, he no longer has the enthusiastic support of Western countries, and Turkey's once strong economy took a downturn.

In this volume, we attempt to give voice to progressive public intellectuals activitists who experienced these dramatic transformations up close and who have dared to take a position on them. As the AKP government ruled by Erdoğan was moving the country's economy from that of a massive neoliberal project toward an authoritarian capitalism, Turkey also witnessed unprecedented protests, including the 2013 Gezi Park protests and the 2015 Kurdish uprising. Gezi protests were grounded in the decades-long struggles of feminists, environmentalists, human rights activists, a budding LGBTQ rights activism, and the struggle for the recognition of minorities. At a time when democracy movements around the world are under attack, we believe there is much to be learned from Turkey's unique and not so unique experiences. One could argue that the Gezi protests in Turkey were a part of a global movement that swept the world from Syntagma Square in Athens to Tahrir Square in Cairo, from the Indignados (Outraged) movement in Spain to Occupy Wall Street in the US. This book is thus also an attempt to open a dialogue with those who are interested not just in Turkey, but also in democracy struggles of the 21st century taking place under neoliberal and authoritarian regimes cross the globe.

This volume brings together not only academics, but also people who have devoted themselves politically and have chosen to take personal risks in exercising their democratic rights. Both the interviewees and the interviewers are public intellectuals and experts on their topics. It is striking how many of the contributors to this volume are either in jail (Ahmet Şık), or have been in and out of jail (Şebnem Korur Fincancı, Pınar Selek), have been dismissed from their positions and have had their passports cancelled (Ahsen Deniz Morva Kablamacı, Yüksel Taşkın, İbrahim Kaboğlu, Bülent Şık), or have been forced to live in exile (several). And had we not been able to rely on our personal contacts within the internationally located progressive movement of Turkish citizens, we would not have been able to persuade such brilliant interviewers to conduct these interviews for us.

References

OSCE Office for Democratic Institutions and Human Rights. (2017). Turkey, Constitutional Referendum, 16 April 2017: Statement of Preliminary Findings and Conclusions. Retrieved November 20, 2017 from http://www.osce.org/odihr/elections/turkey/311721.

Spencer, R. (2016). Turkey's president says all he wants is same powers as Hitler. *Telegraph*. http://www.telegraph.co.uk/news/worldnews/europe/turkey/12077703/Turkeys-president-says-all-he-wants-is-same-powers-as-Hitler.html.

Srivastava, M. (2017). Erdogan's blacklist. *Financial Times*. https://ig.ft.com/vj/turkey-purge-victims-voices/.

Author Biography

Esra Özyürek is an associate professor and the chair for contemporary Turkish studies at the European Institute, London School of Economics. She received her BA in sociology and political science at Boğaziçi University, Istanbul and her MA and PhD in anthropology at the University of Michigan, Ann Arbor. Before joining LSE, she taught in the anthropology department at the University of California, San Diego. As a political anthropologist, Dr. Özyürek seeks to understand how Islam, Christianity, secularism, and nationalism are dynamically positioned in relation to each other in Turkey and in Europe. She is the author of *Being German, Becoming Muslim: Race, Religion and Conversion in the New Europe* (Princeton University Press, 2014) and *Nostalgia for the Modern: State Secularism and Everyday Politics in Turkey* (Duke University Press, 2007). She is also the editor of *The Politics of Public Memory in Turkey* (Syracuse University Press, 2007) and *Unuttukları ve Hatırladıklarıyla Türkiye'nin Toplumsal Hafızası* (İletişim Yayınevi, 2002).

Part I
An Overview of History

Kemalism and the Republican People's Party (CHP)

Baskın Oran and Karabekir Akkoyunlu

Abstract From the late 18th century onward, the twin revolutions of industrialization and nationalism posed existential threats to multireligious, multiethnic, multicultural territorial empires like those of the Hapsburgs and the Ottomans. During this period, the imperial ruling elite responded to these new challenges using various ideological interventions. In the Ottoman Empire, these were, respectively, Ottomanism, Islamism, and Turkism. Kemalism is the offspring of this turbulent process, borne out of the rise and fall of the three ideologies of Ottomanism, Islamism, and Turkism and the experience of a decade of war and destruction between 1912 and 1922. It emerged as the ideology of revolutionary Westernization from above, conceived and carried out by the modernized intelligentsia of a largely premodern society.

Keywords Turkey · Kemalism

Where should we locate Kemalism in the genealogy of governing ideologies of the Ottoman Empire and Turkey?

From the late 18th century onward, the twin revolutions of industrialization and nationalism posed existential threats to multireligious, multiethnic, multicultural territorial empires like those of the Hapsburgs and the Ottomans. During this period, the imperial ruling elite responded to these new challenges using various ideological interventions. In the Ottoman Empire, these were, respectively, Ottomanism, Islamism, and Turkism.

In the 19th and early 20th centuries, a group of Ottoman bureaucrats and intellectuals sought to keep the empire's territories intact and its subjects content

B. Oran
Ankara University, Ankara, Turkey
e-mail: baskinoran@gmail.com

K. Akkoyunlu (✉)
University of Graz, Graz, Austria
e-mail: karabekir.akkoyunlu@gmail.com

© Springer International Publishing AG, part of Springer Nature 2019
E. Özyürek et al. (eds.), *Authoritarianism and Resistance in Turkey*,
https://doi.org/10.1007/978-3-319-76705-5_2

through a series of Westernizing reforms, particularly in the education and justice systems. They promoted a civic Ottoman identity, whereby all subjects of the empire would be treated as equal citizens before the law, regardless of their faith (Çiçek 2010). But it was too late; these reforms failed to stem the rising tide of nationalism, especially among the Christian populations of the Balkans. The Greeks rose against the sultan and became independent in 1829, followed by Serbia, then Bulgaria, and so on.

They also proved deeply unpopular with the empire's Muslims, who, thanks to the Ottoman *millet* (religious community) system, had enjoyed a superior legal status over non-Muslims for centuries, but had their social status threatened with the rise of a wealthy and European-backed non-Muslim bourgeoisie. The failure of Ottomanism and many Christian uprisings led to an attempt to forge a new bond among the empire's diverse Muslim communities. The rise and decline of Islamism followed the fate of its main sponsor, Sultan Abdülhamid II (r. 1876–1909). Its final collapse came with the British-backed Arab uprising against the Ottoman Empire in 1916 and the advent of World War I.

The third ideology, Turkism, became the empire's final governing idea following the coup d'état of January 1913, which brought to power the Committee of Union and Progress (*İttihat ve Terakki Cemiyeti*), the radical wing of the Young Turk movement. Inspired by the pan-ideologies of Europe and Russia (some of its main ideologues, such as Yusuf Akçura, had escaped persecution in tsarist Russia) the Turkists imagined a land for all ethnic Turks, called Turan, extending from the Adriatic Sea to the Bering Strait (Ersoy 2010). It was discredited with the Ottoman defeat and the annihilation of the Anatolian Armenians in World War I.

Kemalism is the offspring of this turbulent process, borne out of the rise and fall of the three ideologies of Ottomanism, Islamism, and Turkism and the experience of a decade of war and destruction between 1912 and 1922. It emerged as the ideology of revolutionary Westernization from above, conceived and carried out by the modernized intelligentsia of a largely premodern society.

How much did the Kemalists borrow from their Young Ottoman and Young Turk predecessors? What was the Kemalist vision for Turkey and to what extent were they successful in bringing this vision to life?

In terms of cadres and ideology, Kemalism's closest next of kin is the Committee of Union and Progress and their Turkism. After all, almost all leading Kemalists, including Mustafa Kemal (Atatürk) himself, were former Unionists. But there are two crucial differences between the political program of the Unionists and the Kemalists. The first is that the Kemalists did not make irredentist claims based on the patronage of all ethnic Turks. Unlike Unionist leaders like Enver Pasha, the Ottoman War Minister during WWI, who went chasing pan-Turkist utopian dreams in the Caucasus and Central Asia, Mustafa Kemal had no interest in the so-called external Turks. The disasters caused by the Turkist utopia were still fresh in the minds of Mustafa Kemal and others. These included not only shocking military debacles during WWI, most notably in Sarıkamış on the Caucasian front, where nearly an entire army led by vainglorious Enver perished under harsh winter conditions, but also the catastrophic fate of the Ottoman Christians. Ottoman officers mobilizing against the empire's post-WWI occupation, including Mustafa Kemal, were aware of the violence the Unionist government had unleashed upon the Armenians during the war and were troubled by the potential fallout on the Turkish state's international standing and claim to sovereignty.[1]

They focused, instead, on nation building within defined boundaries, which more or less corresponded to the borders of modern Turkey, plus parts of western Thrace and northern Iraq. This was, of course, a pragmatic decision, first, as Muslims now constituted an overwhelming majority of the population within these boundaries, and second, as any claim on external Turks would have brought the Kemalists in conflict with the Soviet Union. Let us not forget that the Bolsheviks had provided crucial financial and military assistance to the Anatolian resistance led by Mustafa Kemal and fellow patriotic officers against the post-WWI occupation of Ottoman lands, also known as the Turkish War of Independence, 1919–1922.

The second difference is the idea of a *republic*, which was absent in the Unionists' thinking. Enver's ambitions most probably included being crowned sultan. Mustafa Kemal, in contrast, appears to have regarded republicanism as the epitome of civilized government. He abolished the Ottoman monarchy and declared Turkey a republic in 1923, even though this was not a popular idea either among the populace or even among his fellow officers. That he went on to become a sultan-like president does not historically present a contradiction, as few countries during this period associated republicanism with democracy, much less with liberal democracy. We are talking about the interwar era of the 1920s and 1930s, when totalitarianism increasingly became the international zeitgeist, especially after the Great Depression of 1929.

The Kemalists shared with their Young Ottoman predecessors, who espoused Ottomanism and advocated for constitutional government during the final quarter of the 19th century, the belief in achieving modernity through Westernization. This was Mustafa Kemal's ultimate goal. Ending foreign (Western) military occupation and constructing a Turkish nation-state were prerequisites to achieving modernity. To be modern, the dominant thinking went, one needed to *become* Western, and to be Western one had to have an independent national state and identity.

Like many other state-led nation-building projects, the attempt to forge a homogenous national identity on multicultural communities was carried out through assimilation (of non-Turkish Muslims) and ethno-religious cleansing (of non-Muslims). In fact, this process had already started in earnest under the Unionists and continued throughout the republic (Zürcher 2010). It has only been

---

[1]Mustafa Kemal denounced pan-Turkist irredentism in a speech to the Grand National Assembly in Ankara on 1 December 1921: "Gentlemen, we drew the animosity of the entire world upon this country and this nation because of the grand and chimerical things we said we would do but didn't. [...] Instead of provoking our enemies by chasing notions that we will not and cannot realise, let us return to our natural and legitimate boundaries. Let us know our limits. For, gentlemen, we are a nation who wants life and independence. And only for this should we sacrifice our lives." (Arsan 1989: 216; quote translated by Akkoyunlu).

partially successful and remains incomplete to this day, having created many victims and sources of resentment and resistance against the Turkish state, which still constitute the main points of tension in Turkey's politics and society.

When did the Kemalists lose their grip over Turkey's state and society? Can we still talk about a Kemalist Turkey after the Democrat Party victory of 1950, during the Cold War, or after the 1980 coup? Or was it finally dismantled with the AKP government in the 2000s?

Kemalism was a product of its time. But the times changed fundamentally after the Second World War. The defeat of fascism and Nazism, and the rise of the United States as a global superpower promoting democracy and capitalism, led to a division within the ruling elites in Turkey, all of whom were then part of the CHP. Led by Celal Bayar, a prominent former Unionist who became prime minister in Atatürk's final years (1937–1939), and the charismatic Adnan Menderes (prime minister, 1950–1960), a group of CHP members influenced by this change went on to form the Democratic Party, which came to power in 1950 in the first competitive multiparty election.

In other words, both the Democratic Party government—which ruled Turkey for a decade, aligned it with the US axis, and turned increasingly authoritarian in its final years—and the opposition CHP—which put up stubborn resistance to the DP under the leadership of former President İsmet İnönü (1938–1950)—were in fact led by Kemalists. Yet they had rival interpretations of the Kemalist ideology due to its internal contradictions, and, therefore, the contradictions inherent to Turkey's position in the changing world. One internal contradiction, for instance, concerned the state's role over the economy. Mustafa Kemal favored a relatively liberal approach in the 1920s, supporting the rise of a national bourgeoisie. But that had to change with the Great Depression of 1929 and the global rise of statism in the 1930s. So both the economic liberals in the DP and the statists in the CHP could justify their rival position with reference to Kemalism and Mustafa Kemal himself.

Ultimately it was the military-bureaucratic wing of the state that stepped into halt Kemalist Turkey's soft landing into the post-WWII world order. The bureaucrats and the officers, especially the junior ones who carried out the coup d'état of May 27, 1960, opposed the DP's political excesses. Crucially, they also lost out severely because of the DP's economic policies, especially after the currency devaluation and crisis of 1958. As a child, I remember cheering for this coup, which brought down the DP and ended in Menderes' execution. But in hindsight, it was a most unfortunate turning point that not only set the stage for future military interventions and kept the bulk of Kemalists frozen in time, but also, in my view, prevented this soft landing into the postwar era.

From 1960 onwards, we see a continual power struggle between elected officials and appointed bureaucrats and officers, who saw themselves as the custodians of the Kemalist order and justified their interventions in the name of safeguarding Atatürk's legacy, however this legacy was defined. Changing or amending the constitution after every military intervention, the custodians made sure they always had the upper hand over elected governments. This arrangement changed with the rise of the AKP in the 2000s. The AKP government did put an end to this arrangement, but Erdoğan has since replaced it with something more terrible.

You mentioned the collapse of the Islamist ideology during World War I. But Islamism experienced a revival in Turkey after the 1960s. It became a major political force in the 1990s and the dominant ideology by the 2000s. Islamism and Kemalism are often seen as two irreconcilable poles in Turkish politics, the ideological antitheses of one another. How do they differ, and where do they converge, in their approach to state and society?

Kemalism was the ideology of secular nation building, of creating a single, homogenous Turkish national identity. Nationalism, by definition, is intolerant of pluralism and tries either to assimilate or eliminate those who openly espouse a different identity. In contrast, the Islamists look back to a premodern arrangement: the *millet* system of the Ottoman Empire in which religious communities were legally recognized as distinct and autonomous groups under the sovereign's rule. In this sense, Islamists can be much more accommodating toward (religious) minorities than the Kemalists, at least in theory. But in the Ottoman Empire that accommodation came with a price: the acceptance of an unequal status before the law vis-à-vis Muslims. In short, inferior status in exchange for recognition.

In Kemalism, on the other hand, we could talk about a promise of equality before the law in exchange for subdual of identities. This is what Mustafa Kemal implied when he said, "Happy is he who calls himself a Turk," meaning, accept the new Turkish identity and you can enjoy the benefits of a full citizen. Of course, this only applied to non-Turkish Muslims, such as the Kurds. Non-Muslims could not become Turks; they were legally defined as minorities by the Lausanne Treaty of 1923, the legitimizing text of the Turkish republic (Özkırımlı and Sofos 2008). So the *millet* system is actually at the root of Kemalist nationalism too.

Again, this is all in theory. In practice, neither did the Kemalists truly extend equal citizenship to non-Turkish Muslims, nor have the Islamists displayed a great deal of tolerance toward non-Muslims. When possible, both groups used state power to impose their singular will on society and crush dissent. In this sense, they are not too different from each other.

However, in contemporary Turkey under President Erdoğan, I don't think we can meaningfully talk about Islamism as the governing ideology any longer. As Erdoğan has come to dominate Turkey's politics, his ego and hubris have overtaken the cause of Islamism. Therefore, in the context of Turkey today, instead of Islamism, it is more appropriate to talk about *Erdoğanism*, which is little more than leadership cult, rather than a coherent ideology.

Ironically, what the Erdoğanists are trying to achieve in Turkey looks not so much like a revival of the Ottoman Empire, as they often claim, but rather like a return to the autocratic arrangement of the 1930s, with its strictly hierarchical vision of one leader, one party, and one people. Whether this is what Erdoğan always aimed for, or if he changed his mind along the way, moving from being a genuine Islamist to a conservative reformist and finally to an autocrat, is an issue of endless polemic in Turkey.

The CHP was established by Mustafa Kemal as the young republic's main political vehicle for mediating between the state and the people. But since the end of the single-party era in 1950, with the exception of a brief surge in popularity under Bülent Ecevit in the 1970s, it has failed to capture the imagination of large swathes of the population. It has been the main parliamentary opposition party since 2002, but has almost no expectation of being in government. What do you make of this underwhelming electoral performance and what does it mean for democracy in Turkey?

Kemalism was the project of reforming the state and society from above, carried out by the modernized intelligentsia in a largely premodern setting. One of the six principles of Kemalism—populism—was put into practice with the express aim of acting "for the people, despite the people." It is little wonder that a party founded on such a premise and mission would struggle to adapt to popular politics in a multiparty electoral setting.

What Bülent Ecevit briefly succeeded in doing in the early 1970s, as the new leader of the CHP and as prime minister, was to replace this elitist attitude with a more relatable social democratic platform that reflected both the spirit of the times and the socioeconomic needs of larger segments of the population. He framed his politics as "for the people, *with* the people," not despite them.

Of course, we should remember that what made Ecevit temporarily a hero in the eyes of so many people was not only the bread-and-butter politics of the CHP. It was also very much his role as head of government ordering the military operation into Cyprus in 1974 (Oran 2010). He was dubbed the "Conqueror of Cyprus" and his popularity soared for the first time above 40% in the following election. Offering a sacrifice on the altar of nationalism has always been a guaranteed way of shoring up popular support, especially in otherwise difficult times. This is something that populist politicians like Menderes or Erdoğan know well and exploit masterfully.

The CHP of today has been suffering from a different but not entirely unrelated malaise (Ciddi 2009). For years the party has been split into two wings: anachronists who look back to the single-party era of the 1930s with nostalgia and those who are in tune with the social democratic norms of our time. Not being able to fully reconcile or formally divorce, these two poles give the party a schizophrenic character. One side supports the EU, the other side views EU reforms as a plot to weaken secularist Turkey. Some speak up for minority rights, others stick steadfast to nationalist bans under the guise of anti-imperialism. Trying to be both pro- and anti-globalization, social democratic and nationalist at the same time, it ends up being none of them. As a result, it has become a stagnant party, not going away, but not seriously challenging the government either. And this is one of the pillars that enables the Erdoğanist regime to carry on: no meaningful rival.

What do you make the key symbols of the republic's foundational period represent in today's Turkey? I have in mind, for instance, the Atatürk flags at the Gezi Park protests in 2013 or even at some of the HDP rallies during 2015. Can these symbols serve as popular banners of a secular, democratic, and inclusive Turkey in the 21st century?

Symbols represent what people see in them. Of course, as the world changes, so can the meanings associated with flags, figures, or slogans. For decades, the face of Atatürk, present in every schoolyard, classroom, and public office around the country, symbolized the omnipresent authority of the Kemalist state. For many a Kurd or devout Muslim, that face was—and still is—a symbol of the suppression of their identity or faith. It is not impossible to change that perception, but it would take a lot of time and effort, as it touches on many open wounds and deep-seated resentments. And in Turkey, far from healing our wounds, we have a tendency to dig them even deeper.

Yet at the same time, the context in which such symbols are being used is changing. Previously the symbol of state authority, the face of Atatürk is now used in opposition to an increasingly repressive political authority. In the mid-2000s, it was part of the monochrome secularist rallies against the AKP and the West, including the liberal democratic norms championed by the European Union. During Gezi, it became part of a colorful protest against a government that, in pursuit of its dream of a new Ottoman Empire, violated the very basic democratic rights and liberties of its citizens. Perhaps we could say that in Gezi, Atatürk came to symbolize modernity, understood in the context of the EU and the 21st century, and not in terms of a nostalgia for the interwar years. In a sense, it caught up with the times.

What made Gezi or some of the pro-Kurdish HDP rallies you mentioned special was not the presence of a single symbol or flag, but the presence of many flags, many symbols, and people from very different, even clashing backgrounds, all in the same square. Remember that famous photograph in Gezi of a Kemalist, a Turkish nationalist, and a supporter of the Kurdish movement, standing side by side? That was the kind of synthesis that made Gezi such a powerful moment and, of course, such a potent threat to Erdoğan's hegemonic ambitions. It showed that on their own, no single symbol, party, flag, or person can symbolize the vision of a democratic, pluralistic Turkey. It can only be symbolized by a synthesis, a picture of pluralistic coexistence itself.

References

Arsan, N. (Ed.) (1989). *Atatürk'ün Söylev ve Demeçleri* [*Atatürk's Speeches and Statements*] (Vol. 1–3). Atatürk Araştırmaları Vakfı. Ankara: Türk Tarih Kurumu Basımevi.

Oran, B. (2010). *Turkish Foreign Policy (1919–2006): Facts and Analyses with Documents* (M. Akşin, Trans.). Salt Lake City: University of Utah Press.

Zürcher, E. J. (2010). *The young turk legacy and nation building: From the Ottoman Empire to ataturk's Turkey*. London: I. B. Tauris.

Çiçek, N. (2010). *The young ottomans: Turkish critics of the eastern question in the late nineteenth century*. London: I. B. Tauris.

Ciddi, S. (2009). *Kemalism in Turkish politics: The republican people's party, secularism and nationalism*. New York: Routledge.

Özkırımlı, U., & Sofos, S. A. (2008). *Tormented by history: Nationalism in Greece and Turkey*. New York: Columbia University Press.

Ersoy, A. (2010). Yusuf Akçura: Three types of policy. In A. Ersoy, M. Górny, & V. Kechriotis (Eds.), *Modernism—the creation of Nation States* (Vol. I, pp. 218–226)., Discourses of Collective Identity in Central and Southeast Europe (1770–1945) Budapest: CEU Press.

Baskın Oran is a professor emeritus of international relations who has repeatedly challenged the ideology and practices of Turkish state institutions. As assistant professor at the School of Political Science, Ankara University, he was twice dismissed, in 1971 and 1982, by ruling military juntas for a total of nine years. Oran is the author and editor of 22 books on Turkey's international relations, nationalism, minority rights in Turkey, political satire, and oral history. As a member of the prime ministry's Human Rights Advisory Council, he wrote the *Minority and Cultural Rights Report* (2004) and edited the three-volume history, *Turkish Foreign Policy: 1919–2012*. Since 2000, Oran has been a regular columnist at the Armenian-Turkish weekly *Agos*, has served as national liaison officer to the Council of Europe's European Commission Against Racism and Intolerance (1999–2009), and also served in the official Wise People Committee during the Kurdish Peace Process in 2013. In 2008, Oran was one of the four launchers of the online campaign *Apology for Armenians*, which called for a collective apology from the Turkish side for the Great Catastrophe/Metz Yeghern of 1915.

Karabekir Akkoyunlu is a research associate of the Centre for Southeast European Studies, University of Graz, and a visiting scholar at the Institute for International Relations, University of São Paulo. He holds a BA in history from Brown University and an M.Phil. in international relations from the University of Cambridge. His research lies at the intersection of comparative politics, democratization theories, and Middle East studies, with a focus on modern Turkey and Iran. Akkoyunlu completed his Ph.D. at the London School of Economics where he researched the transformation of Turkish and Iranian tutelary regimes and taught courses on theories of democratization and Middle East politics. He is the coeditor with Kerem Öktem of *Exit from Democracy: Illiberal Governance in Turkey and Beyond* (Routledge, 2018), coauthor of *The Western Condition: Turkey, the US and the EU in the new Middle East* (SEESOX, 2013), and author of *Military Reform and Democratisation: Turkish and Indonesian Experiences at the turn of the Millennium* (Adelphi Paper 392, 2007).

The 1980 Coup d'État

Ertuğrul Mavioğlu and interviewed by Eylem Delikanlı

Abstract The 1980 coup d'état is seen as a turning point in terms of Turkey's social and economic history. If we are to understand the September 12 coup, we need more than an accounting of the murders committed, the tortures executed, and the human rights violated. Knowing whose side the junta was on, we must take it a step further and ask the following question: "Why did the coup take place and against whom was it organized?" To answer this question, it is important to highlight the transformation the world has undergone since the 1970s. The traditional investment strategies for maximizing capital, which is able to move much faster than before due to new investment opportunities, changed rapidly. The fluidity of capital led to resource abandonment and to imperialist looting of the third world. Industrial production was transported to where the resources were, leading toward the end of 1970s to the emergence of free trade zones in both underdeveloped and developing countries. Thanks to these new opportunities, investors did not have to run off with foreign resources. By changing the investment location, capitalists could reduce both the cost of transportation and the cost of labor.

Keywords Turkey · 1980 junta · Military intervention

The 1980 coup d'état is seen as a turning point in terms of Turkey's social and economic history. How might we best characterize the 1980 coup? Who was the target and why? What differentiates it from previous coups in Turkey?

The coup that took place at 4:00 a.m. on September 12, 1980, was an assault against the people. As with other coups in places like Chile, Argentina, Brazil, and El Salvador, the goal of the 1980 coup in Turkey was to install a brutal military dictatorship. If we take a closer look at what actually happened, our definitions will

E. Mavioğlu (✉)
Independent Researcher, Istanbul, Turkey
e-mail: emavioglu@gmail.com

E. Delikanlı
Oral Historian, Research Institute on Turkey/Columbia University, New York, USA

© Springer International Publishing AG, part of Springer Nature 2019
E. Özyürek et al. (eds.), *Authoritarianism and Resistance in Turkey*,
https://doi.org/10.1007/978-3-319-76705-5_3

become more comprehensive and more specific. The violence and sophistication of the coup should force us to answer the question of what September 12 really was. Only such an effort will allow us to accurately analyze the coup and give us the tools with which to categorize it.

Military tanks occupied the streets, the parliament was abolished, and five generals of the junta took control of the judicial, executive, and legislative branches of government. These actions ran contrary to what they claimed to be doing. General Kenan Evren, presiding over the junta, advocated publicly for the restoration of democracy, but he took the world's most brutal dictatorships as his example. He publicly called the bloodshed to stop while the news reported youngsters being shot in the streets or murdered while under torture.

The junta was judge, jury, and executioner all at the same time and used their power to torture and kill. Over the years, it became normal for everyone to speak only from their pain—let's name it—just to survive. The coup thus meant death, torture, and prison for tens of thousands of people in this country. For millions of others, it meant irrational and inhumane assaults on their freedom. What was expected of society was that it oppose the deaths, the torture, the imprisonments—that it resist the coup. But we are talking about human beings, so not everyone will react to the same situation in the same way. Not only did some people acquiesce to these measures very quickly, but some also voluntarily contributed to the restrictions on freedom by becoming informants. These were the ones who snitched on their neighbors and wanted them dead. Not only did these people support the death penalties, the executions, the detentions and imprisonments, but they were also the ones in the crowds that filled the squares during rallies. These informants were the first circle, built on the slogan "We stand against both the left and the right." The second circle represented a wider part of society, people who were scared of the violence they witnessed during the first months of the junta. These were the people who acquiesced to the violence so as to avoid being subjected to it. They did not snitch on anyone, but preferred to remain silent so as to lessen the level of violence. They preferred to be invisible and therefore did not object. Although this was not their intention, they created the conditions for the junta to declare victory. As a result, those actively resisting the junta became such a minority that the junta was able to proceed. Immediately after the first wave of violence, the first executions, and the first bullets aimed at people on the streets, the junta only dared seize ordinary life once the space was cleared.

The five generals of the junta had a two-handed strategy: with one hand they increased the volume of torture and the number of coffins carrying young bodies out of back doors, and with the other hand they kept the pressure on social life. The junta granted the Turkish Industry and Business Association the status of an "association working for the benefit of the public" and closed all other associations. It closed down the Confederation of Progressive Trade Unions (Devrimci İşçi Sendikaları Konfederasyonu, hereafter DİSK), but allowed the work of the Confederation of Turkish Employers Unions (*Türkiye İşveren Sendikaları Konfederasyonu*, hereafter TİSK) to continue. All strikes and resistance were outlawed by a National Security Council resolution. Since unions were closed and the executives of DİSK were in jail, it became impossible to carry out strikes legally. After the suspension of unions and associations, agricultural and consumer co-ops were also outlawed, thereby preventing poor peasants from organizing as workers. By doing that, the junta revealed the purpose and the character of the coup right from the beginning. The employers were the first to understand this and openly supported it. TİSK secretary Halit Narin's statement regarding the workers was, "Until now the workers laughed, and we cried. Now it's our turn to laugh." As Turkey's richest ever businessman, Vehbi Koç's declaration of support expressed in a letter to the junta leader Kenan Evren was not for nothing.

This scene clearly demonstrates if we are to understand the September 12 coup, we need more than an accounting of the murders committed, the tortures executed, and the human rights violated. Knowing whose side the junta was on, we must take it a step further and ask the following question: "Why did the coup take place and against whom was it organized?" To answer this question, it is important to highlight the transformation the world has undergone since the 1970s. The traditional investment strategies for maximizing capital, which is able to move much faster than before due to new investment opportunities, changed rapidly. The fluidity of capital led to resource abandonment and to imperialist looting of the third world. Industrial production was transported to where the resources were, leading toward the end of 1970s to the emergence of free trade zones in both underdeveloped and developing countries. Thanks to these new opportunities, investors did not have to run off with foreign resources. By changing the investment location, capitalists could reduce both the cost of transportation and the cost of labor.

Free trade zones were geographically and legally autonomous and isolated areas where foreign capital was given advantageous conditions, particularly in terms of security, taxation, and workers' rights. To attract international firms to these free trade zones, governments invariably chose locations close to the ports because of their suitability for export and reexport. The right to strike or to unionize was outlawed in the free trade zones. Wages were low and working hours were long. Capitalists investing in free trade zones were exempt from taxation. Free trade zones developed first in East Asian countries such as Taiwan, South Korea, and Singapore, and then in North Africa.

The system implemented in Turkey was inspired by free trade zones, but was much more advanced. Especially in Mersin, several trade zones were established, but establishment of a zone was not the main goal. If these zones worked, everywhere in Turkey was to become a free trade zone. The first clues as to the real goal can be seen in the economic package put together by the Demirel government on January 24, 1980, only months before the military September coup. This package, known as the January 24 Decisions, involved a series of measures designed to overcome Turkey's economic crisis. What we know now is that in reality it foreshadowed an important break. The former import-based industrialization policy that had been secured by customs walls was abandoned, and the country's economic strategy was redefined as integration into the world economy. This was termed the "free market economy" where domestic capital must inevitably integrate with foreign capital. The first measure of the January 24 Decisions was a 32.7% currency devaluation. With its fashionable idiom of "realistic parity," this policy opened the door to foreign capital and oriented economic policy toward export-oriented industrialization.

The January 24 Decisions impeded public intervention in price regulation, and favored price determination according to the supply-demand balance of the market. This bitter pill also included the reduction of public shares in markets, the establishment of stock exchanges, the determination of interest ratios by the market with absolute interest as its basis, and realizing structural measures to liberalize the exchange-rate regime. Another interesting detail is that it was none other than Turgut Özal who prepared this stability package. Özal had been appointed secretary of the treasury by the then prime minister, Süleyman Demirel. As the former manager of the Union of Metal Industrialists (Madeni Eşya Sanayicileri Sendikası), which had been defeated by the resistance of the DİSK, Özal saw these measures as retaliation against the working class. The consequences of these measures for the working class were immense. And they were no secret, given what we knew about International Monetary Fund and the World Bank policies in other countries. Shocking devaluation, increased interest rates, tight fiscal policies, and austerity measures were contracting the economic welfare of ordinary people. Tightly-controlled wages meant an assault on labor organizations. Before the coup, when trade unions and the working class were strong, it was not possible for parliament to pass economic measures like those of 1980. The only way to realize such measures was to by illegal means involving oppression and brutality. Eight months after the January 24 Decisions, the mechanism for realizing this economic package was the military coup of September 12.

The September 12 coup constituted a significant shift, especially for the labor class. The number of workers associated with trade unions reduced significantly following the coup. It goes without saying that this sharp reduction was a direct outcome of the coup. But if we look at statistics worldwide—for example, in the US, France, England, Germany, Greece, and Japan—starting in the mid-1970s, the number of workers who were members of trade unions reduced dramatically. By the early 1980s, trade union-associated wage labor had reduced from 22 to 15% in the US, from 17.5 to 8% in France, 49 to 38% in Italy, and 31 to 25% in Japan. Deunionization in these countries continued over the course of subsequent years. And these are only the statistics. The ideological transformation of the trade unions as they became more aligned with the capitalists, constitutes the other dimension of the deunionization process. This transformation in alignment entailed diminished wage differences between union members and nonmembers, the silent consent of unions on the extortion of workers' rights, and the transformation of unions into bureaucratic settlement organizations as they peeled away from their original role as labor organizations.

In short, before 1980, the rule of thumb for the working class was that you were a union member. Globalization reversed this. The organized culture of the working class was swiftly smashed by capitalism. The membership incentives of some European trade unions notwithstanding, it became a unspoken rule for capitalists to employ workers without any trade union affiliation. With this new stage, capitalists gave the world a clear message: "If you wish to work and live, you work and live by our rules!"

In this period, there were two main features of capital: the first was to be disconnected from the center and the second was to not have to follow the rules. Under globalism, as the term was coined, capital was much more ruthless. By forcing workers into competition, capital lowered workers' wages worldwide and launched a hostile attack on all forms of organization for workers' rights. In the old days, for example, if Germany would fall short in providing a work force locally, it would compensate with foreign workers. But now, local and foreign workers shared the same threat of unemployment. The reason was that local industry tied to a country was evaporating. Are wages high in Germany or do they have more social rights or do the workers insist on becoming union members? The solution was simple. You disassemble the factory, move it to a haven where workers will agree to lower wages and fewer or no rights, a place where workers would not even imagine becoming a member of a union. Does this galvanize workers in the new country? There was no force against capital that could stop it from moving from one county to another overnight. What was interesting in Turkey was that the junta attacked the unions and workers' rights around the same time that the wave of neoliberalism hit the world. Paul Henze, head of the CIA's Ankara Division in 1980, stated in his cable to the White House about the coup, "Our guys did it." To be in line with global capitalism, this economic regime could only come into being thanks to the military coup. This is what Turgut Özal, the rising star of the post-September coup period, termed "export-oriented industrialization." Supported by the coup, Özal could concentrate on energy investments and communication technologies, investments that would play an important role in the transformation of the culture of consumption in Turkey. Özal's dream of "whatever exists in the US, will exist in Turkey" was slowly becoming a reality.

Yes, the political outcomes of the coup are hotly debated, but those kinds of discussions disguise the real reasons behind the coup. As with the 1980 coup, which is viewed only as an impediment to democracy and the wholesale embrace of executions and torture, the 1960 coup is also seen within this democracy discourse as a democratic outburst against a brutalizing Democratic Party. However, all the numbers point to the fact that immediately following the coup, Turkey took a major step toward capitalist development. Mechanization in agriculture, the elimination of feudalism, a limited land reform, rural to urban migration, certain traders being promoted from franchisers to industrialists, industrial developments in cities, and irregular urbanization—all were made possible by the 1960 coup, which mainly served to remove obstacles to capital rather than to further democracy. Some relatively democratic steps were to erase the remaining feudal classes rather than emancipating the masses. If not for the 1960 coup, capitalism in Turkey would not have developed so fast, and the country would not have been affected by the ensuing global crises so directly. In turn, Turkey would not have put the austerity measures in effect and would not need the March 12, 1971 military memorandum. From this perspective, what we should be talking about are not the minor differences between the various Turkish coups, but the common goals from which these coups originate. Today we can clearly state that the 1960, 1971, and 1980 coups were all undertaken to fulfill the needs of capital. Although the military appears to be onstage in all three coups, the path to be followed had been previously been determined by big capital. The following sentence is true: since 1960, the real organizer and executor of the military coups in Turkey has been big capital.

It is enough to look at the general setup of the junta's 1982 constitution, which dictated changes and left society without a say in the matter. This setup proposed a silent, obedient, submissive society. The actions of the Özal government after the 1984 elections, which took place with two and a half political parties and many vetoed by the junta, would take its meaningful place in the big picture. Özal could see from which direction the wind was blowing and sailed out into this wind. He was thereby able to execute the otherwise impossible October 24 measures, which synchronized investments in infrastructure with emerging global technology. In this way, Turkey became a symbol for the economic giants of the world. With the high thresholds against mobilization, trade union organizations became mere decorations, strikes became impossible, every demonstration was categorized as "destructive and separationist," and even a small objection could mean running the risk of huge consequences. In other words, all of Özal's actions were made possible by the thornless rose garden created by the 1980 coup. Unsurprisingly, politicians who had seemed to oppose the 1980 coup, strongly embraced the 1982 constitution. With the coup and the extensive support of their international mentors, they had found the recipe for how to rule Turkey. They then opened Turkey up to world monopolies, institutionalizing it all with an authoritarian form of governance that left no string untied. What remained for their successors was to preserve fascism and take harsher measures in times of crisis. That was it.

As a journalist, you were jailed for eight years after the coup. Can you please tell us about the conditions you experienced? What does it exactly mean to say that "the country has been turned into an open prison?"? Is there a relation between what we experience today under, what many people call, an 'authoritarian' rule and the human rights violations during and after the 1980 coup?

I was arrested in March 1980, therefore, I witnessed the coup while in the prison. What we experienced in prison before the coup was not any different from what we experienced after the coup. However, on the night of the coup, we recognized clearly the start of a new and brutal period. The first thing the prison management did was to pump up the volume of the speakers at midnight while they played fascist and racist marches. To threaten us, they brought in armed soldiers for the morning count. I remember the commander of the Davutpaşa military prison, Major Adan Özbey, telling us, "Get ready! We will interrogate you one by one again." As a matter of fact, they moved two of our friends to a larger cell next door right away. The psychological war was heightened in an attempt to force us to give up. When we heard that our friend İrfan Çelik committed suicide by hanging himself on the heating pipes in an isolation cell, we all started to think that our end was near. In a very short period of time, oppression and torture increased to the highest level in every prison in Turkey. They even started military education in some of the prisons they controlled in the first days of the coup. Police and gendarme, working full-time, took people on the streets into custody if they had not already been shot, then tortured them severely while in custody. The courts ordered people to be imprisoned no matter who the detainee was or whether there was a case or evidence against them. In any case, people who were already heavily tortured would face a longer period of being tortured in whichever prison they were sent to. Even though these are official numbers prepared by the Grand National Assembly of Turkey (Meclis Araştırması Komisyonu 2012), they show the severity of what society had to endure between 1980 and 1984 under the ruling junta: 7,000 people were given the death penalty; 517 people were sentenced to death; 50 of those given the death penalty were executed; the files of 259 people who had been given the death penalty were sent to the National Assembly; 444 people died in a suspicious manner; 171 people were documented as having died during torture; 299 people lost their lives in prison; 14 people died on a hunger strike; 16 people were shot while fleeing; 95 people were killed in combat; the cause of death of 43 people was announced as "suicide"; 73 people were given 'natural death' report; 650,000 people were arrested; 1,683,000 people were blacklisted; 230,000 people had judgments against them in 210,000 lawsuits; 71,000 people were prosecuted on account of articles 141, 142, and 163 of the Turkish Penal Code; 98,404 people were prosecuted on charges of being members of a leftist, rightist, nationalist, conservative, or other organization; 388,000 people were denied a passport; 30,000 people were dismissed from their job because they were under suspicion; 14,000 people had their citizenship revoked; 30,000 people went abroad as political refugees; 30,000 people were dismissed from their posts; 23,677 associations had their activities stopped; 3,854 teachers, 120 lecturers, and 47 judges were dismissed; 937 films were banned; 400 journalists were sentenced to a total of 3,315 years 6 months of imprisonment; 300 journalists were attacked; three journalists were shot dead; newspapers were not published for 300 days; 303 investigation cases were opened for 13 major newspapers; 39 tons of newspapers and magazines were destroyed.

This horror scene is based on the official numbers and is likely to reflect only a portion of what actually happened. But what is important is not only how many people faced this brutality. Torture and bullying spread across the entire country and detainees constituted only a small part of those who witnessed violence. People released after heavy torture returned to their places of work, their neighborhoods, their villages and told their stories everywhere they went. The listeners were affected by the tales from the underworld as though they had experienced it themselves. In addition to the physical effects of torture, the widespread awareness of its existence led to an ever-growing mountain of fear. In other words, the success of the junta in generating the submissiveness of the people stemmed not only from detention and torture. More than the torture itself, the tales that were told of the brutality was a decisive player in the establishment of the empire of fear. If people were afraid, the junta could rule with greater ease and could legislate as it pleased. Whoever expected these rules to disappear as the junta turned their power over to civil governments was clearly mistaken. On the contrary, subsequent governments not only took advantage of the climate of fear, they went so far as to uphold the laws and rules generated by the junta.

Notwithstanding the ostensible support from liberals who claim that the AKP was against coups and detentions, the AKP government, which came to power 18 years after the 1980 coup, has also benefitted from the fascist junta's legal infrastructure. Because of this, defining the AKP's ruling regime as "authoritarian" is inadequate, and because it is inadequate, it is wrong. The AKP is a political party that embraces the 10% election threshold, preserves the ban on political activity of the foundations and trade unions, crushes all demands for freedom with violence, and diminishes the freedom of the press. A clearer definition would be to call the AKP a fascist party that has strengthened the laws that isolate society from political decision-making, and which has adopted all the regulations of the 1982 constitution, which restricted all basic human rights and liberty.

What is the role of the Turkish-Islamic synthesis within the American imperialist strategy? What is the role of the coup and its constitution in today's political setup?

After the coup, the supporters of the Nationalist Movement Party (*Milliyetçi Hareket Partisi*, hereafter MHP) were jailed. However, they did not react because they were jailed for their bloody acts. They reacted because "their ideas were in power and they were in jail." Indeed, after the coup Turkism gained power under the name of Kemalism. The junta leader Kenan Evren went out to the rallies insulting Kurds, Greeks, and Armenians, and praising Turks. The junta also utilized those MHP militants who had not been detained within the National Intelligence Organization for its own purposes. Racist and nationalist tendencies gained power after the coup, but so did political Islam. The executives of the National Salvation Party (*Milli Selamet Partisi*), including Necmettin Erbakan, were jailed, but the junta preferred not to interfere with Islamic organizations, cults, and communities. The junta made secret deals to shore up the Islamic community youth, making them into neighborhood informants. These young people were not jailed like so many of their peers were; they had already met the dark side of the state and were linked with it. Obviously, Kenan Evren's citations of the Qur'an at rallies and the increase in the number of Imam Hatip Islamic school openings would have political consequences. The junta criminalized political thought and books by attacking neighborhoods, factories, and schools. Within a few months, the gaping ideological hole that followed from this criminalization was filled with another form of thought: soft Islamism with a touch of nationalist tendency. This new form of thought was delineated within the framework of the American "green zone" project which included those soft Islamist countries that had ties with the US and supported the global consumer culture that fed the needs of capitalism. The September 1980 coup was the necessary starting point in order for Turkey to be included in the green zone project. After the coup, the strongest political proclivity was the Turkish-Islamic synthesis, a Turkish version of the United States' green zone project. This movement had dynamic management and had gone into a kind of partnership with the state. This was the only formula for a strong conservatism that would embrace both nationalists and Islamists. This mechanism worked like clockwork. Even those who were against authority, met it in their youth and found ways to deal with it. In the end, authority served these meek characters so devoted to their own self-interest. Green-zone Islamists were eventually to part ways with the radical National View movement, which they collaborated with for a while. They would benefit tremendously by taking this new step, and did not need to wait too long for the doors to open before them. The coup depoliticized and disorganized the working class. Workers could not use working-class knowledge as a way out of their predicament when lived in a country where a book could be proof of a crime, where they feared for their families, their children, their future. In an effort to survive and perhaps one day reach the dim light at the end of the tunnel, they set aside their own interests and began choosing political parties designed to protect the interest of the ruling class. All the political parties in government after the junta did everything to ensure the continuation of the conditions that had originally brought them to power. The steps taken toward building structural fascism in Turkey were both preserved and strengthened. The best-held secret of the long life of the September 12 constitution was that its tenets never expired in relation to capitalism.

If we evaluate the coup in a more global context, what was its meaning for the US and regional politics?

Shah Reza Pahlevi's overthrow in Iran, which ended in the Ayatollah regime, meant that the US lost a significant ally in the region. We have to note here that not only were US interests harmed, but also those of Israel. The Islamic Republic of Iran's prestigious win against the US and Israel also empowered regional fundamentalist Islamist groups. Meanwhile, Egypt and Israel reached an agreement at the Camp David summit, which led to the isolation of Egypt from the Arab world. The United States' interest in Turkey was in keeping with its larger aim of strengthening regional alliances. We cannot therefore ignore the role the US played during the path to the September 12 coup. Given the special importance of the Camp David summit, the US was known to be seeking support from Muslim countries, and the "green zone project" emerged in due course. Another reason for this project was the Soviet Union's close relationship to Arab countries after the invasion of Afghanistan. Because of their secular identities, the Ba'athi regimes of Syria, Libya, and Iraq were very distinct from sharia regimes. This situation would mean a new threat, and a loss of power for the US. In short, to preserve the interests of the United States, Turkey must be in the green zone project. To achieve this, the US began to deepen and strengthen its relationship with the Islamic world via Turkey, which was already part of NATO. But for this, Turkey must first restore stability, which would mean easing up all opposition to US policy. So in addition to the overarching need of capitalists to suppress opposition and diminish the freedoms and civil rights of the working class, US interests in the Middle East would necessitate an overt fascist junta in Turkey. The 1980 coup thus has both a direct and indirect relationship to US interests.

From the 1960s through to the 1980s, coups had been useful tactics for the furtherance of US foreign policy in Turkey. President Jimmy Carter's national security adviser, Zbigniew Brzezinski, started to work in Turkey at this point. It is no longer a secret that Brzezinski held numerous meetings with representatives of the Turkish Industry and Business Association and coup general Kenan Evren, discussing how to restore a "stable" Turkey and set the stage for the coup to take place. For the US, the only way to restore stability in the region was to appoint Turkey as the border guard in the Middle East. Long after the coup, Brzezinski commented that he had defended the idea that the best solution would be a civilized military regime in time; the armies were disciplined, well organized, and strong; in places like Turkey, Egypt, and Brazil, the armies could both seize power and rule. After the coup, as the junta experienced major problems with the Turkish people, the comprador monopolist bourgeoisie was good with the IMF and the US. That was why John Tower, chair of the Senate Armed Services Committee, would say that it was the Golden Age for the relationship between Turkey and the United States. These good relationships would also enable Greece's return to NATO's military committee, which had been vetoed several times by Turkey. Then the rest unfolded: US contingency forces were based on Turkish territory, the restrictions on the use of Incirlik military base were removed, Turkish radar bases were renovated, and the US was given unlimited use of them.

When we take all of this into consideration, the 1950s may be defined as the era of affinity-building in Turkish-American relations, while the post-1980 coup era may be defined as the era when these relations were rapidly transformed. Subsequent governments adopted the political perspective the junta who had built a strong relationship with the US. Even if these governments wanted to, they could not initiate a change. In this way, the junta's political perspective on the Middle East formed the basis of Turkey's foreign policy for years to come, and as a result, Turkey continued to be a player in US regional policy.

The 2010 referendum was a breaking point for paving the way to the structural changes that would end the republic as we know it. Making the 1980 Coup as their focal point, the hotly debated "Yes, but not enough" political position triggered a discussion that continues to date within the Left. Considering the outcome of the 1980 Coup trial, we can conclude that it did not follow any of the mechanisms necessary to confront the past. Put differently, during the trial, there was no truth-finding commission or a fully operational legal process. There was no compensation for the emotional and material damage inflicted, no public acknowledgement of human rights violations. Why was the September 12 trial important for the AKP? What is the hardship for those who work towards confronting the past and the collective memory of the era?

The big gain for the AKP with the September 12, 2010 referendum was the takeover, of power over the judiciary together with its coalition partner Fethullah Gülen movement. When you take over the judiciary, you can turn laws into cudgels against your political enemies and hide your bullying behind the legal shield of the "rule of law." This method, used in other countries, creates the appearance of legitimacy while allowing you to still achieve your goals. Parliamentary fascism is created in exactly this manner. This process was carried out by the AKP masterfully. An arrangement removing the temporary 15th clause of the constitution, which provided the legal shield for the 1980 coup, was inserted into the referendum package. The AKP chose the referendum date of September 12 as a distraction. Thus, the bulk of the electorate would focus on the judgment of the bloody dictator Kenan Evren and his cronies, without questioning the rest of the package. The AKP was able to wrangle into its pocket vociferous liberals who were outside its base, and this intellectual class came forward with the slogan "Yes, but not enough." The impact of this intellectual class was not as big as has been assumed. The AKP was given a boost primarily by the boy

cott of the referendum by the Kurdish political movement, making the referendum a relatively easy win. The Kurds did not go to the polls; even if they did not vote yes, they also did not vote no. In the end the referendum was voted in by 57% of the electorate and the AKP was able to move on with its plan to take over the judiciary in the advertised name of reform. This plan went off without a hitch and in a short time the courts began to act as inquisitions on behalf of the partners in power. The unwarranted arrests and trumped-up evidence of the ongoing trials after 2010 were all products of this plan.

Then, with the referendum result, cases were opened against the two surviving leaders of the September 12 coup, Kenan Evren and Tahsin Şahinkaya. But the case included neither the tortures, executions, unwarranted years-long detentions, street beatings, nor the dismantling of democracy. Evren and Şahinkaya were charged with "attempting a coup" because "perpetrating a coup" was not on the books as a crime in Turkey. For this reason, the case was opened on the pretense of attempting to change the constitutional order set in place after the 1980 coup. This was of course a sideshow. The main goal was to exclude from legal judgment all the crimes committed within the chain of command. The counterguerilla forces were thereby left untouched, no headache caused to the torturers and murderers, the mountains of case files of unsolved murders perpetrated in the name of the government left unopened. In a case where the prosecutor was seeking hardened life sentences, no order was made to arrest Evren and Şahinkaya. They were not even brought to the courtroom, but were instead connected to it via an audiovisual system. Finally, on June 18, 2014 the court gave both defendants hardened life sentences, but then commuted them to regular life sentences on account of good behavior. Again there was no order given for their arrest. The case then went to the Supreme Court of Appeals. While that court was still in process, Evren died on May 9, 2015 and Şahinkaya died on July 9, 2015. Due to their deaths, the appeals court decided to drop all charges and the lower court obeyed. So the September 12 case, opened to much fanfare, did not do anything but feed the AKP's end to military tutelage scheme. In short, the case strengthened the AKP's hand in its fight against its social foes.

That fact that the case was restricted from the beginning to Evren and Şahinkaya, and excluded all the other crimes committed during the coup, did not satisfy the people wishing to hold those involved in the coup accountable, nor did it create

hope for a democratic future. Because the coup-era crimes were to be examined by
the government apparatus that committed them, it was implied that the government
would have to guarantee to no longer engage in such crimes against humanity. But
since the 1980s, the government has continued to use torture, unsolved murders, the
breaking of its own laws, and unwarranted arrests and punishments. These methods
have kept their legitimacy as a form of rule. Put differently, as long as the government did not take on a more democratic character, it was not possible to judge
the crimes of the coup. The work of those recording the collective memory of that
era was harder than expected, because to uncover the truth and see the big picture, it
is not enough to simply document the crimes of the junta era. The inheritance left
by the junta for the next administration, the legal framework set by the junta, its
final developments and institutions: only by questioning these issues will it be
possible to understand what happened. From this perspective, the work of
researchers of the recent history on the junta era must focus also on today, so that
we can build a solid bridge between yesterday and today.

**On the coup attempt of July 15, 2016, Recep Tayyip Erdoğan is known to have
said, "This move was a great gift from God for us." In light of the developments after the coup, what exactly is this gift Erdoğan referred to? Was the
social transformation, whose main foundation was laid on September 12, 1980,
furthered by the attempted coup of July 15? How do you evaluate this process
where a large segment of society remains cynical and silent?**

First, it is important to stress the fact that we are currently unable to see the full
picture on the coup attempt of July 15, 2016. What happened before July 15? Did
the government know about the coup attempt? What did the CHP leader
Kılıçdaroğlu mean when he said "this is a controlled coup?" Were the coup-makers
all soldiers tied to the Fethullah Gülen movement or did the coup attempt have a
broader spectrum of participants? Who was the leadership of the coup and what was
their main goal, had they been successful? Were the coup-makers able to get the
support of big capital? Or, as former military chief of staff İlker Başbuğ said on
television, was it that "Those who organized the coup also organized its failure"? It
is possible to come up with more questions, but it is not very necessary. Eventually
the answers to these questions will be revealed by the relevant documents. Beyond
trusting our intuition on all this, I think we are trying to feel our way in the dark,
because the documents are being ferreted away in a highly secretive manner.

The extraordinary effort of the AKP government, and especially of Erdoğan, to
turn July 15 into a heroic epic reveals that there is a large shadow lurking in the
background of this situation. This has not stopped the AKP from stubbornly
pushing its own narrative of events. It is intolerant to any declaration besides "The
traitorous Fethullahist terror organization attempted a coup, but the people came to
the streets with a democratic fervor and, by stuffing underwear into tank gun
barrels, standing in front of bullets, and running after F-16 planes with brooms, they
thwarted the coup." The AKP wants everyone to chime in on this ridiculous chorus
so that there are no discordant voices. The goal is to create a country with one

voice, and the AKP will censure journalists who ask questions, arrest them if they are insistent, and shut down media organizations that do not comply.

The data we have right now is what we lived through. The AKP, using July 15 as a pretense, quickly organized its own coup. First it declared a state of emergency. Then it began ruling the country by cabinet decrees. It imprisoned opposition MPs and mayors. It bombed cities. People died, got arrested, were left unemployed and starving. The AKP did not recoil from any cruelty in its rush to turn the country into a thornless rose garden for itself. In other words, by using both the suppression methods developed by the junta and the cruel laws and institutions left over from it as weapons against the people, the AKP became the biggest inheritors yet to the legacy of 1980.

But running a country cannot be done solely through bullying. From this angle, the AKP being this aggressive is related to the fact that it is experiencing its weakest period to date. We are talking about an administration that has no neighbors left with which is on good relations, stuck in a Middle Eastern quagmire, inconsistent in its foreign policy, domestically repressive, allowing no room for freedom of speech, cracking down on democratic institutions, financially corrupt—all this, and still it assumes that it will never be held accountable. In a country with such a government, we cannot talk about people sustaining peaceful lives, and we don't talk about it. Hopelessness, pessimism, silence, docility are the bywords now.

But no matter how much they may be oppressed, people are not creatures that can remain docile forever. Honor, pride, morality—such concepts exist precisely for this reason. It is perhaps meaningful in this context to repeat the words of optimism spoken by the imprisoned leader of the People's Democratic Party, Selahattin Demirtaş, during an interview: "While the darkness thinks that it is forever, and that it has destroyed the light, it takes its first hit at sunrise. At that moment, darkness is done, and light begins to dawn."

Reference

Meclis Araştırması Komisyonu. (2012). Ülkemizde Demokrasiye Müdahale Eden Tüm Darbe ve Muhtıralar İle Demokrasiyi İşlevsiz Kılan Diğer Bütün Girişim ve Süreçlerin Tüm Boyutları İle Araştırılarak Alınması Gereken Önlemlerin Belirlenmesi Amacıyla Kurulan Meclis Araştırması Komisyonu Raporu [Parliamentary Research Commission. (2012). The Report of the Parliamentary Research Commission that was established towards determining the measures to prevent them, to elaborate all the process and attempts that leave the democracy dysfunctional and all the coups and memorandums that intervenes in democracy 37 (Vol. 1). Türkiye Büyük Millet Meclisi, Ankara.]. Retrieved November 10, 2017, from http://www.tbmm.gov.tr/sirasayi/donem24/yil01/ss376_Cilt1.pdf.

Author Biographies

Ertuğrul Mavioğlu was 19 years old at the time of the September 1980 military coup and spent eight years in jail for political reasons during the period of 1980–1991. During his periods of freedom, he completed his degree in journalism. He worked for nearly 30 years as a journalist at various newspapers and television stations. He has received two awards for investigative journalism from the Progressive Journalists Association (Turkey). He is the author of an oral history trilogy about the September 12, 1980 junta, as well as a coauthor with Ahmet Şık of a two-volume work about counterinsurgents in Turkey. Mavioğlu's last book was published in 2012 and was an analysis of the media. In 2006, together with Sedat Yılmaz he codirected a 26-minute short documentary entitled *Justice by Epaulette* (*Apoleti Adalet*). *North* (*Bakur*) is Mavioğlu's first feature-length documentary.

Eylem Delikanlı is a founding member and an oral historian at the Research Institute on Turkey (RIT), a grassroots research cooperative based in New York City. She holds an MA in Sociology (CUNY) and an MA in Oral History (Columbia University). She published several articles about American politics in the Turkish dailies. As an oral historian, Eylem's work focuses on theories of post memory, collective memory, silence and resentment. She is the co-author of the oral history book *Keşke Bir Öpüp Koklasaydım* (with Ozlem Delikanli) about the 1980 Coup D'État in Turkey, published in 2013. Her current research, forthcoming book in 2018, as a sequel focuses on the political refugees living in Europe and North America after the Coup. She is working on a digital oral history archive for the 1980 coup, which is part of RIT's collective memory working group. She continues her research as an Institute for the Study of Human Rights fellow at the Alliance for Historical Dialogue and Accountability Fellowship Program at Columbia University.

Historicizing the Gezi Protests

Sungur Savran and interviewed by Erol Ülker

Abstract The period between May and June 2013 witnessed the outbreak of an enormous wave of mass movements in Turkey aimed at stopping government attempts to demolish Gezi Park, located in the Taksim area of Istanbul, and put up a shopping center designed to resemble the old Taksim Military Barracks. The street actions that began in Istanbul around Taksim Square swiftly spread across Turkey, many parts of Europe, and even some cities in the United States. It is true that the single most important site of this people's protest was Gezi Park, occupied for a full fortnight, with the otherwise ubiquitous police nowhere to be seen. This was a genuine local commune with all needs being met in a communal manner. But to restrict the understanding of the movement to this location because it was so spectacular implies a kind of reductionism and prevents us from understanding the many different manifestations of opposition against the oppressive AKP government of Recep Tayyip Erdoğan, then prime minister, currently president of the republic.

Keywords Turkey · Gezi protests

The period between May and June 2013 witnessed the outbreak of an enormous wave of mass movements in Turkey aimed at stopping government attempts to demolish Gezi Park, located in the Taksim area of Istanbul, and put up a shopping center designed to resemble the old Taksim Military Barracks. The street actions that began in Istanbul around Taksim Square swiftly spread across Turkey, many parts of Europe, and even some cities in the United States. A variety of descriptors have been used for the Gezi or June protests—that the protests were an uprising, a resistance, a revolt. How would you explain the character of these movements? What happened in May and June 2013?

S. Savran (✉)
Istanbul, Turkey
e-mail: sungur.savran@gmail.com

E. Ülker
Altınbaş University, Istanbul, Turkey

© Springer International Publishing AG, part of Springer Nature 2019
E. Özyürek et al. (eds.), *Authoritarianism and Resistance in Turkey*,
https://doi.org/10.1007/978-3-319-76705-5_4

33

I would characterize the Gezi events of 2013 in Turkey—themselves part of a much wider cycle of popular struggle around the world and especially around the Mediterranean basin in the period of 2011–2013—as a popular rebellion. One should beware of reducing the significance of these events to what was little more than their trigger—the struggles around the future of Gezi Park. The movement was much wider and more varied than that. According to figures provided by the Ministry of the Interior, the movement spread to 80 out of the 81 provinces of Turkey and brought out on the streets a full three and a half million people, not counting the multitudes who stayed home, but joined in with the clamor of their pots and pans, a form of protest that in Latin America is called the *cacerolazo*. Even that figure is in all probability an underestimation. It is true that the single most important site of this people's rebellion was Gezi Park, occupied for a full fortnight, with the otherwise ubiquitous police nowhere to be seen. This was a genuine local commune with all needs being met in a communal manner. But to restrict the understanding of the movement to this location because it was so spectacular implies a kind of reductionism and prevents us from understanding the many different manifestations of opposition against the oppressive AKP government of Recep Tayyip Erdoğan, then prime minister, currently president of the republic.

One can safely say that if the felling of trees by the municipal workers in Gezi Park was the triggering event, the clearly sectarian pro-Sunni, anti-Alevi Syria policy of the Erdoğan-Davutoğlu duo—the latter was first foreign minister and later prime minister—was the fundamental driving force behind the mass movement. The Alevis were a major force in the protests. The revolt encompassed a large section of wage workers, but was not a working-class struggle in the classical sense of the term: it did not advance any specifically working-class demands, nor did any section of the working class engage in methods of struggle such as strikes or workplace occupations that are the hallmark of class struggle.

I believe the popular rebellion was not confined solely to the month of June, as many seem to think, but it in fact extended all the way to mid-September. It is true that Gezi Park was forcibly evacuated by the police in mid-June, and other cities followed suit. But then there followed a bustling public forum movement, where thousands of people come together in neighborhood parks to discuss a way forward without any predetermined hierarchy. That was somewhat alien to the political culture of the country. This, I believe, is one important dimension of the durable legacy of the popular rebellion.

How can we historicize the Gezi protests? Are they a unique development in the modern history of the Ottoman Empire and the Republic of Turkey?

In certain respects, the Gezi protests are unique in Turkish history. But in other respects, there are precedents. The mass movement that formed both the background and the sequel to the Constitutional Revolution of 1908 is one important precedent. This was when Turkey came closest to having a classical bourgeois revolution, one in which a newly emerging bourgeoisie mobilizes the popular toiling classes. The moment was filled with promises that subsequent historical developments simply did not fulfill. On the one hand, that movement was the product of a series of struggles, revolts, and insurrections. Some of the Young Turk leadership had been engaged in fighting a counterinsurgency war against Macedonian guerrillas in the Balkans before they turned their arms against the "Red Sultan," Abdul Hamid II. On the day the sultan conceded the demands of the revolutionaries, Ottoman–Turkish officers and Macedonian irregulars embraced each other.

The revolution was also preceded by a series of tax revolts in many cities of the empire, including cities such as Erzurum in the eastern part of present-day Turkey, a bulwark of conservatism nowadays. Another dynamic behind the revolution was the series of mutinies that took place in many barracks against abominable working conditions, poor pay, and discrimination against officers of humble background. Once victorious, the revolution opened up a Pandora's box of discontent throughout society. A very strong mood of working-class activism created a wave of strikes the like of which would not be seen again until the 1960s. In every city, down to the backwaters of provincial towns, thronging crowds came out chanting the catchword of the revolution: "Liberty! Liberty!" A large number of new periodicals saw the light of day and numerous political parties were formed in the immediate aftermath of the revolution.

But this was not exclusively a Turkish revolution. In an empire that still extended from the Balkans to the Indian Ocean, this was truly a multinational revolution. The imam, the Orthodox or Gregorian priest, and the rabbi all rubbed shoulders in the empire. Macedonian and Armenian revolutionary parties were as important in the uprising as the Young Turk Committee of Union and Progress (the Unionists). The 1902 and 1907 Unionist congresses were attended by the minority revolutionary parties as well. Given the later tragedy that befell them during the Great War (WW I), it is interesting to note that the Armenians cooperated with the Young Turks for the first five years of the revolution. The popular image recently in vogue of the Young Turks as bloodthirsty power seekers from day one of the revolution is a caricature. This perception is noxious in that it obscures the possibility of retrograde tendencies within every revolution, as with the wave of retreat and repression during the Thermidor of the French revolution. It was only as a result of their ill-prepared response to material developments in the real world that the Young Turk movement turned to the monstrous policy that led to the Armenian Genocide of 1915.

Why did the liberal and multinational spirit of the Ottoman constitutional movement fall apart so fast between 1908 and 1915?

In a nutshell, this was a result of the disintegration of the multinational Ottoman project during the revolution's early years. The Albanian revolt and subsequent independence in 1912 and the Balkan Wars of 1912–1913 led to the loss of the entire European territory possessed by the empire. The Unionists despairingly turned to a different strategy of pan-Turkism cum pan-Islamism in place of Ottomanism—although interestingly enough, the Young Turk leaders were atheists and agnostics. This new strategy pitted the Turks, the politically ruling ethnic group, against the Greeks and Armenians, the economically dominant ethnic groups. The new economic strategy adopted from 1913 on of promoting a "national economy" implied that the Turkish element would be promoted to the position of being the economically dominant group. The Unionists jumped on the opportunity created by the outbreak of World War I in the hope of solving the quandary faced by an ailing empire. In what amounted to a *fuite en avant*, a doubling down, the Young Turks, prodded on by the German Kaiser Wilhelm II, worked to spread Ottoman influence to distant Muslim and Turkic lands. The Armenians were thus perceived as a barrier between Turkey and the Turkic-Muslim peoples of the Caucasus and Central Asia. The genocide was willfully planned by the Ottoman General Headquarters under the leadership of Enver Pasha and Talaat Pasha, who were encouraged by their German allies. The genocide also acted as a primitive accumulation process for the incipient Turkish bourgeoisie: Armenian possessions were turned over to the Turkish propertied classes. This was a classic case of a revolution turning reactionary, while at the same time remaining on the terrain of the revolution—a Thermidor of monstrous proportions.

How did the Turkish national struggle develop? Did the Unionists involved in the persecution of Ottoman Christians impose this struggle on society from above?

The overambitious entry of the Ottoman state into World War I was an adventure of the worst kind, resulting in a double tragedy. Not only were the Armenian people massacred wholesale and driven almost to the last individual from historic Armenia, but the Ottoman Empire itself crumbled within the space of four years. So Enver Pasha, a sickly personality who reputedly compared himself to Napoleon Bonaparte, destroyed an empire as a result of entertaining misplaced dreams of establishing a commonwealth of 300 million Muslims under an Ottoman sultan cum caliph (the Islamic counterpart to the Catholic pope).

Having lost the Balkans before the war and the Arab territories during the Great War, the Turks were now losing large parts of the rump state in Asia Minor (Anatolia) to the great powers, as well as to the Greeks and the Armenians. From an oppressor nation they had been converted almost overnight into a nation without a country. This was what set in motion the so-called National Struggle, the retaking of territories where the Turkish–Muslim population remained in the majority. These were the social bases of what one could call the second Turkish revolution of 1919–1923. The differences with 1908 were twofold. First, this was no longer a multi-national revolution. Second, the popular classes, the laboring peasantry, the urban petty bourgeoisie, and the fledgling working class all remained aloof to the whole enterprise. The Associations for the Defense of Rights were home to the newly expanding bourgeoisie, notables from the western region of the country, and the sheikhs and aghas of the Kurdish territories in the east. Hence the second Turkish, or Kemalist, revolution was very much an affair of the ruling classes, with scant participation of the popular classes—a bourgeois revolution without the masses.

What is Kemalism? In your book, Class Struggles in Turkey 1908–1980 (Savran 2011), you speak of a "Kemalist revolution." Can you explain what you mean by this term?

The government that was set up in Ankara in 1920 created a situation of *dual power*, very different from the Istanbul government of the sultan. This was a clear sign that a revolution was brewing. The social basis for this government was the movement that was organized in the associations I just mentioned. Once the war against the occupying Greek armies was won in 1922, the new government under Mustafa Kemal (better known internationally by the name he adopted later, Atatürk) moved against the sultan. The republic was declared in 1923, and Turkey moved very radically toward the abolition of the ancien régime. The new Republic of Turkey was a bourgeois republic par excellence. An avalanche of laws were promulgated to guarantee private property and establish the legal framework for the smooth functioning of the capitalist market. Social life was reshaped with a view to the adoption of modern bourgeois mores. State banks and enterprises were established aiming to develop capitalism. One peculiarity of the new Turkish polity was its extreme secularism, modeled after the French *laïcité* (secularity) with all its radicalism. This gave Turkey an exceptionalism among countries with a predominantly Muslim population. Although many Arab revolutionists later adopted measures to curb the sway of religion over social and political life, to this day, even the word *secularism* has remained anathema to Arab ears; they use "civil state" as a proxy. However important this was, though, two characteristics of the new regime stand out. First, this was imposed on the masses from above. In contrast to the French revolution, for instance, which mobilized the peasant masses against the Church, the Kemalist revolution attacked the privileged position of religion in spite of the masses. Second, this onslaught against the prerogatives of Islam was only one part of a much larger *civilizational shift*, whereby the young republic attempted to cut the umbilical cord that tied Turkish society to Islam and the East. These two elements generated a situation of alienation of the masses—in particular those from the interior and the countryside—from the new regime.

How did the Kurdish question evolve in this context of a "bourgeois revolution without masses," as you call it, and the transition from the Ottoman Empire to the Republic of Turkey?

The picture depicted above may have already suggested to the perceptive reader that the process of forging a nation-state out of a multinational empire lies at the basis of much of the violence in the period extending from the Berlin Conference of 1878 to the Armenian Genocide of 1915. By the time the republic was declared in 1923, there remained relatively few Armenians and Greeks on the territory of the new Turkish state. The Armenians had been decimated by the genocide of 1915 and by the earlier massacres of 1894–96 under Abdul Hamid II. The Greeks had been sent away as a result of the Population Exchange of 1923 agreed to between Greece and Turkey. The young republic was faced with a situation where the rising Turkish bourgeoisie had already attained a "final solution," to put it cynically, with respect to the non-Muslim nationalities. The major stumbling block in the way of building a Turkish nation-state remained the Kurdish question.

Kurdistan is the historic homeland inhabited by the Kurdish people, partitioned into four parts under the international order established by British and French imperial powers and the main regional powers of Turkey and Iran. The four parts of Kurdistan were distributed among the latter two countries and Iraq and Syria, which were at that time colonial possessions of Britain and France respectively. The Kurds thus remained a stateless people although their number figures anywhere between 30 and 40 million. That is why the century that has passed since World War I has been replete with Kurdish revolts and revolutions.

Under the Ottomans, the division really was between Muslim and non-Muslim. But alongside the increasing emphasis on Turkism—first by the Unionists, later by the Kemalists—there grew a national awakening of the Kurds. The Kemalist republic responded virulently. Its cruelty in smashing the many Kurdish rebellions in the interwar period, especially in the case of Dersim in 1936–1938, is only matched by Unionist savagery vis-à-vis the Armenians during the war. Despite the tragedy that befell them each time, these rebellions have left behind a legacy of struggle for national dignity and freedom within the ranks of the Kurdish people. The present-day Kurdish struggle, much more modern and progressive than all of the earlier ones, is a descendant of that tradition.

What were the effects of the Cold War on Turkey in the 1940s and 1950s?

After the single-party regime of the 1920s and the 1930s, Turkey kept away from World War II and in its aftermath turned its face to the victors in the West. As a result of a combination of domestic and international factors, it made a paltry transition to a multiparty parliamentary system. A new political tradition was born at this stage that has marked Turkish political life to the present day. It is bourgeois through and through, yet distinguishes itself from Kemalist ideology by emphasizing a return to what it considers to be the "authentic" traditions of the Turkish people, in opposition to the civilizational shift undertaken by the Kemalists. The relative weight given by the different representatives of this political tradition to Islam as a ruling force in social and political life has varied, and has now soared with the present AKP government. Four major political leaders representing this new tradition stand out in the 70 years since the end of the Cold War and Turkey's transition to multiparty democracy: Adnan Menderes in the 1950s, Süleyman Demirel in the 1960s and the 1970s, Turgut Özal in the 1980s and early 1990s, and Recep Tayyip Erdoğan in the 2000s.

This whole period was dotted with military coups and interventions that brought down the governments led by these leaders. Menderes was even hanged along with two of his cabinet ministers. And so a whole mythology has been created around the nature of this tradition. A large section of the intelligentsia, including major components on the left, has naively come to believe that this tradition, representing the "periphery" of Turkish society as against the despotic "center," is the bearer of democracy in Turkish history. This has been disproved in practice time and again, but coups have come to the aid of the mythology. Another section of the intelligentsia, also comprising large segments of the left, has embraced Kemalist ideology because of the conservative, pro-Islam, and openly pro-imperialist policies of this new tradition.

Turkey saw the rise of an unprecedented number of social movements and labor struggles during the period from 1960 to 1980. Why is this period exceptional in terms of the intensity of street actions and revolutionary activism? What were the underlying dynamics of the mass movements in the 1960s and 1970s?

The 1960s and the 1970s stand out in the history of modern Turkey in several respects. First, as you rightly point out, there was a feverish tempo of activity on the part of the downtrodden masses of society: workers, poor peasants, students, the Kurdish people, and people from the professions—engineers and architects in particular—all joined the fray.

Second, this was the time when the proletariat, the modern working class, really ascended to the stage of history in Turkey. There were very militant strikes, huge marches, strong politicization, a new and militant labor union movement called DİSK (Confederation of Progressive Trade Unions, *Türkiye Devrimci İşçi Sendikaları Konfederasyonu*)—which threatened the very existence of the earlier bureaucratic, domesticated, docile union movement. The first workers party (TİP) made its brilliant debut in the elections of 1965, sending 15 socialist members to the Turkish parliament for the first time ever. Indeed, in the very middle of this two-decade period, an event happened that was the closest the Turkish working class ever came to an insurrection: the so-called June 15–16 incident of 1970, when more than one hundred thousand workers across the huge industrial conurbation surrounding Istanbul laid down their tools and took to the streets to repel a piece of legislation whose practical aim was to paralyze and eventually liquidate DİSK. This incident terrified bourgeois Turkey and led to the declaration of martial law, but also to the repealing of the legislation in question. It was subsequently DİSK that set the tone of the whole sociopolitical life of the country in the 1970s. One can even sum up the meaning of the military coup of 1980 by conceptualizing it as the savage response of the bourgeoisie to the June 15–16 incident. Despite the very many differences in content and form, the June 15–16 incident is the only turning point in modern Turkish history that can be compared to the Gezi protests.

How did political Islam increase its popular base after the coup of 1980? Is there a significant correlation between the application of neoliberal policies and the rise of political Islam in Turkey?

Without going into the intricacies of the struggles between the different wings of the Islamist movement, the whole quarter century that extends from the 1991 elections to the present may be considered to be the period of ascendancy of Islamism. As with all social phenomena of historical significance, this has many different causes. Leaving aside the international factor of a general rise in the Islamist movement since 1979—the year of the Iranian revolution and of the occupation of Afghanistan by the Soviet army—one can say that there were four major factors peculiar to Turkey.

First, the military dictatorship of the early 1980s cleared the ground for Islamism by smashing the militant union movement and the left, on the one hand, and by turning officially to an arch-conservative ideology called the "Turkish-Islamic synthesis," on the other.

The second factor is the impoverishment and helplessness of the working masses in Turkey in the context of an all-out assault on the gains of the past effected through neoliberal strategies adopted by all the parties.

Third, the most important single factor that explains the recent rise of Islamism in Turkey is the intraclass struggle now taking place. A new wing of the Turkish bourgeoisie is challenging the vested power of the old faction that emerged throughout the formative decades of the republic. This wing has adopted Islamism as its ideological mantle in opposition to the firmly entrenched Westernizing and secular orientation of the earlier wing. It is this intraclass contradiction that explains both the very acute contradictions within the establishment and the resilience of the AKP government.

One should finally call attention to a structural factor of immense importance, usually disregarded by the secular intelligentsia. As I have already pointed out, the Kemalist republic effected a civilizational shift, thereby alienating major sections of the population. Many political leaders have harped on this raw nerve successfully since the transition to the parliamentary system in the wake of World War II. But only Islamism has taken this to its logical conclusion. The Islamist bourgeoisie can pretend, hypocritically of course, to have emanated from the bosom of the popular classes for this very reason. That is what forms the substance of the charismatic hold that Erdoğan has succeeded in establishing over the masses. Without understanding how to tackle the trauma visited on the people of Turkey as a result of this civilizational shift, it is very difficult for the left to win over the masses.

How would the Gezi protests change the future of this society?

The most important lesson to be learned from Gezi is that the people are not incapable of changing the world. I say this because very large sections of even the left really did not believe deep down inside what it had been saying aloud all these years: "Another world is possible!" It may perhaps be too audacious to even contemplate this, but one would hope that the present situation in Turkey might finally liberate the younger generation from the dual shackles with which the left in Turkey has been bound. The reactionary nature of the Erdoğan regime is now clear for all to see, and therefore all the idiotic illusions about the democratic nature of the anti-Kemalist ruling class have finally been decimated. From the other side, a full decade has gone by with major sections of the Turkish left expecting salvation from a Kemalist army intervention to save secularism, the republic, women's rights, and so forth. That has not come.

What *has* come is something very few people expected: a heroic attempt by the people to emancipate themselves from the exploitation and oppression to which they have been subjected. The history of modern Turkey is full of precedents to Gezi, be it the 1908 revolution in its earlier phase, or the Kurdish revolts—in particular the current one—or the massive workers' struggles, or the very advanced student movement of the 1960s, or the more recent rise in areas such as women's and LGBTQ rights or ecological movements. If only the mighty working class of

Turkey could rise again, Turkey would definitely join the band of countries that are fighting for a different future. Whatever new forms are thrown up by the future, one thing is certain: salvation will come from the self-activity of the masses and not from Kemalism or the bourgeois opposition to Kemalism.

Author Biographies

Sungur Savran is an author and political activist based in Istanbul, Turkey. He received his BA from Brandeis University in political science and completed his PhD in economics at Istanbul University, where he taught for 10 years until resigning in 1983 in protest against military repression of Turkish universities. He has taught as a visiting professor at various universities in the United States, including in the graduate faculty of the New School for Social Research in New York City. He is the author of several books in Turkish and coeditor of two volumes in English on Turkey: *The Politics of Permanent Crisis* (2001) and *The Ravages of Neo-Liberalism* (2002), both published by Nova Science Publishers. He has written for various US and British journals, including *Monthly Review, Capital and Class, Socialism and Democracy*, and *Khamsin*. He is on the editorial board of the Turkish-language theoretical journal *Devrimci Marksizm* (Revolutionary Marxism), and is a founding member of the Revolutionary Workers' Party of Turkey (DIP in its Turkish acronym).

Erol Ülker is an assistant professor of history at Altınbaş University in Istanbul. He has published several articles on the Turkification policies of the late Ottoman state, the migration and settlement policies of early republican Turkey, and the socialist and labor movements in Istanbul under Allied occupation. Ülker received his PhD in history from the University of Chicago in 2013. His dissertation was entitled "Sultanists, Republicans, Communists: The Turkish National Movement in Istanbul, 1918–1923." He holds two MA degrees from the Political Science Department of Boğaziçi University (2003) and the Nationalism Studies Program of Central European University (2004). He obtained his BA in international relations from Istanbul University in 1999.

Part II
Politics and Economics

Turkey's Economy Since the 1980 Military Coup

E. Ahmet Tonak and Ümit Akçay

Abstract The political economic program of the 1980 military coup was designed by Turgut Özal, at the time an adviser to the thenprime minister, Süleyman Demirel. Özal was later to becomedeputy prime minister under the military junta, and eventually prime minister and president of the republic. The program was based on the overarching assumption that markets operate more efficiently to produce a functioning economy than any kind of government intervention or involvement. All aspects of the International Monetary Fund and World Bank-sponsored debt and loan restructuring program of 1980—the so-called "January 24 measures"—as well as similar programs that followed it, were fully consistent with that assumption. With these measures, the internally oriented, partly planned, hybrid development model based upon import substitution industrialization (the replacement of foreign imports with domestic production) was abandoned and superseded by the market-based policies of an export-incentivizing growth model.

Keywords Turkey · Economy · 1980 coup

What are the main characteristics of the political program of the 1980 coup, which brought about the beginning of the neoliberal era in Turkey?

This political program was designed by Turgut Özal, at the time an adviser to the then prime minister, Süleyman Demirel. Özal was later to become deputy prime minister under the military junta, and later prime minister and president of the republic. The program was based on the overarching assumption that markets operate more efficiently to produce a functioning economy than any kind of government intervention or involvement. All aspects of the International Monetary Fund and World Bank-sponsored debt and loan restructuring program of 1980—the

E. A. Tonak (✉)
University of Massachusetts, Amherst, MA, USA
e-mail: eatonak@gmail.com

Ü. Akçay
Berlin School of Economics and Law, Berlin, Germany

© Springer International Publishing AG, part of Springer Nature 2019
E. Özyürek et al. (eds.), *Authoritarianism and Resistance in Turkey*,
https://doi.org/10.1007/978-3-319-76705-5_5

45

so-called "January 24 measures"—as well as similar programs that followed it, were fully consistent with that assumption. With these measures, the internally oriented, partly planned, hybrid development model based upon import substitution industrialization (the replacement of foreign imports with domestic production) was abandoned and superseded by the market-based policies of an export-incentivizing growth model.

In a globalized world economy, export-oriented growth requires competitiveness, and therefore the reduction of production costs. The military coup of 1980 suspended trade union activities, thus creating the conditions in which the January 24 measures could be implemented. The new constitution and other legal measures drafted under military rule facilitated the economic policies of the governments headed by Turgut Özal (1983–88), which reduced real wages, incentivized exports, and kept the balance of foreign trade under relative control.

Although the short-term goals of the January 24 measures were ostensibly the reduction of the balance of trade deficit and the control of inflation, it was clear from the beginning that they were in fact intended to completely dismantle the existing development model based on import substitution industrialization. The goal was to construct a neoliberal order based on the free flow of capital and goods. In this sense, even though privatization and the complete liberalization of capital flow were not implemented immediately, it is fair to say that the fundamental tenets of neoliberalism pervaded the January 24 package.

Of course, these general remarks imply neither that neoliberal policies were smoothly implemented, nor that they met with no resistance. Indeed, workers' activism in 1989 and 1990 compensated in part for the losses suffered by labor in the preceding period, while relations of distribution under the coalition governments during 1991–1998 also suffered from instability from the viewpoint of capital.

The crisis of 2001 was one of the most significant economic crises ever experienced in Turkey. The IMF's Transition to a Strong Economy program, designed by Kemal Derviş of the World Bank that year as a monetary policy exit strategy, determined the trajectory of the economy during the 2000s. What were the significant features of the neoliberal program during the 2000s?

Starting with the January 24 measures, Turkey rapidly became integrated into the world economy. It is therefore impossible to understand the recent trajectory of Turkey's economy independently of that of the world economy. Prior to the global crisis of 2007–2008, the world economy went through a roughly decadelong cycle consisting of a recession spanning 1998 to 2001 and a recovery in the years of 2002–2007. It is important to analyze the crisis of 2001 with reference to this background.

The 2001 crisis and its aftermath, during which total control of Turkey's economy passed to the World Bank and the International Monetary Fund, represent a period that can be said to have begun in June 1998 when an agreement was signed with the IMF. With the subsequent stand-by arrangements of 1999, 2002, and 2005, the economy was fully reshaped according to the preferences of international finance capital.

The basic purpose of the 1999 stand-by arrangement was to reduce the long-standing uncontrolled inflation down to single digits within a short period, specifically by the end of 2002. However, capital flight began before the program's goal could be achieved, and the need arose for further borrowing from the IMF. This was followed by news of a clash between Prime Minister Bülent Ecevit and President Necdet Sezer, which brought the already fragile markets to their knees. In February 2001, overnight interest rates reached 4,000%. The inflation control program tied to the foreign exchange anchor was abandoned, and the Turkish lira was allowed to float and quickly lost 50% of its value. The GNP itself declined by 9.4% in 2001. This was the context in which Kemal Derviş, a former vice-president of the World Bank, implemented his Turkey Program for a Transition to a Strong Economy as minister of economic affairs.

This was a generalized program enforced by the IMF, itself responsible for the crisis of 2001, but this time pushed through by Derviş. In contrast to earlier programs, foreign currency rates were now allowed to float, tighter financial and monetary policies were adopted, and "structural reform" was on the agenda. In exchange, the IMF promised 30 billion US dollars of credit by the end of 2004.

When we compare the years 2001–2007 with the preceding decade, the 2000s can be said to have been a time of relatively stable growth, but low job creation. Moreover, all indicators show that this growth was tied to foreign resources: a significant increase in foreign investment (from 10 billion to 55 billion US dollars), a steadily growing current account deficit (from 1.5 billion to 38 billion US dollars), and increasing foreign debt in the private sector (from 128 billion to 247 billion US dollars).

In Turkey's experiment with neoliberalism, which has now continued for more than three decades, the 2000s stand out by virtue of the fact that they solidified the economy's dependence on foreign resources. This demonstrates the fragile, crisis-prone structure and unsustainability of the economic program implemented by the ruling AKP government. While the ratio of the current account deficit to GDP during the 1980s and 1990s remained in the neighborhood of 1.5%, it increased to 5.4% during the period 2002–2012. Even more striking is the fact that the inflow of foreign capital, used during the Özal governments to finance the foreign trade deficit, became independent of the trade deficit during the AKP governments. The inflow of capital has added to the current account deficit. Thus, control of Turkey's economy has been relinquished to global finance capital, which has added to the economy's fragility.

What is your assessment of the Gezi protests of June 2013 in terms of the protesters' origins, class character, and short-term results?

It has been suggested that Gezi was a spontaneous, middle-class movement. It is true that the protests were neither the work of a single organization, nor were they triggered by a single cause reaching its boiling point. I think it is necessary to go beyond this qualification and see the cumulative effects of the structural, political, and cultural factors that paved the way for the protests.

As for the structural factors, it is clear that since the late 1960s, advanced capitalist countries have faced severe profitability issues in their productive sectors. After 1979, attempts were made virtually simultaneously by Thatcher, Reagan, and Özal to fix this problem by means of neoliberal policies, such as minimizing social spending and liberalizing the flow of capital and commodities. In Turkey, these policies have been implemented by every government since Özal, serving to weaken trade unions, give hand-offs to capital through the privatization of state economic enterprises, and in short encroached on the people's rights. These policies were an attempt to solve the crises and bottlenecks manifested in the 1970s as a reduction in profitability, but the crisis of 2008 made it clear that they did not work. Those who participated in the June protests were the children of this 30-year process.

Labeling the protesters as middle-class is both incorrect and harmful. It is incorrect because the term describes income groups and lifestyle preferences (or consumption patterns, if one prefers) with parameters inspired by American sociology, then goes on to generalize the description in an artificial manner to the entire population of participants in the June protests, said to exceed 3.5 million people, according to official sources. It is not for nothing that the slogan "work by day, resist by night" (*gündüz iş, gece direniş*) was used. Most of the participants were wage workers. Unemployed students and working-class youngsters mobilized from the urban fringes and other poor neighborhoods were also present among the protesters. Some identified the middle class with the petty bourgeoisie. This is conceptually incorrect, however, because the petty bourgeoisie are those who own their own means of production and also work in their own workplaces. Unlike what some may think, the petty bourgeoisie is not comprised of the small-scale bourgeoisie. My personal, albeit impressionistic, observation is that the segment of society least involved in the protests was precisely the petty bourgeoisie.

The short-term results of the June protests in Gezi Park have been what one might have expected given the despotic approach of the AKP regime. The government adopted a set of measures, ranging from passing laws further curtailing the people's freedom of speech and of assembly, to equipping the police with even more hazardous chemical weapons. Moreover, rather than seeking to understand the reasons underlying the protests, they constructed an ideological environment based upon conspiracy theories, a situation that continues to this day. This has established both the AKP's ideological superficiality and incompetence, and its inability even to manage the instruments of repression of which it disposes.

What would you highlight on the balance sheet of the three-and-a-half decadelong neoliberal experiment of Turkey?

Under the AKP government, the so-called neoliberal experiment continues in full force. The goals of this experiment have not changed at all. Rather, they have been consolidated and deepened since the adoption in 1980 of the neoliberal model and the January 24 measures, effected by a number of important policies: the complete dismantling of the public sector, particularly the state economic enterprises, by way of extensive privatization; turnover of basic service provision, such as health and education, to the private sector; full liberalization of the flow of goods, services, and capital; and limitation of wage and salary increases through enforcement of labor market flexibility and the restriction of the ability of workers to unionize.

Even with these harsh policies, Turkey's growth performance over the last 37 years has been highly erratic and mediocre when compared to the earlier import-substituting, semi-planned industrialization period. Considering the fact that the predicted growth rate for 2017 is in the neighborhood of 4–5% per annum, it would not be an exaggeration to claim that the economy can achieve such performance only with a substantial amount of capital inflows.

The neoliberal era has created two new constraints for the Turkish economy. First, Turkey has become excessively dependent on foreign investment, mostly short-term inflows, rather than direct new productive investment. Second, the foreign debt of the private sector has become excessive, currently around 216 billion dollars. Both constraints obviously make the situation more fragile than ever, even though they temporarily provide the momentum for short-term reasonable growth rates. It is clear that foreign capital flows will take into account global conditions and opportunities—for example, the contractionary monetary policies of the US Federal Reserve and the Eurozone policies of the European Union—and seek the most stable and profitable countries. Furthermore, since extreme liberalization makes sudden capital flight more likely, as we saw in 1994, 1999, 2001, and 2009, it is quite probable that Turkey will experience an external shock in the not too distant future.

The most important product of 35 years of neoliberalism remains, as I have already had occasion to point out, the accumulation of class contradictions along with the accumulation of capital. The period since Gezi has been instructive in this sense. The spring of 2015 saw tens of thousands of metalworkers rise in opposition to the company-dominated yellow union that has regimented the metallurgical industry since the military coup of 1980. They staged a widespread wildcat strike, coupled with occupations in certain plants, in several industrial basins of the country to demand the exit of that union, which the bosses had supported and continued to support unreservedly. First among the striking enterprises were the workers of multinational companies such as those of Renault, Fiat, Ford, and the like, both in plants employing up to six thousand workers and in those of more modest size. Although unsuccessful in the medium term, this experience shows the irrepressible tensions that exist within the working class, confirmed by the actions, in the same three-and-a-half years, of glass workers, municipal workers, and others. It is these contradictions first and foremost that are going to shape the evolution of Turkish society in the medium and long terms.

References

Akyüz, Y., & Boratav, K. (2003). The making of the turkish financial crisis. *World Development, 31*(9), 1549–1566.

Balkan, N., Balkan, E., & Öncü, A. (Eds.). (2015). *The Neoliberal Landscape and the Rise of Islamist Capital in Turkey*. New York and Oxford: Berghahn Books.

Balkan, N., & Savran, S. (Eds.). (2002). *The Ravages of Neo-Liberalism: Economy, Society and Gender in Turkey*. New York: Nova Science Publishers.

Köse, A., Şenses, F., & Yeldan, E. (Eds.). (2008). *Neoliberal Globalization as New Imperialism: Case Studies on Reconstruction of the Periphery*. New York: Nova Science Publishers.

E. Ahmet Tonak is a Visiting Professor in the Department of Economics at University of Massachusetts Amherst. He holds a BS in mechanical engineering from Istanbul Technical University, an MS in applied mathematics and statistics from the State University of New York at Stony Brook, and an MA and PhD in economics from the New School for Social Research. Tonak has taught courses in economics in various universities in the US for 25 years, including Bard College at Simon's Rock, New York University, and the New School for Social Research. Tonak is the author of many articles and has published several books including Measuring the Wealth of Nations: The Political Economy of National Accounts (with Anwar Shaikh), Turkey in Transition: New Perspectives (with İrvin C. Schick), and in Turkish, Marksizm ve Sınıflar (Marxism and Classes, with Sungur Savran and Kurtar Tanyılmaz), Kapital'in Izinde (In the Footsteps of Capital, with Nail Satlıgan and Sungur Savran), Kent Hakkı'ndan Isyan'a (Right to the City to the Uprising). He has been doing freelance journalism since 1972, has written columns for various Turkish dailies, and currently writes a weekly column for sendika.org.

Ümit Akçay is a visiting lecturer at Berlin School of Economics and Law. He previously held positions at Istanbul Bilgi University, Atılım University and METU in Turkey between 2016 and 2017, at the Department of Politics and at MEIS in New York University in the US between 2011 and 2015, and at the Department of Economics of Ordu University in Turkey, between 2009 and 2011. He has a Ph.D. in development economics from Marmara University, Turkey. He is the co-author of *Finansallaşma Borç Krizi ve Çöküş: Küresel Kapitalizmin Geleceği* (Financialization, Debt Crisis, and Collapse: The Future of Global Capitalism, Notabene Press, 2014), and the author of *Para Banka, Devlet: Merkez Bankası Bağımsızlaşmasının Ekonomi Politiği* (Money, Bank, State: The Political Economy of the Central Bank Independence, SAV Press, 2009) and Kapitalizmi Planlamak: Türkiye'de Planlamanın ve Devlet Planlama Teşkilatının Dönüşümü (Planning of Capitalism: Transformation of Planning and the State Planning Organization in Turkey, SAV Press, 2017). He writes a weekly column in Turkish at Gazete Duvar on various aspects of international political economy. His other works are available at https://hwr-berlin. academia.edu/UmitAkcay.

Branding as a Neoliberal Project

Aslı Iğsız and interviewed by Elif Sarı

Abstract Neoliberalism was introduced to Turkey alongside the 1980 military coup. But it is often discussed with reference to the 2000s, especially as a project of the AKP government. There are three reasons for it. First, neoliberalism has been transnationally consolidated as a hegemonic mode of capitalism over the last 10 to 15 years. Second, when the 1980 military coup happened under the leadership of General Kenan Evren, the military framed the intervention as a requirement for bringing about stability and security. In the name of stability, the military also crippled the trade unions, favoring right-wing nationalist ones over the unions on the left, and brought the 10% parliamentary threshold to the electoral system. Third, With the advent of the AKP governments, we see the victory, based on the 10% parliamentary threshold, of a strong majority for four consecutive general elections, and we see that such "stability" has brought with it tremendous power that has enabled the implementation of the neoliberal logic across a number of fields, including the health care system, and the distribution of environmental resources and property.

Keywords Turkey · Neoliberalism · AKP · 1980 coup

Neoliberalism was introduced to Turkey alongside the 1980 military coup and found its first practical applications during the Özal regime. But why is it that neoliberalism is often discussed with reference to the 2000s, especially as a project of the AKP government? What is new about the institutionalization of neoliberalism under the AKP government?

A. Iğsız (✉)
New York University, New York, NY, USA
e-mail: asli.igsiz@nyu.edu

E. Sarı
Cornell University, New York, NY, USA
e-mail: e5858@cornell.edu

© Springer International Publishing AG, part of Springer Nature 2019   51
E. Özyürek et al. (eds.), *Authoritarianism and Resistance in Turkey*,
https://doi.org/10.1007/978-3-319-76705-5_6

First, neoliberalism has been transnationally consolidated as a hegemonic mode of capitalism over the last 10 to 15 years. During that period, it so happened that the AKP was in power in Turkey. In addition to the AKP's own neoliberal policies, the transnational context made it easier to associate neoliberalism with the AKP—as if it were an exceptionally AKP phenomenon, even though, yes, this is historically inaccurate.

Second, we must remember that when the 1980 military coup happened under the leadership of General Kenan Evren, the military framed the intervention as a requirement for bringing about stability and security. The 1970s in Turkey were marked by a civil war between ideologically divided camps that were also sectarianized in many ways. The bloody massacre of more than one hundred Alevis as part of the anti-Alevi pogrom in 1978 in Maraş is an example of this. This civil war was never called by its proper name, but was instead referred to as anarchy. In that period, among many other things, there were also a series of trade union strikes, IMF programs, and coalition governments with short lifespans. The PKK was also founded in those years.

The military, which claimed to be bringing security and stability to the country, proclaimed its mission as one to protect citizens from what officials called "deviant" ideologies—read, various interpretations of Marxism or communism. For this purpose, an ideology dubbed the "Turkish-Islamic synthesis"—reminiscent of the national Catholicism of the fascist dictator General Franco in Spain—was promoted as a policy both in the cultural field and in education. Citing security reasons, the military suspended the rule of law and declared a state of emergency. Prisons such as Diyarbakır and Metris became infamous symbols of brutality. It was very clear from the onset that the real target of these repressive policies was what they called "deviant" ideologies associated with the left, which the military deemed incommensurable with Turkish "traditions." It should come as no surprise then, that they tried to fortify these Turkish "traditions" by endorsing a Turkish-Islamic synthesis as a nationalist cultural policy against what they deemed to be deviant.

In the name of stability, the military also crippled the trade unions, favoring right-wing nationalist ones over the unions on the left, and brought the 10% parliamentary threshold to the electoral system. The latter is equally important, as it harmed the electoral system. This meant that a party needed to gain more than 10% of the vote nationwide, not locally, in order to return MPs to parliament, thus allowing parties that met the national threshold to win more seats than correspond to their share of the vote. Turkey has the highest national threshold level worldwide. The rationale for imposing the 10% threshold was to bring stability to the country by keeping small parties out of parliament. To the military, this meant stopping coalitions from happening. Under former World Bank economist Turgut Özal's leadership and later his prime ministry, IMF-imposed measures of deregulation were implemented. Overall, the Evren-Özal decade was the historical precursor to the AKP.

It is ironic that the AKP's victory for four successive electoral terms would qualify as the kind of stability that Evren and his companions wished to establish. Still intact, the 10% threshold has detrimental implications for plurality and democracy. As an example, the 10% threshold generates a concrete obstacle for the Kurdish political parties, and the AKP appears reluctant to change it. Furthermore, it is possible to view the Turkish-Islamic synthesis being reinterpreted as neo-Ottomanism under the AKP rule. We can therefore say that, historically speaking, there is a direct correlation between the AKP and the 1980 coup, both in terms of conservative cultural and educational policies, and with regard to the neoliberal measures they embraced. This is the second link.

The third connection I want to address here is directly related to these issues: majority-yielded power and what might be at stake when we talk about stability. Despite the fact that remarkably corrupt governments were characteristic of the 1990s, they arguably did not do as much damage as they could have. This is for the very simple reason that they were coalition governments, and therefore no single party could establish its own hegemony. With the advent of the AKP governments, we see the victory, based on the 10% parliamentary threshold, of a strong majority for four consecutive general elections, and we see that such "stability" has brought with it tremendous power that has enabled the implementation of the neoliberal logic across a number of fields, including the health care system, and the distribution of environmental resources and property. In that sense, this might be another reason why the AKP is viewed as an embodiment of neoliberalism in Turkey, simply because of the unrivalled power they have had, how they have used that power, and the scale of the policies they were able to implement in that regard.

In short, in addition to the AKP's own neoliberal policies, there are conjunctural, historical, and political links that consolidate the AKP as an embodiment of neoliberalism in Turkey, but it would be inaccurate to consider them as the historical originator of such policies.

In your articles (Iğsız 2013 and 2014), you wrote that the AKP has been trying to create a "Brand Turkey" by establishing new partnerships with global institutions such as the World Economic Forum and the United Nations, and spearheading transnational projects like the UN Alliance of Civilizations initiated in 2005. Could you explain this branding process?

In 2005, the Spanish and Turkish governments cosponsored an initiative to address issues raised by *The Clash of Civilizations* (Huntington 1993 and 1996) discourses that gained traction in the aftermath of the September 11 attacks of 2001. This initiative, called the Alliance of Civilizations, was quickly institutionalized by the United Nations. My critique of the Alliance of Civilizations is its emphasis on "alliance" in place of putting the very notion of "civilization" into question. If we remember, Samuel Huntington's thesis was that after the Cold War, the division of the world in terms of political and economic systems was no longer relevant, and that therefore we should consider grouping countries in terms of their culture and civilization. This entailed a elision of important differences under the overarching rubric of civilization. It was also precisely for this reason that Huntington was against multiculturalism in the United States. In his books *The Clash of Civilizations and the Remaking of a World Order* and *Who Are We? The Challenges to America's National Identity*, Huntington (1996 and 2004) argued that the recognition of minorities had resulted in diluting white American ties to what he called "Western civilization"—read, Western Europe. His essentialist approach to difference is mirrored in his assessment of multiculturalism in the domestic context in the United States, and in the transnational context, in his equally problematic grouping of different countries in terms of "civilizations." This implies that for Huntington, minorities in the US do not come from the same "civilizational" background as white, Protestant Americans, and minority recognition as part of multiculturalism is detrimental to the civilizational ties of the US with the so-called "Western civilization." In short, he also racializes civilization.

With the UN Alliance of Civilizations at the time, Turkey's leading role comes across as an "Eastern" and "Muslim" interlocutor who favors such an alliance. Yet adopting a subject position within the same discourse in order to negate it—in other words, promoting "alliance" instead of "clash" of civilizations—reifies the very category of a civilization instead of debunking it. In fact, putting the stress on *alliance* without problematizing civilizational narratives risk reifying the East versus West dichotomy. Regardless of any good intentions that might have been part of such initiatives, does the term *civilization* not imply the very polarized and frozen cultural identification and worldview that a project of alliance is attempting to remedy? *Civilization* is a very problematic term with a heavily loaded history that includes colonial civilizing missions, imperialist knowledge production, and the alignment of various nation-states as hierarchized constellations within "essentially different civilizations," among others. The fact that none of this is questioned is distressing, because, even if this is not the intention, what all this implies is that this unquestioned history is in fact taken as a point of departure for conceptualizing and approaching various countries.

The problem of civilizational identification does not end there, unfortunately. In 2006, a series of "rebranding" initiatives was launched during the World Economic Forum (WEF) meetings to repair the image of the Middle East. There, Turkey was proposed as a "bridge between civilizations." In that context, there is a complete cross-fertilization between the UN Alliance of Civilizations and the WEF meetings. For example, on November 13, 2006, the first UN High-level Group report on the Alliance of Civilizations was presented in Istanbul (United Nations 2006). Ten days later, Istanbul hosted another transnational organization: the WEF in Turkey. Equally concerned with civilizations and national image, the knowledge produced for the Alliance of Civilizations projects and the categories of relevance it utilized —East-West, a Muslim country as a bridge of civilizations, and so on—were then transferred to the WEF platform. It is therefore not only a political alliance, but now also clearly an economic alliance, built upon the same premises of essentialist East-West divisions and assumptions about "civilizations" that have deeply religious implications.

In the case of the WEF, bridging civilizations was used as a tool to market Turkey, with bold references to the Alliance of Civilizations, so as to attract foreign investment and thereby rebrand the Middle East. Unsurprisingly, Turkey was widely praised for its "stability" in an unstable region. (Of course we are talking about a while ago, and not the current situation). At the 2006 WEF meeting in Turkey, the

European Union was advised by the United States to accept Turkey in order to show that an alliance of civilizations was possible. Incidentally, it was that same year that Istanbul was selected as a European Capital of Culture for the year 2010. In the mid-2000s, we therefore see a concentrated effort to frame Turkey as a bridge, and to turn that into a positive image for Turkey. Yet the way this effort was implemented through platforms such as the Alliance of Civilizations or the WEF rebranding sessions was very problematic. For the most part, this is because such measures to improve the image of a predominantly Muslim country were taken without actually questioning power discrepancies, the radicalization of inmates in places like Guantanamo, and attributing violence by Muslims to their putative "culture." Instead, the attention shifted to image and perception, and the saving of appearances. It is my sense that Turkey became an emblematic case for "bridging civilizations" in transnational organizational contexts such as within the UN, the WEF, and to a certain extent, some platforms of the EU. It is in this light that we should contextualize branding Turkey.

Brand consultants meet government officials and important actors in the business world to encourage a combined effort to promote the image of a country. One of their major concerns is to improve the negative image of a country, which they deem to be unjust. According to country brand consultants, this treatment is unfair because some countries get a bad reputation, and then foreign investors do not want to invest there, and consumers do not want to consume their products. As a result, a negative image has economic consequences. For some consultants, rebranding is a means to bring justice to a country and its image. To concretize their point, some brand consultants use the examples of France and the US versus Bangladesh and Chile. As true as this may be, we do not see an attempt to unravel why countries like France have a positive transnational image to begin with. In the case of the Alliance of Civilizations, the is just a cosmetic gloss aimed at fixing public perception, without actually opening space to question why it is that certain economic powers are invisible to such scrutiny. In other words, why are certain countries immune to such hierarchized image-making in the first place, even though they are home to disparities, rights abuses, racism, and imperial legacies?

What branding does is to render the neoliberal logic dominant in approaching nation-states. Rather than resolving political and socioeconomic disparities in national and transnational contexts, it is the culturalized image that must be fixed in order to render the country profitable for all parties. Perception and image are privileged over an analysis of the historical, political, and economic reasons for disparities, illiberal interventions, and their legacies.

It is precisely in this context that we should locate the branding of Turkey. It has become the officially embraced approach to politics. The AKP's political academy textbook (Turşucu and Beriş 2011), assigned to AKP politicians and citizens in attendance, is an example of this. Because the textbook explains nation branding in detail, we often encounter branding in the discourses of the politicians. In my opinion, the project of rebranding Turkey was successful to the extent that Turkey was promoted as a "model democracy," even when this statement obscured ongoing problems. Branding appears to bring to Turkey the same kind of invisibility that certain economic powers enjoy in terms of an absences of scrutiny of rights abuses or the rise of authoritarian measures in the name of national security. In many ways, this rhetoric reproduces Orientalism. Because when problems like the Gezi Park protests emerge, those who declared Turkey a model democracy turn around and demonize the political officials. What has changed? Is it just the reaction to the Gezi Park protests that made a difference? If anything, these swinging images from one extreme to the other risk reifying the sense of Orientalist superiority in the Euro-American context. It is astonishing that none of this was put into question.

Since the Gezi Park protests, the international press has criticized the AKP government's authoritarian tendencies—the extensive use of the police force against protesters, human rights violations, attacks on the rule of law. These critiques have only increased with the ongoing state of emergency, implemented in the wake of the coup attempt of July 2016. Because the state of emergency rule allows the government to bypass parliament through the issuing of emergency decrees, many have noted that the government seems to use the emergency rule to silence and criminalize all dissenting voices. To what extent do you find these critiques to conflict with the AKP's concern with marketing a positive national image? How would you explain the tension between the AKP's growing isolation in foreign relations and its project of creating and promoting Brand Turkey?

In the mid-2000s, the AKP was widely circulated as a success story in the transnational media. At that time, Turkey was held up as a model of democracy in the Middle East. Of course, this is an Orientalist approach at best: why does the Middle East need a model in the first place? This approach obscured what was happening in Turkey beneath the surface. After the AKP was reelected in 2007, Turkey continued to have problems with bureaucracy, civil and political rights, and plurality. In that period, mass trials and loosely interpreted anti-terror laws resulted in the arrest of roughly one out of every 6,000 citizens in Turkey under the guise of terrorism. These numbers were crystallized in an Associated Press survey conducted in 2011 on the impact of the post-9/11 anti-terror laws (Mendoza 2011). The lack of transnational visibility of these problems during those years is as problematic as their "rediscovery" now. As for the present state of emergency declared in the aftermath of the horrendous coup attempt in July 2016, it is a predictable outcome of what was already happening on the ground. In the current global climate of neofascism as well as securitarian discourses and practices, branding might come across as a better case scenario. And yet, if the pendulum can swing so sharply from one end to the other, how much were such initiatives as branding helpful in addressing the ongoing issues is a question that begs an answer. Branding was a cosmetic touch-up that didn't solve anything.

In the meantime, those who are not content with the AKP's neoliberal policies are accused of threatening the country's national security and stability and harming the marketing of a positive national image, and are criminalized. For instance, Erdoğan has repeatedly referred to Gezi protesters as "terrorists,"

and the minister of culture and tourism accused the international press of trying to diminish the value of Turkey's brand name with their coverage of human rights violations and police brutality during the Gezi Park protests. What is the relationship between branding and security discourses?

There are three major issues with regard to the relationship between branding and security discourses. First, as the official responses to the Gezi Park protests crystallized, branding appeared to be adopted at the expense of civil and political rights in Turkey. State officials such as the minister of culture and tourism or Abdullah Gül, who was the president of Turkey at the time, made it clear that the press coverage and police reactions to the Gezi protests shattered the image of Turkey. Other officials called Gezi protesters "traitors" who destabilize Turkey. And of course, stability is essential for a country's image, brand, and the economy. Second, the term *traitor* demonstrates how branding reconfigures the relationship between the citizen and the state and informs nationalism: protesting is not considered a right of citizenship, but rather a threat to stability. And because stability is essential for this model of economic growth to attract foreign money, the protesters are easily configured as a threat to the "best interests" of the nation. What we see then is a dangerous nationalism informed by branding that extends the neoliberal logic into the nationalist discourse. The preservation of the profitability of the national image becomes a national duty. Once the discourse of betraying the nation and being a traitor starts circulating, taking security measures against the so-called traitors has been legitimized. In this model, it is the citizens who are at the service of the state, and not vice versa, in order to serve the best financial interests of the country by keeping the brand image intact, even if it is at the expense of civil and political rights.

Third, the value attributed to branding the nation and preserving its positive image at the expense of the citizens informs security discourses and facilitates criminalization of protesters. One might argue that this was not the initial intention of brand consultants. But promoting branding as a way of bringing about justice through the repair of a country's image and then convincing state officials across the board that this is public diplomacy allows officials to put the emphasis in the wrong place. Straightaway, it opens the door to assigning excessive importance to the national brand as image, rather than to addressing and providing solutions for actual national problems. It should then come as no surprise that security measures are taken to protect the national image for the sake of maintaining stability, seasoned with civic duty discourses, at the expense of civil and political rights. What we get then, is the unfortunate dissemination of neoliberal logic into nationalism, put into practice via criminalization policies and security measures.

The present climate makes it looks as though we must choose between a neoliberal discourse packaged as a positive image that does not attend to actual societal issues, or securitarianism. But as the work of Matthieu Rigouste (2013, 2016) shows, securitarian capitalism constitutes the core of securitarianism, and if so, branding and securitarianism have a dialectical relationship within the capitalist system.

Does neoliberalism feed authoritarianism? What kinds of connections can we draw between neoliberalism and the high-security state in Turkey?

If we were to rethink Loïc Wacquant's work on the United States (2009), he argues that the high-security state is an essential component of the neoliberal state in the American context. State funding is not related to social security and welfare, but to the securitarian state whose aim is to protect the interests of the field of economics. This is done at the expense of the people. This system clearly overshadows democratic principles and favors the criminalization of socioeconomically disadvantaged groups.

That said, technically speaking of course, the main difference between authoritarianism and democracy is the electoral system. During the Cold War era, this distinction of whether or not a country has a transparent and reasonably fair competitive electoral system might have appeared sufficient for identifying a democracy. But in the context of today's world and shifting dynamics, these definitions are in need of serious revision. I do believe more and more security-based measures will be taken to protect capitalist interests. It is important to remember that in the post-9/11 transnational context, national security has become a hegemonic discourse that informs distressing practices that are far from transparent. One of the symptoms of this has been the overexpansion of anti-terror laws. In that respect, the lack of transparency in counterinsurgency—as Laleh Khalili's research has demonstrated (2013)—coincides with increasingly securitarian measures taken in countries with a respectably democratic electoral system. We should thus rethink amalgamated forms of *authoritarian democracies* which consist of differing shades of authoritarianism and democracy, depending on the context.

There is a complex transnational dynamic behind neoliberal policies that feeds authoritarian tendencies. Indeed, in the vast majority of countries, it is the militarized law enforcement, and no longer the Cold War-empowered military, that has undertaken the task of domestic guardianship of capitalist interests. In this changing world order, considering the military as the sole obstruction to democracy conveniently obscures the widespread growth of a militarized riot police and the deployment of nonlethal technologies against those who protest neoliberal policies around the world.

Further, the Minerva Initiative, established by the Department of Defense in the United States, funded a research project in 2014 to analyze what they called the "digital traces" of protests like the one for Gezi Park. The goal of this academic research is to identify who gets mobilized in a protest, why, and when. It is striking that the military funds such a project.

To come back to your question, yes, I believe there is a relationship between authoritarian policies and neoliberalism with differing degrees and shades, depending on the local context. On the other hand, if in a country there are signs of authoritarian tendencies, it would be simplistic to automatically assume that it is directly because of neoliberalism. Rather, the relationship between the two, in addition to the local and transnational dynamics that pertain, needs to be analyzed; stakeholders need to be concretely identified and policies need to be examined. In other words, the relationship between authoritarian tendencies and neoliberalism needs to be materially concretized. Authoritarian measures taken in the name of securitarianism need to be better laid out for both liberal and illiberal democracies.

As in many countries, urban transformation and renewal projects in Turkey constitute an important element in neoliberal transformation. Public and green spaces across the country are increasingly turned into construction sites. The interesting part is that the government continues these projects by issuing decree-laws, despite allegations of unlawfulness and legal efforts to block them. Could you elaborate on the judicial system in Turkey in light of these controversial urban projects?

Urban transformation policies have become central to neoliberal discussions in Turkey over the last few years. This has various implications, and one of them is the authoritarian implementation of decree-laws to authorize aggressive urban development. As I have discussed in detail elsewhere (Iğsız 2013), these decree-laws in Turkey undermine expert reports, legal cases, and environmental protection measures with regard to land, and open them to potential development. This is especially true for the decree-laws of 2011. Overall, the point we have reached is that of a dysfunctional system of laws and rights.

On the other hand, as we have learned from the work of social scientists Gönen and Yonucu (2011), for example, IMF-implemented policies after the 1980 military coup had a detrimental impact on agriculture in Turkey. With subsequent deregulation, state-subsidized agriculture was no longer sustained, and this, according to Gönen and Yonucu, had a big impact on migration to big cities and demographic accumulation around urban centers. These policies coincided with 15 years of a state of emergency in Kurdish regions between 1987 and 2002 and the forced "evacuation" of a large number of Kurdish villages, resulting in increased internal migration. More recently, we can also add the urban warfare that leveled Kurdish cities to ground zero, which exasperated this situation. Urban accumulation has thereby increased over the last few decades. These are among the groups that are gentrified today, together with Alevi neighborhoods, as Yonucu also discusses in her work (2013a, b, 2017).

Overall, what we see is a massive reconsideration of land for development and not for agriculture. National parks that are protected by law are also in danger. One last thing I want to interject here is that it is very important to protect the environment and not let protected sites disappear under neoliberal policies. But equally important, if we redefine the struggle for these lands in terms of development, we will be limiting ourselves. As with many national parks around the world, Turkish national parks too are being dehistoricized and depoliticized, and the history of blood shed on those sites becomes conveniently demarcated under the rubric of "national park," thus muting histories of violence and dispossession at multiple levels.

Authoritarian tendencies and instability in the country have increased dramatically in recent years—since 2015 there has been a wave of bomb explosions and gun attacks in city centers and then the coup attempt in July 2016. How can we rethink neoliberalism, security, and branding efforts in light of these recent developments?

Overall, the rise of neofascism and securitarianism across the globe appears to mobilize capitalist interests in racialized terms at yet another level. In such an environment, authoritarian and securitarian logics are reproduced in varying degrees depending on the local dynamics. The political landscape in Turkey today may appear to be very different to an outsider, but in fact, the present climate in Turkey is a predictable outcome of decades of problematic transnational policies. These policies expose global economic powers as the strange bedfellows of authoritarian figures and regimes, beginning with the successive military juntas in general, and with General Kenan Evren, the leader of the 1980 junta in particular. Locally speaking, policies and regulations established by the military are the tools that are being deployed today. The July 2016 coup attempt appears to provide the public consent to authoritarian policies such as the state of emergency. I therefore do not believe the problem can be reduced to just one person's leadership; it is a systemic and bureaucratic issue. Many bureaucrats contributed to passing laws, endorsing practices that contributed to the present dynamic. In an environment where democracy is reduced to majoritarianism rather than a plurality of peoples and institutions—and this was the direct legacy of the 1980 coup d'état, supported by the United States to meet neoliberal ends—there is always a danger of authoritarian tendencies. I firmly believe that as long as the transnational system and Turkey's problem with bureaucracy is not resolved, then if it is not one given strongman, there will always be others willing to assume the role. All branding strategies did was to shine a positive light on what was happening in Turkey, thus enabling problematic representations of Turkey and the broader Middle East. In sum, there are local dynamics but also transnational collaborations and partnerships that gave rise to the landscape that we see in the Middle East today, with Turkey being a particular instance. The Turkish case needs to be better contextualized within the current global rise of securitarianism and neofascist tendencies, so that we can put things into the proper perspective, avoid generating Orientalist exceptionalisms, and still be able to remain critical of local dynamics.

References

Gönen, Z., & Yonucu, D. (2011). Legitimizing violence and segregation: Neoliberal discourses on crime and criminalization of urban poor populations in Turkey. In A. Bourke, T. Dafnos, & M. Kip (Eds.), *Lumpencity: Discourses of marginality, marginalizing discourses* (pp. 75–103). Ottowa: Red Quill Books.
Huntington, S. P. (1993). The clash of civilizations? *Foreign Affairs, 72*(3), 22–49.
Huntington, S. P. (1996). *The clash of civilizations and the remaking of the modern world.* NY: Simon and Schuster.
Huntington, S. P. (2004). *Who are we? The challenges to America's national identity.* Simon and Schuster.
Iğsız, A. (2013, July 12–13). Brand Turkey and the Gezi protests: Authoritarianism, law, and neoliberalism (Part 1 & 2). In *Jadaliyya.* http://www.jadaliyya.com/pages/index/12907/brand-turkey-and-the-gezi-protests_authoritarianis.
Iğsız, A. (2014). From alliance to civilizations to branding the nation: Turkish studies, image wars and politics of comparison in an age of neoliberalism. *Turkish Studies, Special Issue: Turkish Studies from an Interdisciplinary Perspective., 15*(4), 689–704.

Khalili, L. (2013). *Time in the shadows: Confinement in counterinsurgencies*. Stanford: Stanford University Press.

Mendoza, M. (2011, September 5). AP analysis: 35,000 worldwide convicted as terrorists since 9/11. The Mercury News, Retreived from https://www.mercurynews.com.

Rigouste, M. (2013). *Les marchands de peur: La band à Bauer et idéologie sécuritaire* [Merchants of fear: the Bauer gang and the securitarian ideology]. Paris: Libertalia.

Rigouste, M. (2016). *Etat d'urgence et business de sécurité* [State of emergency and the business of security]. Ariège, Paris, Marseille: Niet!Editions.

Turşucu, H., & Beriş, H. E. (2011). *AK Parti siyaset akademisi lider ülke Türkiye (10 Dönem), Ders notları elektronik kitap [AK Party Political Academy Leader Country Turkey 10th Period Lecture Notes Electronic Book]*. Ankara: AK Parti AR-GE Başkanlığı Yayınları.

United Nations Alliance of Civilizations (UNAOC). (2006). Alliance of civilizations: report of the high-level group, 13 November 2006. United Nations. https://www.unaoc.org/resource/alliance-of-civilizations-report-of-the-high-level-group-13-november-2006/. Accessed 14 November 2017.

Wacquant, L. (2009). *Punishing the poor: The neoliberal government of social insecurity*. Durham: Duke University Press.

Yonucu, D. (2013a). European Istanbul and Its Enemies: Istanbul's Working Class as the Constitutive Outside of the Modern/ European Istanbul. In D. Reuschke, M. Salzbrunn, & K. Schönhärl (Eds.), *The Economies of Urban Diversity*. New York: Palgrave Macmillan.

Yonucu, D. (2013b). Devlet Şiddeti ve "Mimli" Mahalleler [State Violence and Stigmatised Alevi Neighborhoods]. *Express, 138,* 31–33.

Yonucu, D. (2017). The absent present law: An ethnographic study of legal violence in Turkey. *Social & Legal Studies.* 1–18.

Author Biographies

Aslı Iğsız is an assistant professor in the Department of Middle Eastern and Islamic Studies at New York University. Her teaching and research interests include cultural representation and cultural history, narratives of war and displacement, and the dynamics of alterity in late Ottoman and contemporary Turkish contexts. Her publications span a variety of issues that include the politics of memory, nation branding, the alliance of civilizations and image wars, law, neoliberalism, and the Gezi Park protests in Turkey. Her forthcoming book, *Humanism in Ruins: Biopolitics, Culture, and the Entangled Legacies of the 1923 Greek-Turkish Population Exchange* (Stanford University Press, 2018), offers a multidisciplinary cultural analysis of the management of alterity via the legacies of the 1923 exchange in the post-1945 transnational context with a special focus on Turkey. She is currently working on an article on race and civilization, and her second book tentatively titled *From World Exhibitions to Branding: Image Wars and Politics of Comparison.*

Elif Sarı is a PhD student in Sociocultural Anthropology at Cornell University. Her research interests include gender, sexuality, and queer theory; immigration, asylum, displacement, and borderlands; and law and violence in the Middle East. She received her bachelor's degree in Political Sciences and International Relations at Boğaziçi University, and her master's degree in the Near Eastern Studies at New York University, where she studied the intersections of sexuality, law, and violence by examining LGBTI asylum in Turkey. Her current research project explores the practices and processes of LGBTI asylum from the Middle East to the US and Canada via Turkey, as well as the lives and experiences of Middle Eastern queer refugees waiting in Turkey. She is a Co-Editor of the Turkey Page at Jadaliyya Ezine.

Urban Transformation in Istanbul

Mücella Yapıcı and interviewed by Esin İleri

Abstract Turkey is experiencing a very rapid urbanization. Today, 70% of the country's population is living in urban areas. When mass domestic migration toward big cities began in the mid-1950s, the population of metropolitan Istanbul was 1.5 million; today it is home to more than 15 million inhabitants. The interview discusses the transformation of the Istanbul through the lens of political transformations.

Keywords Urban transformation · Istanbul · Turkey

Turkey is experiencing a very rapid urbanization. Today, 70% of the country's population is living in urban areas. When mass domestic migration toward big cities began in the mid-1950s, the population of metropolitan Istanbul was 1.5 million; today it is home to more than 15 million inhabitants. Can you briefly explain this process?

In the 1950s, the decision was made to move away from state capitalism and move closer to the private sector. In Turkey, the first factories belonged to the state; for example those producing shoes, iron and steel, and sugar. When the private sector was permitted to invest in industry, the process began with the elaboration of 5-year development plans and political decisions made by the state planning agency. As a result, industry was relocated to the Marmara region.[1] This was the first turning point for urbanization and development in Istanbul and the Marmara region.

---

[1]Turkey is subdivided into seven regions, defined during the First Geography Congress of 1941, held in the capital of Ankara. These include Marmara, the Aegean, the Mediterranean, Central Anatolia, Eastern Anatolia, and Southeastern Anatolia.

M. Yapıcı (✉)
Tmmob Mimarlar Odası Istanbul Büyükkent Şubesi, Istanbul, Turkey

E. İleri
Ecole Des Hautes Etudes En Sciences Sociales, Paris, France
e-mail: esinileri@gmail.com

© Springer International Publishing AG, part of Springer Nature 2019
E. Özyürek et al. (eds.), *Authoritarianism and Resistance in Turkey*,
https://doi.org/10.1007/978-3-319-76705-5_7

It is important to keep in mind that Istanbul is a natural harbor with many streams feeding into it. In the Ottoman period, most of the land belonged to the sultan, and private ownership of the land was very rare. Starting in the 1950s, all these public lands, especially those along the banks of streams such as the Kağıthane and the Levent, were given to industrial producers and private investors. Because of this, the residential problems associated with urbanization were difficult to resolve. Istanbul urgently needed capital accumulation and the state gave all the help they could. Agriculture was undermined despite the existence of Turkish agricultural equipment corporations, and the major part of unemployment was absorbed by industry. An incredible wave begun in this period: the rise of the assembly industry, the implementation of the Marshall Plan (1948–1952), the shift from railroads to motorways, all these factors contributed to a population increase in the Marmara region. As a matter of fact, the government threw cheap building materials to the market and tolerated the development of *gecekondu* shanty dwellings in districts like Zeytinburnu, Levent, and Kağıthane because it solved the housing crisis and cut the costs of companies.

What about the 1960s and the 1970s? How did the 1968 students movements, the 1971 Turkish coup d'état, and the 1970s oil crisis affect urbanization in Istanbul?

At first things went smoothly. The 1968 student protests, the strong unionism, the rise of the labor movement, and the Great Workers' Resistance of June 15–16 1970[2] indicated a certain class consciousness and the coalescence of left currents among the youth. In this process, worker's housing zones were important places where workers and the workforce were created and reproduced, and there was an amazing culture of solidarity. But these strong networks of solidarity inconvenienced the system. At the same time, one could see the effects of the oil crisis, and then the coup d'état of March 12, 1971 happened. I find it very interesting that in Turkey, the historical shifts for urbanization coincide with those for democracy. At the time, besides the oil crisis, we were transitioning to a unipolar world, the automation industry was in trouble, they were trying to reduce costs in industry, and we also saw a shift from a production economy to a consumption economy. Meanwhile in Istanbul, the First Bosphorus Bridge was constructed between 1970 and 1973. Although *gecekondu* shanty dwellings were being developed in the old industrial districts of Istanbul like Kağıthane, Alibeyköy, and Gülsuyu, the construction of the First Bosphorus Bridge sped up the process, and a different Istanbul started to come into existence. On the other hand, since the 1970s, there have been projects to market Istanbul to foreign capital, to transform Istanbul to into Beirut—

---

[2]Following amendments made in laws on labor and unions, workers affiliated to form the Confederation of Progressive Trade Unions (DİSK). They organized demonstrations in multiple neighborhoods of Istanbul, with 75,000 participants. The following day, 150,000 protesters rallied in multiple cities across Turkey. Martial law was announced. The amendments were later annulled, but many union leaders were also arrested and stood trial. The events are commemorated each year, and are considered one of the most important protests in the history of Turkey.

because Beirut had been demolished, it was assumed that Istanbul could replace it. And as Turkey abandoned the promotion of development and neglected agriculture in Southeast Anatolia, encouraging industry to move to the Marmara region, tourism was given more and more importance. Factories in valuable areas near major thoroughfares like Kağıthane, which is connected to the First Bridge, and those behind Büyükdere, were exiled to the outskirts in İzmit, Çorlu, and Dilovası. The deindustrialization, or in better terms, the *decentralization* of industry in order to promote Istanbul as a city of culture and tourism is an important phase in the city's history.

The coup d'état of September 12, 1980 had crucial impacts in all spheres, from society to politics and economy; but also in urban matters. Can you explain in which ways the coup affected Istanbul and how urban change evolved during the 1980s?

Both military coups of that era—March 12, 1971 and September 12, 1980—were moments of significant historical change, but much less is known about the September 12 coup and its consequences for urban space. During the 1980s, a series of amnesty laws for *gecekondu* shanties were introduced, and *gecekondu* dwellings were subdivided and transformed into private property. The new shanty settlements were regarded as a source of electoral votes, and as a consequence illegally added floors were tolerated. This contributed to the disintegration of working-class, solidarity-based spaces of reproduction. However, with the construction of the Second Bosphorus Bridge in 1988, new areas were opened up to settlement, allowing for a different population to migrate to Istanbul—those fleeing from the "dirty war" between Turkey and the Kurdish guerillas and from the forced evacuations of villages in southeast Turkey.

Cities like Antep and Mersin received an important wave of migration, too. But Istanbul was regarded as a city where "stones and earth are made of gold," where you could somehow put a roof over your head with an affordable rent in the illegally constructed *gecekondu* neighborhoods and get a job with the help of fellow townsmen, even if it was only selling water on the street. In the same period, in connection with the downsizing of industry and the advent of the flexible manu-facturing system, we observed an augmentation in a new *invisible working class* which wasn't connected to a specific workplace. This situation put significant pressure on urbanization. Solidarity weakened. People discovered urban rent and land profit. They built on public property, obtained title allocation documents via amnesty laws, and then started to transform their *gecekondu* dwellings into apart-ment buildings by adding floors. In a way, the government tried to compensate for the unemployment problem by allowing the *gecekondu* owners to rent out the extra floors they were allowed to build. What they did not realize at the time was that labor demand decreased, and while unemployment was particularly high, no one was starving. It's still like this. When Bedrettin Dalan was the mayor of Istanbul between 1984 and 1989, major axes of a deindustrialized Istanbul were being traced. For example, the Tarlabaşı and Büyükdere boulevards, and the new tourism axis in Florya were promoted in this period. And then, in the darkness of the 1980 coup d'état, with the construction of the second bridge, we lost our water basins. All these things are dreadful. At the same time, while the construction boom had started, neoliberal laws and decisions concerning urban space were not yet put in place. Some protective laws that came with the Constitution of 1961, in particular the coastal law,[3] remained in place. Although some laws were repealed, as the Union of Chambers of Turkish Engineers and Architects, we began to struggle concertedly. The governments of that time didn't have strong legislative powers, and the legal grounds for the pressure brought to bear on underdeveloped countries like Turkey by global real estate and foreign capital had not yet been established. In 1995, Turkey became a member of the World Trade Organization and the General Agreement on Trade in Services. But behind all these developments, there was nothing related to industry. The sole aim was to attract capital, mainly real estate capital. And the only city that could be sold was Istanbul. They were selling the city. They were using phrases like, "How should we *sell* Istanbul?" "We should *sell* Istanbul like this." And where to begin? They began with the historically important areas, and with areas with a beautiful natural environment like Beyoğlu, Haydarpaşa, and Galata.

The August 17, 1999 earthquake struck the Marmara region—the industrial heartland of Turkey—with a magnitude of 7.5. It was one of the deadliest earthquakes in the history of Turkey, and the epicenter was just 100 km east of Istanbul. Experts predict that another major earthquake will occur along the North Anatolian Fault that passes below the Sea of Marmara, about 20 km south of Istanbul. Since 1999, the government has announced various projects and urban renewal plans designed to protect us from earthquakes. Yet the areas selected for the so-called Earthquake-Oriented Renewal Projects are not neighborhoods at major risk, but are in fact the most profitable areas. Is it possible to say that these urban renewal projects are a cover for state-led gentrification?

The third historical shift for Istanbul came with the 1999 earthquake. Between the 1970s and the 1980s, and also between the second half of the 1980s until the 1990s, universities became treacherous entities promoting globalization. They claimed that staying out of globalization would be a disaster, that cities had to create their own opportunities, and that Istanbul should be sold to the global market as a product. Phrases such as "urban renewal," "global city," "alpha and beta cities," and "competing in the urban hierarchy" entered into the urbanization vocabulary. Istanbul inflated like the Aesop's frog who envied the size of the ox. In 1999, the World Bank published a major report about Turkey which basically said, "If you want to integrate into the world economy, you need to get one or two cities into the world city hierarchy." Ali Müfit Gürtuna, the longtime mayor of Istanbul from 1988

---

[3]Known as *kıyı kanunu* in Turkish, this law aims to protect the natural and cultural properties of the coastlines along seas, rivers, and lakes dines the use of the costline, the coastlines along seas, rivers or otu olarak ekle lütfen edenler için verdiğim kaynakçad.

to 2004, said something like, "It's not countries that compete anymore, it's the cities." And therefore Istanbul was going to compete along with other cities with the help of urban transformation and megaprojects. Barcelona was pointed to as an example. And bam! The 1999 earthquake happened. Official numbers say 20,000 deaths, but we never believed it. The real numbers are around 30,000. All the capital and industry was in the Marmara region, so we experienced a collapse of the Turkish economy. I will never forget it. A few weeks after the earthquake, contractors from the UK and the US, and even the American president Bill Clinton came to Istanbul. They organized meetings at the Conrad Hotel where they talked about urban megaprojects just the way construction companies go to postwar countries to rebuild. In a sense, the earthquake legitimated the implementation of megaprojects, and the megaprojects became Earthquake-Oriented Renewal Projects. Today, 80% of the economy rests on the construction industry; the finance sector is completely dependent on it. All these megaprojects are undertaken in order to solve the national deficit.

Urban transformation, originally shaped by the market, is now carried out by the state. Turkey's Public Housing Development Administration (*Toplu Konut İdaresi Başkanlığı*) has an clear role in this process. Created as the provider of social housing for low-income residents, this government branch has become a business that produces luxury housing. Could you comment on this transformation?

Before the maps for the Marmara Earthquake Master Plan and the Plan of Istanbul were drawn to a scale of 1/100,000, the AKP came to power with an incredible legislation authorization—zoning plans were ready before the Earthquake Master Plans were. One by one, the projects were announced with the words, "We are presenting Istanbul to prospective husbands." The 1970s slogans were updated: instead of "How to sell Istanbul?" and "How can Istanbul be the new Beirut?" it was now "Istanbul will be the new Manhattan," "Istanbul will be the new Venice." It all began with the Haydarpaşa train station. After the historic Haydarpaşa train station—one of the busiest in Turkey—was damaged by a fire on November 28, 2010, traffic was gradually suspended. In 2012, the Istanbul Metropolitan Municipal Council approved a zoning plan of nearly one million square meters to transform the area into a center of tourism and commerce called "Haydarpaşa Port." Then came the Küçükçekmece and Kartal renewal projects. More than 20 such projects were marketed to prospective investors at the MIPIM International Real Estate Show for Professionals in Cannes.

After 2004, both the Public Housing Development Administration and the *Gecekondu* Settlement Building Land Office, established in the 1970s to provide credits to low-income and poor residents, were equipped with absolute power and brought directly under the prime ministry. The aims of their urban projects were to decrease the national deficit, to increase the growth rate, and to prevent economic crisis. Historic districts such as Haydarpaşa and Galata would inevitably to attract local and national investors; megaprojects such as the Third Bridge, the Istanbul Canal, the Eurasia Tunnel, Marmaray, and the Istanbul New Airport were prepared in order to attract foreign investors. The government was pushing hard to get these projects underway, but one institution stood against the urban pillage—parliament. There were constitutional rights still on the books and significant urban resistance to overcome. In response, the AKP overturned the laws during the 2010 referendum, claiming to do so in the name of democratization, but they began to weed out those who spoke out. As we can see, they all but demolished parliament. We arrived at a chaotic point in the end.

On the website of the Directorate General of Infrastructure and Urban Transformation Services it says, "The main objective of the renewal of buildings under disaster risk is to prevent the loss of life and property. With urban renewal, we aim to improve quality of life, and to create environmentally-conscious, energy-saving living spaces and a Turkey featuring tomorrow's brand cities." Urban renewal, gentrification—these concepts claim to have positive implications. What does urban renewal mean? How is it carried out in Turkey? Who are the main actors?

In 2004, not long after the AKP had to power, the government made the urban renewal law. In 2005, the Council of Ministers approved Law No. 5366 on the Preservation by Renovation and Utilization by Revitalizing of Deteriorated Immovable Historical and Cultural Properties, allowing the sale of property very quickly in cultural and historical districts such as Sulukule and Tarlabaşı, where they evicted inhabitants and opened the neighborhoods to profit and speculation. But even that wasn't enough. They needed more profit, and all of a sudden, the Law on Disasters sprang up after the Van earthquake of 2011.[4] Later on, other municipalities wanted their share, and with article 73, they obtained the right to establish urban renewal zones. The main cause for all this has been economic and social policy change. Urban renewal is nothing more than the reflection of these changes upon space. Urban space in the city acquired real estate property value. Rights to housing and shelter disappeared. Use value was replaced by exchange value. The story of Earthquake-Oriented Renewal Projects in Turkey is a fishy one. Why? Because 15 years after the 1999 earthquake they related urban renewal with the earthquake.

Earthquake preparedness is proposed as the main reason for state-led urban renewal projects. While geotechnical earthquake engineers reported 700,000 houses under earthquake risk, Erdoğan Bayraktar, Minister of Environment and Urban Planning (2011–2013), announced that 7 million houses would be demolished, an increase by a factor of 10. On the other hand, the money levied through earthquake taxation[5] is used to build divided highways. After the Marmara earthquake, 232 out of 470 parks and green spaces designated as

---

[4]Law No. 6306, on the Renewal of Areas under Disaster Risk, also known as the "Disaster Law."

[5]This was a temporary, one-year tax imposed in 1999, designed to raise funds for those who had suffered during the Marmara earthquake. The tax law became permanent and the funds have subsequently been used for other purposes, such as the construction of highways.

gathering places in case of an earthquake are being allocated to development projects. What does this contradiction mean, and what kind of urban state policy does it relate to?

I would like to reply this with a thesis from Milton Friedman. In times of crisis and disaster, you can make people do anything out of fear. This is quite doctrinal. I do not believe that people are acting out of fear in Turkey. Our society is not afraid of earthquakes at all. People realize the dangers posed by an earthquake from their experience of the last one 16 years ago. Where have they been these past 15 years? How could they just sit there, waiting for the next one? Don't they feel any responsibility toward their children? They've all been waiting for the rise in the imputed value. It's horrifying. There is obviously a huge profit to be made, and everyone wants to legitimize their indecency by using the pretext of earthquake preparedness. If people were moral, this corrupt order would not endure. The economic system needs fresh money and Turkey is trying to solve this with the construction and sale of private property. The construction and housing industries are nourishing the finance sector, and, not coincidentally, the biggest enterprises accumulating interest by exploiting the city are the energy corporations and media companies.

What is the role of the Ministry of Environment and Urbanization, created in 2011, in this urban renewal process?

Today, the Ministry of Environment and Urbanization has plenary power to make all zoning plans. The minister orders a plan, the plan is prepared, and he then approves it. Look at this file. This is about Haliç Port, the Golden Horn. Plans have been prepared for the Golden Horn, the board didn't agree, alas it's been approved, end of story. The ministry announces that they have chosen the Golden Horn as a special project zone for landscaping. It's a fait accompli. Why bother to pass the plan from the district council, to circulate it, and wait for the chamber of architects and the chamber of agricultural engineers to see it and file a lawsuit? Instead of handling it fairly, they start constructing. It's not legal, but they begin construction anyway. Today, the law doesn't exist anymore, especially zoning law.

Do we have to oppose urban renewal as a whole, or is there another form of urban transformation possible?

The urban renewal concept is problematic. It appeared in the urbanization vocabulary sometime in the 2000s. And they're trying to legitimize it by showcasing the rapid urbanization and the irregular construction we're experiencing in the city. Cities always change, they transform. Buildings are renovated, they wear out, and are abandoned. You can prevent things going that far with a properly planned settlement policy and a solid economic policy. And then you can try to improve the city. But this is not the case in Istanbul. A healthy city is a city where children go school without having to take cars, where we can reach clinics and hospitals without transportation. Current urban renewal projects have no concern for these issues. The type of urban change we're experiencing is transformation—it's turning something into something else. Just look at the new definition of a "park." It's defined as places where you can retain a certain amount of earth in which to grow plants, where you can construct underground parking lots, or taxi stands, or police stations. This is the official definition given in the municipality's documents.

It is as though we were living in the middle of a big construction site. Although many cities in Turkey are affected by this flood of construction, large-scale urban projects are particularly concentrated in Istanbul. There is ongoing state-led gentrification, combined with "crazy projects"—that's how Erdoğan himself calls them—like the Third Airport and the Istanbul Channel, which aim to link the Black Sea to the Sea of Marmara by carving Istanbul into two peninsulas. You stated that in destroying the northern forests and polluting water resources, the Third Bridge would cause an ecological disaster. Could you please explain what kind of city Istanbul would become if these projects are implemented?

Let's look at the environmental impact assessment for the Third Airport. Funds were allocated even before the environmental impact assessment was announced. State auctions were held and the foundations were quickly laid, yet there was no construction or development plan yet. They drew out the construction plan seven days after the foundation was laid. What else can I tell you? Look, they will build the Third Tubular Passage. The project was accepted in the municipal council with only three PowerPoint slides. They claim to construct a rail passage but it's impossible to construct a railway underwater where there is a 6.5 km inclination; they cannot construct it.

What are they going to do?

They will build a motorway instead. They plan to erect two new towns in Istanbul, and they will need this motorway to connect those new towns to the airport, which needs customers.

After Gezi, new forums, new urban commons and local initiatives sprang up in order to protect those squares, parks, gardens, and historic buildings open to public use, places like Haydarpaşa train station. A common struggle to protect urban public spaces seems to have been born. Is it possible to say that a new citizen is being born, aware and able to think broadly about urban space, beyond their own neighborhood? Are there differences between the pre- and post-Gezi urban struggle?

Of course there's a difference. Something important happened after Gezi. But we're also fragmenting. It's like after the Paris Commune. Public forums became more active, but we still need to find a way to organize around big themes like public space, the Third Bridge project, and the like. One way or another, this fragmentation will end. But we're passing through hard times in terms of urban planning and the economy. The government is interfering in an authoritarian fashion because they're very much trapped. All these new laws they pass—for example, the internal security law—shows that we're in deep trouble. So what have we learned from

Gezi? We learned that we have to unify our approach. Neoliberalism has divided and dismembered us. It made each of us into the specialist of a tiny part of the bigger picture—it forced me to think about the door handle and you to think about the potted plant. This is not consistent with the philosophical approach of engineering. It made us forget the philosophical foundations of our work. We rediscovered this after Gezi. We no longer do projects alone. When we look into a project, we do it together—the construction engineer, the urban planner, and the locals. We're insurmountable that way. That's why Erdoğan wants to shut parliament down. He wants to destroy this unified consciousness.

References

Turkish Ministry of Environment and Urbanization. http://yalova.csb.gov.tr/il-mudurlugu-olarak-kentsel-donusum-bilgilendirme-calismalarimiz-devamediyor-haber-95573. Accessed December 2017.

World Bank. (1999). Title of report. http://siteresources.worldbank.org/INTDISMGMT/Resources/TurkeyEAM.pdf. Accessed December 2017.

Mücella Yapıcı is an architect (MArch) and an activist. She graduated from the Istanbul Technical University's Faculty of Architecture and served as secretary-general of the Chamber of Architects Istanbul Branch and head of the Environmental Impact Assessment Commission in the Union of Chambers of Turkish Engineers and Architects. She is also a member of the union's Urbanization and Disaster Committees. She was a key figure in the Gezi Park protests where she was one of the spokespersons for Taksim Solidarity, a platform of 128 NGOs dedicated to the protection of Gezi Park. After Gezi, she was accused of "establishing an organization with the purpose of committing crime," "being one of the leaders of a criminal organization," and "contravention of the Law on Public Gatherings and Demonstrations," and face up to 29 years in jail. She was acquitted in April 2015.

Esin İleri is a Ph.D. candidate in Sociology at EHESS (Ecole des Hautes Etudes en Sciences Sociales). She holds a B.A. in Sociology from Galatasaray University (2004), and M.A. in Sociology with a specialisation on Social Movements from EHESS (2005). Her main research and teaching focus evolves around individual/collective political activism and the urban. She is a member of CADIS—Centre d'analyse et d'intervention sociologiques (EHESS—France) and SMAG—Social movements in the global age research group (Université Catholique de Louvain—Belgium). She is currently working for the national daily newspaper Cumhuriyet.

Part III
Political Islam and the AKP

The Justice and Development Party (AKP)

Yüksel Taşkın and interviewed by Burak Cop

Abstract By actively supporting Turkey's EU membership process, the AKP had placed itself in the democratization wagon and had thereby gained the sympathies of the US and European capitals. This was the most secure way to counterbalance the military, which carried out a "postmodern coup" in February 1997. Erdoğan openly declared that the AKP was not Islamist but was rather a conservative democratic party. The question is, had the AKP elite truly internalized the new discourse of democratization or was it just a Machiavellian strategy of deception? They were neither committed democrats nor inflexible Islamists with a hidden agenda. Having opened the Pandora's box, they were not ready to deal with the new actors that came on the scene with their diverse and sometimes clashing demands.

Keywords AKP · Democracy · Islamisim · Turkey

The AKP has been in government for 14 years. Have they changed ideologically over that period, or have they retained their originally staunch Islamist stance?

Before the rise of the AKP, there were lively debates within Islamism and between Islamists and liberals on the compatibility of Islam and democracy. It would be misleading to conclude that these debates eventually produced a consistent democratic program ready to be put in practice. There were other factors as well, for example the rise of Islamic business groups that wanted to see a new party that would avoid clashes with the state while pursuing the main goals of the neoliberal agenda introduced by Turgut Özal in the 1980s. For these actors, the main goal was neither intraparty democracy nor democratization of Turkey as a whole.

Y. Taşkın (✉)
Istanbul, Turkey
e-mail: yuxelina@yahoo.com

B. Cop
Istanbul Kültür University, Istanbul, Turkey
e-mail: m.cop@iku.edu.tr

© Springer International Publishing AG, part of Springer Nature 2019   75
E. Özyürek et al. (eds.), *Authoritarianism and Resistance in Turkey*,
https://doi.org/10.1007/978-3-319-76705-5_8

Having accepted the main rules of the game, they simply wanted to replace the secular actors in the economic, cultural, and political realms. These business groups admired Turgut Özal's Motherland Party (*Anavatan Partisi*) yet wanted to color it with a more conservative identity.

It should not be forgotten that newly rising Islamic media outlets were largely created and sponsored by these Islamic business groups. The Islamic media had interacted with liberal circles to promote the AKP as the exclusive actor of belated democratization in Turkey. This was essentially a strategy to bypass the increasingly obsolete politics of fear that had been imposed by the secular Kemalist regime guardians of the state.

By actively supporting Turkey's EU membership process, the AKP had placed itself in the democratization wagon and had thereby gained the sympathies of the US and European capitals. This was the most secure way to counterbalance the military, which carried out a "postmodern coup" in February 1997. Erdoğan openly declared that the AKP was not Islamist but was rather a conservative democratic party.

The question is, had the AKP elite truly internalized the new discourse of democratization or was it just a Machiavellian strategy of deception? They were neither committed democrats nor inflexible Islamists with a hidden agenda. Having opened the Pandora's box, they were not ready to deal with the new actors that came on the scene with their diverse and sometimes clashing demands.

Despite Erdoğan having promised intraparty democracy by de-linking the AKP from the one-man tradition of the National Outlook (*Milli Görüş*) movement, within two years he had changed all restraining articles in the party bylaws and had made himself an autocrat who demanded unquestioning loyalty.

Can a leader asking for unquestioning loyalty from his party members recognize other political groups as equally legitimate players? Even when the party introduced certain democratic reforms, it never accepted rival political groups as legitimate. The AKP elite has always avoided power-sharing with others. In so doing, they have exploited the center-right tradition of reducing democracy to a tyranny of the majority by claiming themselves to be the unique voice of a long-silenced Muslim majority.

The majoritarian fallacy seems to be the most enduring hindrance to the consolidation of the democratization process in Turkey. Political actors, including the AKP, must recognize their limits by accepting power-sharing as the underlying principle for a new civilian constitution. A new constitution based on power-sharing or decentralization of power may be the only answer to the persistence of authoritarianism in Turkey.

But there is a dilemma here: will the ruling party accept power-sharing and impose constitutional limits upon itself? The AKP elite appear all too happy to control vast amounts of state power and resources and are busy empowering their economic, cultural, and political cadres with the various state resources at their disposal.

However, the new actors that have become more visible after the opening of the Pandora's box of democratization will not accept the "Old Turkey" political style of authoritarianism. The AKP seems to have positioned itself as the sole obstacle to democracy in Turkey.

After a time, parties in government typically weaken and fall from power. This has not yet been the case with the AKP. Can this be explained solely with reference to the opposition's inability to succeed?

The AKP won landslide victories in the last three general elections held in 2002 (34%), 2007 (47%), and 2011 (50%). The party also won two consecutive elections in June and November 2015 with 40 and 50%. The AKP also had clear victories in three local elections in 2004, 2009, and 2014, two referendums in 2007 and 2011, and two presidential elections—one indirect in 2007, and one via popular vote in 2014. In 15 July 2016, pro-Gülen community sympathizers in the army staged an abortive coup. After the failed coup, the AKP imposed a state of emergency and severely restricted existing freedoms in Turkey. Finally the AKP, in collaboration with the ultra-nationalist MHP, imposed a referendum in April 16, 2017 to introduce a presidential system without accompanying checks and balance mechanisms. The AKP-MHP alliance won the referendum with a slight margin (51%). Turkey has turned into a one-man rule as Erdoğan now controls almost all political power defined in the constitution.

There are economic, cultural, and political reasons to explain AKP's successive electoral victories. The AKP has developed some very flexible redistributive mechanisms which have significantly benefited underprivileged sectors. The local governments assumed an active role in this line of clientelist and flexible redistribution politics that Erdoğan calls *hizmet siyaseti*, politics based on the provision of services. Millions of poor people receive some 500–700 US dollars monthly. Because these supports are not based on regular state policies and programs, the poor people who are dependent on them feel that they can lose them if they do not support the ruling party. The AKP has also made the strategic choice of granting these informal aids to the women in the family—a choice that has thus far produced disproportional support for the party among women.

This is also the reason many Kurds in the metropolitan areas vote for the AKP. In fact, a majority of Kurds vote for the AKP, while the HDP openly voices Kurdish discontent, ranks second among Kurdish voters. Here again, the support of Kurdish women in the western cities seems to be crucial.

On the political and cultural level, Erdoğan and his AKP cadres also benefit from their claim to authentic representation. The AKP positions itself as the sole representative of the silent Muslim majority, which they pit against a "disproportionally active" Westernized secular minority. This is not just about a politics of resentment. There is also an implicit promise to refill the empty seats of power created by the marginalization of the old-guard secular elite. Even poor people who support the party are vulnerable to being manipulated by the promise of upward mobility.

The main opposition parties—the CHP, the Turkish nation-state's founding party, and the MHP—seem to be deadlocked in their reactionary discourses and therefore fail to produce hope for large sectors of the population. The CHP is in the middle of an identity crisis, caught between its secular-republican identity and its officially declared social democratic orientation. In order to attract voters from the larger pool of ordinary Muslims and from Kurds, the party needs to reform itself. Today, the CHP is a party solely supported by the peoples of the western shores of Turkey who come from relatively privileged social and economic backgrounds. While the party is giving signs of softening its militant secularism, it is still reluctant to recognize the sociological roots of the Kurdish question.

The MHP also suffers from its reactionary nationalist discourse. The object of reaction during the Cold War were the communists, to be replaced in the post-Cold War era by the Kurds. The MHP is still too far away from recognizing the historical and sociological roots of the Kurdish question. Due to its obsession with the Kurdish "problem," the party fails to garner the support of many sectors of society. Thus, it has reduced itself to the defense of a lost cause.

What are the differences between the AKP and previous right-wing parties in terms of the social networks they created?

In the past, the center-right parties had managed to gain support from politically passive people mostly living in the countryside. In this regard, the AKP may be credited with having urbanized the type of representation that center-right parties had created long before.

When we look at the people who live on the outskirts of the metropolitan areas, they have been more active in the AKP than they were in the former center-right parties. They have not only been active in the AKP party rank-and-file, but also in the party leadership. This gives some credit to the party's claim to authentic representation.

The AKP have also benefited from building clientelist networks within the local governments, which in return have contributed to the AKP national electoral performance. The Islamist movement was successful at the local level before setting its sights on the national power center in Ankara. It can even be claimed that they have set a precedent: "the road to national power must begin with the building of power networks within the local governments."

Right-wing governments before the AKP had a tradition of including a liberal or pro-Western wing. Members of this wing of the party tended to be from an influential minority with strong links to urban business circles. Such a wing has never existed in the AKP. Former center-right parties also had a tradition of working with nationalist cadres in the state bureaucracy. The AKP has also distanced itself from this tradition. The party has its own Islamist cadres, a significant part of whom were socialized in the radical Islamist movements of the 1980s.

Unlike Turgut Özal and his Motherland Party in the 1980s, the AKP does not feel obliged to cooperate with secular businessmen and media elites. The AKP was made possible by the newly rising economic, political, and cultural Islamic elite whose main concern was to take possession of those powers long enjoyed by the secular elites. This struggle for conquering and redefining the center of power, rather than complying with its main premises, makes the AKP radically different from former center-right parties.

Are there any leftish elements in the AKP's social policies?

The AKP has managed to develop a very flexible model of redistribution. This model has been criticized for its informal nature. Many critics have argued that rather than contributing to the creation of a strong welfare state based on citizenship, this model promotes clientelist favoritism by selectively promoting some people at the expense of others. Is this a leftist element we see in AKP practices? I think the right term is populist. At the end of the day, millions of poor people seem to be happy about the mechanisms that have been put in place. Criticism should promote the establishment of a more permanent welfare system, rather than fall into the trap of elitism.

The AKP has given hope to many people in their search for upward social mobility. While poverty remains a serious problem that has also accelerated due to the AKP's neoliberal agenda, many people are optimistic about their future. While this development does contain an element of democratic aspiration, it is not supported by clearly defined liberties that are valid for all citizens. The implicit message presented by the AKP is that the old elites will not make space for the Islamic newcomers. This is typical populism rather than a leftist position.

Can Erdoğan's regime survive in the absence of the Western linkage?

First, we need to clarify the issues. Is the AKP trying to uncouple Turkey from the Euro-American zone, or is it trying to raise Turkey's relative autonomy vis-à-vis the US and Europe? I believe that the second point is still valid, even after the 2013 Gezi protests. After the Gezi protests, the AKP leadership and the pro-government media have improvised some conspiracies in order to delegitimize the protesters as "antinationalist puppets of foreign powers." I think this strategy was not very well planned out and was partly the outcome of widespread panic.

This intensification of anti-Western discourse has also coincided with Turkey's increasing isolation over its active interventionism in Syria. When the AKP's fight with the Gülen movement became visible in December 2013, the anti-Western discourse intensified. I believe that this is a dilemma for the AKP leadership. They would have preferred a controlled anti-Westernism, as they are still trying to follow a pro-US foreign policy line in many respects. Many circles in the US have become increasingly AKP-skeptic. I do not think that this is a sustainable style of interaction for Turkey and the US. In the name of a common hatred of the Gülen movement, the AKP has allied itself with Islamist groups who are visibly nationalist and anti-Western. In order to keep its coalition intact, the AKP has resorted to an Islamist discourse reminiscent of 1970s. This is the current dilemma of the AKP. There is now only one possibility: escalation of populism at home coupled with an anti-Western discourse. But is this contradiction sustainable? The domestic use of anti-westernism seems to resrict Turkey's room for maneuver in her foreign policy options.

Do you think there is any hope for the restoration of secularism in Turkey?

Here I need to begin my answer by asking a question: which secularism? The Kemalist idea of laicism (*laiklik*) was based on the active control of religion by the state, rather than on dividing the two realms. The state first defined and then attempted to promote its own version of "true Islam." Those Kemalists who were critical of religion or Islam have always used the pretext of "good Islam" versus "bad Islam." In this way, they sidestepped the task of having to create an intellectual-popular tradition of religious criticism.

The AKP has simply borrowed from the same tradition of promoting "true Islam." Unlike the Kemalists, however, they now promote a more assertive and public Islam around Sunni-Hanafi principles. Now is the time to defend the institutional separation of the state and Islam, not the time to bring Islam under the control of the state, or the state under the control of Islamist ideas. Such a move requires a critical stage of consciousness defined around twin tolerations: the state must be respectful of religious freedoms and religious authorities must be respectful of the temporal functioning of state institutions. At present, we are far away from this mutual recognition.

However, I do believe that the more Islam is defined as a state-promoted public religion, the more we will see reactions against it in society, as we saw in Iran after the 1979 revolution. Religious groups will also object thus emboldening calls for a secular state. A truly secular state will only be institutionalized once religious groups begin to demand it. Secularists now have the difficult task of developing more creative and inclusive forms of secular state.

Author Biographies

Yüksel Taşkın was a fulltime faculty member and professor in the Department of Political Science and International Relations at Marmara University, Istanbul from 2002 to 2017. Because he had been one of the signatories to the Academics for Peace petition, he was dismissed from the university during the state of emergency decree law issued on February 7, 2017. He is coauthor with Suavi Aydın of *AKP Devri: Türkiye Siyaseti, İslamcılık ve Arap Baharı* (The AKP Era: Turkish Politics, Islamism, and the Arab Spring, Birikim Yayınları, 2013). He is the author of *1960'tan Günümüze Türkiye Tarihi* (The History of Turkey from 1960 to the Present, İletişim Yayınları, 2014) and *Anti-Komünizmden Küreselleşme Karşıtlığına: Milliyetçi Muhafazakar Entelijensiya* (From Anti-Communism to Anti-Globalization: Nationalist Conservative Intelligentsia in Turkey, İletişim Yayınları, 2007).

Burak Cop is an associate professor in the Department of International Relations at İstanbul-Kültür University. Between 2012 and 2015, he taught at Galatasaray and Boğaziçi universities as a part-time lecturer. He received his PhD from University of Nottingham, his LLM from the University of Kent at Canterbury, and his BA from Galatasaray University. His research and publications focus on Turkish political life and institutions, Turkish electoral and party systems, democratization issues, and social democratic politics in Turkey.

The Gülen Community and the AKP

Ahmet Şık and interviewed by Deniz Çakırer

Abstract The Gülen movement has two wings. The civil wing runs operations that a civil society institution would run, does charity work, and has a broad base of followers. The second wing is militarist, organized both horizontally and vertically within Turkish bureaucracy. The Gülen movement is most densely organized within the substructures of the security bureaucracy; these include the police force, the military, the National Intelligence Agency (NIA), and the judiciary. Although the Gülen movement argues that it is not involved in politics, actually it is right at the center of politics. Having organized within the security bureaucracy means owning the state. The goal of the community is to have an organizational network that can shape the state in line with their interests; they want to have more say within the state bureaucracy so that they can implement their social engineering policies with more ease. The Gülen movement has a presence in the education community, in charity work, in all parts of the security apparatus, in every one of Turkey's bureaucratic institutions from the Ministry of Education to the Ministry of Agriculture, and in the business community from small grocery stores to large factories with 10,000 workers.

Keywords Turkey · Gülen movement · AKP · Islamism

How would you define the Gülen movement?

The Gülen movement has two wings, which I refer to as the civil and the militarist wings.[1] The civil wing runs operations that a civil society institution would run, does charity work, and has a broad base of followers. I do not have a critical stance

---

[1] The term *militarist* is used here to denote the Gülen movement members who are regarded as being employed by the state to promote the Community's interest by using state power. Authors discussing the Gülen movement refer to Gülen movement members in the Turkish Armed Forces and the Police force as the "militarist" wing, but the term is also used to denote Gülen movement members in other parts of the security bureaucracy, such as the judiciary.

A. Şık (✉) · D. Çakırer
London, UK
e-mail: ahmetinadresi@yandex.com

toward the civil wing. Let everyone live the way they like. The second wing of the Gülen movement, what we refer to as the militarist wing, is organized both horizontally and vertically within Turkish bureaucracy. The Gülen movement is most densely organized within the substructures of the security bureaucracy; these include the police force, the military, the NIA, and the judiciary. Although the Gülen movement argues that it is not involved in politics, actually it is right at the center of politics. Having organized within the security bureaucracy means owning the state. The goal of the community is to have an organizational network that can shape the state in line with their interests; they want to have more say within the state bureaucracy so that they can implement their social engineering policies with more ease. The Gülen movement has a presence in the education community, in charity work, in all parts of the security apparatus, in every one of Turkey's bureaucratic institutions from the Ministry of Education to the Ministry of Agriculture, and in the business community from small grocery stores to large factories with 10,000 workers. In other words, they exist in every possible sector of society you can think of.

What is the relationship between the civil and militarist wings? Are there disagreements between them?

These two wings reinforce one another, but there is an important disconnect between them. The religious laypeople within the civil wing are unaware of the existence of the militarist wing. In their eyes, the Gülen movement is simply a religious organization that does charity work, opens schools, and whose main activities are in the field of education. The militarist wing, of course, knows that there are two wings. Above the two wings is Fethullah Gülen, who directs them both.

The purpose of the militarist wing is to open the way for the civil wing. We saw how this relationship works during Ergenekon trials. Two civil society institutions ideologically opposed to the Gülen movement—the Association for the Support of Contemporary Living[2] and the Contemporary Education Foundation[3]—were drawn into the investigations. Their leaders were detained in April 2009 as part of the Ergenekon trials, accused of supporting Ergenekon, an alleged terrorist organization that aimed to topple the AKP government (Milliyet 2009). In this way, rivals of Gülen movement's civil society institutions were eliminated. As the conflict between the AKP and the Gülen movement intensified, the government launched operations against Gülen movement's civil society institutions and revoked some of their rights; for instance, the government revoked the Gülenist *Kimse Yok Mu* (Is

---

[2]*Çağdaş Yaşamı Destekleme Derneği*, the Association for the Support of Contemporary Living, is a Turkish nonprofit organization whose declared mission is "the promotion of contemporary education and reforms implemented by Atatürk," the Turkey's secular founder (Çağdaş 2017).

[3]*Çağdaş Eğitim Vakfı*, the Contemporary Education Foundation, is a Turkish nonprofit organization whose declared mission is to "secularize education in Turkey" (Çağdaş Eğitim Vakfı 2017).

Anyone There?) foundation's permit to collect donation.[4] Later, the Council of State annulled the government's decision. The permit to collect donations is very important for Gülen movement; during the month of Ramadan, with one cell phone text, a charity can collect five liras[5] from one million people simultaneously. For Gülen movement, it is about becoming economically stronger under the guise of doing charity work.

How did the Gülen movement become economically so strong?

I believe Gülen movement to be the richest holding company in Turkey; an Islamic holding company that has no problem with neoliberalism. *Himmet* refers to the regular contributions of Gülen movement followers to the activities of the Gülen movement. In the public sector, the standard rate of *himmet* is 10%. Contributions are usually arranged on a monthly basis and constitute a certain percentage of a follower's income (see Hendrick 2013, pp. 152–158). *Himmet* rates change according to the income group. If there are two million wage earners in the Gülen movement, imagine taking 100 liras from each one every month. This structure is very similar to the organizational structure of a state. Although the AKP uses the term *parallel state* to refer to the Gülen movement with the aim of consolidating its electorate against the Gülen movement, it is a term that reflects reality quite accurately. Gülenists have established a state-like organization. Similar to a state, it has an income, and an authority that decides how people should be organized and who should be appointed to which position within the Turkish state bureaucracy.

What are the characteristics of the Gülen movement that distinguish it from other Islamic communities in Turkey? How did it manage to become so politically and economically powerful in comparison to other Islamic communities?

The Gülen movement always gets along well with the state. This is what distinguishes the Gülen movement from other Islamic communities. Because Fethullah Gülen himself is pro-state, so is the organization, which always follows its leader. Turkish military and state policies have been behind the Gülen movement's expansion. Both the Gülen movement and the National Outlook (*Milli Görüş*), a movement associated with a succession of variously named political parties led by Necmettin Erbakan, emerged at the beginning of the 1970s.[6] Fethullah Gülen was trying to organize in a few cities around İzmir, with İzmir at the community's center. Around this time, Erbakan entered the political scene with his National Outlook premise. The National Outlook's vision, outlined in Erbakan's 1975 book,

---

[4]*Kimse Yok mu* (Is Anyone There, in Turkish) was a foundation affiliated with the Gülen movement, shut down in July 2016 (Radio Free Europe/Radio Liberty 2016). It described itself as an "international nonprofit humanitarian aid and development organization" (as cited in Akçali 2015).

[5]Around USD $1.31 in December 2017.

[6]After Erbakan's Virtue Party was banned by the Constitutional Court in 2001, a group within the party parted ways with Erbakan and founded the AKP.

Milli Görüş, "proposed a national culture and education, industrialization, and social justice based on the principles of Islam" (as cited in Eligür 2010, p. 66). At the time, the state viewed the National Outlook as a strict pro-Sharia movement, and in contrast, saw the Gülen movement as a representative of what in today's terminology would be called "moderate Islam." For this reason, the Gülen movement was considered an antidote to the National Outlook. This is one of the most important reasons behind the Gülen movement's expansion. Gülen movement has always forged friendly relations with government and political parties that have the potential to be in government. It uses its potential votes as a bargaining chip in all its dealings with different candidates of power.

What was the relationship between Gülen movement and the National Outlook movement, from which the AKP emerged?

One of the most important differences between National Outlook and the Gülen movement is their view of the West in general and their view of the US and Israel in particular. When National Outlook first emerged, it was a movement that identified itself with anti-Westernism. Because the Gülen movement knows that there is no chance for an Islamic organization that is opposed to Israel and the US to grow, the Gülen movement's political and religious operations are carried on under the shadow of and within the limits allowed by the US and Israel. You will not find one declaration by Fethullah Gülen or the Gülen movement against US and Israeli policy. Until now, there has been no such declaration, and there will never be one.

Until the advent of the AKP government in 2002, Gülen and Erbakan cooperated only once, during the 1973 general election. This cooperation provided the Gülen movement with an opportunity to access every part of Turkey through the National Outlook's extensive political organization in cities and districts. After the election, they had a falling out and never cooperated again (see Şık 2014, pp. 52–57). The next fracture occurred during the February 28 Process of 1997, during the deposition of the coalition government at the time, headed by Necmettin Erbakan, the leader of the Islamist Welfare Party. The government was deposed as a result of a military memorandum on February 28, 1997, and the ensuing effort of the Turkish military to restrain the activities of Islamist media outlets, businesses, and other Islamist actors (see Cizre and Cinar 2003).

In the beginning, the February 28 Process seemed to be directed against Erbakan and his Islamist Welfare Party. But the secondary target was the Gülen movement. To avoid being targeted by the military, Gülen movement supported the coup zealously by calling for the Erbakan coalition government to resign and by making declarations indicating that the concerns of the military were legitimate. The current conflict between the AKP and Gülen movement notwithstanding, this constitutes the biggest historical fracture between the National Outlook and the Gülen movement. From the point of view of the National Outlook and its offshoot successor, the AKP, the gravity of the fracture is quite understandable: the Gülen movement played quite a substantial role in the National Outlook's fall from power.

It is therefore extremely interesting that they once again became allies under the AKP.

In light of the conflicts between the Gülen movement and the National View before and during the February 28 Process, how did they again become allies?

Before the 2007 presidential elections, there was a political crisis in Turkey related to Abdullah Gül's candidacy and the fact that his wife wore a headscarf. After the military's memorandum of April 27, 2007, indicating that it would defend Turkey's secular system (BBC News 2007), I think Erdoğan realized that whatever he might do, the military would remove them from government. In Özden Örnek's diaries, which were used as evidence in the military coup trials, Erdoğan is portrayed as having accepted the military as a natural partner to government. In the wake of the memorandum, Erdoğan realized that partnership with the military would not be sufficient. During advance preparations for the Ergenekon trials, Erdoğan was convinced by both the Gülen movement's arm in the government and by his own people that they could eliminate military tutelage with the trials. So he took a risk. For his point of view, this was a good move. He took the country to early elections and solidified his power. This is how the Ergenekon trials began, with the Gülen movement and the AKP coming together to cooperate against the military. The AKP's biggest partner in government between 2007 and 2012 was the Gülen movement. It looked as though they had begun again with a clean slate, but they were very cautious. The partnership between the AKP and the Gülen movement was one based on a common enemy. In general, they view anyone who does not think like them as an enemy, so in this light, it was perhaps not very difficult for them to collaborate.

The whole Ergenekon trial is rightfully disputed and involves many injustices. It was not an investigation that tried the real culprits within the boundaries of the law. Between 2007 and 2012, the period when the Gülen movement was a partner to the AKP government, was one of the darkest parts of the dark period Turkey is going through right now. This was a period where everyone was silenced by being pulled into one of the trials, and all opposition to the Gülen movement and the AKP was eliminated. A crime was fabricated for everyone. The Ergenekon and Balyoz ("sledgehammer") trials and related trials were concocted to investigate and try military personnel and nationalists with a worldview similar to the worldview of the military. For the Kurds, there was the KCK trials, targeting the PKK umbrella organization (International Crisis Group 2012). For the socialists in Turkey there was the Devrimci Karargah (Revolutionary Headquarter) investigation. Aside from these, there were also various trials aimed at reshaping society through social engineering; an example is the corruption trial that targeted the Fenerbahçe sports club in 2011 (Hürriyet Daily News 2014). Is there corruption? There absolutely is. However, the trial did not have as its purpose the investigation of football corruption.

The only good that came out of this entire process was that the military was pushed back inside its rightful boundaries. But there was a problem: counter-guerillas had been eliminated using counterguerilla-style measures. For this reason, what was achieved cannot in any sense be called "democracy." A new kind of tutelage, far weightier, replaced that of the military.

What role did the Gülen movement serve in the functioning of the political system during the AKP governments?

The Gülen movement had considerable influence at the most important levels of state bureaucracy, especially between 2007 and 2012. The Gülen movement was directing everything. It was even dictating the government position on each of the trials. No one from the government opposed the trials, because the two powers had an agreement based on the existence of a common enemy.

What would dominating the security apparatus bring them? The answer becomes clear when we think of the leaked tapes on the private lives of certain MHP parliamentarians and of Deniz Baykal, the chair of the CHP.[7] Their political lives came precipitously to an end. How can one organize such a thing? You need to tap the phone lines, you need to go to the appointment place ahead of time and place cameras, and then you need to publicize it. This can only be accomplished by a unit organized within the state bureaucracy. The name of this organization is the Gülen movement. I used to call it "today's illegal counterguerilla group." In the past, counterguerilla forces used to kill you with a bullet. The new counterguerilla would rather bury you alive. They produce ridiculous pieces of evidence against you, and throw you in jail.

What kind of a role did the AKP play in this partnership?

The AKP is the governmental authority that sanctioned the whole thing. It created the perception that only the Gülen movement is virtuous and clean. The AKP government was the prime contributor to the Gülen movement's accumulation of power, particularly within the judiciary, the police force, the military, and the NIA. During the 2014 corruption scandal revealed by Gülenists in the police force Erdoğan rhetorically asked Gülenists: "What is it that you wanted and we did not give to you?" What he says is correct: the AKP gave the Gülen movement whatever it wanted.

The AKP cannot therefore be exempted from an accounting of the Gülen movement's crimes. The AKP provided political sanction to the Gülen movement precisely because it benefited from what the Gülen movement was doing. Now Erdoğan says that everything went wrong was the Gülen movement's responsibility, that the Gülen movement fooled them. That's not true: the AKP was aware of everything the Gülen movement did. The Gülen movement and the AKP acted together. They are accomplices. When you are organized within the judiciary and the police force, you fabricate crimes and manufacture evidence via the police, and then you reach over to the next link in the chain, the judiciary, and you arrest

---

[7]Deniz Baykal was the chair of the CHP when tapes from his private life were leaked. Baykal resigned from the chairmanship after the incident (Ete et al. 2014, p. 28).

people. Consent was manufactured by the manipulation of public perception through the AKP–Gülen movement coalition media. The financial structure of mainstream media in Turkey does not allow it to oppose the government; it is silenced through tax penalties.

As you explain in your book, *The Imam's Army* (Şık 2012), the Gülen movement has always been careful to be on good terms with whomever is in power in Turkey. Why did the Gülen movement change its strategy and challenge the AKP government?

The ultimate objective of the Gülen movement is to control the state. This is the most important reason for the current war between the AKP and the Gülen movement. All the opposition was eliminated, one way or another, and then the internecine war broke out over how to share power.

The Gülen movement and the AKP had had disagreements before. The first publicly visible manifestation was to be seen in the differing positions taken by the AKP government and the Gülen movement during the Mavi Marmara flotilla massacre of 2010.[8] Gülen expressed his disapproval of the flotilla, while Erdoğan was in favor of them; the public opposition between them was an indication of a deeper tension.

By far the biggest indication of disagreement came during the NIA investigation that began on February 7, 2012. The objective of the NIA investigation was to arrest Erdoğan. It was a direct challenge. It requires courage to target such a strong government, but whatever they were counting on did not work. The Gülen movement is an organization that is capable of arresting anyone—professors, police officers, even the Chief of General Staff—without due process and damage their reputation. They might have thought, "We can take down Erdoğan, too." The most important characteristic of the Gülen movement is its patience. They are very patient. If they had waited two or three more years, and combined the NIA investigation with the corruption investigation initiated on 17 December 2013,[9] we might be experiencing a more terrible darkness now. For once, they acted impatiently, and it was a big mistake.

Why did the conflict between the AKP and the Gülen movement initially focus so much on the NIA?

The most important weapon of this century is information. If you control information, you can shape society and politics. During all the reputation-ruining and the

---

[8]Mavi Marmara is the name of the lead ship of a six-vessel convoy carrying humanitarian aid to Gaza. As a result of an Israeli raid on the flotilla on May 31, 2010, nine activists form Turkey were killed (UN General Assembly 2010).

[9]The corruption scandals referred to involved two successive police operations on December 17 and 25, 2013. The trials, which targeted numerous state officials, businessmen, and cabinet ministers, forced the resignation of four cabinet ministers. The investigation is widely regarded as the Gülen movement's attack against the AKP government (Ulusoy 2015, pp. 69–73).

investigations, both accurate and false information was spread around in the public sphere. With the aid of technological advances, the Gülen movement organization within the state bureaucracy was already accessing new information. They would tap phone lines and bug rooms for audio surveillance, physically follow people, and they used the capabilities provided by the state to carry all this out. They also found a legal pretext with which to do it. If a Gülen movement police officer was going to listen in on someone, they got authorization from a Gülen movement judge. Gülen movement prosecutors would instigate legal proceedings. The NIA archive is Turkey's black box. It is the power of that archive that is behind the struggle over the NIA. The Gülen movement understood that the only way to control information about everyone's past was to take control of the NIA. You can blackmail the most powerful corporations in Turkey if you are able to find and interesting piece of information about them.

During the 2012 NIA trials, voice recordings of the Oslo talks (2009–2011) between the Turkish state and the PKK were leaked. In the recordings, Hakan Fidan, who did not have an official position at the time, said that Erdoğan himself had appointed him for the talks, and that he represented Erdoğan. In other words, he named Erdoğan as the instigator of the talks. Later, it became clear that the NIA had prepared reports outlining the approaching danger represented by the Gülen movement's organization in the state bureaucracy, and as a result, some Gülen movement people were fired. As head of the NIA, Hakan Fidan was the one coordinating this effort. I think this is the reason for the Gülen movement's demonization of Hakan Fidan. The Gülen movement sensed that the conflict would escalate and tried to preempt government action against them by targeting Fidan.

During the NIA crisis, police officers and NIA agents pulled guns on each other. What could have been a gunfight between state institutions did not escalate, but this event constitutes the beginning of open conflict between the AKP and the Gülen movement. It is their most significant public contest, and the target was without doubt Erdoğan. Erdoğan himself said that he was the target. He could have been arrested, too, because the crime he would have been accused of was a constitutional crime that does not fall under parliamentary immunity. The NIA crisis was a very big move on the part of the Gülen movement and it caused a rift that is not going to heal.

The Gülen movement has been attempting to gain influence in majority-Kurdish areas by providing health and education services. At the same time, the Gülen movement tried to eliminate its rivals in Kurdish politics through the KCK trials. Is the Gülen movement's approach toward Kurdish politics one of the reasons underlying the rift between the AKP government and the Gülen movement?

There is not one rift that separates the approach to the Kurdish issue taken by the AKP, the Gülen movement, nationalists belonging to the far-right MHP, and other nationalists; there are many rifts. For a while the AKP and Gülen movement media presented the Kurdish question only as a PKK question, assuming that if the PKK were eliminated, the Kurdish problem would also go away. Articles were published explaining that the way to eliminate the PKK was through the adoption of the state practices of the 1990s, which applied the Tamil Tigers model. At that time, numerous major military operations were conducted against the PKK. Horrible atrocities were committed, not only by the government, but by the PKK as well. The motivation behind the military operations came from reports provided by the Gülen movement to the bureaucratic cadres. The project was to eliminate the PKK units in the mountains by means of large-scale military operations, and to eliminate those operating in the cities by arresting them as part of the ongoing KCK trials. In this way, the Gülen movement and AKP would have been able to fill the gap left by the absence of the PKK and the KCK with a religious identity. In other words, nationalist assimilation was to be replaced by Islamist assimilation, to the benefit of both the Gülen movement and the AKP government. Once the gap was filled with AKP and Gülen movement religious cadres, that region would be transformed into a voter base for the former. Erdoğan initially supported this plan, but changed his mind once he realized that this would not work.

As a group, the PKK and the Kurdish movement in general understands the state better than anyone. It understood immediately what was going on and worked to prevent the Gülen movement from expanding in that region, using questionable means. They killed an imam. When an Abant Platform meeting of the Gülen movement's Journalists and Writers Foundation was going to be held in Diyarbakir, the PKK openly threatened the Gülen movement, saying, "If you come to Diyarbakir, we will kill you." The meeting could not be held in Diyarbakir.

In time, Erdoğan realized that the Kurdish problem would not be solved through war. He thought that a change in his position might eliminate the risk to his political future. The Gülen movement was guiding the military operations against the PKK, legal operations against Kurdish politicians, and the Ergenekon trials. The directing, and enforcing of power belonged to the Gülen movement, and the final decision-making resided with the AKP. The Gülen movement has no legal identity; the AKP does. That meant that all the political risk entailed in these various operations fell squarely on the shoulders of the AKP. Erdoğan saw this. As a result, Erdoğan and the Kurdish movement sat down together at the negotiating table. The Gülen movement, which had hoped to solve the Kurdish problem militarily and then rush into fill the gap left by an absent PKK, saw that they were being cut out of the deal.

One should be careful not to conclude from my explanation that the AKP is pro-peace and the Gülen movement pro-war. Both of them are clearly pro-war. Both of them conceive the Kurdish problem as solely a PKK problem. The PKK is not the cause of the Kurdish problem; it is a result of it. None of these actors are developing a solution that focuses on the cause. In this sense there is not a difference in the way they approach the Kurdish question. It is because they attempt to eliminate the result of the problem—the PKK—via military, judiciary, or illegal means that the Kurdish issue does not end.

What has been the Gülen movement's strategy to protect itself from AKP government pressure?

The Gülen movement adopted the same survival strategy it used during the February 28 Process of 1997—to hide itself as an organization as much as possible and defend its position. Its strategy is one of lying in wait, attending to one's wounds, and gathering strength. When there is an opportunity, it will reemerge with the power to destroy everyone all over again. During the February 28 Process it was easier for them to hide. Now it is harder, because this time around Gülen movement's adversary also has a support base composed of devout Muslims. The AKP has a better idea of who is who—who is Gülen-affiliated, and who is not.

What do you think will happen to the Gülen movement after Fethullah Gülen is gone?

I think that the Gülen movement will splinter and become smaller. This is what has happened in the past to similar Islamic organizations. When the leader dies, there is definitely a process of disintegration and fragmentation. The most important issue at play here is the large amount of money that the Gülen movement commands. We are talking about billions of US dollars. More than any other problem, there will definitely be problems in sharing those funds. It is conceivable that Fethullah Gülen has designated someone to replace him. I am also curious as to how this is going to happen, but I have no doubt that the Gülen movement will shrink.[10]

References

Akçali, Y. (2015). Two paths of modernization: A comparative analysis of Turkey and Egypt.

BBC News. (2007). Excerpts of Turkish army statement. BBC News, April 28 2007. Retrieved November 15, 2017, from http://news.bbc.co.uk/2/hi/europe/6602775.stm.

Çağdaş Eğitim Vakfı. (2017). Hakkımızda [About us]. Retrieved November 15, 2017, from http://www.cev.org.tr/Default.aspx?pageID=3.

Çağdaş Yaşamı Destekleme Derneği. (2017). Hakkımızda [About us]. Retrieved November 15, 2017, from https://www.cydd.org.tr/sayfa/hakkimizda-2/.

Cizre, Ü., & Çınar, M. (2003). Turkey 2002: Kemalism, Islamism, and Politics in the light of the February 28 process. *South Atlantic Quarterly, 102*(2–3), 309–332.

Eligür, B. (2010). *The mobilization of political Islam in Turkey.* Cambridge: Cambridge University Press.

Ete, H., Akbaba, Y., Dalay, G., Ersay, S. O., Kanat, K. B., & Üstün, K. (2014). *Turkey's 2014 local elections.* Ankara: SETA.

---

[10]Ahmet Şık was once again taken into custody on December 29, 2016, on charges of promulgating "propaganda for terrorist organizations." His defense statement, given on July 24, 2017, can be read in English as translated by the Solidarity Group for the Freedom of Ahmet Şık at Pen International: http://www.pen-international.org/newsitems/ahmet-siks-defence-statement-on-the-trial-of-cumhuriyet-24-july-2017/. He was released on March 10th pending trial.

Hendrick, J. (2013). *Gülen: The ambiguous politics of market Islam in Turkey and the world*. New York: New York University Press.

Hürriyet Daily News. (2014). Turkish football politics: A mesh of murky politics and alleged corruption. *Hürriyet Daily News*, March 17 2014. Retrieved November 15, 2017, from http://www.hurriyetdailynews.com/turkish-football-politics-a-mesh-of-murky-politics-and-alleged-corruption-63643.

International Crisis Group. (2012). Turkey: The PKK and a Kurdish settlement. *ICG Europe Report*, No: 219. Retrieved November 15, 2017, from https://www.crisisgroup.org/europe-central-asia/western-europemediterranean/turkey/turkey-pkk-and-kurdish-settlement.

Milliyet. (2009). Çağdaş Yaşam Derneği hedefte [The Association for the Support of Contemporary Living in the crosshair]. *Milliyet*, April 14. Retrieved November 15, 2017, from http://www.milliyet.com.tr/cagdas-yasam-dernegi-hedefte/guncel/gundemdetay/14.04.2009/1082823/default.htm.

Radio Free Europe/Radio Liberty. (2016). Turkey targets security agency in anti-Gulen crackdown, September 27. Retrieved November 15, 2017, from http://www.rferl.org/a/turkey-targets-intelligence-agency-gulencrackdown/28016360.html.

Şık, A. (2012). *İmamın Ordusu*. [The Imam's army]. Retrieved November 15, 2017, from http://xeberler.files.wordpress.com/2011/04/51984426-dokunan-yanar.pdf.

Şık, A. (2014). *Paralel yürüdük biz bu yollarda: AKP-Cemaat ittifakı nasıl dağıldı? [We walked these roads in parallel: How did the AKP-Cemaat alliance unravel?]*. Istanbul: Postacı Yayınevi.

Ulusoy, K. (2015). Turkey's fight against corruption: A critical assessment. In Aydın-Düzgit et al. (Eds.), *Global Turkey in Europe III: Democracy, trade, and the Kurdish question in Turkey-EU relations*. Rome: Edizioni Nuova Cultura.

UN General Assembly, Human Rights Council. (2010). Report of the international fact-finding mission to investigate violations of international law, including international humanitarian and human rights law, resulting from the Israeli attacks on the flotilla of ships carrying humanitarian assistance, A/HRC/15/21. Retrieved November 15, 2017, from http://www2.ohchr.org/english/bodies/hrcouncil/docs/15session/A.HRC.15.21_en.pdf.

Ahmet Şık is an award winning investigative journalist known for his books and reports that shed light on the human rights violations and police violence in Turkey; Ergenekon trials and the connections between the state and the Gülen Community, which arguably was the most powerful Islamic community in Turkey before the coup attempt in July 2016. He worked in several newspapers in Turkey including Cumhuriyet, Evrensel, Yeni Yüzyıl, Radikal; in periodicals such as Aktüel and Nokta and in Reuters as a reporter. A member of Turkish Trade Union of Journalists and Association of Progressive Journalists, Şık wrote articles and gave talks on freedom of press and ethics of journalism. As he was working on his book, *İmamın Ordusu* (The Army of the İmam), which investigates the Gülen Community's organization within the police force, he was arrested in relation to the Ergenekon investigation in March 2011 and released pending trial in March 2012. The copies of the book draft were confiscated and the book was banned from publication. He explained the unlawful practices during Ergenekon trials in his book *Pusu: Devletin Yeni Sahipleri* (Ambush: The New Owners of the State), published in 2012. Ahmet Şık is the recipient of numerous awards including the Metin Göktepe journalism award (2002, 2003 and 2007); Progressive Journalists Association News Story Award (2002, 2003 and 2005); Turkish Publishers Association Freedom of Thought and Expression Award (2011); UNESCO/Guillermo Cano World Press Freedom Prize (2014). On December 29, 2016 he was arrested in his house for allegedly being a member of the Gülen movement which he had publicly and outspokenly criticized. While in prison he won the Raif Badawi Award for his courageous journalism. Ahmet Şık was released from prison on March 10th 2018 pending trial. This interview was conducted in June 2015, before the Gülenist coup attempt in July 2016 and the ensuing dismissal of Gülenists from state institutions.

Deniz Çakırer received her B.S. in International Relations from Middle East Technical University and her Ph.D. in International Relations and Politics from University of Southern California. She taught classes on the political economy of the Middle East; ethnicity and nationalism; theories of International Relations and quantitative methodologies in political science at the University of Southern California and the California State University, Dominguez Hills. She continued her research as a Visiting Post-Doctoral Fellow at the Center for Middle Eastern Studies at Harvard University. Her research focuses on the evolution and political economy of political Islam in Turkey, Islamic communities, politics of the developing world, gender and International Relations, critical theory of International Relations. She is currently working on a book that analyzes evolution of the discourses of two Islamic communities in Turkey, Gülen and Erenköy Communities, in the context of changes in Turkey's political and economic structure.

Political Islam in Turkey

Hayri Kırbaşoğlu and interviewed by Gülay Türkmen

Abstract In this interview, Gülay Türkmen discusses the trajectory of political Islam in Turkey with Hayri Kırbaşoğlu, professor of theology at Ankara University's Divinity School. One of the main figures of the "Ankara school" in theology, known for their liberal interpretation of Islam, Kırbaşoğlu was among the founders of HAS Parti (The People's Voice Party), a religiously oriented party that was later coopted by the ruling Justice and Government Party (AKP). Coming from an Islamic background, he remains staunchly critical of the dominant interpretation and implementation of Islam in today's Turkey. In what follows, Kırbaşoğlu provides a detailed look at "Islam's crisis", both in Turkey and in the world, and offers ways out of it.

Keywords Political Islam · Islamism · Turkey

Following the attacks over the last two decades of self-declared Islamist armed groups such as Al-Qaeda and ISIS we began hearing more frequently, both in Turkey and in other Muslim-majority countries, the argument that "this is not real Islam." Is it possible to come up with a definition of "real Islam"? Would "real Islam" provide a way out of the current cycle of violence? In the face of increasing violence of this kind, how, do you think, Muslims should react?

The expression "real Islam" has both political and theological components. From a political angle, it is quite clear that this discourse is little more than a pragmatic tool Muslims frequently use to fight off accusations made by various publics and medias. However, from a theological angle, "real Islam" does actually correspond

H. Kırbaşoğlu (✉)
Divinity School, Ankara University, Ankara, Turkey
e-mail: hayrikirbasoglu@hotmail.com

G. Türkmen
Forum for Interdisciplinary Religious Studies, University of Goettingen,
Goettingen, Germany
e-mail: gulayt@gmail.com

© Springer International Publishing AG, part of Springer Nature 2019   93
E. Özyürek et al. (eds.), *Authoritarianism and Resistance in Turkey*,
https://doi.org/10.1007/978-3-319-76705-5_10

to a real entity. In that sense, one could certainly say the following: Yes, there is genuine confusion in the field of Islamic knowledge and practices. There is also a serious gap between Islamic teachings and the acts carried out in the name of Islam in the Muslim world. Because of this confusion, and because of the obvious rupturing of Islamic teachings, quite a number of issues that in reality have nothing to do with Islam are unfairly attributed to it. In summary, it is not possible to claim that those Muslims who seek refuge in the proposition that "this is not real Islam" are actually knowledgeable about what real Islam is. Still, one may roughly assert that the founding text of Islam, the Qur'an, is the basis of "real Islam," and all interpretations that contradict its teachings fall outside of "real Islam."

It's worth emphasizing that I consider violence to be a multifaceted problem that cannot be evaluated in isolation from the systematic state terrorism of global sovereigns. If this problem is not addressed comprehensively and multidimensionally, no progress will be made in solving it. "Real Islam" is only one among many factors that could play a positive role in this solution, but it is the most important and effective one. There will always be disagreements about what real Islam is, but I believe that a satisfactory common ground will eventually be found.

In dealing with violence, there are several steps that must be taken in the Muslim world. People must first become aware of the political, military, economic, and cultural interventions of external powers, and they must then form a "consciousness of resistance" to them. Next, society must differentiate between the legitimate and illegitimate use of violence. It should carry out a critical analysis of the religious, cultural, and sociological arguments used to justify illegitimate violence, as well as a sociocultural analysis of the social groups in which these arguments circulate. It must also seriously consider the many grievances that have been caused by the oppressive and collaborationist policies pursued by the governments of Muslim countries over the last hundred years. Particular attention should be paid to the defeats experienced in the face of Western imperialism—cases like Palestine, Afghanistan, Iraq, Lebanon, and Yemen. Although the democratization of Islamic countries is usually presented as an important part of the solution, in Muslim countries where the culture of pluralism and democracy is fairly weak, democracy can easily turn into democratic despotism. Unless the problem of violence is understood as a multidimensional global phenomenon (that is also present in Islamic countries), and unless the West, in addition to Islamic countries, also engages in self-criticism and takes the necessary steps, the long awaited solution—global peace and justice—will remain nothing but a utopian dream.

In your interviews, you often quote Muslim thinkers like Roger Garaudy, Alija Izetbegović, Ali Shariati, Muhammad Abduh, Jamal al-din al-Afghani, and Fazlur Rahman. You define their line of thinking as "Qur'an- and *hadith*-centered, based on *ijtihad* (reform), politically oppositional, and intellectually critical" (Kırbaşoğlu 2014).[1] Can you please summarize the main tenets of this intellectual strand, which, in Alija Izetbegović's words, "proposes the Islamization of Muslim societies" (Izetbegović 2010)?

Actually, for me, it's quite clear that this line of thinking could provide the most accurate answers, at least in the 20th and 21st centuries, to the question of what "real Islam" is. Hence, it would not be wrong to claim that there is indeed an "alternative Islam" that stands against the popular perceptions of Islam in the Islamic world. The importance of this approach can be summarized as follows: some may claim that the relationship between the dominant, traditional Islamic conceptions of our age and those of Western civilization are categorically mutually exclusive, but modernist-reformist Islam, which began with Afghani and Iqbal and has developed through to today, lays the foundations for a possible dialogue between the West and the Islamic tradition. This modernist-reformist Islam does not categorically reject either Islam or the West, but, in Garaudy's parlance, approaches both critically. Also, because critical thinking is very weak in traditional, popular perceptions of Islam, one could claim that the modernist-critical perception of Islam provides the most suitable approach for the formation of a tradition of self-critique in the Muslim world. Add to this the fact that the traditional, reformist, Salafist, and Sufi mystical perceptions of Islam, which have dominated the Muslim world over the last two hundred centuries, have failed in the political, social, and economic arenas. Nor have they been able to produce feasible political, social, or economic models that could serve as alternatives to Western ones. Indeed, some of their experimental models have utterly failed. This shows rather clearly that the Muslim world needs a new point of view and a new approach. That is why I think that the only way out for the Muslim world is to embrace a line of thinking that is Qur'an- and hadith-centered, based on renovation and reform, and is politically oppositional and intellectually critical. This view is represented not only by the names you mention above, but also by hundreds of other contemporary Muslim intellectuals whose names are not often mentioned, such as the Tatar scholars Musa Jarullah (Dzharullakh) Bigiev and Rizaeddin bin Fakhreddin. This is not only a theoretical assumption; it is a practical finding based on the observations and analyses of an activist academic who has been dealing with the realities of the Muslim world for the last several decades.

At this point, it would be quite useful to remind the reader that, in contrast to the empty accusations and slanderous remarks often emanating from conservative circles, these reformist intellectuals are not Westernists. On the contrary, they embrace a line of thinking that criticizes the West as much as it criticizes the Islamic tradition. So much so that, as Munir Shafik points out in his works on contemporary

---

[1]Please see http://www.hayrikirbasoglu.net/?p=292 for the full quote.

Islamic thought, almost all of these reformist intellectuals could be considered anti-imperialist activists. Hence, it is possible to claim that the Westernist label placed on these reformist Muslim thinkers is a reflection of the dislike for this line of thinking that circulates in conservative-traditional circles.

Why do you think that the calls for *ijtihad* (reform) voiced by these thinkers fall on deaf ears in Turkey and the Muslim world? Why is it that, quite the reverse, a radical interpretation of Islam is growing stronger? What should be done to spread this reformist line of thinking?

It is not that difficult to understand why the calls for reform fall on deaf ears in the Muslim world. It is quite clear that these attempts would, first and foremost, shake the foundations of the political and civil *status quo*, which has been built on religious perceptions in need of reform. As is known, in order to keep the masses under control and to further their own political aims, rulers in the Islamic world employ certain institutions—for example, the Directorate of Religious Affairs in Turkey, al-Azhar in Egypt, the religious structure dominated by the mullahs in Iran, or the official religious institutions in Gulf countries, beside religious educational institutions—to spread throughout society a religious culture that values obedience rather than criticism, submission rather than questioning. Embellished with religious maquillage, this culture of obedience and submission functions as a valuable tool for administrators, equivalent to Karl Marx's "opium of the masses" (1997) or to Ali Shariati's "religion" in his conceptualization of "religion against religion" (2013). This same perception of Islam also exists among the religious orders (*tarikat*) and communities (*cemaat*) that act in concert with the rulers. After all, it is a pragmatic requirement for these so-called non-governmental—but in reality, quite governmental—religious groups to defend a perception of religion centered on obedience and submission in order to keep their members under control and to manipulate them in line with the aims of the political entities they are in cooperation with.

One should not forget, however, that this problem is also closely related to social psychology. Because the religious perceptions and approaches that need to be reformed rest on a tradition that's been there for centuries, and because they in some measure worked in the past, people tend to consider the continuation of this tried and tested tradition as the most reliable way forward. In line with this, because there is a degree of uncertainty about what new approaches and perceptions might bring, people opt to preserve the status quo rather than take a risk on something new. In order for reform attempts in Islamic thought to take root in society, there must either be a very strong social consciousness movement or a political project that would incorporate reformist Islamic tendencies at all levels of the education system. Such a project would help to spread the reformist approach to Islam through the collaborative efforts of official religious institutions and institutions of higher religious learning. It should not be forgotten that for either project to be successful, delicate and well-thought-out strategies would have to be developed. It is also obvious that one should not ignore the positive and negative roles the media plays (and will play) in all these developments.

In an interview you gave in the journal *Birikim* (2014),[2] you state that after 1980 Islamism in Turkey tagged along with those in power, and that Muslims went through a profanization (*dünyevileşme*) process. In light of this explanation, would it be possible for you to summarize the evolution of political Islam and Islamism in Turkey since the foundation of the Republic?

Drawing on the Moroccan intellectual Muhammad Abed al-Jabri's formulation, I think we can summarize the situation at hand as follows. Al-Jabri summarizes the whole of Islamic history with three designations: *nubuwwah*, *asabiyyah*, and *ghanima*. *Nubuwwah* stands for the period of idealism distinguished by the sincerity that existed at the birth of Islam. *Asabiyyah* stands for the tribal solidarity or monopoly of the Banu Umayyah tribe in charge of both political and economic power during the Umayyah period. The *ghanima* period begins with the rule of the Abbasids, during which time Umayyah domination came to an end and people from many different races and tribes took part in governance. This is a period marked by conquests and the acquisition of wealth generated by them, which gained speed during Abbasid rule and continued at the same pace throughout the rule of the Seljuk Turks and the Ottomans.

Building on this threefold classification, we can say that the social and political Islamic movements of the 1970s were sincere and idealist in that their main aim was to spread Islamic values throughout society rather than take control of political and economic power. This period, which lasted from the 1970s to the 1990s, could be called the *nubuwwah* period. Then the negative impact of profanization began to surface in the late 1990s during the rule of the Welfare Party (*Refah Partisi*), which became a coalition partner in the 1997 Refahyol government (it had previously served as a coalition partner in the 1970s under the name of the National Salvation Party (*Milli Selamet Partisi*)). It could be argued that the rent (*rant*) system within municipal administration accelerated the profanization process and helped spread corruption in both the Welfare Party and among the various religious groups—the *jamaat*s and *tariqah*s—that supported the party. This period, characterized by the control of political and economic power by a party oligarchy within the Welfare Party, could be seen as the *asabiyyah* period.

It should also be added that it was during the rule of the religious-conservative politician Turgut Özal in the 1980s that Islamic groups moved closer to power and began to be corrupted by it. But profanization has reached its peak with the ascent to power of the AKP, which has come under the shadow of accusations of

---

[2]Koca, Bayram. 2014. "M. Hayri Kırbaşoğlu ile söyleşi: İslâm, sol ve AKP". *Birikim* 303/304: 181–190.

corruption, robbery, injustice, rentiership, nepotism, and degeneration. Because the AKP government manages to share the government rent with various groups both within and outside the party much more generously than the preceding governments, it would not be wrong to argue that this period corresponds to the *ghanima* period. As a matter of fact, because the primary aim in this period has been to share the economic rent, both the government and the civil organizations that support the government—which I prefer to call civil-state institutions—have come to be associated with the negative aspects of rent-seeking, such as corruption, extravagance, wastefulness, and vanity. This is quite telling in that it shows that the axiom "power corrupts, absolute power corrupts absolutely" is also perfectly applicable to Islamic groups and Islamic movements. The Islamic movements of the 1970s—especially political Islam—which began with the aim of fighting pervasive immorality and injustice in society, ended up 40 years later being associated with profanization, or, worse, with corruption, bribery, patronage and nepotism—practices that directly contradict the values of Islam. This fact shows very well the dire need for a new conceptualization of Islam, from a reformist perspective, that puts social justice, social morality and the morality of the system rather than ritual (*ibadet*) at its center.

In an interview on the website *Geniş Ufuk* (2014), you suggest that Turkey needs a "morality-centered political culture."[3] Then you go on to talk about the People's Voice Party (*HAS Parti*)—which you were also involved in—and the New Politics Initiative (*Yeni Siyaset Girişimi*), both of which have attempted to fulfill this need, but failed. Why do you think these attempts failed? Why is it that, in a Muslim-majority country, the masses do not support movements that underline Islam's emphasis on morality and justice?

Even though these movements are quite important and necessary, it can be claimed that the actors involved in them are not sufficiently qualified to carry out the movements' ultimate goals. Surprisingly, both initiatives resulted from a cooperation between socialist and Islamist groups. The New Politics Initiative failed because several former deputies from the CHP decided to join the AKP. The People's Voice Party failed because several former deputies and bureaucrats from the National Outlook (*Milli Görüş*) movement decided to join the AKP. This shows quite clearly that, be they rightists or leftists, religious or nonreligious, the average person in Turkish society still sees politics only as a source of rent. In all fairness, it must be said that in both of these unsuccessful movements, contrary to expectations, socialists had a much more principled and moral stance than pious Muslims.

In your book *Ahir Zaman İlmihali* [Catechism of the End Times], you write: "Turkish Muslims are moving away from Islam. Muslims are bowing down to conformism. Muslims are losing their cause (*dava*). *Mujahideen* are turning into contractors (*müteahhit*), devoted mystics (*tasavvuf ehli*) are turning into sly entrepreneurs (*tasarruf ehli*). Green capital (*yeşil sermaye*) has given birth

---

[3]Please see http://www.hayrikirbasoglu.net/?p=292 for the full interview.

to a class of abluted (*abdestli*) capitalists who are only pursuing status/political power, cash/money, and women (*masa-kasa-nisâ*) and, while doing so, are captured in the triangle of passion, fame, and bribery" (2014: 245–246). What do you think is triggering this negative transformation of Islam in Turkey? Is it possible to put an end to this course of events? If so, how?

Actually, one could say that it is not only the Islamic segments of the society that are going through such turmoil but all segments of it. It would be quite spurious to think that the degeneration experienced not only in our country but in many other Muslim societies is particular to only pious Islamic groups. For as much as the members of Muslim societies, including our country, belong to different religious, philosophical, ideological, and ethnic circles, it is quite normal that the degeneration among the religious in society—who claim to be quite attached to moral values—should draw more attention. What we need to focus on in all these developments is the process of globalization—or more correctly the globalization of capitalism—experienced over the last few decades. It is possible to state that this worldview, which may also be seen as the founding ideology of the USA, the EU, and transnational capital, aims primarily to spread consumerism across the globe.

Having witnessed the cost that the National Outlook parties led by Erbakan had to pay because of their uncooperative attitude toward the imperialist and colonialist West, the AKP government and its Muslim supporters decided not to challenge the global powers that be and so they came to an agreement on globalization. As a result, cash flow into the country increased, the West backed Turkey economically, and Turkey took part in numerous Western projects as a subcontractor. In particular, the rent created via municipal administrations has contributed to the financial well-being of the government and its supporters. The incentives given to the construction sector helped boost the economy, and the resulting aggregate rents have largely benefited the capitalists and the supporters of the government. Currently, the total wealth of the 100 richest people in Turkey is 102.9 billion dollars, which means that around 13.5% of the GDP is controlled by these people. Lured by the benefaction and patronage of the government and embracing an accommodation of capitalism and consumerism, Islamic groups have given into the enchantment of the luxurious and ostentatious life of the rich, and have embraced the lifestyle of those they have been criticizing for the last 40 years. As a result of an evolutionary process that is well-expressed by the axiom "the way you live shapes the way you believe," they have now ended up in the midst of a continual struggle to justify and legitimize this lifestyle. This so-called "new Islamic bourgeoisie" is now striving to come up with arguments that would justify their mounting wealth, which is the result of corrupt and illegitimate financial practices. On certain occasions, I personally have heard people close to government circles say that in order to transform the oppressive system in Turkey, in order to fight against the previous system's elite and media—and nowadays also against the Gülen organization's [*Gülen örgütü*] capital and media power—they will create their own capitalist groups and media circles. In the name of doing just this, they say, it is perfectly legitimate to put on hold or ignore certain values. I have lost count of the number of times I have heard people in these circles say, "So far, others have been amassing unlawful gains; now it is time for Muslims to do so." Even if the government and its supporters do not say these things officially, we know that such an interpretation is quite widespread in the pro-government circles.

For the last 15 years, a self-proclaimed religious party has been ruling Turkey. You argue that Islam/Muslims have degenerated during the rule of AKP. Yet, it's also during this period that we have seen the birth of groups like the Labor and Justice Platform (*Emek ve Adalet Platformu*) and the Anti-Capitalist Muslims (*Antikapitalist Müslümanlar*) who embrace an oppositional religiosity and emphasize labor, justice, and rights. Can we trace back the emergence of these groups to the disappointment caused by the AKP government among those Muslims who were hoping that everything would be better when the pious were in power? To what extent do you think these groups can contribute to the fight against a degenerated Islam/Muslims or to the spread of an understanding of Islam based on *ijtihad*?

There's no doubt that the degeneration among those in government circles has greatly disappointed the sincere and idealist Islamic segments of the society, especially the youth. There is a constant increase in the number of oppositional and dissident voices among those in Islamic circles. These voices stand in opposition to groups that collaborate with globalization and that have embraced the consumer-society model, and have, as a result, degenerated. The self-proclaimed religiosity of these groups, and the conceptualizations of Islam which give birth to such religiosity, are also increasingly criticized. However, this wave of protest has yet to reach the power it needs to shake the government. With the cooptation of the People's Voice Party, the possibility of having an Islamic opposition in the political arena—one that emphasizes social justice, morality and is even a bit leftist—against the so-called Islamic government, seems to be off the table. Opposition groups that criticize the profanization and degeneration of the government and its supporters are still quite marginal. Importantly, they still haven't been able to agree on a common discourse and strategy. In short, an Islamic-socialist oppositional position critical of the conservative government's ideology and actions is still in the very early stages of its formation. These groups are closer to reformist Islamic approaches. However, given that the government and its supporters are in complete control of politics, the economy, and the media, it would be unrealistic to claim that this opposition—anti-imperialist, anti-capitalist, open to reformist Islamic approaches and displaying some of the features of an Islamic-socialist solidarity—will be able to have any say in Turkey's future any time soon. It looks like we will have to wait for quite a while to see this happen. Still, we should not give into hopelessness and we should not forget that it's always darkest just before dawn.

Since 2011, Turkey has been witnessing a struggle for power between once-close allies—the AKP and the Gülen movement. As a result of this clash, a coup attempt, allegedly spearheaded by Gülenist soldiers, took place on July 15, 2016. Overall, what harm do you think this fight has done to Islam and Islamists in Turkey?

In fact, policies that have harmed Islam and Islamists have been increasingly practiced since the AKP's second term in office. It was not only the Islamists who believed that the government was sincere in its steps toward democratization during its first few years in power; the liberals and social democrats also supported the government back then. All these groups would later on realize that they had been mistaken and would start claiming more vocally that they had been deceived.

Rather than characterizing what is happening as a fight between the AKP and the Gülen organization it would be more realistic to say that this is a fight between Erdoğan and Gülen. Both groups are based on one man's will and are ruled through a top-down hierarchy. Although one is a political entity and the other is a religious one, the same authoritarian-totalitarian mindset is strongly present in both. As such, one could easily talk about this as a commonality between the two. Despite their claims of piety and the discourse of the "Islamic cause," both sides started fighting not over Islam, but over power and rent. This rentier power project—whose political infrastructure was established by the AKP, and whose civil society infrastructure was established by the Gülen organization—has, over time, become the prize in a wrestling match between the two partners who now compete for dominance. This fight resulted in the failed coup attempt of July 15—most probably supported by the USA and the EU. The coup attempt showed to what lengths these two supposedly pious Islamic groups can go to in order to monopolize power. It also served as a wake-up call for broad segments of society. The most common-place accusations against the current government—corruption, rentiership, discrimination, religious exploitation, sectarianism—are valid not only for the AKP, but also for the Gülen organization.

To put it differently, the degeneration of those in power has resulted from joint policies perpetuated by mutual agreement and cooperation. It is not difficult to see that neither side has the right to accuse the other as they are equally corrupt. In that sense, in thinking about the damage they have done to Islam and Islamism, it is clear that the political and civil society components of the government's fifteen-year-long policies cannot be separated and should be evaluated together. It has now been revealed that the fight between the constituents of this government—and the attempt by the Gülen organization to organize a coup—is not a fight over morality, but rather a worldly struggle over power and rent-sharing presented as a religious struggle. As such, it is not surprising that this is labeled as "the end of Islamism" or "the end of political Islam." Yet, it should be noted that these labels do not denote the end of Islamism or political Islam categorically; rather, this "end" refers to the failure of and the disappointment with the Turkish case, as well as that of the Egyptian Muslim Brotherhood.

Several religious orders in Turkey—the Menzil, the İsmailağa—are trying to fill the void left by the Gülen movement. In your opinion, which of these orders is the AKP more likely to collaborate with? What would the repercussions of such a collaboration be for Turkey?

It looks like there are only two criteria for the AKP government in terms of filling the positions they had systematically stuffed with Gülenists in the past: submission and loyalty. In this sense, the government's mentality is no different than that of the Gülen organization or any other religious order. Yet while the Gülen organization is more homogenous and organized, the others act more like religious orders or communities. Because of that, they end up getting into power struggles among themselves or with the AKP government. There is no guarantee that in the future these orders, communities, and groups will not take the same steps as the Gülen organization has. In this sense, these groups' being granted certain cadres is a serious threat for both the AKP and the country. It is a threat for the AKP because they could easily take a stance against the AKP once the power- and rent-sharing is over. It is a threat for the country because these groups have no acquaintance with scientific knowledge or critical thinking; when it comes to the type of religious mentality they have embraced, they are no different from the AKP or the Gülen organization. They are just as fanatic, unrealistic, patronizing, confrontational, and pragmatic. More worrying are the hysterical delusions, among members of the AKP and of these groups, which point to a complete loss of touch with reality. If this mentality in both its political and religious form is not curtailed, there is no obstacle that would prevent them from taking crazy steps in the near future.

What are your predictions for the future of political Islam in the post-AKP period, particularly keeping in mind the existence of various religious orders, as well as of the ISIS cells claimed to be rapidly spreading in Turkey?

That the AKP and pro-AKP religious groups have been corrupted by power is a view that is now being voiced not only by opposition groups, but also by some government representatives. Even in the pro-government media one can see increasing number of journalists reporting this type of confessions. It is becoming quite apparent that in order to stay in power, the government will not hesitate to cooperate with the most radical and repressive groups, even with violent, mafia-like organizations, and that all parties involved are acting recklessly with the euphoria of victory. As a result of such groups' endorsement by the government—especially within the compass of a conspiracy/collaboration mechanism composed of the Ministry of Education, the Higher Education Council, and the media—the fanatical pro-government staffing of cadres (*kadrolaşma*), and pro-government propaganda, it is very likely that local entities that are not any different from ISIS and Al-Qaeda will emerge soon.

Add to this the question of where ISIS militants or the ISIS-like armed groups within the Syrian opposition—supported by the AKP government—will go when they withdraw from Syria. Unfortunately, all analyses point to the conclusion that should these groups enter Turkey, even as they head for other countries, they will pose a serious security threat. The recently increased police operations against ISIS in Turkey could be seen as a testament to the immanency of this threat. Sadly, this frightening picture has resulted largely from the government's grossly flawed policy in Syria. In line with these policies—the failure of which have been accepted even by the government—and with the financial support of Qatar and Saudi Arabia, the government has given logistical and tactical support to numerous armed oppositional groups in Syria and has turned a blind eye to the movement of these groups across Turkish borders. It is not surprising that these groups are now hitting Turkey like a boomerang.

In order for one to reach the optimistic supposition that Turkey will be much safer in the future than it is today, one needs to overlook these security threats. What makes things even worse is that this threat is no longer only an external threat. On the contrary, it is likely to reproduce itself as a local threat within Turkey. According to research conducted by various institutions between 2015 and 2016, the number of ISIS sympathizers in Turkey ranges from 500,000 to 6,000,000. As such, this threat should not be underestimated, as it has the potential to turn increasingly into an internal threat.

In light of these developments, one could speculate that a number of different factions in Turkey—be it the government and the opposition, rightists and leftists, Turks and Kurds, religious conservatives and secularists—will eventually have to agree on the need to reevaluate religion and political Islam as social realities, and stop using it as a tool for politics and rent-sharing. Turkey direly needs such an agreement. If not, it will not be possible to prevent the current polarization in society from navigating down dangerous paths.

References

Izetbegović, A. (2010). *İslam Deklarasyonu*. (Islamic Declaration) İstanbul: Fide Yayınları.
Kırbaşoğlu, H. (2014). *Ahir Zaman İlmihali* (10th ed). (Catechism of the End Times) Ankara: OTTO Yayınları.
Marx, K. (1997). *Hegel'in Hukuk Felsefesinin Eleştirisi*. (Critique of Hegel's Philosophy of Right) İstanbul: Sol Yayınları.
Şeriati, A. (2013). *Dine Karşı Din*. (Religion against Religion) Ankara: Fecr Yayınları.

Author Biographies

Hayri Kırbaşoğlu is a professor at Ankara University Divinity School. After graduating from Ankara University Divinity School in 1978, he completed his Ph.D. in hadith studies at the same university in 1983. Between 1985 and 1987 he worked as an assistant professor at Imam Muhammed Ibn Suud University in Riyadh, Saudi Arabia. Between 1988 and 1989 he served as a consultant at the Presidency of Religious Affairs [*Diyanet İşleri Başkanlığı*]. Between 1986 and 1998 he served as the assistant editor of the journal *İslâmî Araştırmalar* (Islamic Research). Between 1998 and 2007 he was an editorial board member for the journal *İslâmiyât* (Islamiyyah). Between 2011 and 2012 he worked as a faculty member at Qatar University, Faculty of Sharia and Islamic Research. Some of his books include *İslam Düşüncesinde Sünnet—Eleştirel Bir Yaklaşım* [Sunnah in Islamic Thought: A Critical Approach] (Ankara 1999); *İslam Düşüncesinde Hadis Metodolojisi* [Hadith Methodology in Islamic Thought] (Ankara 1999); *Sünni Paradigmanın Oluşumunda Şâfi'î'nin Rolü* [The Role of the Shafiite in the Formation of the Sunni Paradigm] (Ankara 2000); *Alternatif Hadis Metodolojisi* [Alternative Hadith Methodology] (Ankara 2002); *Namazların Birleştirilmesi* [The Joining of Prayers] (Ankara 2002); *Eskimez Yeni Hz. Peygamber'in Sünneti* [The Ever New: Prophet Muhammad's Sunnah] (Ankara 2010), *Ahir Zaman İlmihali* [A Muslim Cathecism for End Times] (Ankara 2010); *Ehl-i Sünnet'in Kurucu Ataları* [The Founding Ancestors of the Ahl al-Sunnah] (Ankara 2011);*Üçüncü Yol Mukaddimesi* [Introduction to The Third Way] (Ankara 2014).

Gülay Türkmen is a postdoctoral researcher at the University of Goettingen's Forum for Interdisciplinary Religious Studies. She received her Ph.D. in Sociology from Yale University in 2016. She is a comparative-historical sociologist with research interests that stand at the intersection of culture, politics and religion. She is specifically interested in how certain historical, cultural and political developments inform questions of belonging and identity-formation in multi-ethnic and multi-religious societies. Under that rubric, her research focuses on how religious, ethnic and national identities intersect, intertwine and compete with each other, especially in Muslim communities in the Middle East and Europe. She is also interested in cultural politics of nationalism, especially in cultural trauma and collective memory in the context of national identity formation. Her work has appeared in the *Annual Review of Sociology*, *Nations and Nationalism*, *Yale Review of International Affairs*, and the *Routledge Handbook of Religion and Security*. She has also written opinion pieces for *Open Democracy*, *Jadaliyya*, *Policy Trajectories*, and *the European*.

Part IV
Social Movements

The Gezi Revolts

Y. Doğan Çetinkaya and interviewed by Bilge Seçkin Çetinkaya

Abstract Until the events of the Arab Spring, the Middle East and North Africa were described with words like stagnation, unchanging, subservience, and submission. But after 2010, it became a region that inspired protests worldwide. People began to revisit the history of Middle Eastern social movements, and it became common to assess the current protests in their historical context. The Gezi revolts, too, are a part of this history, in that sense. However, we must differentiate what happened at Gezi Park from political movements and organized social movements. Few spontaneous social upheavals can push state forces to retreat from a public square located at the heart of a country. Hundreds of thousands of people came together for change in the most central location of a country governed by a strong neoliberal government that is itself integrated into a neoliberal world. They also dared to stand up to the police. In that sense, it was an important experience for the western part of the country. Although there have been effective social movements and resistances throughout Turkish history, there are few examples of such a spontaneous social explosion.

Keywords Turkey · Gezi protests

With the Gezi Park protests of May–September 2013, millions of people poured into the streets in a way we had never seen before. We were all immediately aware that we were witnessing an historical moment. And they did this just for the sake of a few trees. During the Taksim Solidarity meetings, we repeatedly heard that the Gezi revolts were the largest demonstrations in the history of modern Turkey. How do you, as a participant in the protests, as an activist, and as someone who writes about social movements, historicize Gezi now, in hindsight?

Y. Doğan Çetinkaya (✉) · B. S. Çetinkaya
Istanbul University, Istanbul, Turkey
e-mail: dogancetinkaya@gmail.com

B. S. Çetinkaya
e-mail: bilgeseckin@gmail.com

© Springer International Publishing AG, part of Springer Nature 2019
E. Özyürek et al. (eds.), *Authoritarianism and Resistance in Turkey*,
https://doi.org/10.1007/978-3-319-76705-5_11

The most important reason Gezi could be very quickly and easily defined as Turkey's largest protest to date is related to some generally accepted ideas on social movements. It is commonly believed that the main actors in the Middle East are elites, administrators, states, and imperialists. Everyday insurgencies and the organized struggles of common people are quickly forgotten.

Until the events of the Arab Spring, the Middle East and North Africa were described with words like stagnation, unchanging, subservience, and submission. But after 2010, it became a region that inspired protests worldwide. People began to revisit the history of Middle Eastern social movements, and it became common to assess the current protests in their historical context. The Gezi revolts, too, are a part of this history, in that sense. However, we must differentiate what happened at Gezi Park from political movements and organized social movements. Few spontaneous social upheavals can push state forces to retreat from a public square located at the heart of a country. Hundreds of thousands of people came together for change in the most central location of a country governed by a strong neoliberal government that is itself integrated into a neoliberal world. They also dared to stand up to the police. In that sense, it was an important experience for the western part of the country. Although there have been effective social movements and resistances throughout Turkish history, there are few examples of such a spontaneous social explosion.

Where is Gezi positioned in this global and regional wave of protests? Is it positioned with the Occupy movement in the US, which claims to reject all kinds of power struggles? Or with Tahrir Square in Cairo, which successfully removed the nondemocratic rulers from power, but then had the revolution stolen by the military coup? Or with the dignity of Puerta del Sol in Madrid and the rage of Syntagma Square in Athens at the deepening financial crisis? Iran, Yemen, Tunisia, Russia, Bulgaria, Armenia, Lebanon. The list of uprisings after Gezi goes on.

The mass protests against the 1999 WTO Ministerial Conference in Seattle were an important milestone. Following those events, the anti-globalization movement spread worldwide. It gained momentum as a social and political reaction against neoliberal globalization. In 2001, in Porto Alegre, Brazil, which was governed by a workers' party, the World Social Forum proclaimed that "another world is possible." In that same year, the social explosion in Argentina demonstrated that spontaneous struggles against neoliberal capitalism were spreading. During those years, social media forums were still led by formal political and social organizations. Although a few Turkish activists followed these events closely, it is difficult to claim that Turkish organizations were involved in these forums. The Kurdish freedom movement, which is one of the largest social movements in Europe, wasn't really involved in the anti-globalization movement. The most organized and mobilized group, the Revolutionary Teachers Movement, was stuck in its own problems. Socialists were following the process more closely, and some got involved on an individual basis.

Despite this, toward the end of the 2000s, there was a significant transformation in the history of social movements globally. The protests after the murder of young Alexis in Athens during the last days of 2008 marked the beginning of a new era of social explosions. Before that, urban street clashes and skirmishes with police occurred in the context of prior organization, in a much more controlled manner, during global meetings or social forums. But a new era began after 2008, an era where social explosions occurred spontaneously outside the control of an organization or movement. The financial crisis hit all the countries of southern Europe heavily and thrust them into social turbulence. Austerity measures intensified the ill effects of prevailing neoliberal policies, and as a result the Mediterranean region as a whole was thrown into social turmoil. Between 2010 and 2012, Greece was shaken by the largest spontaneous mass demonstrations in its modern history. The anti-austerity movement became a turning point. Simultaneous occupations, sit-ins, protests, and looting occurred in countries like Iceland, Italy, Spain, Portugal, and England. But the most significant developments of this period occurred in the southern Mediterranean and the Middle East.

Ever since the 1977 Egyptian Bread Riots, significant insurgencies against repressive regimes have occurred throughout the Middle East. Prior to the Arab Spring events and Tahrir, and developing through the 2000s, there had been protest coming from the political opposition and from the organized working class. Protests and direct actions occurring after 2008 carried the struggle into the streets and occupied town squares. These involved mostly unemployed people hurt by the neoliberal system, workers without job security, students and young people who believed that their future had been stolen, groups denied of their rights, victims of urban transformation, immigrants forgotten in the suburbs, villagers, refugees, victims of ecological destruction, people fighting against patriarchy. It wasn't hard for them to unite their varying demands on the streets. Uniting in the public squares of the world, people were now coming out to protest financial and political systems, demanding political freedom and representation, requiring recognition of their various identities. So class, feminist, and environmental movements—which had been compartmentalized in their struggles—began to stand together side by side. The Gezi protests are part of this world. After having followed the moves of the anti-globalization movement and social forums from the sidelines throughout the 2000s, Turkey finally become an important part of this period of social explosion— of course, with its own specificities.

About these specificities, Gezi surprised all of us—including those who were involved—what with its massiveness and outrage. We had all been rather hopeless, so no one expected such a massive protest. In hindsight, were there prior indications which could give us an idea of how big Gezi was going to be, and did we miss them?

As with many other protests, the 2013 spring demonstrations surrounding Gezi Park took us all by surprise. But again, as with other upheavals, it is possible in hindsight to detect its origins, which are not much of a mystery. It is not often that these kinds of resistances turn into massive uprisings. A number of events occurred during the lead-up to Gezi, and although they did not bring with them such widespread social explosion, they're still important to know in order to understand the background to Gezi Park. A number of workers' activities happened just before Gezi: Denizli Deba, Meha LC Waikiki, United Parcel Servie, Turkish Airlines, Şişe-Cam, Antep Tuğla, Teksim, Hey Tekstil, the metal factory at Bursa, egg protests, bus protests, the occupation of Starbucks at Boğaziçi University, student protests at the Middle East Technical University from the previous winter, demonstrations against exam cheating scandals. There were countless student protests. We still remember the protests against urban transformation and urban gentrification—and these protests continue today. The Başıbüyük protests, the struggle for Sulukule, demonstrations for the Emek theater hall, marches against the prohibition of abortion, widespread protests in the countryside against gold mining, actions against hydroelectric dams which eventually became a movement in and of itself, clashes between people and the police at Gerze, Tortum, and Çıralı. These happened not long before Gezi. Football team fans joined together to protest the policing of stadiums and clashed with the police on the streets. People were protesting against the Turkish Intelligence Agency draft bill, phone tapping, debates concerning abortion and women, interference with how many children a family should have, tight regulations against alcoholic beverages, restriction of public spaces as with Taksim during last year's May Day celebrations or during Gezi, increasingly conservative legislation, demolition of statues, kissing bans at metros, official discourse against Alevis, and many others. Although the government seemed powerful and hegemonic, all these protests were little drops in the making of an oceanic social reaction. Although there was a standard overlay of neoliberal destruction and a new proletarianization process creating a precariat in Turkey, there was no financial or debt crisis as in some other contemporary protests worldwide. As in Tahrir, the demand for political freedom was more notable in Turkey than it was in other European countries. Hatred erupted particularly against Erdoğan's personality, his expressions and political discourse. It was his public statements that sparked the fire again and again during the protests. We must mention here that even though the prime minister claims to represent the country's vulnerable and to defend the periphery against the center, his words concerning the protests were blatant displays of elitism. It was he as well who named the protesters "looters" (*çapulcular*).

It is puzzling that everyone finds it so difficult to determine who participated in the protests. Whose movement was it? Where were the Kurds?

Perhaps it is easier if we begin with the last question. Had there not been a ceasefire between the PKK, and the government as part of the peace negotiation process, the Gezi protests probably would not have happened. Or at the very least it would not have happened in that way. The negotiation process, which the Kurdish freedom movement viewed as an achievement of its long struggles, created a relaxed atmosphere for the Gezi revolt and other protests that I mentioned before. The Kurdish freedom movement did not participate in Gezi with its mass base in

Kurdistan. However, I find their critics on the Turkish nationalist left quite insincere. When the Kurdish freedom movement goes to the streets, it elicits very different results, as has been seen time and again. We saw it again in another case after Gezi: deaths, missing people. These kinds of results are not comparable to Gezi—they pay a very high price for their resistance. We cannot guess what the results would have been had there been a simultaneous Kurdish revolt during Gezi. It may have posed a threat to the prime minister's power or perhaps people would have had to return to their homes in the west. But it is not true that the Kurdish freedom movement was not there at Gezi Park. They were there alongside other organized political groups. Herein lies the problem: the Turkish and foreign literature on Gezi is produced by people with no real experience at Gezi Park, or by people did not participate in the Taksim Solidarity meetings where some 128 organizations were represented.

Here we must examine two arguments about Gezi that came to the fore during and after the protests. The first interpreted the protests as a manifestation of a new middle class which had arisen as a result of the global transformation in capital, a transformation that includes Turkey. This argument was repeated many times in liberal and left-liberal circles. The second argument appeared soon thereafter as a response to the first. This view stressed the common idea that capitalist societies consist of two conflicting classes: the owners of capital and the working class. According to this view, those who participated in Gezi were part of the working class.

Although I cannot discuss these arguments in-depth in this interview, I must point out the unreasonable nature of their premises. The argument about the new middle class fails to explain how the members of this so-called new middle class can have the same cultural and political values, the same democratic sensitivity, while they are segmented across very different income groups and employed in very different job sectors. In this explanation, it is impossible to understand why these new middle classes are intrinsically against all types of oppression and hegemonic power. The answer offered is invariably that such views are due to new communication technologies, lifestyles, and consumer patterns. But these answers are no less reductionist than the classical class analyses put forward in the second argument.

Those segments of society relevant to our subject are members of the middle class currently experiencing rapid proletarianization. The generation I belong to experienced up close the class position of this new middle class, that of paid white-collar professionals. Their university education has lost value within this neoliberal order; the education system has increasingly lost its autonomy and the academic structures which allow critical thinking and free thought, and its graduates have now been transformed into ordinary technical personnel. Outside a tiny executive group that controls the means of production, these white-collar office employees work under very oppressive conditions that are defined by performance criteria and which eventually lead to the corrosion of character. In short, as in other countries, we are not experiencing a rising middle class in Turkey, but rather a falling one. These people are losing their social status, their salaries, and their position in the relations of production, and are clearly aware of it. In many cases, their salaries have dipped below those of blue-collar union workers. Employees of corporations and large businesses aside, there are numerous studies on the prole-tarianization of the professions—lawyers, doctors, teachers. Simply declaring this rapidly growing segment of society a part of the working class does not help us to understand Gezi, or to understand or transform society.

Various kinds of proletarianization and the social elements shaping these types have created a separation within the working class. This is why the bulk of the working class wasn't involved in Gezi. For example, a significant number of workers voted for the AKP, and they didn't participate in the protests. This doesn't mean that their class consciousness is wrong, or that they lack a specific type of class consciousness. What we must see here is that the process of proletarianization in domestic work, in illegal factories and business centers, has very different social and political consequences; organized workers, illegal factory workers, domestic workers were not involved in Gezi. Those who stood out at Gezi are workers who have experienced a specific form of proletarianization, those with a very specific class culture—youth who are losing their futures, working or unemployed educated professionals Alevis who experience oppression and proletarianization based on their religious identity, secular women who are excluded from all kinds of own-ership, LGBTQ youth who are victims of conservative patriarchy, those for whom secular concerns are paramount. The masses experiencing their own specific pro-cess of proletarianization created Gezi with limited intervention from the left. There are other workers' groups who come with a very different class culture and politics; they are among the reasons the AKP regime still stands, despite all its setbacks.

Superficial observers and unreliable surveys have gotten it wrong; participants in Gezi also differed according to their social base and the place where they were involved. There was a significant difference—visible even to the uninitiated—between those who clashed with the police on the night of June 1, those who held ground at the barricades for a week, and those who remained within Gezi Park. There are enormous differences between those who occupied and remained in Gezi Park, and those who came as tourists. Had they gone to Gezi Park and Taksim Square, researchers would have obtained very different information. Protesters in other cities or protests organized by the Turkish left had a very different organi-zation than the Gezi Park occupation. Researchers who would have gone to the park in the morning, midday, or night would have seen very different participants and event, and therefore would have come to very different conclusions. The main point is that there was a clear gap between the spontaneous social explosion and orga-nized structures, especially at Taksim Square.

Immediately after the uprising, we entered a long period of election campaigns. Do you think there is an irreconcilable contrast between Gezi and the elec-tions? On one side there is the ballot, on the other there are the streets. What kind of social residue did Gezi leave behind?

When Gezi Park was occupied by masses and the state security apparatus was sent out of the Taksim district, an attempt was made to show that another world, another social life was possible. That was indeed symbolic. But there were already serious rifts. Very quickly, a rift emerged between those who stood watch at the barricades around Taksim and those who remained in Gezi Park. There were a number of different groups involved in the street clashes, especially on the night of the occupation and the following day, and they differed both socially and politically. Shortly thereafter, the stage was left to the socialists and the nationalists, and people at the barricades, the square, and Gezi Park became fragmented. People at the barricades would leave even without visiting the square or Gezi Park. While the socialists defended the existence of the barricades at Taksim Solidarity meetings, they did not defend them in practice. They failed to coordinate with their auxiliary committees concerning security and organization of the park. In order to allow people to speak and participate in decision-making, they also chose not to take the lead in the forums, at least not until the last days; in fact they did their best to stop that kind of railroading. Actually, the left prevented the protests from taking a nationalist course—as you've stated. That was their chief success. People who came to the park arrived with a nationalist CHP mentality and left transformed at some level. The old slogan "We're all soldiers of Mustafa Kemal" was fended off with a counterslogan: "We won't kill, we won't die, and we are no one's soldier." These are the contributions Gezi has made. In cities outside Istanbul, people tried to create public occupations resembling Gezi. Soon, we heard claims like, "We are clashing on the streets; people at Gezi are having fun at the park." When the police recaptured the square and the park by force, people spread out to parks all around Istanbul and across Turkey and began to create forums, from which a significant debate culture arose. There were even forms of occupation that we've rarely seen in Turkey, for example the squatter occupation at Kadıköy. These were very important, substantive experiences for social movements in Turkey. But in time, these forums, too, died out and disappeared.

I said before that Gezi participants were generally concerned with political freedom, and that they came out especially against Erdoğan. This is why the Gezi movement tried to beat Erdoğan democratically at the first opportunity: the elections. Although some leftist groups were against this effort, saying "Gezi won't fit into the ballot box," we can easily assume that those who participated in Gezi supported the centrist CHP party in order to beat the AKP. Another significant result of Gezi was the establishment by the Kurdish freedom movement of the HDP party, which later achieved a success in the elections. All this is to say that Turkey's most important spontaneous social protest turned into an appetite for participation in mainstream parliamentary politics. Their efforts were of course defeated by Erdoğan, both in presidential and local elections. Everyone assumed that millions clashing on the streets would have resulted in a win for the centrists.

But in this sense, no one could claim Gezi for themselves. Another Turkish left-wing group calling themselves the June Movement claimed ownership of the dynamics produced by Gezi. The HDP picked a tree reminiscent of Gezi Park as its symbol. But as I mentioned before, even if the socialists were an important presence in Taksim Solidarity meetings and on the streets, they displayed utter short-sightedness during the Gezi protests. This was related to their lack of organizational strength and focus. This is why all attempts to claim to politically represent the Gezi movement have resulted in disappointment. The only success was that of the Kurdish freedom movement when they stood against AKP in the presidential and parliamentary elections. Only time will tell how successfully the HDP will be able to organize the Gezi audience for in the short term.

The most important legacy of Gezi was that it expressed the need for the people to communicate their demands in the streets, in a spontaneous and direct manner, without delegating their voice to a representative. After Gezi, active political struggle became more commonplace than it had been for a long time. Street protests, demonstrations actions organized around urban transformation, environmentalism, or within the working-class movement became legitimate modes of engagement.. The lack of conflict in Turkey and the region, the relative peace, created significant space for social movements. When HDP's election success added to the moment, the AKP government realized that the opposition was reaping the benefits of peace, and it started to sound the drums of war. The situation in the Middle East, especially the Syrian civil war, facilitated this. In the long term, what we do as a society to counter the ongoing government warmongering will be a testament to the extent and political durability of Gezi.

You have recently compared the resistance of AKP followers and Islamists against the coup attempt of July 15, 2016 with Gezi. Why do you think Islamists and the AKP keep referring to Gezi and do they also compare the coup attempt with Gezi?

When the HDP surpassed the 10% parliamentary threshold in the June 7, 2015 elections, the political establishment—particularly the state elite—recognized the threat it posed to their power. For the first time in the course of modern Turkish history, the right-wing government was confronted with potential unity between groups who had theretofore acted apart: Kurds, Alevis, socialists, liberals, organized workers. Although the vote garnered by the HDP in the election was to a great extent that of the Kurdish constituency, the HDP emerged as a potentially powerful opposition party. They were a threat not only to the AKP, but also to the CHP. Because the HDP had a massive base and links to the PKK, an armed organization, it was also a threat to the entire political system of the country. Such a coalition might have undermined the dominance of the AKP across different social classes. For this reason, following the June 2015 elections, the state declared war against all opposition parties and groups with a propensity to unite around the HDP. They were successful. The bombings and street fights in the eastern Kurdish towns and cities alienated many groups, particularly those who were active in Gezi-related protests in the western parts of the country. The level of struggle involved in the armed street fights in Kurdish towns was beyond the capabilities and predilections of those active in the Gezi protests. They could do little more than watch the clashes over social media. This destroyed what was left of the Gezi protests. The sole declaration against the hostilities by Academics for Peace confirms the impotence of the opposition. Erdoğan's new coalition with the Turkish nationalists and with groups who had once been active in the state security forces shut down the public sphere to any kind of political, social, or civil activity. Those who claimed to be the representatives of Gezi are restricted to social media now. The HDP leaders and members of parliament are in prison as we speak. This is a total defeat.

It is important note here that the first to resist the coup attempt, even before Erdoğan called upon citizens to go to the public squares and resist the army, were the Islamist groups. Erdoğan has the unqualified support of organized Islamist groups behind him; they know that they must stand with Erdoğan, lest they lose the freedoms and power they have gained over the last 15 years. Their support enhances Erdoğan's position.

In this context, the resistance of the Islamists on July 15, 2016, and the demonstrations mobilized by Erdoğan in public squares were also a reply to the Gezi protests. Resistance to the coup attempt was actually characterized by its participants and by Islamist groups specifically as a reply to Gezi. Islamic journals compared every aspect of their actions to Gezi, claiming that, in contrast with Gezi, theirs was a "true" resistance. Gezi, they asserted, was a conspiracy against Turkey perpetrated by the "Great Powers." This also indicates the significance of the Gezi protests: it lingers about, a specter still haunting Erdoğan's New Turkey.

Author Biographies

Y. Doğan Çetinkaya is an assistant professor in political science at Istanbul University and gives lectures and organizes workshops at the Free University-Istanbul. He was an activist in the student movement of 1990s. He earned two MAs, the first from Boğaziçi University in 2002 and the second from Central European University in 2004. He received his PhD at Leiden University in 2010. In 2012–2013, he was a visiting scholar at Panteion University in Athens. Between 2003–2008, he served as a member of the board of directors of Istanbul's Eğitim-Sen University Section, one of the largest trade unions in Turkey. Between 2005–2007, he was a member of the party council of the Freedom and Solidarity Party. In 2017, he became the vice-president of History Foundation, the largest independent organization of historians in Turkey. He is on the board of the journal *Toplumsal Tarih* (Social History). Among other publications, his book *The Young Turks and the Boycott Movement: Nationalism, Protest and the Working Classes in the Formation of Modern Turkey* was published in 2014 by I.B. Tauris.

Bilge Seçkin Çetinkaya graduated from Istanbul University, Faculty of Political Sciences. She received her MA at Boğaziçi University with her thesis on Theater of the Revolution in the Ottoman Empire. She is still a PhD student at the same university. She worked as actress, producer, director in many theater plays (1994–2003). She wrote and worked in Radio Mega and Olay TV (1992–1994), feminist journal *Pazartesi Kadına Mahsus Gazete* (1999–2001), Yol TV (2008–2010). She was a columnist in *Birgün* newspaper (2010–2016). She worked in Mor Çatı Women's Shelter (2001) and at Boğaziçi University as a Research Assistant (2006–2007). She was an activist in the organization efforts of DESA workers and worked in Deri-İş Trade Union. She started to work in the Amsterdam based Clean Clothes Campaign in 2006 and became one of its founders in Turkey in 2012. She was the co-president of the Freedom and Solidarity Party in between 2012 and 2016.

Women's and Feminist Movements

Aksu Bora and interviewed by Nil Uzun

Abstract The major achievement of the feminist movement has been the spread of word *feminizm*. Although the state dictates that there is no such thing as "the equality of women and men," women' demands for equality, including within the governing party, have increased. Equality within the judicial system has been achieved to a great extent. The civil law statute which declared the head of the family to be the man was removed, and regulations pertaining to the division of labor between men and women were modified to reflect a more egalitarian legal stance. In response to the demands of the women's movement, regulations in the penal law regarding violence against women have improved. Sexual crimes against women are now regarded as violations of individual liberty rather than as crimes against the family, with harsh sentences imposed for those who commit honor crimes. Almost all political parties have quota bylaws, although the AKP is both against this approach to equality generally and does not include it in their party bylaws.

Keywords Feminisim · Turkey · Women's movement

Can you give us a brief historical outline of the women's and feminist movements in Turkey?

During the Ottoman era, beginning in the last quarter of the 19th century, a feminist movement arose alongside the movements for modernization and began to spread. Feminists came together in "White Conferences" to discuss their demands. There were also several feminist magazines, some short-lived, but a few long-lasting as well. If we also take into account the magazines that Armenian and Kurdish women

A. Bora (✉)
Middle East Hacettepe University, Çankaya, Turkey
e-mail: bora.aksu@gmail.com

N. Uzun
Rutgers University, New Brunswick, NJ, USA

© Springer International Publishing AG, part of Springer Nature 2019
E. Özyürek et al. (eds.), *Authoritarianism and Resistance in Turkey*,
https://doi.org/10.1007/978-3-319-76705-5_12

in the Ottoman Empire published, as well as the organizations they formed, we can say that feminism in Turkey has a 150-year-long history.

Throughout the process of transformation from a cosmopolitan Ottoman Empire to a nation-state, the feminist movement continued. Immediately after the declaration of the Republic of Turkey in 1923, an attempt to form the first women's political party, the Women's People's Party (*Kadinlar Halk Firkasi*), was made. Women did not enjoy suffrage at the time, and thus the purpose of this initiative was to achieve the right to vote, as well as the right for women to hold elected seats in government. The newly formed republican government refused the latter demand on the grounds of the former: individuals who do not have the right to vote cannot be elected and therefore have no right to form political parties. Women's demands for political participation were thus quickly sacrificed to the nationalist project whereby women were to serve as the "guardians" of the newly formed nation-state. The group of women who had initiated the effort to form a political party then established the Union of Turkish Women (*Turk Kadinlar Birliği*). With the achievement of suffrage in 1935, the Union of Turkish Women dissolved, and the women's movement was relegated to functioning as the "women's branch" of the new administration. Henceforth, women's issues were subsumed under the aegis of the Turkish modernization narrative and defined as a cultural problem rather than a political one. Feminists also pushed feminism aside and embarked upon the project of "enlightening the people" within the Kemalist secular modernization project.

This was a strategic choice: educated middle- and upper-middle-class women cooperated with Kemalist male elites in order to open up a space for themselves. These were elite women who called themselves the "daughters of the republic." With this strategy, they achieved very limited political influence, but also significant gains for women in the workplace. When the Union of Turkish Women was reestablished in 1949, it was represented in all the women's assemblies through to the 1980 coup d'état. The education of girls and women and women's employment in essential fields such as law, medicine, and education was expanded.

For broader sections of women living beyond the elite circles of these daughters of the republic, however, political empowerment and emancipation were delayed until much later. The consent of elite feminists to organize solely within the confines of the cultural arena and to withdraw from the political scene resulted in the feminist movement in Turkey being removed from the political agenda until the 1980s.

Women who had been active in the leftist opposition of the 1970s initiated the second wave of feminism in Turkey after the 1980 coup d'état. Initially coming together in consciousness-raising groups, these women brought the issue of private space into the political discussions of the time. Violence against women was the leading topic of these discussions. This second-wave feminism, which began in the big metropolitan centers, soon spread throughout Turkey and began mobilizing thousands of women.

After 1980, the major themes within the feminist movement centered around the methods of feminist organizing, horizontal and nonhierarchical organizing, violence, motherhood, and sexual freedom. Topics that had been on the agendas of their predecessors 100 years earlier continued to be central to these discussions: legal versus de facto equality and political participation and representation. They demanded equality with regard to legal regulations primarily related to civil law, and sought to create shelters and legal safety mechanisms for women who were victims of violence. Throughout the 1990s, the feminist movement created its own institutions and organizations. In this period, as a reflection of Turkey's political agenda, religious women and women within the Kurdish movement organized and began to make their own unique voices heard in the public arena. This resulted in both the spread and diversification of the feminist movement. At the same time, new fractures and conflicts within the movement began to intensify.

The major achievement of the movement has been the spread of word *feminizm* (feminism). Although the state dictates that there is no such thing as "the equality of women and men," women' demands for equality, including within the governing party, have increased. Equality within the judicial system has been achieved to a great extent. The civil law statute which declared the head of the family to be the man was removed, and regulations pertaining to the division of labor between men and women were modified to reflect a more egalitarian legal stance. In response to the demands of the women's movement, regulations in the penal law regarding violence against women have improved. Sexual crimes against women are now regarded as violations of individual liberty rather than as crimes against the family, with harsh sentences imposed for those who commit honor crimes. Almost all political parties have quota bylaws, although the AKP is both against this approach to equality generally and does not include it in their party bylaws. Rather than a party quota system or the pursuit of true gender equality within the party, the AKP party leadership has set a party goal of electing a minority of women candidates under the slogan "81 provincial capitals, 81 candidates."

There are of course many more things to do, and the achievements made thus far are not irreversible. More recently, the struggles concern conservative policies regulating women's bodies. Alternative policies have been put forward to counter the utilization of the family as a social policy tool and the placing of the burden of social policies onto women.

You mentioned the diversification of the women's movement after 1980 and throughout the 1990s, women within the Kurdish movement and religious women's organizations. Can you talk a little bit more about this?

The 1990s was a moment when feminism started to diversify and split up. Although it was not explicitly stated, the signs of serious divisions could already be seen. The predominant nationalist narrative which subsumes women's issues into the project of modernization and secularization continued to dominate. The unease with this narrative within feminism and the subsequent critique of the modernization project from a feminist perspective became possible in the 1990s, but discussions at the practical and political levels—which could at times become very difficult—intensified in the 2000s.

While the feminist movement has long worked toward a shared consciousness of what it means to be a woman through campaigns and consciousness-raising activities, it did so by emphasizing a shared identity as women, enshrined in a document entitled "The Women's Liberation Declaration" (*Kadınların kurtuluşu bildirge*), drafted in 1989 by an ad hoc group of feminists. This declaration, which began with the words "We, as women," was the embodiment of this emphasis on a shred identity: "We, as women, are oppressed and exploited. Our bodies, labor, and identities have been seized" (Kadinlarin 1989). This shared identity or collectivity (*ortaklik*) defined by feminists was a negative shared identity stemming from the experience of being oppressed. It meant that while we may be different from one another, we are all oppressed. Addressing the sites of oppression as the "bodies, labor, and identities" was a conscious gesture toward these differences—differences between feminists and between women.

This ground of negative shared identity upon which the feminist movement in Turkey today stands signals a break with the old state feminism that equated women's emancipation with modernization. The reference to *oppression* rather than to *underdevelopment* was meant to define feminism as a political struggle, rather than an enlightenment project.

When feminists said in 1989 "we, as women," they envisioned a collectivity big enough to embrace all women. Declaring that educated women also face domestic violence and abuse was meant to emphasize this shared identity. It meant that the "light" of an enlightened modernity was not falling upon women. But instead of saying it explicitly, instead of laying out their critique of modernity in a political statement, they used domestic violence as evidence of gender as a category that cuts horizontally across class and other differences. In taking this less direct strategy, I think they missed out on a very important opportunity to break with the old sponsored version of the women's movement. This break would have make it possible to expose the difference between feminism and that vague group of people that had theretofore bee called "the women's movement." Without such a clear break, it made it almost impossible to address the differences.

In forming their collectivist movement on the basis of a demographic analysis (women as victims of oppression) rather than on a political project of rights and liberties, they paradoxically strengthened their ties with the modernist tradition despite their attempts to break from it. Yes, it was very important to take a stance as "we, as women" and to then define themselves as subjects. Because now the project would have to be about extending women's liberties. Yet to emphasize women's subjectivity and identity on demographic rather than political grounds diminished the radical power of the break between the two movements. If womanhood as a shared identity stems from their common oppression, and their liberation is formed from that common oppression, then there is not much of a difference between women liberating themselves and women being liberated by saviors. The former can only be achieved by defining womanhood as a *political* shared collectivism.

To say that women today are still oppressed distances the movement from the grand narratives of progress, but in doing so, it takes modernization out of the discussion. To say that modernized and traditional women share a collective experience in their oppression is to argue that gender issues arise from some other cause. But which cause?

It wasn't a coincidence that the first major turning point in the fragmentation of the women's movement began at the point where women, primarily religious Muslims, who identified with the image of the modern woman began stating publicly, "We are here, too." These religious women were speaking from within a different interpretation of modernity. Feminists began asking, "Is an Islamic feminism possible?" The very question itself renders the discussion impossible. It poses the question as one addressed not to religious women, but to the secular and feminist woman-next-door. The answers were different back then, but the whole discussion went in very unfortunate directions. Certain feminists were sympathetic to Islamic feminists, others felt differently. There were jokes about it at the time, but it was never seen as a question about the definition of feminism itself.

Of course, we should not reduce the characterization of this turning point only to the question of Islamic feminism. There was already a broader space of struggle within Islamic feminism coded as pro-shariah versus pro-laicite which addressed this question, and which came to the center of the main political discussion. Among those involved in the discussion were feminists who had previously stated that there can be no such thing as a religious feminism. Because of their history, it was impossible for them to side with pro-state secularists in such an explicitly political struggle. The grounds of the debate remained vague. Rather than analyzing the thorny dichotomies of secularity and religion, modernity and tradition and tagging them as important topics of discussion for forging a feminist politics and discourse, they were instead sidestepped. When the question of the headscarf began to dominate the entire political discussion, feminists couldn't come up with a clear and direct position on it. I think that this shows the consequences of having avoided the issue altogether.

The fact that this discussion did not move any further also left another political problem unanswered. Islamists ended up being the only ones with a serious critique of modernism. But where did religious women stand within this critique? Some of them directed harsh criticisms at men in their movements, exposing the serious consequences of polygamy for women or the hypocrisy of men who viewed technological innovations such as washing machines as signs of modernism and so rejected them at home, while using computers at work. When they made these critiques, women Islamists were accused by men of being feminists. At the time, feminists were focusing on whether there was such thing as religious feminism. So Muslim feminist women paved their own path. This was a path that has seen some cross-over with secular feminists—such as in the UN Convention on the Elimination of All Forms of Discrimination against Women—but has mostly been a separate movement, with few exceptions. Since the intersection with feminists were so few, the prominent differences around questions like headscarves and religiosity were inevitable.

Islamic feminism was not the only dividing issue within the narrative of modernity. When Kurdish women became politicized through their identities as oppressed Kurds, it shook the foundation of the modernization and women narrative. These Kurdish women made us see how the modern definition of citizenship in Turkey was built on a nationalist idea of *Turkluk*, Turkishness. The relationship between Kurdish women and feminism in Turkey is not only a question of recognizing difference or the other, but it is also an opportunity for *Turkish* feminism to reflect upon itself.

We need to think about Kurdish feminists and the extensive grassroots movement of the pro-Kurdish HDP separately. We mustn't fixate on the party names so much, particularly given that Kurdish political parties have been so often disbanded by the state; the HDP is currently the official party of the Kurdish movement. Kurdish feminists have tried to develop a two-sided critique. While criticizing the nationalist patriarchal structure of the Kurdish movement they feel close to, they simultaneously criticize the Turkishness in feminism and the Turkish nationalism that exists within Kemalism. At the same time, the Kurdish women's movement has developed and has been politicized for years through demonstrations, prison visits, and party gatherings. It is difficult to say whether it is a feminist movement, because in many ways it is not. As a movement, it is developing very fast and is producing an incredible energy that cannot easily be controlled. While the movement refers to itself as the "Kurdish women's movement," it has many characteristics which cannot be easily categorized as being about women. Their Kurdish identity is the most important factor in their politicization, and they establish their political starting point from that identity.

The political struggle of Kurdish women is another point of divergence for the feminist movement in Turkey, because nationalism is such an important component of the modernization paradigm. That is not only the case for Turkish Kemalist modernization narratives, but also for Kurdish modernization projects.

The Islamic movement and the Kurdish movement have defined the political agenda of the 1990s. These two movements, coded as pro-shariah and pro-separatist respectively, are still important today. However, we see that their definitions are changing. LGBTQ and feminist movements worldwide view themselves as natural allies, and this is the case for Turkey too. But since the growth of the queer movement, this relationship has turned become more contentious.

The question of the hegemony of the AKP and its political approach to women's bodies has recently come to the fore. Throughout the period that the AKP government has been in power, what kinds of changes have occurred regarding the politics of gender and sexuality in Turkey? What kinds of positions have the feminist movements taken in this regard?

It is difficult to say anything in brief about the AKP's policies regarding women and the family, but one thing is certain: it is not a topic we can easily formulate around concepts like *backwardness*, because there are both continuities and disruptions between the policy formulations of previous governments. Patriarchy and the tradition of state dominance did not begin with the AKP, but has always existed. The AKP is also not the only party with those anti-secular policies. But it is the first government to openly joke about women's bodies and explicitly state that they are against the equality of men and women. The government feels empowered to say such things and calculates that making such statements will make it stronger. I don't think they are wrong in that sense. The government uses the old nationalist cliché very cleverly that there are two kinds of women—the shameless feminist and the Anatolian woman. The AKP builds its hegemony on these ideological grounds, while in the economic sphere resorting to social policies. Throughout the history of the republic, social policies have been formulated around the notion of the family. But today, for the first time, the AKP government is addressing women as the head of the family. Remember that this is the same AKP government that removed the status of the head of the family from civil law. The Kemalist regime made upper-middle- and middle-class women its allies, and the current government has allied with middle- and lower-middle-class women. Women in the feminist movement have different positions on this: there are those who defend Kemalism with an anti-AKP stance, offering critiques of AKP policies from the left, and there are those who struggle to break the ideological hegemony of the AKP.

Reference

Kadinlarin. (1989). Kurtuluşu bildirgesi, *Feminist*, 5,11.

Author Biographies

Aksu Bora is a professor of anthropology and sociology in the Department of Communication at Hacettepe University, Ankara. She is a scholar of gender studies, feminism, and feminist politics. Her research and teaching interests include culture and gender, feminist anthropology, sociology of the family. She has authored, coauthored, and coedited a number of books published by İletişim Yayınları: *Boşuna mı Okuduk: Türkiye'de Beyaz Yakalı İşsizliği* (Studied for Nothing: Unemployment of White Collar Workers in Turkey, 2015); *Yoksulluk Halleri: Türkiye'de Kent Yoksulluğunun Toplumsal Görünümleri* (Conditions of Poverty: Social Views of Urban Poverty in Turkey, 2011); *Kadınların Sınıfı: Ücretli Ev Hizmetleri Bağlamında Kadın Öznelliğinin Kurulması* (The Class of Women: The Formation of Woman's Subjectivity in the Context of Domestic Labor, 2005); *1990'larda Türkiye'de Feminizm* (Feminism in Turkey in the 1990s, 2002). She is the author of numerous papers in Turkish and English and is also coeditor with Pinar Selek of *Amargi Dergi*, a journal of feminist politics and theory.

Nil Uzun is a PhD candidate in sociology at Rutgers University. She holds a BA in economics from Boğaziçi University, an MA in cultural studies from Sabancı University, and an MA in social anthropology from Central European University. She is coeditor and contributing author of a forthcoming edited book on social movements and urban public lands and is a contributing author of an edited book on violence and authoritarianism in Turkey. Her recent work focuses on the geopolitics of scientific knowledge production in high-performance computing.

The LGBTI+ Movement

Evren Savcı, interviewed by Şebnem Keniş and İpek Tabur

Abstract When we look at the history of the development of the LGBTI+ movement that first began with small gatherings in private houses in the metropolitan cities of Istanbul and Ankara, we see that over time the movement has given way to independent structures—associations, NGOs, informal initiatives, student clubs—which differ in their organizational approaches, the issues they tackle, and their areas of expertise. As the movement institutionalized, it also assumed a more plural and multivocal character. Following the establishment of the first LGBTI+ organizations in the first half of 1990s, Lambdaistanbul in Istanbul and Kaos-GL in Ankara, today there are approximately 40 LGBTI+ organizations across Turkey that focus on local needs and issues. The LGBTI+ movement in Turkey did not emerge and develop in a vacuum, but rather has, from its onset, been in a close dialogue with a number of social movements—feminist, Kurdish, leftist, and Islamist movements.

Keywords Turkey · LGBT movement · Gay rights

When we look at the history of the development of the LGBTI+ movement that first began with small gatherings in private houses in the metropolitan cities of Istanbul and Ankara, we see that over time the movement has given way to independent structures—associations, NGOs, informal initiatives, student clubs—which differ in their organizational approaches, the issues they tackle, and their areas of expertise. As the movement institutionalized, it also assumed

E. Savcı (✉)
San Francisco State University, San Francisco, USA
e-mail: savci@sfsu.edu

Ş. Keniş
Raoul Wallenberg Institute, Istanbul, Turkey
e-mail: sebnem.kenis@gmail.com

İ. Tabur
Oxford University, Oxford, UK
e-mail: ipektabur@gmail.com

© Springer International Publishing AG, part of Springer Nature 2019
E. Özyürek et al. (eds.), *Authoritarianism and Resistance in Turkey*,
https://doi.org/10.1007/978-3-319-76705-5_13

a more plural and multivocal character. Following the establishment of the first LGBTI+ organizations in the first half of 1990s, Lambdaistanbul in Istanbul and Kaos-GL in Ankara, today there are approximately 40 LGBTI+ organizations across Turkey that focus on local needs and issues. How did this transformation take place and what are the implications of this move toward a multivocal, multi-actor institutionalized politics?

I am really glad that you bring up the issue of needs. As with all organic political and social justice movements, contemporary LGBTI+ politics in Turkey is very much shaped by people's needs. This makes the larger movement quite dynamic, as all of these various organizations keep in touch and are aware of one another's organizing efforts. In other words, when the current set of groups do not meet the needs of a particular constituency, those people do not quietly leave and start up another organization. Historically, the injuries and resentments caused by people feeling that their concerns have not been properly taken into account at the organizational level has led to public articulations of disappointment and demands for organizational self-reflection.

For instance, transgender people, and especially transwomen, have felt structurally excluded from larger LGBTI+ organizations at various points in time, and have left these organizations to start their own associations. The reasons for their experience of exclusion stem very much from the NGO structures you just brought up: when organizations become mostly project-oriented, certain knowledges are inevitably prioritized, let's say proficiency in English or computer skills. This is due to the current transnational political economy where the European Union sets fairly liberal, rights-based standards for social justice and provides grants for projects that follow these standards. Transwomen rightfully pointed out that their exclusion from institutions of higher education often makes them ineligible to work in these projects, and that these projects do not seek any solution to this problem. They have also critiqued the 9:00 a.m. to 6:00 p.m. NGO schedule that is untenable for those who are sex workers and thus work at night and sleep during the day.

A number of local organizations are also informed by local political needs and exigencies. Kurdish politics shapes the survival needs of *Hebun* and *Keskesor*, two Kurdish LGBTI+ organizations, as much as LGBTI+ politics does. There are also differences in what LGBTI+ people and organizations find to be the most effective form of organizing toward social change. For instance, there are groups that find grassroots, street-level action to be the most effective way to create social change. I would say Lambdaistanbul is an example of this. While they flirted with EU-funding-based projects for a while, they soon recognized the inequalities funding-based activism can and does perpetuate. They gave up altogether on this form of organizing for a time, and later began very selectively accepting funding from a few trusted human rights organizations that align with their vision. This might have already changed by now, since the volunteers change every few years, and they are the ones making the decisions. Other groups find engaging with formal politics to be more effective in producing social change. SpoD (*Sosyal Politikalar Cinsiyet Kimliği ve Cinsel Yönelim Çalışmaları Derneği*) initially consisted of

Lambdaistanbul members who believed that their efforts were best spent trying to change the parliament and local governments. Their work focused on supporting LGBTI+ friendly politicians and by becoming active members in the parties.

I think this multitude of voices, levels, and styles of political action is both very exciting and vital. The current heterogeneity of organizations with different approaches to social justice and political effectiveness means that there is a fundamental acknowledgment that there is no one way to engage in activism and social change. This is radically different from homogenized LGBTI+ organizations that have one token transperson, or one token Kurdish gay or lesbian, but nevertheless work from within the same style, values, and understanding of social change—an unfortunate trend under neoliberalism.

The LGBTI+ movement in Turkey did not emerge and develop in a vacuum, but rather has, from its onset, been in a close dialogue with a number of social movements—feminist, Kurdish, leftist, and Islamist movements. Could you please elaborate more on the mutually transformative impact of these interactions with other struggles and political actors?

Based on my experience and interviews with Lambdaistanbul activists, I would say this has been true for many of them. They had been members of feminist, antimilitarist, socialist, or communist organizations, which were sometimes housed in the same building with an LGBTI+ organization. This physical proximity facilitated contact. The level of previous political activism of the Ankara-based *Pembe Hayat* (Pink Life) members was more varied. This of course has a lot to do with the level of acceptance of gender-nonnormative people in nonqueer organizations.

The personal organizing histories of LGBTI+ activists—their previous political experiences and whether they are active in multiple organizations simultaneously—influence their intersectional politics. I was and continue to be extremely impressed with many groups' pronounced critique of global capitalism, militarism, sexism, nationalism, and racism. Many of these political positions do not simply stem from pre-identified issues that LGBTI+ activists decide to take on as central to their cause. On the contrary, their positions and political agendas are very much the result of their lived realities. Lambdaistanbul had, and I believe continues to have, members who are conscientious objectors to the compulsory military conscription, Kurds, and feminists. You mentioned that LGBTI+ activists have also been members of Islamist movements. This I am not familiar with. And while the activists I know might have family members who are religious, I have not met one LGBTI+ activist who was also a member of an Islamist movement. But your next question seems to get at this as well, so let me for now bracket that issue. As a result of this intersectionality, many LGBTI+ activists do not articulate their own issues as distinguishable from other forms of exclusion and inequality.

Now, as for the other side of mutual transformation, I think the effects remain to be seen. Though I will say that the Gezi Park protests have been a great example of political transformation via solidarity. The already sizable Pride March in Istanbul grew enormously after the Gezi Park protests, and there is now more room to bring up sexual politics within organizations and formal politics. Not that this was not done prior to Gezi Park, but the willingness and ability of non-LGBTI+ people to listen to and hear LGBTI+ concerns seems to have increased. I think that the oppressive moral and sexual politics of the AKP regime—as seen in their opposition to abortion, alcohol consumption, coed student housing, and the singles lifestyle, among other things—has also contributed to this. By judging many citizens as "immoral, marginal degenerates," AKP party politics has meant that many people have experience what it means to be excluded from the moral mainstream. Luckily, this newfound marginalization has not led protesters to lay a claim to moral respectability, but rather has led them to question morality politics altogether. I find this to be perhaps the most powerful transformation regarding non-LGBTI+ people' position vis-à-vis LGBTI+ politics. Of course, what needs to follow is a heightened understanding by straight cis citizens of the fact that the AKP positioning many as immoral does not make them all equal in the eyes of the system. Gender-confirming people will never face the same level of daily harassment and violence as those who are gender-nonconforming. And although public displays of all forms of sexual intimacy are now under more scrutiny than they were 10 to 20 years ago, heterosexual intimacies certainly do not elicit the same public reaction as nonheterosexual ones do.

How do you evaluate the relationship between the LGBTI+ movement and religion in Turkey, a predominantly Muslim country where the public space is continually shaped by family-centered, conservative government policies that draw on specific Orthodox Sunni interpretations of Islam intertwined with tenets of neoliberalism and nationalistic propaganda?

I find it rather hard to summarize this relationship, but I think several points can be made. First of all, religion is practiced differently by different constituents. This is true despite the current context in which the Turkish government would like to monopolize what stands for Islam, who is a proper Muslim, and how they are supposed to live their life. Turkish citizens and the LGBTI+ movement witnessed this multiplicity of ways of being Muslim with the presence of Revolutionary Muslims at Gezi Park protests and during the falling out of the AKP government with the Gülen movement. These differences do not change the fact that the AKP government works to mobilize Islam for their very particular conservative agenda, which has alienated many citizens from Islam and religion altogether. This alienation is different from a staunch Kemalist secularist reaction to Islam, in my opinion.

In one of the chapters of my forthcoming book, *Queer in Translation: Sexual Politics under Neoliberal Islam* (Savcı under contract), I write about the particular historical conditions under which an AKP minister, Aliye Kavaf, pronounced the words "homosexuality is an illness and it should be cured" and was supported by a large number of Muslim NGOs. There are no such moments recorded previously in the history of the Republic. I am interested in questions of why here, why now? Instead of generalizing about Islam's relationship to sexuality or LGBTI+ politics,

I find it to be more beneficial to pay attention to the historical particularities of such discourses. In my experience, LGBTI+ activists are also varied in their relationship to Islam and pious Muslims. During my research, some activists had religious family members, some of whom knew about their sexuality and were supportive. During the summer of 2008—a time when the AKP government seemed rather democratic—a number of LGBTI+ activists were quite sympathetic to the party and its politics, were critical of the militaristic and secular past of the country, and were supportive of the lifting of the headscarf ban. Now that the AKP has deeply disappointed so many liberals who at some point felt aligned with its politics, I think that many also have taken a position that does not wish to see how Islam and democracy could be compatible. By 2010 or 2011, I remember attending a Pride Week panel in Istanbul on religion and LGBTI+. The dominant tone of the event was that religion was a man-made nonsense that some fools were brainwashed into believing. Mild objections from the audience were not even entertained. Of course, that one panel cannot stand for the entire LGBTI+ movement by any means, but that tone regarding religion was simply not present in 2008 in the circles I knew.

Again, I think this is a different position than the old Kemalist secularism. But it is nevertheless one that treats Islam as a homogenous, unified entity. Your question very aptly points out that this is an orthodox Sunni position married to neoliberalism and nationalism. But because it has managed to transform many pious citizens' understanding of Islam—Cihan Tuğal's ethnography, *Passive Revolution* (2009) details this beautifully, I understand how one could be compelled to see it as a bounded particularity.

One significant discussion concerning the LGBTI+ movement pertains to the limitations and possibilities of what is called "identity politics." Considering the critical stance taken by queer theory and politics toward identity politics in general, what are the political impacts of queer politics on the LGBTI+ movement in Turkey?

What this brings to my mind immediately is a matter that also connects to your previous question. A little while before the 2014 Pride Week in Istanbul, a group that called itself the LGBTI+ Individuals of AKP (*AK Parti LGBTI Bireyleri*) announced that they were going to join the Pride March with an AKP banner. Now, the pride parch is a nonpartisan affair, and the LGBTI+ associations organizing it for years had always to tell different constituents that no flags, banners, or signs of any parties are allowed. So, there would be no exception for AKP either. But I have seen a number of social media responses to this by LGBTI+ folks, for whom the issue was not a partisan banner. The real issue for them that these were people who supported a government party that has proven itself to be very authoritarian, autocratic, and excessively violent toward dissenting civilians, a party with sectarian, as well as extremely conservative gender and sexual politics. So, for many LGBTI+ folk, they were simply not welcome at the march, no matter their gender or sexuality.

These are moments where identity politics hit up against very clear limits. Do activists in various LGBTI+ organizations have much in common with the gays and lesbians of the AKP simply because of their sexuality?[1] Most likely not. Does anyone have the right to ban a self-identified group of gays and lesbians from the annual LGBTI+ Pride March? I do not think so. What I find productive in this case is that the pro-AKP group was not banished from the March, but they were also not made to feel welcome simply because they were gay. This means that for many activists in Turkey, politics goes beyond one's gender and sexuality, and no one is interested in crafting an easy-going faux community where everyone gets along because everyone is LGBTI+. In other words, while I have not heard this debated in these specific terms, in my understanding many LGBTI+ activists do not believe they belong to a homogenous community where everyone better get along and suppress differences, political and otherwise. I think these are the very lived implications of queer theory's anti-identitarian position. It might not lead to a complete dissolution of identities altogether for LGBTI+ subjects, but I think that a healthy distance from the presumed unity of identity categories had already been taken by Turkey's LGBTI+ activists before their access to queer theory texts.

In Turkey, it has been commonly recognized that the Gezi Park protests that ignited on May 31, 2013 in Taksim Square and spread in no time to other cities around the country marked a turning point for the LGBTI+ movement. Gezi offered the movement the opportunity to gain further visibility and public acceptance. How do you think this became possible? What are the challenges and prospects for the LGBTI+ movement in Turkey now?

I certainly agree with this statement. It is no coincidence that participants in the annual Pride March the summer following the Gezi Park protests multiplied compared to previous years. There also seems to be more openness among parliamentarians in entertaining the needs put forth by LGBTI+ activists, as well as more doors opening to activists becoming official political representatives in local government.

How this became possible brings us back to our conversation about identity movements and international LGBTI+ activism. What Gezi Park protests did so effectively was to disrupt the government and national narratives that rendered different solidarities unthinkable through something I refer in my book as a *deployment of marginality*. LGBTI+ activists were among many disenfranchised groups involved in the protests. What brought people together was opposition to the increasingly authoritarian and autocratic AKP government, which often deployed a rhetoric of marginality against any person who did not perfectly align with their politics. This, I find. led to many theretofore mainstream citizens to experience exclusion, marginalization, and lack of a sense of safety due to their newly-found nonnormative, "undesirable" status. If anything, this had a huge influence on

---

[1]Here I am bracketing the fact that sexuality is a lot more complicated than just "gay" or "lesbian," and that it is best not to presume that everyone who identifies as gay has the same sexuality.

people's ability to think differently about forms of existence they either had previously paid no attention to, or about which they had completely and unques-
tioningly believed the official narrative—not only about queers, but also Kurds,
Alevis, Armenians, and other disenfranchised groups.

The protests were, in a way, an exercise in trust, which is the necessary ground
for solidarity. But to reiterate, if this was simply a moment of coming together as
the largest common denominator—together demanding freedom from state violence
and a right to public spaces and goods—it would not have had lasting effects. Let's
say the AKP government ceases to be in power in the future, and we have a more
democratic government that respects the public's right to public goods, does not
concentrate wealth in the hands of a few, and does not jail people for their publications. If Gezi were simply a moment of the biggest common denominator, for
many privileged citizens in the country that cause would no longer have any
importance, and solidarities would cease to exist. But I think because the AKP gave
so many citizens a taste of marginality, I am hopeful that the effects will be
longer-lasting, even if some citizens embrace a return to being mainstream subjects.
One of the reasons I am hopeful this will be the case is because many embraced the
marginality they were pushed into. An example of this is when many protesters
took on the epithet *çapulcu* (looter) as a beloved term and positionality, rather than
making counterclaims to respectability.

It is hard to say how the LGBTI+ movement in Turkey will change and transform. Since I actively started following it in 2008, it has been such an active
movement full of dynamism and surprises. For instance, after the significant growth
in interest it experienced after Gezi, the Pride March was banned by the Istanbul
Governor's Office and protesters have been attacked every year since June 2015.
Each year, activists try to respond to the difficult question of how to organize under
these circumstances. In my book (Savcı in press), I write a little bit about the 2016
strategy of disbursing into the artilleries of the city instead of gathering as a massive
crowd at Taksim Square, which I found to be a very creative and interesting
response. This new technique demands not only that we rethink the value we place
on the old strategies, such as public gatherings, but it also provides a way for
something akin to the Pride March to take place in various neighborhoods of the
city instead of concentrating in the center. The Pride March is just an example; by
no means does it have to be the central issue of the movement. I bring it up as an
instance of political circumstances making some forms of political protest impossible. What do we do then? The responses do not have to mean that the movement
simply consists of "reactions" to what the power structures enable and foreclose.
The responses also become productive moments to rethink values, priorities, and
strategies.

What I really hope might happen going forward is a continued emphasis on the
contextual nature of marginality and exclusion, rather than an identitarian project of
LGBTI+ rights. This has proven so powerful, both during and since the protests,
that I think many people are ripe to question systems that produce exclusion,
violence, and premature death for many citizens. If LGBTI+ activism could

continue pushing their projects along these lines, I do not see how it would not be the one of the most refreshing, effective, and intersectional sexual movements to date.

References

Savcı, E. (under contract). *Queer in translation: Sexual politics under neoliberal islam*. Durham: Duke University Press.
Tuğal, C. (2009). *Passive revolution: Absorbing the islamic challenge to capitalism*. Stanford: Stanford University Press.

Author Biographies

Evren Savcı is assistant professor of women and gender studies at San Francisco State University. She received her Ph.D. at the University of Southern California in sociology and gender studies in 2011 and completed a two-year postdoctoral fellowship at the Sexualities Project at Northwestern University. Her areas of interest include gender, sexualities, globalization and transnationality, queer, feminist and social theory, cultural sociology, and epistemology. Her ongoing book project, *Queer in Translation: Sexual Politics under Neoliberal Islam*, traces the travel and translation of Western concepts and discourses on nonnormative genders and sexualities (gender identity, sexual orientation, hate crimes, and LGBTI+ rights) to the context of contemporary Turkey.

Şebnem Keniş holds a Bachelor of Arts in Political Science and International Relations (Boğaziçi University, Istanbul) and a Master of Arts in International Relations (Koç University, Istanbul). In her master's thesis *Islam and Homosexuality Debates in Turkey: Discursive Contestations among Muslims over LGBTI Rights*, she examined the basic premises of the Islamic political opposition to LGBTI rights in Turkey and analysed how and with what coping strategies LGBTI Muslims tackle and dispute these hegemonic homophobic Islamic views and are able to develop a Muslim defence of LGBTI rights. She held the position of the Gender Equality Rapporteur of the Council of Europe's Joint Council on Youth between March and December 2016. Since August 2016, she has been working for Raoul Wallenberg Institute of Human Rights and Humanitarian Law (RWI)'s Turkey Programme as programme officer.

İpek Tabur holds a BA degree in History from Boğaziçi University, Istanbul and a MA degree in History from Oxford University. She is currently pursuing her PHD studies and working as a freelance editor and translator.

The Labor Movement

Aziz Çelik and interviewed by Emrah Altındiş

Abstract Proletarianization in the Ottoman Empire came much later than in Europe. At the beginning of the 20th century, the percentage of paid workers among the labor force was around 1%, numbering around 200–300 thousand. To understand this quantitative picture, we should look at similar processes in England of the mid-19th century. In those days, there were 3.3 million workers in England, and 42% of the eligible population were employed in industry. Yet in Turkey, even during the 1960s, industrial employment was only around 10% whereas agricultural employment was close to 70%. The capitalist-industrial shift—and therefore the emergence of the working class—began quite late here and followed a different course compared to the Western path. During the state-managed industrialization of the republican era, the Turkish working class appeared more in the form of public workers. Another difference was the lack of a strong federalist-corporatist tradition in Turkey, unlike in the West. This caused a delay in the organized representation of the social classes and in the development of industrial relations.

Keywords Turkey · Workers · Labor movement · Trade unions
Working class

In which period did the working class begin to emerge in the Ottoman Empire? What are the similarities and differences between the beginnings of the working class in Europe—let's say in England—and in the Ottoman Empire? Did this beginning play an active historical role in the abolition of the sultanate and the establishment of the republic?

A. Çelik (✉)
Department of Labour Economics and Industrial Relations,
Kocaeli University, İzmit, Turkey
e-mail: azizcelik@gmail.com

E. Altındiş (✉)
Harvard Medical School, Boston, USA
e-mail: altindise@gmail.com

© Springer International Publishing AG, part of Springer Nature 2019
E. Özyürek et al. (eds.), *Authoritarianism and Resistance in Turkey*,
https://doi.org/10.1007/978-3-319-76705-5_14

Proletarianization in the Ottoman Empire came much later than in Europe. At the beginning of the 20th century, the percentage of paid workers among the labor force was around 1%, numbering around 200–300 thousand. To understand this quantitative picture, we should look at similar processes in England of the mid-19th century. In those days, there were 3.3 million workers in England, and 42% of the eligible population were employed in industry. Yet in Turkey, even during the 1960s, industrial employment was only around 10% whereas agricultural employment was close to 70%. The capitalist-industrial shift—and therefore the emergence of the working class—began quite late here and followed a different course compared to the Western path. During the state-managed industrialization of the republican era, the Turkish working class appeared more in the form of public workers. Another difference was the lack of a strong federalist-corporatist tradition in Turkey, unlike in the West. This caused a delay in the organized representation of the social classes and in the development of industrial relations.

Due to its small size and very limited organizational structure, the working class could not play a prominent role in either the 1908 or the 1923 revolutions. The 1908 revolution did, however, open the way for the birth of a labor movement. Following the declaration of the Second Constitutional Monarchy (İkinci Meşrutiyet), massive strikes took place with the involvement of tens of thousands of workers. It would not be incorrect to designate the 1908 strikes as the onset of the modern labor movement in Turkey. However, the rise of the labor movement was hindered by the Work Stoppage Act (Tatil-i Eşgal Kanunu) of 1909, which prohibited the creation of trade unions for public workers. That was followed by a 10- to 15-year period of war and a state of emergency—the Balkan Wars, the First World War, and the National War of Independence—which in turn negatively affected the quantitative growth of the working class.

Similarly, the working class did not play an influential historical role in the abolition of the sultanate and the establishment of the republic. The labor movement was limited in quantity and oppressed in quality; its role in the early political evolution of the country was accordingly next to nothing. Yet it is possible to say that a tradition of workers' campaigns began in Turkey in the early 20th century.

Could it be said that the experiences and traditions of workers in the Ottoman period were carried through to the republican era? Given their close relations with the Soviet Union, how did the founders of the republic of the 1920s connect with the Turkish working class? How did the Armenian Genocide or the 1923 population exchange between Greece and Turkey affect the collective consciousness of the working class?

Although limited, the experiences of the labor movement during the last period of Ottoman rule did carry through to the republican era. But it is also true that the progress of the labor movement was hindered, particularly during the authoritarian single-party period of 1925–1946 when workers were banned from organizing. Yet it is still possible to say that the cumulative experience of the last period of the Ottoman era did partially influence the trade unionism of the 1940s and 1950s.

Cadres within the socialist movement had tried to pass the baton on to future generations of the labor movement. We must approach the relations of the republic's founding elites with the Soviet Union and their approach toward labor and the leftist movement with two different contexts in mind. Relations with the Soviet Union intensified both during the period of the War of Independence and in the statist industrialization period of the 1930s. In fact, in parallel to the relationship with the USSR in the early 1920s, a so-called Communist Party, separate from the Communist Party of Turkey of the time, was established by the Turkish state itself. Shortly thereafter, an era of repression of the left and of the labor movement began. By the end of 1920s, workers' organizations were being suppressed, and the police began widespread operations against Communist Party of Turkey. In the 1930s, authoritarianism intensified. Class descriptions were rejected and a solidaristic populism was embraced. Because class designations were deemed irrelevant, so too were class organizations such as trade unions and socialist parties. In 1936, Turkey's first labor law was accepted. While it did introduce important rights to individual workers, the law was still authoritarian in terms of its stance toward collective labor rights. Strikes were banned and trade unions prohibited. The early republican era could be described as a period of intense paternalism with regard to labor relations within Turkey.

The ethnic composition of the newly emerging working class of the late Ottoman era is quite striking. In the 1910s, only 15% of workers employed in industry were Turks. Occasional serious struggles took place between workers of different ethnicities. It is possible to say that the ethnic structure of the Ottoman working class had a distinctly hampering effect on the progress of the labor movement, and that the simultaneous strengthening of nationalistic tendencies within different ethnic groups weakened the labor movement and the development of class solidarity.

After the Second World War, we see a Turkey that had entered a multiparty period with a Democratic Party, a Turkey that had integrated into the capitalist block and had become a member of NATO. Then came the Cold War. How would you evaluate this period in terms of class struggle?

Post-WWII Turkey was transitioning into some degree of democracy. During the Cold War, Turkey sided with the Western camp. In the immediate postwar period, a group of politicians who had parted ways with the CHP (Republican People's Party), established the DP (Democratic Party). The DP represented a liberal tendency, both economically and politically. In 1946, the ban on labor unions and left parties was dissolved, followed by the founding of two socialist parties and numerous unions. Because the regime could not tolerate them, they were banned, and their senior leaders were imprisoned. In this way, Turkey's adventures in democracy began by blocking out the left. The mainstream political stance of the time was nationalism and anticommunism.

After the leftist and independent unionism was crushed, a period of state-controlled unionism, in other words, paternalistic unionism, began in 1947 with a new union law. This period, known as 1947 Unionism in the Turkish labor relations literature, created a new understanding of unionism whose affects are still alive today. Post-WWII unionism in Turkey emerged primarily within state-run enterprises. Due to the prominent economic status of these public enterprises, the trade union movement in Turkey did not arise from within the private sector out of a pure class struggle, unlike its Western counterpart. The unionism that appeared in these public enterprises had a paternalistic character. With the 1947 law, unions were defined as national institutions and were heavily banned from political activities. The ban on strikes established with the 1936 labor law continued, and sanctions against striking became aggravated. The membership of unions within international union organizations was taken under governmental permit only. A declawed unionism thus came about that was stripped of its basic function. It was under these circumstances that the CHP, the governing party, began establishing unions in the public sector. The goal was to have all unions under their control and to diminish the effect of the left on them. The unions had been banned from practicing politics, but political parties were openly interfering in the internal affairs of the unions. As most of the unions were under the control of CHP, the DP began establishing unions under its control. Leftist and socialist movements, still banned from politics, were not allowed to take part in this trade union development. Operations conducted by the CHP against the left in 1946–1947 were adopted by the DP in 1951–1952: leftist leaders and several members of the Communist Party of Turkey were arrested and imprisoned. Under these circumstances, unionism ran aground an strong anticommunist ideology. With Stalin's demand of land from Turkey following WWII, anticommunism reached its peak.

Debates concerning the right to strike marked the post-WWII labor movement. The CHP opposed strikes. Its primary thesis was that class struggle was unnecessary: the state would give the workers their rights and thereby establish balance. To this end, the CHP took a number of important social policy steps after the war: the Ministry of Labor and the Social Insurance Institution were established. The DP, on the other hand, defended the right to strike, hoping to gain the support of the burgeoning working class. Once it came to power, however, the DP did not grant the right to strike. Now being in opposition, it was the CHP's turn to include the right to strike in its platform. During its 10-year rule (1950–1960), the DP pursued an oppressive policy toward the unions and did not want them to become powerful. Like the CHP before it, the DP did not take a positive view of collective workers' rights movements, and so paternalistic unionism continued during DP rule.

Another aspect of the 1950s, was the growth of the private sector. This growth paved the way to a larger debate on the unionization of workers outside the public sector, who began to unionize. Trade union organizing in the private sector grew throughout 1960s, resulting in a significant split in Turkey's trade union movement.

You wrote in one of your articles about trade union leaders having been trained in the US under the Marshall Plan. Was trade unionism in Turkey influenced more by the American or the European tradition of trade unionism? Could you elaborate on the emergence of the TÜRK-İŞ, the Confederation of Turkish Trade Unions (*Türkiye İşçi Sendikaları Konfederasyonu*)?

TÜRK-İŞ was founded in 1952 as the first umbrella organization in Turkey. Its precursor was another important umbrella trade union called the Istanbul Association of Trade Unions (*İstanbul İşçi Sendikaları Birliği*). It is inaccurate to claim, as has often been done, that the centralization trends of the labor movement in Turkey are a product of its interactions with American trade unionism. Rather, this trend is a result of dynamics internal to the Turkish case. Centralization of the trade union movement in Turkey was being debated long before American unionism took an interest in Turkey. Both the leftist unions established in 1946, and those under CHP control from 1947 were in favor of a centralized structure for the union movement.

With the Marshall Plan, the US began to interfere in European trade unionism, even to the point of dividing strong European unions. The union alliance that had formed after WWII under the World Federation of Trade Unions split up upon American initiative. Thereafter, the American trade union movement began to show interest in and began communication with Turkish trade unions in the early 1950s. The effects were limited. Although Irving Brown, the representative of the American Federation of Labor, paid several visits to Turkey with the aim of organizing, American unions could not be effective in Turkey due to DP wariness concerning the growth of the union movement. The influence of American unionism on the Turkish labor movement intensified in the 1960s. Large sums of money were transferred to TÜRK-İŞ from USAID funds, and hundreds of trade unionists from Turkey were sent for training to the US through USAID-TÜRK-İŞ programs. These developments strengthened the influence of American unionism on the trade union movement in Turkey. TÜRK-İŞ eventually adopted the political nonpartisanship policy of the American Federation of Labor in 1964, and began operating under another mainstay of American unionism—*bread and butter unionism* focused on collective bargaining rather than on social reform.

In parallel to American unionism's efforts, its European counterpart also tried to influence the labor movement in Turkey. At the time, there was great rivalry between American and European unionism within the International Confederation of Free Trade Unions. European unionism wanted to push Turkey's labor movement away from pragmatic bread and butter unionism and more in the direction of political action. European unionism tried to politicize the union movement in Turkey, and this also had a rather limited outcome. Due to the politically disintegrated structure of Turkey's working class, the American unionism model became more attractive for union leadership in Turkey. In other words, the reasons for the adoption of the American model of unionism were not only external; the distinctive conditions within Turkey also played a part.

In the 1960s, the working class was quite strong, both quantitatively and qualitatively—we saw strikes, the emergence of DİSK (Progressive Trade Union Confederation of Turkey) and TİP (Labour Party of Turkey). How do you evaluate the 1960s in terms of class struggle? What was the climate that created the workers' protests on June 15–16, 1970, and what happened there?

The 1960s were years that saw the strengthening of the working-class movement in Turkey, both in numbers and in quality. Following the 1960 coup d'état, rights and freedoms broadened, ironically. The oppressive government of the DP had come to an end, and after a short period of military rule, a new constitution was approved in 1961, one that embraced the principles of a democratic welfare state governed by the rule of law.

The constitution of 1961 secured a number of trade union rights that had never before been seen in Turkey's history, including the right to collective bargaining and the right to strike. The ban on union political activity was lifted and affiliation with international trade union organizations was allowed. Those changes in the political conditions of union activism had wide-ranging effects on the union movement. Upon securing the right to collective bargaining and strikes, the trade union movement gained momentum and working-class struggle increased. With the growth of industrialization and increasing urbanization, the sociological grounds for the union movement began to expand.

With this, unionization ceased to be limited to the public sector only, and unions started to gain strength in the private sector. This change brought about an important differentiation within the trade union movement between unions operating in the public sector and those operating in the private sector. Another distinctive aspect of this period is the politicization of the working class. In 1961, TİP was established by 12 trade unionists who had organized largely within the private sector in İstanbul. While European unionism had a hand in the foundation of TİP, the main motive was the fact that the mainstream parties had turned away from the unions and the trade union movement. The leadership of TÜRK-İŞ was not involved in TİP and kept its distance. The foundation of TİP in 1961 can be seen as the first step on the path to the foundation of DİSK in 1967, established by the same group of trade unionists. Although TİP did not succeed in its early years, it managed to enter parliament in 1965 following the addition of socialist intellectuals to the party, and once there put up a strong opposition. One year after the foundation of TİP, attempts under the leadership of TÜRK-İŞ were made to establish the Employees' Party of Turkey (*Türkiye Çalışanlar Partisi*), to no avail. But it was an important indication of the politicization of the working class and of the labor movement during that time.

The 1960s were also years when militancy and the class struggle came to the fore and the distinction between the traditional-reformist unionism and class-based unionism were heightened. Within TÜRK-İŞ, strong tensions arose between the unionists who were close to the mainstream parties—the Justice Party (*Adalet Partisi*) and the CHP—and those who supported TİP. The latter initiated numerous strikes and boycotts within the private sector. TİP unionists also rejected the nonpartisan unionism approach that had been embraced by TÜRK-İŞ. Meanwhile, the center-right Justice Party founded after the 1960 coup and which later came to power in 1965, had increased its strength within TÜRK-İŞ and began eliminating unionists who supported TİP. DİSK was founded following these developments. While TÜRK-İŞ was strong in the public sector and embraced principles of American unionism, DİSK was stronger in the private sector and advocated the class-struggle-based approach of European unionism. DİSK began an effective struggle in the private sector right from the start, and the Justice Party government, alarmed by DİSK's growing power, attempted first to impede it at the union level, then to annihilate it indirectly through legislative means. They introduced a new law on union permits requiring a minimum enrollment of one-third of employees sector- and nationwide, a very high percentage that was difficult for DİSK to achieve. The plan was for DİSK to cease operation altogether. DİSK and its members responded harshly: in defense of their union, tens of thousands of DİSK members went on strike on June 15 and 16, 1970, organizing massive protests in the industrial cities of Istanbul and İzmit. Four workers and a policeman died. A state of emergency was declared, and DİSK leaders were arrested. The most important aspect of the June 15–16 strikes is that they were based solely on unionist motivation, and not economic ones: workers acted to protect DİSK.

How would you assess the 1970s, the period when DİSK was strong and progressive movements had massive support?

On March 12, 1971, there was another military coup. As a result, members of the elected government resigned and a new technocrat cabinet dominated by the army was appointed. Marked by the rule of this quasi-military regime, the first half of the 1970s, known as the 12 March era, was a relatively stagnant period for the labor movement. Beginning in 1975, however, we can talk about significant advances for both the labor movement and for public participation. While DİSK was growing stronger, the main body of the working class remained within TÜRK-İŞ. This period that saw both the rise of the Kemalist CHP party and that of left parties was also a time of escalating political turbulence and tension. There was significant fragmentation and introversion within the left parties and within the workers' movement. This led to a deceleration in public actions, which reached their peak with the massive 1977 May Day celebrations at Taksim Square massacre in Istanbul, where 41 people were shot.

What did the military coups d'état of 1960 and 1971 mean to the working class? Could you elaborate on the January 24 decrees and the coup d'état of 1980 in relation to the working-class struggle? What were the outcomes of these coups for the working class?

As a political stance, denouncing military coups wholesale is one thing, but an analysis of the difference in their motivations and outcomes calls for something more. In principle, all three were military coups and as such should be denounced. But it should not be forgotten that each had their own distinctive aftereffects. Following the 1960 coup, political freedoms in Turkey expanded, a democratic

constitution was adopted, welfare legislation adopted. This had very positive outcomes for class struggle. As a result of the ongoing import-substituted economic
policy, a compromise was made with the working class and its unions. Paternalism
slowly gave way to democratic corporatist practices. In contrast, both the 1971 and
1980 coups were aimed at nullifying the political and social rights that had been
established with the constitution of 1961. The aftereffects of these two coups on the
labor movement were completely different. In the constituent assembly following
the 1961 coup, we see the influence of leftist intellectuals and unions. In contrast, in
the aftermath of both the 1971 and the 1980 coups, the parties and unions of the
right wing dominated. While the welfare state gained power following the 1961
coup, after the 1980 coup, neoliberalism grew stronger and in fact took its revenge.
The neoliberal policies adopted in the economic package of January 24, 1980
devised to address Turkey's increasing economic crisis, were given practical
ground with the military coup of September 12, 1980. The September 12 coup was
a natural outcome of the January 24 Decision. Trade union activities were halted,
DİSK members were imprisoned and sentenced to death, strikes were banned—
with this, the hands and feet of the unionist movement were tied.

**In 1989, only nine years after the 1980 coup, workers and public employees
began again the struggle for rights by means of the so-called Spring Actions.
Did the workers involved any pre-1980 experience in unionism? Could you
elaborate on the Spring Actions, which initiated a period of widespread strikes
that carried through until 1995?**

The Spring Actions were the collective reaction of the labor movement, which had
been suppressed by both the military coup of 1980 and the government's neoliberal
policies. The nationwide actions, initiated by public workers which then spilled
over into the private sector, were aimed at the military regime and the erosion in
wages created by the neoliberal government of Özal. The movement was begun by
rank-and-file members of the trade unions, not by the trade unions themselves; the
unions joined in later. The workers and unionists who organized these actions were
mainly from leftist groups with pre-1980 unionist experience. The wave of actions
resulted in important workers' gains, a significant increase in real wages, and an
extremely important political outcome: Özal's right-wing neoliberal Motherland
Party, which had ruled since 1983, lost the elections. The actions continued through
to the first half of the 1990s, reaching its peak in 1995.

**How is it that during the early 1990s we saw the mass expansion of collective
class struggle at the same time that working conditions were being reformed
via neoliberal policies? How did the increase of repression over the Kurdish
people during the 1990s influence the working-class struggle? Why was the
labor movement defeated? Was it defeated?**

The 1990s are years of stalemate in the class struggle in Turkey. Workers who had
gained strength from the Spring Actions continued their struggle at an accelerated
pace up to 1995. The wave of actions over that six-year period delayed privatization

attempts in Turkey considerably. Many neoliberal initiatives were hindered during the years of the Demirel and Çiller coalition governments. In 1989, Turkey ratified the European Social Charter with several reservations. In 1991, it ratified the International Labor Organization Convention No. 87, Freedom of Association and Protection of the Right to Organize. Then the struggle started to decelerate in the second half of the 1990s, especially among public workers. The economic crisis, public-sector shrinkage, the increase in subcontracting and new nonstandard work forms—all of these developments undermined the labor movement. The union leadership began to become dissatisfied when the movement could not sustain the rise that had occurred during the first half of the 1990s. The recession, whose effects endure today, began.

It would be fair to say that the union movement's approach to the Kurdish question was limited to the narrative put forward by the state. The mainstream union movement simply did not comprehend the issue. The Kurdish question was depicted as a conflict of "terror" and "security," and with that, the union movement reflected hegemonic state policy. It would even be fair to say that the mainstream union movement had a more backward attitude than that of the employers' organizations.

Could you summarize the labor policies of the AKP, who have ruled for the last 13 years, since coming to power in 2002? What does the AKP mean to the working class?

Meryem Koray and I edited a book on the topic of social rights under AKP rule entitled *Charity, Fate, Market* (2015): social rights and labor policies during the AKP era can be expressed in these three terms. First, the AKP implements social policy based on philanthropy and charity rather than on rights. In essence, a clientelistic social policy regime has been established whereby the AKP built customer relations with the voters it aided. Second, the AKP prefers the discourse of fate over the discourse of the workers' rights or social security. The discourse of fate has been particularly prominent in discussions regarding working conditions and workplace safety; following large-scale workplace fatalities, the AKP has made declarations based on disposition and fate. Third is the market. The primary AKP party platform goal, aimed at deregulation of the labor market, is the creation of a market society in Turkey. In this respect, the AKP has shown itself to be a standard neoconservative, neoliberal party. In terms of the working class, AKP rule represents a period when corporate social policy regulations have been loosened, subcontracted and precarious work forms have increased, and unionization has declined. Extensive strike bans have been put in place and strikes have been disallowed.

Turkey has a high rate of workplace fatalities. According to official records, four workers are killed daily in workplace accidents in general—fatalities in the shipyards at Tuzla, in the construction industry, and most recently the deaths of 301 miners in Soma. Why does the AKP not take action and stop these deaths?

Workplace fatalities have risen significantly during the AKP period. The reason
the problem is not addressed is not technical. We must look instead to economic
policies for our answer. Throughout the years of the increase in shipyard fatalities,
the shipbuilding sector received an enormous number of orders. Likewise, extensive privatization in the mining sector brought with it an escalation of workplace
deaths. Throughout the 2000s, the death toll in the private mines in the Zonguldak
coalfield was 12 times that of the public ones. Similarly, workplace fatalities are on
the increase in the construction sector, which is currently in highest demand in
Turkey. The precarious work practices that have been institutionalized in recent
years in Turkey, the increase in subcontracting, and the extreme limitations on
unionizing all contribute to workplace fatalities. It is not merely a technical problem. The government does not actively inspect working conditions.

**What did the Gezi protests signify for the working class? Do you agree with
those who regard Gezi as a middle-class act? Did the working class join Gezi?
Was Gezi a working-class movement?**

Gezi was a movement of discontent that involved various segments of society. It
was an act of social and political opposition. I find the middle-class argument
insufficient and vague. I think that a significant portion of those who got involved in
Gezi were from the modern working class and the new proletariat. When we look at
the structure and character of today's working class, we see that an increasing
number of wage laborers now work in the service sector. We see that various
professionals who once belonged to the middle class are rapidly in decline. We see
that there is a rising trend of precarious labor. I think that these are the characteristics of the modern working class. We are experiencing a wave of reproletari-
anization. Although this recurrence of the process of proletarianization differs
significantly in form from its 19th century counterpart, there are quite some similarities between the two in terms of labor-capital relationships and the control of
labor. The differences between factories and shopping malls or assembly lines and
call centers are not matters of substance. The answer to your question—did the
working class participate in Gezi?—could well be in the affirmative. While Gezi
was, to a large degree, a workers' movement, labor-related demands were not in the
forefront. A similar question about the participation of organized labor and trade
unions should be answered more cautiously. While one cannot say that working
union members or industry workers with job security participated in Gezi, precarious workers, service sector employees, and the new proletariat played an
important role at Gezi.

**Could you elaborate on the relationship the AKP has built with the working
class in connection to HAK-İŞ, the Confederation of Turkish Real Trade
Unions (*Hak İşçi Sendikaları Konfederasyonu*) and Memur-Sen, the
Confederation of Civil Servant Trade Unions (*Memur Sendikaları
Konfedarasyonu*)? Would it be accurate to say that the majority of the working
class in Turkey votes or has voted for AKP? How would you explain the strong
support the AKP receives from the working class?**

Like the conservative right-wing parties of the 1950s and 1960s, the AKP wants to keep various public spheres under control. The control over the trade unions is accomplished through two channels. First, TÜRK-İŞ has been effectively neutralized. Second, the union movement is kept under control by means of HAK-İŞ and Memur-Sen. HAK-İŞ was founded in 1970s as a political Islamist workers' organization. Although it initially had limited impact, it gained influence during the 1990s, appearing to depart from political Islamism. With the ascendance of the AKP to power in 2002, HAK-İŞ has strengthened its ties with the government. Having for years carried out joint actions together with other union organizations under the umbrella of the Labor Platform (*Emek Platformu*), HAK-İŞ gradually changed its oppositional stance toward the government and evolved into a government-controlled organization. At politically critical junctures, together with several employer organizations and government support groups, it made declarations of support for the AKP, the government, and Erdoğan.

We see a similar trend with Memur-Sen, the union confederation under which civil servants organize. It had about 40 thousand members when the AKP came to power in 2002. As of 2014, the member count was 720 thousand. This represents a growth ratio of 1,700%. This is a rather unbelievable, "miraculous" growth rate. The reason behind it is the support it now obtains from the AKP government. The relationship of HAK-İŞ and Memur-Sen with the AKP is a symbiotic one. They have both increased their member counts as a direct result of the support they give to the AKP.

We must understand that the majority of Turkish workers voting for center-right or conservative parties is not a recent phenomenon. There was a similar tendency during the 1950s and 1960s. In that regard, the voting behavior of the working class in Turkey differs drastically from that in the West. One of the main reasons for this is that Turkey lacks a Western-style labor party or a left-wing social democratic party. Another reason is that religious and cultural factors influence voting behavior. Specifically, for the AKP, charity mechanisms are highly effective in garnering the support of the electorate. The AKP employs these mechanisms very cleverly in order to attract the votes of the poor and the precariat. Their political strategy has been to shield the public from the damaging effects of neoliberalism and thereby turning opposition into obeisance.

What percentage of the working class in Turkey is organized within trade unions? What portion are members of DİSK or KESK, The Confederation of Public Employees' Trade Unions (*Kamu Emekçileri Sendikaları Konfederasyonu*)? As an academician studying the field, do you have a hopeful outlook on the future of working-class rights?

Among OECD countries, Turkey does not have a high rate of trade union density. But we have to take a closer look at the specifics, because the statistics can be deceptive. Civil servants excluded, trade union density is about 7–8% of all workers, with density in the private sector around 4–5%. Trade union density in Turkey has gradually declined during AKP rule and, in contrast to European countries, coverage of collective bargaining agreements in Turkey has been limited. Civil servants, on the other hand, are in quite a different position, with unionization reaching up to 70%. But because they have no right to strike and no right substantial collective bargaining, the high rate of union density is both hollow and fictitious. Most civil service union members belong to Memur-Sen and became unionized during AKP rule. Their membership fees are paid by the state. As a result, the member count of civil service unions has artificially increased.

Currently, trade unions active in the private sector are members of three confederations: TÜRK-İŞ, HAK-İŞ, and DİSK. In terms of leadership and policy approach, TÜRK-İŞ, the largest, is a center-right organization; HAK-İŞ is a political Islamist union with close ties to the AKP; while DİSK is open to the left and utilizes class unionism. There are also three confederations for the public-sector civil servants: Memur-Sen, Kamu-Sen, and KESK. Memur-Sen is a political Islamist union with close ties to the AKP; Kamu-Sen is center-right and utilizes nationalist conservative policies; KESK is center-left and has a socialist approach to unionism. DİSK and KESK both rank third rank in their sector, claiming around 10 and 15% of the membership in their sector, respectively. Although I am not optimistic for the short term, I believe that the conditions for the labor movement and for social rights generally will improve in the long run. Countless examples can be culled from the past. Several recent developments give us hope and optimism. Gezi was the most notable of these, but we also had the worker's actions at Tekel, a state-run enterprise, and some recent large-scale metal workers' strikes. Although they are not interconnected, workers protests continue. It is perhaps useful here to recall that old Latin saying, *labor omnia vincit*—work conquers all.

After the July 15, 2016 military coup attempt, the AKP government declared a state of emergency and has been extending it. What are the effects of this state of emergency on the working class?

Following the failed coup of 2016, the government chose to declare a state of emergency rather than suppressing the coup by mobilizing parliament. With the state of emergency, the legislative function of the parliament has been largely curtailed.

The state of emergency has had severe outcomes for labor rights. The most salient are a disrespect for the right to work, removal of job security for both public and private employees, and limitations on the exercise of trade union and other labor rights. The state of emergency turned out to be a guarantee for the owners of capital while the rights of employees were violated.

Under the state of emergency, the right to work has been heavily violated right. Over 120,000 public employees were dismissed without any concrete evidence, any means of defense, or access to a fair trial. These individuals have been socially stigmatized, declared guilty of a crime, some deprived of their right to retirement benefits. Many have faced obstacles to finding replacement jobs in the private sector. There are even cases where the passports of dismissed employees have been seized to prevent their employment in foreign countries. Thousands of academics have been removed from their universities by such means of layoffs, firings, and forced resignations or retirements.

The right to strike is another right that has been violated under the state of emergency. While the AKP government barred eight strikes in total in the period between 2002 and July 2016, since the implementation of the state of the emergency less than one year ago, five large-scale strikes have been barred for reasons of national security, public health, and financial stability.

Although these decisions to halt strikes have not been taken within the framework of state of emergency laws, President Erdoğan has stressed twice while addressing employers' organizations that such suspensions are a part of the state of emergency. In his speech on July 12, 2017, at the meeting organized by International Investors Association, President Erdoğan said that, thanks to the state of emergency, the AKP would intervene immediately anywhere there was a threat of strike. The message was that striking workers would not be allowed to disturb business. This is a clear indication that strike suspensions now form part of the state of emergency strategy, and that strikes is no longer regarded as a right, but as a threat.

Reference

Çelik, A., & Koray, M. (Eds.). (2015). *Himmet, Fıtrat, Piyasa*. Istanbul: İletişim Publishing. (Charity, fate, market).

Author Biographies

Aziz Çelik is a professor of Labor Economics and Industrial Relations at Kocaeli University. He holds a Ph.D. degree from Marmara University Labour Economics and Industrial Relations Department. Prior to joining to university Çelik worked for trade unions as an adviser for training, research and, international relations. Çelik was elected a vice president of Turkish Social History Research Foundation (TUSTAV). He lectured on trade unionism and social policy at Ankara University and Istanbul University. Çelik's books in Turkish include Trade Unionism and Politics in Turkey (2010), EU Social Policy and Turkey (2014), Social Policy During the JDP Era (co-editor with Meryem Koray, 2015), Class, Union and State-Scenes of Turkish Labour History (co-author with Ahmet Makal and M. Hakan Kocak, 2016) and Labour in Hard Times in Turkey (co-editor with Ahmet Makal, 2017). He also contributes to the daily BirGün

Emrah Altındiş is a medical scientist. He received his B.S. degree from Ege University (Izmir, Turkey) and completed an M.Sc. at the Middle East Technical University (Ankara, Turkey). He then moved to Italy to start his Ph.D. at Bologna University (Bologna, Italy). After receiving his Ph.D., he joined Harvard Medical School as a postdoctoral fellow in 2011 and is currently working as an Instructor in Medicine (Boston, USA). He has published several scientific research articles in the fields of microbiology and diabetes. He has also been a human rights activist, and for over a decade wrote political opinion pieces to various Turkish newspapers (Radikal, BirGün, Cumhuriyet), journals (Birikim) and news websites (Diken, Bianet) and has given interviews to several national and international media outlets.

Environmentalism

Bülent Şık and interviewed by Cana Ulutaş

Abstract Before the 2000s, Turkey's environmental scorecard was not very good. It makes sense to take the military coup of 1980 as a turning point. Neoliberal government policies implemented in the aftermath of the coup aggravated already-existing environmental problems. The coup crushed and weakened leftist movements in Turkey. Right-wing governments dominated in the Turkish parliament and were keen to apply the new neoliberal policies. But the AKP government that came to power after 2002 has been the strongest implementer of neoliberal policies thus far. If we compare Turkey to other countries, we should underline that current government representatives have a conceptual void in terms of environmental issues. In Turkey, one of the top five countries in ship dismantling, we are without proper environmental regulation. Such a lack of government regulation of these types of hazardous materials is only seen in underdeveloped, low-income countries.

Keywords Turkey · Environmentalism

What does Turkey's environmental score card look like since the 2000s? What are the endemic reasons for environmental degradation in this country?

Before the 2000s, Turkey's environmental scorecard was not very good. It makes sense to take the military coup of 1980 as a turning point. Neoliberal government policies implemented in the aftermath of the coup aggravated already-existing environmental problems. The coup crushed and weakened leftist movements in Turkey. Right-wing governments dominated in the Turkish parliament and were keen to apply the new neoliberal policies. But the AKP government that came to power after 2002 has been the strongest implementer of neoliberal policies thus far.

If we compare Turkey to other countries, we should underline that current government representatives have a conceptual void in terms of environmental issues. For

B. Şık (✉) · C. Ulutaş
Antalya, Turkey
e-mail: bulentilgaz@gmail.com

© Springer International Publishing AG, part of Springer Nature 2019   147
E. Özyürek et al. (eds.), *Authoritarianism and Resistance in Turkey*,
https://doi.org/10.1007/978-3-319-76705-5_15

instance, after Fukushima, antinuclear movements intensified all around the globe. In contrast, Turkey has recently finalized a nuclear deal with the Russians to realize a long-suspended plan, first attempted in 1965, to build its first nuclear power plant in Akkuyu. Meanwhile, even Germany and Japan are preparing to phase out nuclear power. Around the world the disposal of industrial waste and environmental pollution of all kinds is either handled properly or, when not, is protested publicly. Yet in Turkey, one of the top five countries in ship dismantling, we are without proper environmental regulation. Such a lack of government regulation of these types of hazardous materials is only seen in underdeveloped, low-income countries.

Compared to other similarly developed countries, we do not have adequate laboratories or a working and comprehensive monitoring and assessment program that can measure and evaluate the pollution of soil, water, air, and natural habitats. Other middle-income countries successfully implement assessment programs and monitor toxic chemicals contaminating food, water, soil, and air. Although there is a similar program in Turkey on paper, the planning and application of it is a complete disaster. In the developed world and in many middle-income countries, there is both massive public investment as well as government subsidies aimed at boosting private investment in the production of renewable energy sources and in energy saving schemes, such as building insulation and solar panels.

Despite this, I believe that a different approach is needed to fully answer your question. In this context, it makes more sense to underline the similarities between countries, rather than the differences. When we talk about efforts to prevent and solve environmental issues, no country can be labeled as successful. There are certainly countries with better legal statutes, countries where public institutions actually work or where NGOs have had a positive impact on environmental policies. But in essence, their differences are a matter of degree. There is no country in the world that takes a holistic view of human existence to the point where they favor environmental conservation, convergence, and economic de-growth over the constant increase of gross domestic product and per capita household consumption. This certainly does not justify the fact that the current Turkish government has an outmoded and largely uninformed understanding of most environmental issues.

Having a majority in parliament for three successive terms has given the governing party extensive legislative powers. This has enabled it to remove or circumvent some of the barriers to implementing its economic policies, specifically in the realm of environmental conservation laws and international agreements. Could you give some examples of laws and regulations that have been modified, abolished, or circumvented and which have had an adverse effect on environmental management and conservation?

The AKP government was so successful in disrupting the Turkish legal system (which was already patchy), that we cannot talk about a functioning legal system anymore. Dismantling and then suspending the legal system in the name of aggressive privatization has facilitated a number of crises: the destruction of natural habitats, the deprivation of local livelihoods, the depredation of public lands, and the termination of small-farm agricultural production—or what we call a peasant-type agriculture. From where we stand today, it is clear that we failed to stop this destructive process through legal means. For example, the internal security law that is being debated in parliament includes articles that would consider as a crime any objection or protest coming from people whose land and water is to be confiscated by the state.

I can give countless examples of malevolently designed and implemented laws: the law on seed growing, the law on the establishment of the Ministry of Environment and Urbanization, the bio-security act. The law on seed growing banned farmers from producing and using their own seeds. Because of this ban and other regulations that corporatized agricultural production, small-sized family farming has suffered greatly. In just 10 years and without proper planning, the number of farmers has declined from 3 to 2 million. This accelerated decline caused millions to migrate from rural areas to join the urban poor, because there were no complementary economic and social policies designed to absorb these newly unemployed masses. With recent regulations designed to increase the extent of contiguous built-up metropolitan areas, rural populations decreased from 23 to 10% overnight. Rural populations have lost both their entitlements to public lands for pasturing and their access to public local water sources. Vast areas of pastureland have been recategorized as urban areas. They have thus lost their conservation status and may well be opened up for urban construction projects.

Was there a widespread environmental movement against this blend of 19th, 20th, and 21st century types of economic growth and the constant attack on environment and public lands? Ideally, large-scale projects such as energy investments affecting fragile ecosystems or urban renewal projects affecting millions of people should be planned ahead of time. They should be implemented with the cooperation of scientists, experts, and NGOs. They should encourage public participation. Was this the case in Turkey before the 2000s and how has it been since then?

Before 2000, the situation was not promising, but there were campaigns that resulted in long-term positive outcomes. In those days, environmental campaigns were weaker and got less attention. But there were some successful cases. For example, the construction of Gökova Thermal Power Plant was delayed for years with lawsuits, and similar suits were launched for the application of environmentally safe flue gas filters. These successes were the result of the struggles of a persistent and determined few who deserve to be remembered with respect. There was a decadelong struggle against a gold mine in Bergama, a town inhabited since antiquity and located on fertile lands in the west of Turkey. The prolonged protest of the gold mine by the local population in this olive-oil producing region could only slow the mine's construction and disrupt its operation for a time. But these protests were important in many respects. The participation in the campaign of a majority of the people living in the area was a great opportunity for us to incorporate environmental awareness into daily life. With the help of NGOs, professionals, and a legal suit, the project was delayed for years.

Examples of governmental abuse of environmental laws and entitlements, and of environmental movements after 2000s are also abundant. A series of small hydroelectric power plants were planned for every single stream in Turkey, without prior notification or consultation with the people living around them. The most concrete example is the small hydroelectric power plant project on the world-famous Ahmetler Canyon in Antalya, where no local community, NGO, or academic institution was aware of the project until heavy-duty construction equipment arrived in the canyon and began working. Although the government had a legal obligation to inform the local inhabitants beforehand, everything was handled in great secrecy. The notice issued by the state institution in charge of such announcements was posted on a corner where no one could see it. So nobody knew it was happening. The government is also legally obliged to obtain an environmental impact assessment report wherever an industrial investment will alter the environmental characteristics of a region. Yet, these reports are so carelessly prepared that they do not have any function. The environmental impact assessment report for the Ahmetler Canyon hydroelectric power plant was prepared without even physically inspecting the canyon. It was nothing more than a dummy report designed to fulfill a bureaucratic requirement. When such reports contain negative findings concerning an investment, it does not mean that the project will be abandoned. Aside from environmental impact assessment reports, new laws permit formerly archaeological or natural protection areas, untouchable areas like national parks opened to construction investments claiming public interest in the project.

Under AKP rule, public lands, natural and historical protection areas have been turned into construction areas, without consideration for legal or regulatory controls. The primary justification for these investment decisions is always that it is in the public interest, and it is always for the cabinet to decide whether a project will result in the public interest or not. In many cases, local people never know about these plans or decisions. This way, the objection period is shortened or completely eliminated. If legal objections halt or delay the project, new legal changes are prepared in order to overturn court decisions. A concrete example of this technique is the ongoing dispute over a coal power plant project in Yırca, Soma. The company in charge of the project needed to cut down 6,000 olive trees in order to start construction. The local community strongly opposed the plan and took the project to court. The court then decided against the project and cancelled the rapid expropriation decision that gave way to the plant project. Despite the court decision, the company managed to cut down the trees by ignoring the law. Even though the project was halted in the name of the public interest and environmental health, the construction company was able to take revenge, if you will, and get away with it, showing the inhabitants that it does not need to recognize legally binding court decisions.

Realizing that such a court decision was on its way, the government prepared a new regulation that would change the legal framework so as to nullify the legal excuse of a stay of execution—the very one that would have prevented the destruction of the olive trees. If they had ever finally managed to get it through parliament, the "Olive Grove Bill" would have affected not only Yırca, but every olive tree in the entire country. The project in Yırca would start up again, and this time there would no legal barrier that could save the trees. I personally believe they tried their best to pass this bill, which came to parliament six times for a vote and was every time postponed. Nevertheless, the struggle continues, in our country as everywhere else, between those who want to protect life and those who try their hands against it.

Do you see the Gezi Park protests as the culmination of all previous environmental mobilizations? Was the proposed destruction of Gezi Park the inspiration needed to revitalize all the demoralized peace and justice groups, as if saving the park could change our destiny?

The protests at Gezi Park are certainly connected to previous environmental movements in Turkey, but they cannot be reduced to just that. The Gezi protests are connected to every struggle that is rights-based. I do not think that we will ever arrive at an explanation of exactly how it is connected. All we have are partially true opinions that fly through the air. In my opinion, we live in an era where we should frankly ease up on the opinions, we should resist them. In fact, it is essential that we take a step back and view the incident objectively, and this was rarely the case with Gezi. What I am trying to say is that using Gezi as a foil to debate political views or to prove a personal opinion keeps us from understanding the real nature of the resistance.

I believe that we are far away from victory (or whatever we understand our goal to be), that the country I live in is swiftly turning into a totalitarian regime, and that we are going to have worse days. Yet I am not without hope. I believe that this government, wallowing as it is in corruption, bribery, and depravity, will eventually collapse. That is my hope.

Author Biographies

Bülent Şık has a PhD in environmentally friendly food analysis techniques. From 2009 to 2016, he was an assistant professor in the departments of Food Engineering and of Gastronomy and Culinary Arts at Akdeniz University, Antalya. From 1990 to 2009, he worked for the Ministry of Food, Agriculture, and Animal Welfare. He served as assistant technical director of the Food Safety and Agricultural Researches Centre at Akdeniz University until he was dismissed from his position during the state of emergency purges after the attempted coup of July 2016

Cana Ulutaş is an environmental activist working as a freelance translator and educational consultant. She has a BA in economics from Boğaziçi University and an MA in environment and development from the London School of Economics. Her MA thesis was about the environmental movement against the Bergama gold mine. She has worked as a project coordinator for several environmental NGOs and as the editor of IMC News Channel's Green Bulletin. She is an active member of the Rural Development Initiative of Turkey

Part V
Minorities and Conflicts

The Kurdish Movement

Nazan Üstundağ and Interview by Güney Yıldız

Abstract Since the mid-1990s the PKK also changed its strategy in three ways. First, it forged new diplomatic relations with the relevant states and entered into dialogue with women's movements, ecologists, and leftists. The peace process in Turkey was part of that. Second, it began to localize itself at the grassroots level by creating neighborhood assemblies. In Turkey and Syria, it created official neighborhood organizations with the aim of reorganizing the economy, society, and politics. Third, it declared itself an organization that works on behalf of all Middle Eastern peoples, women, and the oppressed in general, alongside the Kurds.

Keywords Kurdish movement · PKK

Let's begin with the goals of the PKK. What is it that the group is fighting for? How would you characterize the PKK politically?

The PKK is primarily fighting for the rights and liberation of Kurds living in Turkey, Syria, Iran, and Iraq. Initially, the PKK aimed at creating a united and independent Kurdistan. However, since the mid-1990s it has changed its goals: it now aims to create a solution for Kurds without changing the existing borders of the states Kurds live in. Since the arrest and imprisonment of Abdullah Öcalan in 1999, the PKK has altered its analyses of power significantly and has declared itself against a triad of nationalism, patriarchy, and capitalism. According to Öcalan's prison writings (Öcalan and Happel 2007), the three problems of contemporary civilization are the nation-state, male oppression of women, and capitalism. Together, these constitute what he calls *capitalist modernity*. He defends what he

N. Üstundağ (✉)
Department of Sociology, Boğaziçi University, South Campus,
34342 Bebek, Istanbul, Turkey
e-mail: nazanust@hotmail.com

G. Yıldız
BBC, London, UK
e-mail: guneyyildiz@gmail.com

© Springer International Publishing AG, part of Springer Nature 2019   155
E. Özyürek et al. (eds.), *Authoritarianism and Resistance in Turkey*,
https://doi.org/10.1007/978-3-319-76705-5_16

terms *democratic modernity*, by which he means a society inspired by the diverse struggles of women, workers, and minorities. In this context, there is no need for a new Kurdish state. On the contrary, the separation of Kurds across four different countries is seen as a strength, and Kurds in these countries are tasked to democratize their respective states by constituting gender-equitable, ecological, noncapitalist, multicultural communities.

With this shift in ideology and analysis, the PKK also changed its strategy in three ways. First, it forged new diplomatic relations with the relevant states and entered into dialogue with women's movements, ecologists, and leftists. The peace process in Turkey was part of that. Second, it began to localize itself at the grassroots level by creating neighborhood assemblies. In Turkey and Syria, it created official neighborhood organizations with the aim of reorganizing the economy, society, and politics. Third, it declared itself an organization that works on behalf of all Middle Eastern peoples, women, and the oppressed in general, alongside the Kurds.

With the collapse of the peace process in Turkey and the war in Syria, however, it has been difficult to call attention to the strategy changes the PKK has made on the ground, the new dialogues it has established, its emphasis on women's rights, or the ecological communities it encourages. It is still viewed primarily as an militant organization that means to bring about change through armed struggle.

In the mid-1970s, the future leaders of the PKK set out to establish what was to become the most successful Kurdish liberation movement. Can you tell us about the Kurdish national liberation movement before the 1970s? What gave rise to the emergence of the PKK?

The Kurdish national liberation struggle didn't begin in the 1970s. The original Kurdish nationalists attempted to launch a Kurdish struggle around the time that the Ottoman Empire was disintegrating. In the first Turkish parliament of 1920, the Grand National Assembly, there was a draft constitution recognizing Kurdish national identity. This consensus was broken in 1923 when the Republic of Turkey was declared, and all mention of the Kurds was removed from legal texts. Since then, there have been many Kurdish liberation movements bearing different political characteristics. Protests and rebellions were launched across Kurdistan in defense of the autonomous structures of their cities and towns. The Koçgiri, Sheikh Said, Ağri (Ararat), and Dersim rebellions were brutally repressed with mass slaughter. These genocidal massacres and the attendant mass trials targeting prominent Kurdish individuals temporarily suppressed the Kurdish national liberation struggle. But new attempts resurfaced as waves of Kurdish youth began studying in universities and an intellectual class was born. These new attempts were suppressed by means of imprisonment and forced exile. By the 1970s, there existed many different Kurdish organizations, most of which were influenced by the left-wing ideologies prevalent in that time. They were in conflict among themselves and fought against the feudal lords still powerful in Kurdistan. Following the military coup of 1980, the PKK emerged as the sole Kurdish organization to survive. This was thanks to organizational discipline within the PKK, the resistance of PKK members at the notorious Diyarbakir military prison, and to the PKK leadership decision to withdraw to the Syrian-controlled Beqaa valley in Lebanon. That decision allowed the PKK to organize for a guerrilla movement rather than to become a political refugee organization in Europe. With this, the PKK became the most powerful Kurdish liberation organization, enjoying wide popular support.

What was the situation with the Turkish left, especially during early 1970s when Abdullah Öcalan and his set began operating as a political group?

As with much of the world in those days, there were many leftist organizations in Turkey: Maoist organizations, organizations that were under the influence of the Soviet Union, and those particular to Turkey. All these left-wing organizations defined socialism and communism as their ideals. They were organized in trade unions and in certain districts and cities and as armed groups. We know that Öcalan was deeply influenced by Mahir Çayan, the leader of the People's Liberation Party-Front of Turkey. In that period, many Kurdish cadres and sympathizers left Turkish left-wing movements to join the PKK because they believed that the Kurds should organize separately since they faced not imperialism but direct colonialism.

Why did the PKK leadership think it necessary to organize independently of Turkish left-wing groups?

Ever since the elimination of Ottoman Greek and Armenian leftists during the transition from the Ottoman Empire to the Republic of Turkey, nationalism has been the dominant mindset of the Turkish left. Their approach to the Kurdish question is no exception. There were a few leaders who thought differently— İbrahim Kaypakkaya, for example, who recognized Kurdistan as a Turkish colony. Some Turkish leftists argued that Kurdistan and Turkey have different class structures which necessitate different tactics and strategies of struggle. But in terms of positive approaches on the left to the Kurdish question, we can only talk about individuals and moments rather than a consistently progressive approach. For this reason, the inclination to organize independent from the Turkish left has been a prevalent one.

In 1974, Abdullah Öcalan and other PKK members established together with Turkish leftists a youth organization that was not exclusively Kurdish—the Ankara Higher Education Democratic Youth Association. What does this experience tell us?

Abdullah Öcalan has never given up on his dream to liberate both Kurds and Turks. The Ankara Higher Education Democratic Youth Association is an example of that. Even after he went to Syria, he continued to seek alliances with the Turkish left. The PKK have provided opportunities for training the Turkish left. Whereas the PKK managed to come out of the military junta of 1980–1982 stronger, the Turkish left suffered greatly and thereafter continued a limited existence. This imbalance of power between the PKK and the Turkish left was one obstacle to further alliances between them.

Which political movements both in Turkey and abroad inspired the PKK? We know that the PKK's name comes from the Workers Party of Vietnam; you've already mentioned Mahir Çayan and his movement; the 1968 movements also had an influence. But we cannot count Kurdish movements in other parts of Kurdistan as inspiration, such as those headed up by Mullah Mustafa Barzani or Abdul Rahman Ghassemlou in Iran.

At the Diyarbakır Prison Truth Commission, a civil initiative, we have interviewed many PKK cadres and sympathizers who spent time in Diyarbakir prison. During those interviews we found that among the books people had read before going to prison were many concerning the Vietnamese experience. The primary difference between the PKK and other Kurdish national movements in Iraq or elsewhere is that the PKK struggle is not only against Turkish colonialism; it is also against global colonial and imperialist systems. In this sense, especially in the 1970s and 1980s, Vietnam and other anti-imperialist movements in places like Argentina or Angola have had a strong influence on the PKK. There are indeed many parallels between Vietnam and Turkey, particularly with regard to repression tactics, torture in prison, and such.

Today things have changed. Environmental, anarchist, and feminist movements now inspire the PKK. We know that Murray Bookchin is a great influence. Almost all the books of Michel Foucault, Jurgen Habermas, and Antonio Negri are read. The women in the movement read Western and postcolonial feminism and have created their own strand of women's science, which they call *jinolojî*. Readings in theory are now more influential than programmatic readings. Then again, the PKK does have close relationships with the radical left opposition in Nepal, Afghanistan, and Argentina, Colombia, and the Zapatistas in Mexico.

Is it significant that the PKK leadership looked to Vietnam, rather than to the Mustafa Barzani Kurdish movement or the PLO? Could it be that because the PKK could not count on external powers pressuring Turkey, they had to design their own strategy?

When the PKK was in Beqaa Valley in Lebanon, many other national liberation movements and European left-wing groups were there. What I see in documents from that time is that Öcalan was very keen to exchange ideas with other groups. Even today we know that the PKK in Qandil receives visitors from around the world.

Following the collapse of Soviet Union, many left-wing and national liberation movements either collapsed or shifted to the right. Why hasn't this been the case with the PKK?

There hasn't been enough research done on the effect the Soviet Union's collapse had on these left-wing movements. Remember that the diminishment of left-wing movements after the demise of the Soviet Union was followed by the rise of Islamist movements. The uniqueness of the PKK is that it kept the channels of communication open with other left-wing political movements across the globe; it never let itself become isolated. It has also been very flexible in terms of its ideology, adapting itself to new circumstances and new ideas. As a movement, it never backed away from a critical assessment of its own tactics and strategies and was always willing to undertake across-the-board change.

We know that Öcalan came from a lower-class family. What about other members of the movement? What were their class backgrounds?

Most were Kurds, but there were also some with a Turkish background. The difference between the PKK and the Turkish left is that PKK members were primarily workers and peasants who came from poor backgrounds, whereas those in the Turkish left had included more members coming from the middle and upper-middle classes.

Is this a significant difference? PKK members were almost exclusively working-class. Middle- and upper-middle-class cadres either left the organization or were expelled early on.

Yes, I believe this is a very significant difference between the PKK and Turkish groups. Another important point is that the PKK first confronted the Kurdish upper classes and feudal lords, even before beginning their struggle against the Turkish state. Their first ever military actions were against feudal lords. They only took on the Turkish state after coming under heavy attack by the Turkish police and military.

Another difference is the PKK's formation around a leader. Öcalan himself personally participated in the internal political training of thousands of his supporters. What effect has this had on the organization?

While the PKK is formed around its leader Öcalan, this does not mean that Öcalan's ideas are followed without critique. It means that just about everyone has a personal relationship with Öcalan, and that their personal approach and character was formed in the course of their relationship with Öcalan. Öcalan was always very sensitive to the formation of revolutionary and ethical subjectivities among the PKK membership.

Since his imprisonment, Öcalan's leadership has taken a new form. The fact that he is now largely inaccessible makes him a mythological leader. His writings are diligently studied, and the PKK struggles to fully understand his theoretical and political assertions and to realize his social model. However, the very fact that he is in prison means that he is not sovereign. Quite the opposite, he is the opposite of sovereign. He is in the hands of the state and continuously under the threat of execution. His influence and his life depend entirely on the Kurds' voluntary recognition of him as their leader.

Despite leading a successful guerrilla organization, Öcalan himself was never a military commander. What's your take on that? Why did the PKK decide that they had to start an armed struggle against the Turkish state?

Öcalan always emphasized the importance of ideological formation and theoretical education vis-à-vis military training. This has been the case since the beginning of the struggle.

After the military coup of 1980 there was widespread repression in Turkey. In Kurdish cities, martial law was imposed. But this is only part of the story. I think the problem is that Turkey was waging an ontological war against the Kurds. The state's policies, discourse, and violently repressive measures of that time were designed to prove that Kurds do not exist—not in Turkey, not elsewhere. Armed struggle was therefore an ontological resistance to show that Kurds do indeed exist. How do you exist in relation to modern law if your existence is denied? By breaking the law that does not recognize your existence. Kurds had to break the law collectively in order to be recognized and named.

The fact of Kurdistan extending across the borders of Turkey, Syria, Iraq, and Iran poses difficulties for the Kurdish movement. These countries belong to different geopolitical blocs: Turkey is a member of NATO, Syria is an ally of the Soviet Union/Russia, Iran is a pivotal Shia country, and Iraq and Syria represent currents of Arab nationalism. What is your take on this complicating factor of Kurds facing enemies from different camps?

I believe that this is a great source of strength for the Kurdish movement. Many intellectuals and political groups refuse to acknowledge the fact that the factional nature of Kurdish enemies is an advantage, not a disadvantage. As a result of these material conditions, the movement has had to develop strategies for negotiating each of the four different regimes and four different geopolitical blocs. Because of this, they have obtained invaluable experience and knowledge concerning different forms of state oppression, destruction, and regulation. The fact that Kurds are spread across four countries and live also in diaspora in Europe makes the movement a global movement. Political knowledge that is created in one part of Kurdistan is quickly transferred to other parts via PKK cadres. This is the most salient way in which the Kurdish movement differs from all other movements.

The PKK emphasizes four distinct periods in its history. The first period of ideological formation extends from the mid-1970s to 1984. Between 1984 and 1993 the movement engaged in a primarily military strategy aimed at creating liberated zones. The negotiation period began with the first ceasefire in 1993 and ended with the resumption of military struggle in 2004. Since 2004, the PKK has emphasized the establishment of democratic autonomy. What is your take on this periodization?

This periodization charts the major changes in the PKK's methodologies, which are in tune with changes similar movements experienced. Throughout this period, repressive states, too, have changed their tactics. Today they resort less often to violence and, through the establishment of comprehensive peace regimes, more often to a strategy of integrating the opposition into the nation-state and the capitalist patriarchal system. Across the globe, we have witnessed the launch of various peace processes aimed at ending longstanding ethnic and political conflicts. The PKK attempted to relocate itself politically in order to better confront this new reality—look at Öcalan's theses on the democratization of the republic. I believe that we should not read the history of the Kurdish movement as being isolated from global events, but rather as part of them.

Now things are changing once again, and peace regimes are being replaced by regimes of war. In the context of the new global wars, the PKK's Kurdish allies in Syria have for the first time been able to declare self-administration and begin establishing institutions. Öcalan and the PKK has been advocating for this for quite some time. But as we are witnessing in Turkey this new war era now also means more violence in urban areas, the securatization of space, image wars..

The PKK describes itself as a Kurdish freedom movement rather than as a Kurdish national movement. Since its beginnings, there has never been much talk of the borders of a prospective Kurdish state. Since the early 2000s, the PKK has openly denounced the idea of establishing a nation-state. Do you see it as viable for a national movement to denounce the idea of the nation-state?

The PKK is very adaptive and pragmatic, but also very ideological. In the Barzani movement, capitalism and nationalism go hand in hand. But the PKK has never given up on its class identity and dos not agree with the nationalist-capitalist model. According to the PKK, the nation-state confiscates the means of production, reproduction, and defense from the people. The PKK wants to create an alternative system by opening up these reified means to the use of the people. Hence it is also against the reification of the state. Rather, it tries to profane it by creating multiple organizational and institutional structures that are always in dialogue and contestation.

Kurdish female fighters are very visible in the PKK's struggle in the Middle East. Why? What are the roots of this phenomenon? Does it come from the PKK's organizational culture or is it part of Öcalan's ideology?

From its first day forward, there have been women in the PKK. Öcalan sees the liberation of women as being equal in importance to the anti-colonial struggle, and he links women's liberation to the liberation of society as a whole. There is also the fact that patriarchal society in Turkey and Kurdistan are quite different from one another. In Kurdistan, the patriarchy allows women to live a separate life. It is therefore acceptable for Kurds to see women organizing among themselves as separate from men. You do not see this so much in a society where the nuclear family predominates.

The Kurdish movement in Turkey has also led the way in being able to organize a leftist political party with broad mass support in the form of the HDP party. The party received 13 and 10% of the national vote in two consecutive elections. How do you see that experience?

These elections mark a turning point in the political history of Turkey. The HDP is an embodiment of the Kurdish movement's new paradigm. It contains many different groups, including feminists, LGBTQ activists, socialist Muslims, Alevis, ecologists, leftists, and Kurds. Until the foundation of the HDP, Kurdish political parties in Turkey had never succeeded in passing the 10% threshold that determines whether a party will sit in parliament. In the span of a bit more than a year, the HDP became a defining actor in Turkish politics, setting agendas and influencing political and social discourse. It was seen as a demonstration of the possibility of Turks and Kurds living together, and it reposed the decade long question of the Turkification of Kurdish politics. Rather than pursuing an assimilative politics, Kurds were now candidates to rule Turkey as a whole—not Kurdistan alone—on the basis of democratic, inclusive, and gender-equitable principles. It was not anti-capitalist, but it defended a mixed economy whereby a space for a communal economy would be opened up and worker's rights, which were eroded by neoliberal policies, would be regranted. This was a very exciting time where we had a glimpse of an alternative future. But it didn't last. The war resumed, and Kurds were once again criminalized, demonized, and marginalized within Turkish politics and social life.

Following a two-year peace process, the Turkish state and the PKK have now resumed military conflict. This time around the fighting is more intense than ever. Armed clashes have taken place inside city centers, producing high numbers of civilian casualties. Can you elaborate on the peace process and the subsequent intensification of the conflict?

The peace process was a hopeful time, but the two sides in the peace process had very different expectations of it. While the Turkish state hoped that through the peace process it could open Kurdistan to capital investment, reinstate its own rule of law, and assimilate Kurds into a new national Muslim identity, Kurds expected that the peace process would provide them with the legal ground to continue their struggle for democracy and liberation, albeit without recourse to violence. While Kurds demanded legal changes and the legal structures to support and monitor the peace process, the state was reluctant to create any legal mechanisms whatsoever and refused to create a peace-monitoring mechanism. It did not help that the Turkish state remained hostile to the newly declared autonomous regions of Syrian Kurdistan and was alleged to secretly be assisting ISIS in its war against the Kurds. Toward the end of the process, the two sides demanded conflicting prerequisites to peace: while the government insisted on PKK disarmament as a first step, the PKK demanded the establishment of a monitoring mechanism as a first step. Meanwhile, the state continued to build new army posts in Kurdish areas and to arrest Kurdish HDP mayors.

I suspect that what happened is that with the HDP's success, the AKP government decided that the peace process wasn't going to benefit them and allow them to monopolize power as they had expected. Instead, the peace process became an opportunity for the opposition, which came together to find voice and visibility under the HDP's umbrella. The AKP received far fewer votes than it had expected. War then became a more viable tactic for consolidating their power militarily, politically, culturally, and economically.

What is your take on the urban war that took place in 2015 and 2Ü016 between the youth and the army, which cost the lives of hundreds and ended with the reoccupation of Kurdish cities by the Turkish Armed Forces?[1]

Once the peace process collapsed, the struggle for autonomy in the towns and cities of northern Kurdistan has undergone a significant shift from a nonviolent reorganization of social and political life to a militant movement of self-defense. The declaration of round-the-clock curfews in the summer of 2016 left many Kurdish cities under de facto military siege, setting the scene for an urban war. Local youth dug trenches and built barricades to protect their neighborhoods and their democratic autonomous initiatives from police raids. When the guerrillas who had until then remained in the mountains came down to support the youth, Turkey's special forces tore apart towns and cities and razed entire neighborhoods to the ground. According to a UN report, hundreds of people died during these clashes.

The devastation of the war was not just material, however. Turkish special forces burned civilians alive, stripped people naked, forbid the burial of those killed, and widely circulated images on social media of mutilated dead bodies and cutoff limbs in celebration of their victory. This made a lasting mark on the Kurdish people. Today, the experiment with democratic autonomy in Turkey's Kurdistan has come to an end, with thousands imprisoned, organizations closed down, elected officials removed from office, and towns and cities occupied by heavily armed security forces.

Can you explain to us what the organizations of democratic autonomy were? How did they function? Were they modelled after existing organizations?

Social scientists have long debated why it is that post-conflict societies—from Ireland to South Africa—often face the disempowerment of emancipatory social forces. Some believe this to be a result of the fact that national regimes and peace processes have often been formulated by global capitalist actors whose primary goal is to secure capital accumulation, consolidate the nation-state, and invalidate ideologies alternative to neoliberalism.

---

[1] **The remaining section of this interview was adopted from Nazan Üstündağ's article in Roar magazine under creative commons license** (Üstündağ 2017).https://roarmag.org/magazine/democratic-autonomy-municipalism-kurdistan/.

Having learned from the negative experiences of the past, latecomers to the conflict resolution process like the PKK and the Colombian guerrilla FARC movement therefore argue that the peace process should be seen more as a social and political struggle than a diplomatic endeavor—peace processes as a *means* rather than an *end*. Society must exercise its self-defense and increase its capacity for freedom during the peace process. In other words, the spaces that open up during peace negotiations and peace struggles have to be seized upon as spaces for exercising freedom here and now. Only a society that can defend and govern itself can achieve peace without losing its potential for radical social transformation and its capacity to build alternative worlds.

This explains why the Kurdish freedom movement in Turkey has created various local, national, and international institutions, has brought various sections of the Kurdish and Turkish public together, and has formed new alliances during the peace process. Through the many conferences it held and the three political parties it created—the DTK (which aimed at bringing all Kurdish actors and NGOs together), the HDP, and the DBP (a pedagogical party that educates people and helps them create neighborhood assemblies)—it aimed to expand the space of negotiation by including new actors in the process. Meanwhile, as the key negotiator for the Kurds, Abdullah Öcalan used the negotiating table as a platform to formulate a legal framework for the larger struggle for liberation.

The AKP government had very different expectations of the peace process. Its aim was to increase its own regional power by declaring itself as the representative of Kurds and Turks alike and to disempower the Kurdish freedom movement's discursive, representational, and operational capacity. It hoped to secure Kurdish territories for the investment of capital and to consolidate state power by promoting a collective Islamic identity that was to unite the disparate historical trajectories of Kurds and Turks. In 2015, two years after it began, the Turkish government abandoned the peace process and resorted once more to military means of handling the "Kurdish question." This decision appears to have been motivated at least in part by the fact that Kurdish groups had been much more effective at using the peace process as a way to address disaffected groups inside Turkey and bring them together in opposition to the policies of Erdoğan's AKP government.

What did people in Turkey think about Kurdistan's democratic autonomy project?

While Öcalan had introduced the concept of democratic autonomy to the vocabulary of the Kurdish freedom movement as early as the 2000s, it only became a subject for debate, criticism, and elaboration by a wider public beyond the movement's cadres after the launch of a key meeting in Diyarbakır in 2010. At the meeting, Kurdish activists invited Turkish journalists and intellectuals to evaluate their proposed solution to the Kurdish question, presenting their ideas of democratic autonomy. They encountered fierce opposition—not because the invited journalists and intellectuals were hostile to the recognition of Kurdish identity, but because they deemed this proposal to be both unrealistic and utopian.

Apart from a reform to the constitution that would exclude any reference to ethnicity, the proposal promoted by the Kurds had little to say about the restructuring of the Turkish state and the correcting of past wrongs. Rather, it included an elaborate model of self-governance and power-sharing where references like "people's parliaments," "communes," "peasants," and "women" expressed a desire to build a radical democracy in the political and economic realm, as well as in health, education, and other fields.

For the intellectuals of Turkey, who at the time were heavily invested in the fantasy of liberal democracy and the rule of law, the proposal seemed to distract energy and attention away from "real issues." Only a few years later, however, that which was once deemed unrealistic was already being practiced in many cities and towns across Kurdistan. Moreover, and somewhat ironically, the desires that informed the Gezi protests of 2013, when a million people took to the streets of Istanbul and cities across Turkey, had an undeniable affinity with the demands for democratic autonomy as formulated by the Kurdish opposition.

What did democratic autonomy involve?

Democratic autonomy in Kurdish cities primarily involved the creation of unofficial assemblies at the local and regional level. Residential assemblies in neighborhoods, towns, and cities would make decisions concerning infrastructure and other important social issues. In the local elections of 2009, the Kurdish opposition gained 97 municipalities and expanded this number to 99 in 2014. Now, however, these new municipal authorities had to respond to the demands of the unofficial people's assemblies, limiting their decision-making capacity and devolving the power of educated, middle-class elites and professionals to everyday people and workers. In addition to the general popular assemblies, there were also thematic assemblies on health, justice, the economy, and education that aimed to democratize social policy and local governance.

While the economic assembly encouraged the formation of cooperatives and held meetings with businessmen, trade organizations and entrepreneurs along with the poor and the unemployed, the assemblies on public health provided free services and educated health workers. Academies opened up around Kurdistan providing ideological formation and skills training for those who participated in the construction of democratic autonomy, while truth and justice assemblies aimed at resolving local disputes to ensure that people in Kurdistan would stop using formal institutions of law and to promote the dissemination and democratization of community justice.

Between 2009 and 2015, various local, regional and national institutions and organizations—including assemblies, parties, and congresses—continued to spread across Kurdistan. The Kurds already had extensive experience in building new models of self-governance. They had developed various organizations throughout the 1990s and 2000s to document human rights violations in the Kurdish regions—

including forced displacements, disappearances, and extrajudicial killings—and to assist villagers who had come to city centers as a result of the government's evacuation and destruction of their villages. The new forms of democratic autonomy built on these past experiences and were quickly put in place.

Were there any problems?

First of all, the model had been delineated in fairly detailed fashion beforehand, first by Öcalan and then by the PKK more generally, allowing it to become a means of social engineering. Second, the language of democratic autonomy was foreign to most people; as such it produced movement elites who were expert in speaking this language at the expense of lay people on whom it imposed an alienating vocabulary. Third, autonomy was often interpreted as national autonomy and was understood to be the provision of services by the Kurdish movement rather than the state. This neglected to problematize the wider relationship of "service provision" under capitalism, statism, and patriarchy. Finally, certain sections of the population, especially the disadvantaged youth, could not be successfully incorporated into the institutions of democratic autonomy and remained isolated in their own organizations.

At the same time, however, this period was also one in which the Kurds further developed their repertoire of oppositional action. For one, the emergence of an autonomous government within the context of the war against ISIS in Rojava in northern Syria influenced the struggle in Bakur immensely. In Rojava, the Kurdish freedom movement achieved universal recognition by means of armed struggle, and Kurdish youths learned and disseminated the tactics and strategies of urban warfare there.

Moreover, the peace process and the ceasefire between the Turkish army and the Kurdish forces allowed different people to visit and consult with the guerrillas at the headquarters in the Qandil mountains of northern Iraq. Notably, the visibility and legitimacy that the freedom fighters acquired during the peace process firmly lodged the struggle in the imagination of ordinary Kurds. As opposed to the claustrophobia of urban spaces shaped by colonialism, capitalism, and the patriarchal family, as well as the everyday conflicts that the formation of democratic autonomy inevitably entailed, guerrilla warfare represented an escape from family and work, an intimacy with nature, friendship, and power. This was especially true for the urban youth. To the extent that they felt excluded from both formal political institutions and spaces of democratic autonomy, they popularized new practices within the cities that mimicked guerrilla warfare and transformed urban spaces into spaces of liberation here and now by means of armed resistance. Starting as self-defense units in neighborhoods fighting against the drug trade, prostitution, and theft, these armed squads increasingly turned into urban guerrilla formations protecting neighborhoods from state violence.

Finally, people's relationship to rural areas underwent a major change during this time. Whereas in the previous period their relationship with the rural areas had been uprooted by the experience of state violence and forced displacement, now urban actors slowly began to reattach themselves to the villages and the mountains.

Children, women, men, party members, and lay people, educated and uneducated, youngsters and elders walked along long roads into the countryside, resisting security forces and risking their lives together, engaging in multiple horizontal negotiations and conversations among themselves and with the guerrilla and security forces alike.

In the Kurdish cities, the youth and police often clash, with the former using stones and Molotov cocktails, and the latter rubber bullets, gas bombs, and pressurized water. Already in 2013, however, these regular skirmishes had developed into more violent confrontations. While the guerrilla forces and the army maintained their ceasefire, a number of youth were shot during protests in the city. Moreover, those in urban areas also faced long prison sentences whenever the police caught them. Many of the youth were sons and daughters of the displaced, with little prospects in formal education and employment, contributing to an explosive social situation in the cities.

When ISIS attacked Kobanê in 2014 and it began to look like the Turkish state was enabling the Kurdish city's siege, the youth took to the streets all over Bakur. That was the first time when the Turkish state realized the size and power of the Kurdish youth movement, and the fact that many of these youths were now lightly armed and well organized. After the defeat of ISIS at Kobanê, the youth dug trenches in their neighborhoods to stop police raids aimed at arresting them. While the trenches were filled up at Öcalan's request for de-escalation during the peace process, they were dug out again once the process collapsed.

Toward the end of 2015, Turkish special forces attacked these trenches with overwhelming force and a number of cities remained under siege for several months, while civilians were bombarded by tanks and targeted by snipers. Some of the guerrilla forces from the nearby mountains joined the youth in their campaign of self-defense. In late 2016, however, all rebelling cities were brought back under state control and reoccupied by state forces. Kurdish urban dwellers were able to survive the siege only because they shared food and safe spaces and had already established some basic autonomous health provision. Throughout 2017, in the wake of the failed coup attempt of the previous summer, the Turkish state engaged in a broad crackdown on all of its opponents, arresting Kurdish politicians, activists and youth. Many of the destroyed urban areas were confiscated by the state with the intention of rebuilding the cities in ways that would prevent future insurgency.

The experiment with democratic autonomy in Kurdish cities and towns might seem like an extreme case in terms of the violence it unleashed from the state. Still, the Kurdish case poses some very important questions for those who want to imagine an alternative future to capitalism, the nation-state, and the patriarchal family. Although short-lived, the Kurds' experiment with democratic autonomy in Bakur, the various institutions they created and the negotiations they engaged in energized Turkey as a whole. On the other hand, because there was always already the external threat of the state, the internal problems that emerged in the process of self-governance remain undebated. Most importantly, the Kurdish case obliges us to rethink the issue of law and violence and how new worlds can be created as well as defended.

References

Öcalan, A., & Happel, K. (2007). *Prison writings: the roots of civilization*. London: Pluto Press.
Üstündağ, N. (2017). Bakur rising: democratic autonomy in kurdistan. *Roar Magazine*, 6. https://
    roarmag.org/magazine/democratic-autonomy-municipalism-kurdistan/. Accessed 10 Dec 2017.

Author Biographies

Nazan Üstündağ received her Ph.D. from the sociology department at Indiana University Bloomington in 2005. Since then she has been an Assistant Professor at Boğaziçi University, Department of Sociology. Currently, she is associated with the Institute for Research Against Anti-semitism in TU Berlin through a scholarship by the Rosa Luxembourg Foundation given to academics at risk. Üstündağ's dissertation concerned the different form of subjectivities and belongings of rural-to-urban women in Istanbul and the life stories they craft in the intersection between the violence of the state, capital and patriarchy. Aside from writing on urban belongings in the era of neoliberalism, Üstündağ wrote extensively on social policy, gendered subjectivities and state violence in Kurdistan in different journals. Üstündağ has also worked as a columnist in the journal Nokta and the newspaper Özgür Gündem and her opinion pieces appeared in web-sites such as Bianet, T24 and Jadaliyya. Üstündağ also conducted research in Argentine, Iraq and Syria. Most recently, she is finishing a book on the cosmology of the Kurdish Movement based on three women figures; the mother, the politician and the guerrilla.

Güney Yıldız is a broadcast journalist with the BBC World Service where he covers international news and current affairs, specializing in Turkey and the Kurds. He has published articles and provided expert opinion on Turkey and the Kurds for various BBC television, radio and online programs. Previously, he worked for the BBC's Turkish Service and for the Turkish Daily News, the country's only English-language daily at the time. He completed his master's degree in politics and communication at the London School of Economics following his undergraduate degree in philosophy at Middle East Technical University, Ankara.

The Armenian Genocide

Lerna Ekmekçioğlu and interviewed by Seda Altuğ

Abstract From very early on the Turkish Republic's attitude toward minorities has been paradoxical. On the one hand, the legal system wants to assimilate them. For example, in 1926 the state forced minority leaders to stop using their canonical and traditional laws in matters of family law. In 1934, the state required that every Turkish citizen receive a Turkish-language last name. Had the state conceived Turkishness as a supraethnic, suprareligious identity somewhat like American identity, this might not have been a problem. In other words, these assimilationist measures are not oppressive per se; but because the same state that forced minorities to identify as Turks has at the same time been treating them as non-Turks in many aspects of their life, these assimilationist policies are discriminatory. For Armenians in Turkey, this is doubly complex: they are genocide survivors who have remained in the unapologetic perpetrators' state, living among a people who clearly did not want continued Armenian presence in their purportedly new country, but in any case forced down the generations to identify as Turks. This is a dizzying process, one so fascinating that I have devoted a decade of exploration to it, focusing in particular on its initial manifestations in the 1920s.

Keywords Armenian Genocide · Minorities · Turkey

As a member of a group whose history has been institutionally denied and silenced, how did you learn about your family history, your local history?

I struggle to find the right words to describe what it was like growing up in the Turkey of the 1980s and 1990s as an Armenian girl. "Weird" probably encapsulates

L. Ekmekçioğlu (✉)
Massachusetts Institute of Technology (MIT), Cambridge, USA
e-mail: lerna@mit.edu

S. Altuğ
Boğaziçi University, Istanbul, Turkey
e-mail: seda.altug@boun.edu.tr

© Springer International Publishing AG, part of Springer Nature 2019
E. Özyürek et al. (eds.), *Authoritarianism and Resistance in Turkey*,
https://doi.org/10.1007/978-3-319-76705-5_17

169

it. On the one hand, I was part of the whole. As we know, there is no visible "racial" or "genetic" difference between Armenians and Turks; I look perfectly like both a Turk and an Armenian. My Turkish is excellent; technically, it is my mother tongue, as my mother who is half Armenian and half Greek does not know Armenian. My last name ends with-*oğlu*, meaning "the son of" in Turkish, a common way of ending last names in Turkey. During the first five years of my school life I was expected to—and did—yell out loud that I was a Turk and that I would devote my whole being to "the existence of the Turks." This was the "Student Oath" that, like every Turkish primary school student, I was required to recite every morning at school. Together with my classmates we would stand facing the teacher and the picture of Mustafa Kemal Atatürk behind her. This requirement remained in effect from 1933 to 2013. But I knew I was not one of "them." My first name was not Turkish, and I attended an Armenian school where by law and regulation only Armenians can attend. I knew that I was an outsider of some sort, and that I should be scared of some of "them". "We" had to be cautious at all times.

I grew up in an educated, left-leaning, nonreligious family whose roots are in Anatolia. Three of my grandparents are descendants of the survivors of the 1915 Armenian Genocide. I learned about their story as a little girl, but I cannot recollect what triggered me to ask about it. I remember that in early middle school I sat down with my father and asked him to tell me about our family history. My father's extended family, a large family from Adıyaman, had always talked about their past during family gatherings, and what happened in 1915 was a regular topic of conversation even during religious holidays. My grandfather wrote his memoirs, which remain unpublished, although I am sure we will find a way of publishing them sometime in the future.

The relationship of my mother's side to their own past, however, has been very different. They don't talk about it. The discrepancy between the two sides as to what they "do" with the family past motivated me in college to interview the eldest family member on my mother's side. I wanted to learn more about my maternal grandfather's side, a family from Tarsus and Mersin that was brutally dispersed during the genocide. My mother either did not know about it or did not tell us. Except for one story, a very short one, one that always, always brought tears to everyone's eyes. This is how my mother told me the story: "They were on the train. They were being deported out of their city." To Aleppo, I assume. "And in one of the stations they sent their little boy to buy bread for the family. But they," the Turks, "started the train as soon as people sent their relatives to buy stuff. Then the train left for the next station. They lost the little boy forever."

This story and others like it here and there made me an Armenian. But because we could talk about them neither in public nor with most of our non-Armenian friends, I am a *Turkish* Armenian. I, like all other Turkish Armenian children, learned to strategize very early on. We had to grasp what to reveal, how much to reveal, how to judge people, and whom to trust. Because the broader public remained hostile to Armenians as a group and had no interest in their stories or history, we Armenians closed in on ourselves.

How did you engage with the official history curriculum during your secondary school education?

I went to Armenian primary, middle, and high schools. Only Armenian students are legally allowed to attend those schools, and the principal and most teachers are Armenian. Historically, the Turkish state has played close attention to the teaching of history. In minority schools, subjects such as history, geography, and Turkish language and literature can only be taught by Turkish teachers who do not belong to minority communities. This means that these teachers are Muslims and quite likely ethnically Turkish. The school vice-principals also had to be ethnically Turkish Turks. All these Turkish teachers were appointed centrally by the Ministry of Education. The vice-principal was seen and expected to function as the eye of the Turkish state inside the minority school, which is, to this day, perceived as a space that opposes the ideals and ideology of the Turkish state, a place where children are raised to be fifth columns. It is illegal to teach Armenian, Greek, Jewish, or any other kind of history but Turkish history. The history textbooks are prepared centrally by the Ministry of Education and are strictly governed.

In general, Turkish history books claim that Armenians are the enemies of Turks, and that they massacred Turks during World War I. This was the part that was so difficult for me to take, because from very, very early on I knew—I don't even know how—that it was a lie. I am sure everyone in my class felt the same way. Some of our history teachers skipped those pages, for which I felt grateful, because it meant that they sided with us against the fabrications of the state. But some history teachers insisted on teaching us that Armenians in the past did not behave well. We had to endure those lessons. I guess all these "weird" processes influenced my decision to become a historian and to study the history of the Turkish Armenian community in its formative years—in the immediate aftermath of the genocide and in the first decade of the Turkish Republic. When I arrived at New York University to do a my PhD in history, I knew next to nothing about Armenian history. But I did know a lot about Turkish history, at least its official version. It took me years to unlearn the Turkish state narrative and to learn the history of Armenians and Turks and Kurds.

Would you be able to single out a period which you think has been formative in your personal history? And would you be able to generalize your time cycle to that of any educated Armenian woman? If not, should we qualify it according to class, place of origin, or time of migration to Istanbul?

I came of age in the late 1980s and 1990s. When I began college in the mid-1990s it was a time of political, social, and cultural changes in Turkey. What proved important for my trajectory was the fact that the broader Turkish public was becoming increasingly familiar with the minorities, their past as well as their present. If this was partially a consequence of larger political transformations such as Turkey's accession process for EU membership, another reason for this heightening of awareness was the active work of certain new minority institutions. Aras Publishing House, for instance, began translating Armenian literature and scholarly works into Turkish. The commencement of the *Agos* weekly was an important historical landmark because this Armenian periodical included more Turkish-language pages than Armenian. Through my father I knew the editors and translators in these types of organizations.

During my years at Boğaziçi University I was a member of the university's folklore club which made a point of performing folk dances of Kurds, Armenians, Turks, Bulgarians, and all others who shared the geography that is today called Turkey. I also found feminists on campus and became active in their clubs. Soon enough, together with my Armenian women friends at Boğaziçi we formed an Armenian women's feminist group and began studying the history of Armenian women. We wrote an article about an important Armenian feminist, Hayganush Mark, and won third prize in a Turkey-wide competition of history writing among university students. It was our professors in Boğaziçi's sociology department who alerted us that we could pursue this topic as an academic study. These college years were formative for me.

Does the term *minority* signify a difference from the (religious) majority in terms of legal status? What are the basic rights that accrue from minority status in Turkey?

Yes, the term minority signifies a legal difference from the majority. In Turkey, from an official standpoint, only religious minorities exist, and they have some extra rights that stem from their legal status as minorities. For example, they have the right to operate their own religious and educational institutions and charitable organizations. These are rights that the 1923 Lausanne Treaty bestowed upon non-Muslims in Turkey. The treaty recognizes "non-Muslim nationals of Turkey" without specifying any group. But because in the Ottoman Empire it was Armenians, Greeks, and Jews who had been the major non-Muslim communities, in the Turkish Republic, too, *minority* had largely come to refer to these specific groups. We should note that the Lausanne Treaty had given minorities many additional rights, but the Turkish Republic breached the treaty terms and reduced minority rights to a bare minimum. Moreover, the treaty also states that minorities are full Turkish citizens and therefore cannot be discriminated against. But this has not been the case. From its very inception, the Republic of Turkey treated its non-Muslims as second- or even third-class citizens. But being an historian, I do not think that you can even begin to understand any of these processes without having a basic understanding of the *longue durée* of history behind them.

Please do tell the history then. I was also going to ask about the role of the Armenian Genocide on dispossession and the ruining of Armenians and other Christian survivors in Turkey. Did a similar process take place for non-Armenian religious minorities as well?

Let me give some historical background so that we can better locate the question of the minorities. The Ottoman Empire joined World War I alongside Germany and Austria-Hungary against the Allied Powers of Britain, France, and Russia. During the war, the Ottoman government, led by three Young Turk pashas—Enver, Talât, and Cemal—decided that Armenians posed a security threat on the borderland that separated Ottoman territory from that of the Russians. That geographical region is called the Armenian Plateau. Armenians are indigenous to that land and consider it the western parts of their historic homeland. Since the 15th century, Armenian territory has been divided between the Russian, Ottoman, and Iranian empires. During the Great War, the Young Turk government decided to eliminate the potential Armenian security threat by eliminating the Armenians, reducing their number to a bare minimum not just in what we today call Eastern Anatolia but also in the western parts of Asia Minor. About a million Armenians perished at the hands of their Ottoman government and their Kurdish, Turkish, Circassian, and other Muslim neighbors. Together, these massacres, abductions of women and children, and forcible conversion to Islam are called the Armenian Genocide, which began in April 1915 and continued, on and off, until 1922 or 1923.

Ottomans emerged from World War I defeated, humiliated, and demoralized. The reigning triumvirate escaped the country. The Allies began occupying different parts of Anatolia and the Ottoman capital of Constantinople. The Allies did this in other defeated countries as well. They justified their occupation by the need to punish the Ottoman Empire for what it had done to its own Armenian population during the war. The leadership of surviving Armenians, like the Greeks in Istanbul, supported the Allies' plans. With the 1920 Treaty of Sèvres, the Ottoman government agreed to the partitioning of Anatolia between Greek, Armenian, Turkish, and potentially Kurdish autonomous or independent states, as well as between "spheres of influence" for the different Western powers. But another group of Ottoman Muslims, organized under the leadership of Mustafa Kemal (later, Atatürk) waged a resistance movement against this plan. From 1919 to late 1922 they pursued a military resistance that came to be known as the Turkish War of Independence. Ottoman non-Muslims were not allowed to participate in this struggle, because it was assumed that they would all betray the cause. The Kemalist movement emerged successful and forced the Allies to renegotiate the Sèvres peace treaty, this time with more favorable terms for the Turks, who negated the partitioning of Anatolia.

Signed between the Ankara government and the Allied Powers of World War I, the 1923 Treaty of Lausanne can be considered as the birth certificate of modern Turkey as we know it today. With this treaty, the international community recognized the Ankara government's sovereignty. This document authorized the 1923 Greek-Turkish Exchange of Populations. About a million Greek Orthodox citizens of Turkey left for Greece, and about 400,000 Muslim Turkish citizens of Greece left for Turkey. This was a forcible exchange; people did not have a say as to which side of the Aegean they wanted to live. The reigning mentality of the time, which was shared by both Great Powers and the Turkish and Greek prime ministers, was that if these people remained together, future violence would unfold and that it would not be possible for these groups to cohabit peacefully. Only the Greeks of Istanbul and the Muslims of Eastern Thrace were exempted from the population exchange. The Turkish government also wanted to exchange the remaining Armenians, but no country was found to exchange them with. The remaining

Armenians, along with the remaining Greeks and the Jews, were recognized by the Lausanne Treaty as minorities. But neither the state nor the majority Muslim population liked this term, which was in fact forced upon the Turkish delegation at the Lausanne Conference. Given the history of the Ottoman Empire and how it had ended, in the Turkish psyche minority still meant treacherous people and fifth columns, extensions of the enemy within.

Do we have any official census figures—from state or religious authorities—concerning the religious origins of Turkish citizens? Are they publicly shared or kept secret? What does this tell us about the minority regime in Turkey?

In 2013, a case involving a Turkish citizen who claimed to have Armenian roots revealed to the public what we, Armenians, have always suspected: minorities have special codes in the Turkish registries, but they are kept secret. From 1923 onward, the state bureaucracy has secretly coded Greeks as "1," Armenians as "2," and Jews as "3." Although these numbers are not written anywhere on Turkish IDs or passports, the Turkish population registry records them and transfers them to each new generation. These codes enable the state to differentiate between its citizens both legally and illegally. On the one hand, it provides proof of minority status which then entitles you to certain rights—if you do not have the right code, for example, you cannot go to the minority school that corresponds to your origins. On the other hand, these codes are used to discriminate against minorities in hiring, promotion, and receipt of various public services. In the end, what the existence of the code tells us is that the state is not religion-blind and does not wish to be so.

What does this reveal about the oft-praised state of Turkish secularism?

Historically, secularism in Turkey never meant state neutrality toward religion. Given the conditions of its birth in the early 1920s, the idea of *laïcité* in Turkey is related to the idea and ideal that the *nation* be independent and free. That nation is conceived as Muslim, ideally Turkish, but not necessarily. Secularism is also connected to being Westernized. Being Western-like means, somewhat ironically, being free from Western, imperial interference and being able to exercise sovereignty. Secularism is also conceived as the opposite of the Ottoman Empire's Islamism and multiethnicity. Minorities are non-Muslims. They are evocative of the Ottoman-era multi-confessionalism and are therefore seen as an extension of the West and its desire to intervene in the domestic affairs of the Turkish state. Minorities are therefore seen as the ultimate others of the Turkish nation. The secret state coding of minorities was further proof of this, serving only to add weight to the countless other proofs we already had.

What are the tools and institutions through which minority groups are assimilated into the hegemonic social order in Turkey? How do violence and memories of violence play out into this?

As I have shown in my work, from very early on the Turkish Republic's attitude toward minorities has been paradoxical. On the one hand, the legal system wants to assimilate them. For example, in 1926 the state forced minority leaders to stop using their canonical and traditional laws in matters of family law. In 1934, the state required that every Turkish citizen receive a Turkish-language last name. Minority students were expected to recite the Student Oath I mentioned before, the one that requires students to yell out that they are "Turks." Had the state conceived Turkishness as a supraethnic, suprareligious identity somewhat like American identity, this might not have been a problem. In other words, these assimilationist measures are not oppressive per se; but because the same state that forced minorities to identify as Turks has at the same time been treating them as non-Turks in many aspects of their life, these assimilationist policies are discriminatory. For Armenians in Turkey, this is doubly complex: they are genocide survivors who have remained in the unapologetic perpetrators' state, living among a people who clearly did not want continued Armenian presence in their purportedly new country, but in any case forced down the generations to identify as Turks. This is a dizzying process, one so fascinating that I have devoted a decade of exploration to it, focusing in particular on its initial manifestations in the 1920s.

Very briefly, might we argue that the Turkish state attempted to colonize the minority psyche? Might there be a process of self-orientalization present among minorities?

I don't think it would be wrong to say that the Turkish state tried to colonize the minority psyche. Of course, they would not use the term *colonize*, but they certainly tried to neutralize the resistant voice and posture of the minorities by punishing those who opposed their discriminatory practices. The latest example of this is the 2007 assassination of Hrant Dink, the editor-in-chief of the Armenian weekly, *Agos*. Hrant Dink was shot dead in front of his office in broad daylight by a Turkish nationalist. We know that the deep state was involved in the organization of this crime, which to this day remains essentially unpunished. Minorities are expected to be grateful, uncomplaining members of society who make themselves useful to the state and to society without demanding fair treatment in return.

What is the state of minority studies in Turkey? How has it changed? Are there any Armenian, Christian, or Alevi studies departments in the universities? Are there any Armenian secondary school teachers or university social science professors in Turkey?

Although minority studies do not exist in Turkey as a specific field of study, over the past 20 years we have observed an upsurge in the study of non-Muslims and non-Turks from historical, political, and sociological perspectives. Rıfat Bali and Rıdvan Akar are the first names that come to mind when I think of this first wave. When I was in high school, my father would buy their books and bring them home for us to read. From the early 1990s onward, publishing houses—most importantly Belge Press—began translating many works, making them available to the Turkish-reading public: English and French works on the Armenian Genocide, the works of Vahakn Dadrian and Yves Ternon, for example. Many Kurdish presses—

Peri Press is one—began publishing work on Armenians and Kurds whose content diverged from the official Turkish narrative. Today, many scholars working in Turkish universities, especially the good ones in bigger cities, are doing research on minorities. While some of these studies inevitably fall into the trap of Turkish nationalism, others are quite free of nationalist baggage. Especially with regard to Armenian Genocide studies, we see a real interest in Turkey among Turkish historians. Another very encouraging development is the fact that more and more Turkish Armenians are studying their own history and are finding employment in Turkish universities as professors and lecturers. My hope is that this process will continue, and that Turkey as a state and a society will face its history directly, honestly, and responsibly (This interview was conducted in Spring 2015).

Author Biographies

Lerna Ekmekçioğlu is the McMillan-Stewart Associate Professor of History at the Massachusetts Institute of Technology, where she is also affiliated with the Women and Gender Studies Program. She specializes in Turkish and Armenian lands at the beginning of the 20th century. Her work focuses on minority-majority relationships and the ways in which gendered analytical lenses help us to better understand coexistence and conflict, including genocide, in the Middle East. She teaches courses on cultural pluralism, women and war, and global revolutions. Her first book, which came out in 2006, was an edited volume in Turkish titled *Bir Adalet Feryadı, Osmanlı'dan Cumhuriyet'e Beş Ermeni Feminist Yazar, 1862–1933* (A Cry for Justice: Five Armenian Feminist Writers from the Ottoman Empire to the Turkish Republic, 1862–1933). Her first monograph, *Recovering Armenia: The Limits of Belonging in Post-Genocide Turkey* (Stanford University Press, 2016), offers the first in-depth study of the aftermath of the 1915 Armenian Genocide and the Armenians who remained in Turkey. She is currently collaborating with Melissa Bilal on a project about the history of Armenian feminism. Titled *Feminism in Armenian*, the project has two legs: an interpretive anthology (book) and a digital archive.

Seda Altuğ is an assistant professor at the Atatürk Institute for Modern Turkish History at Boğaziçi University. She received her PhD from the Oriental Studies Department at Utrecht University in 2011. Her dissertation was an historical anthropology of sectarianism in Syria during the French Mandate. Her research interests include intercommunal relations, Modern Middle East history, the history of empire, and political economy.

Alevi Struggles

Besim Can Zırh and interviewed by Murat Es

Abstract The Alevis are a difficult group to define. The definition I prefer is that the Alevis form the second largest community of belief after the Sunni Muslims in Turkey. This definition involves a few linguistic acrobatics. First, it allows me to avoid employing the term *religion*, simply because the Alevis themselves prefer to use the word *belief*, usually defining Alevism as a *culture of belief*. Second, it points to the question of demographics by locating Alevism statistically after Sunnism in terms of sheer numbers, thus I don't need to struggle with the concept of *minority*.

Keywords Alevism · Turkey

Who are the Alevis? Can you briefly explain their belief systems?

The Alevis are a difficult group to define. The definition I prefer is that the Alevis form the second largest community of belief after the Sunni Muslims in Turkey. This definition involves a few linguistic acrobatics. First, it allows me to avoid employing the term *religion*, simply because the Alevis themselves prefer to use the word *belief*, usually defining Alevism as a *culture of belief*. Second, it points to the question of demographics by locating Alevism statistically after Sunnism in terms of sheer numbers, thus I don't need to struggle with the concept of *minority*. This term has negative connotations in Turkey due to the Treaty of Lausanne (1923), the peace treaty settling the conflict between the Ottoman Empire and the Allies of WWI, which defines minority status only in reference to religion, leaving minorities with a questionable relationship of belonging to the *nation-state*. It is for this reason that Alevis prefer not to be defined as a minority group. Finally, by emphasizing Sunnism as the largest belief group under Islam, it sidesteps the problem of posi-

B. C. Zırh (✉)
Middle East Technical University, Ankara, Turkey
e-mail: besimcan@metu.edu.tr

M. Es
Chinese University, Sha Tin, Hong Kong
e-mail: murates@cuhk.edu.hk

© Springer International Publishing AG, part of Springer Nature 2019   177
E. Özyürek et al. (eds.), *Authoritarianism and Resistance in Turkey*,
https://doi.org/10.1007/978-3-319-76705-5_18

tioning Alevism exclusively in Islamic terms. If we don't approach the category of religion as homogenous and monolithic, there is no need to discuss Alevism specifically in relation to its location within this metacategory. Why do I need these linguistic acrobatics? Because each of these issues serves as fertile ground for polemical questions: Is Alevism a (distinct) religion (from Islam)? If so, should we consider Alevism outside of Islam, non-Islamic, against Islam, or as a *religious minority* in Turkey? These questions are not new, but have gained new prominence in the wake of the Alevi revival that began in the early 1990s.

What makes Alevism a particular belief system is another challenging question and could be answered at two levels. First, certain questions in Alevism are understood completely differently than they are in Sunnism; such as how the cosmic relationship between humans and the creator is portrayed, or how the history of Islam, especially the early years, is narrated. For example, Alevis specifically emphasize the constitutive role of Ali, the Prophet's cousin and son-in-law, for Islam. Their understanding of Ali is different than the way he is represented in Sunnism. To emphasize this difference, Alevis often say, "Our Ali is different than theirs." Alevis recognize Ali, Muhammad, his daughter and Ali's wife Fatma, together with their children Hasan and Hüseyin, as the members of the Prophet's household (*Ahl al-Bayt*). The Prophet's descendants are considered to be the only legitimate source of spiritual charisma, and Alevis differentiate their own interpretation of Islam from that of Sunnism by referring to the tragic events of Karbala, where the Prophet's grandson Hüseyin was killed by an army sent by the caliph Yazid. This event constituted the break between Sunni and Shi'i Islamic traditions. Alevis believe that their spiritual leaders (*dedes*) have directly descended from this holy family. In this sense, Ali is elevated to a higher level of sanctity than in Sunnism, and his name is mentioned along with God (*Hak*) and the Prophet (*Muhammed*). This is why the number three has a sacred meaning for Alevis and is reflected in their daily and spiritual practices as triplication.

It is commonly accepted that there are five basic pillars of Islam, which are: *shahadah* (publicly recognizing that there is no God but Allah, and Mohammad is his messenger), *salat* (ritual prayer five times a day), *zakat* (alms-giving), *sawm* (fasting as an act of self-control during Ramadan), and *hajj* (pilgrimage to Mecca). When Westerners first encountered the Alevis of Anatolia in the early 20th century, they attempted to understand their culture of belief in reference to this normative framework, but doing this would be confusing. Nearly a century later, when Martin Sökefeld met Alevis in his neighborhood in Hamburg, he also had this confusion about how to define Alevism.[1] According to this framework it is hard to accept Alevis as Muslims simply by virtue of the fact that of the five pillars, they only observe the first one, shahadah. Alevis do not deny the prophecy of Muhammad, but they incorporate Ali into the formulation of shahadah. In other words, they triangulate the duality of the heavenly creator and his earthly representative with the formula of Hak-Muhammad-Ali, which used to be understood by Western scholars in reference to the Christian trinity, and thus could also be perceived by Sunnis as blasphemy. Sökefeld therefore argues that Alevis have been defined *negatively* on the basis of who they are not, rather than who they are. But if you talk to Alevi spiritual leaders from a traditional background, they would tell you that Alevism is actually the "true essence" of Islam, and that Alevis actually do observe the five pillars, just not in the formalistic manner that Sunnis do.

How are different definitions of Alevism used?

This second part of your question concerns operationalization: how should we define Alevism so that we can study it anthropologically? First, we need to differentiate the social and cultural domains from the spiritual ones. Yes, in a traditional rural setting, you might be born into an Alevi family, and that makes you a member of that specific village community. However, this blood tie does not guarantee your membership in the congregation in which Alevism may be spiritually practiced. To be able to access the core rituals of Alevism, you need to be initiated through a special ceremony, and you must swear an oath that you are not going to reveal the secrets of your community to outsiders. After going through the initiation ceremony, which is metaphorically described as "dying before dying," individuals may participate in Alevi rituals open only to congregation members.

This aspect is important in understanding the social organization of Alevism. In principle, each of these congregations living in their villages are subjected to the leadership of a specific *dede*, who in turn must be affiliated with a spiritual center or hearth (*ocak*). This organizational system is expressed as "hand-to-hand, hand-to-God," and is presented as a sine qua non, being built into the sociospiritual networks through which the practice of Alevism becomes possible. Under the guidance of these spiritual leaders, Alevis practice their rituals known as *cem*. During cem ceremonies Alevis deal with the social or moral problems of their communities.

Finally, the performative components of Alevism are important. Briefly, *saz* (music), *söz* (hymns), and *semah* (ritual dance) play very critical roles in passing not only spiritual creeds but also social and moral codes from one generation to another. This is facilitated by the fact that all of these components can also be performed during nonspiritual occasions such as weddings or communal meetings. Through the course of internal- and later external migration processes, the sociospiritual organization of Alevism was heavily damaged, but cultural aspects were able to survive rapid urbanization.

What is the size of Turkey's Alevi population?

The fact that a group with such a large population is struggling so hard to attain official recognition might be surprising to those who are unfamiliar with Turkey. This situation is primarily related to the way in which national identity is formulated in modern Turkey. In principle, the constitution states that "anyone who is attached to the Turkish state with the bonds of citizenship is Turkish," implying that Turkishness is not ethnically exclusive, but civilly inclusive. It is also the case that there are some other legal articles prohibiting discrimination on the grounds of "language, race, color, language, gender, political thought, philosophical belief, religion, sect belief, et cetera" (Article 10 of the Turkish constitution). Nevertheless, none of these de jure constraints are sufficient to prevent de facto discrimination. The lack of data on the size of the Alevi population is related to this problem. There are some reliable estimates. Just to illustrate, the Alevi population has been cited as "at least 12 million" (EC, 1998, p. 20) and "12–20 million" (EC, 2004, p. 44) in European Commission progress reports on Turkey's accession, which means that 15–20% of the Turkish population is composed of Alevis.

What can you say about the regional distribution, economic status, and ethnic composition of Alevis in Turkey?

Where Alevis live in Turkey is another critical question because we are able to delineate certain zones thanks to historical and modern studies.[2] This question is also important because we need to be able to talk about the ethnolinguistic, traditional, and regional differentiations that exist within the category of *Alevi*, which functions as a blanket term. In his attempt to map Alevis in Turkey, David Shankland admits that drawing such maps, especially for regions like Anatolia, is very controversial, but that we may make some generalizations. First, Alevi populations have historically been concentrated in mountainous and relatively inaccessible parts of Anatolia. They are absent in the regions dominated by Kurdish-speaking Sunni populations. In that sense, Alevi regions in eastern Anatolia constitute a kind of buffer zone between the Turkish-speaking and Kurdish-speaking Sunni provinces of the country. Second, they are located densely in the east and in much more scattered clusters in the western parts of the country. Finally, in addition to this historical distribution, we need to take into consideration a modern development related to internal and external migration waves. Since the 1950s, Alevism has become an urban phenomenon due to the more generalized of rapid urbanization in Turkey. Because of their concentration in economically underdeveloped parts of the country, Alevis have participated heavily in the waves of international migration since the 1960s.

Defining Alevism—or *Aleviness*—has been a politically contentious matter, particularly given its relationship to Islam. Whether Alevism is a branch of Islam or a religion by itself is a hotly debated topic. What is the historical background of this debate and what are its contemporary political implications?

Attempts to define Alevism gained momentum in the wake of the Alevi revival in the late 1980s when Alevis started making demands as redress for their grievances and thereby articulating their own culture of belief publicly. In the wake of this revival, the question of definition arose as a critical dimension of formulating Alevi demands on two main fronts: first against the Turkish state and the Kurdish movement which were attempting to manipulate the Alevi revival, and second within their own belief community as a way to control the claim for representation. Three main internal fault lines can be defined in relation to the question of definition. At the beginning of the revival, some argued that Alevism should be considered an ethnically Turkic culture of belief since its ritual language is Turkish, something which is actually not true for Kurdish- and Zazaki-speaking Alevis. The second fault line arose during the same period, but was then forgotten until the initiation of the AKP's "Democratic Openings" in 2007. This ideological schism concerns the theological origin of Alevism; namely, whether Alevism should be considered within the framework of Islam or not. The final fault line became apparent again during the same period in parallel to what we could call the Dersim revival. Alevis from the Dersim region began organizing in response to the question of definition by differentiating their particular understanding of Alevism both from Turkish-speaking and Kurdish-speaking traditional Alevism with reference to different ritual practices and cosmological interpretations.

This is a cacophonic and uneasy topography of (self-)designations. One of my research participants from Berlin once described this situation as "mental/intellectual depression," because a consensus seemed to be out of reach. I am neither a theologian nor a historian, yet I must deal with these questions, because how you define Alevism reveals what sort of political stance you will take in response to Alevi demands. In many cases, this question of definition is imposed by actors who may or may not be Alevi, but who are most assuredly pursuing certain political agendas. Instead of playing this game of definitions, we should focus on what Alevis want, because none of their demands are related to the question of definition.

Alevi representatives are aware of this situation and thus usually don't like to address what they feel to be manipulative questions. For instance, in the UK, the England Alevi Cultural Centre formulate their position by conceptualizing Alevism as a "superordinate identity" for Alevis coming from different ethnolinguistic backgrounds. Instead of deepening already-existing tensions among Kurdish-speaking Alevis and the Kurdish movement in the context of migration to London, they seek to establish a bridge between Alevi and Kurdish associations by focusing on demands within the framework of "democracy for all." This is also the case for the Confederation for Alevi Unions in Europe, the umbrella organization established during the early 2000s to coordinate political campaigns organized by Alevi federations in 11 European countries. Especially during the second half of the 2000s, the federation in Germany made a great effort to establish a common platform for all those who have suffered human rights violations in Turkey and had campaigned for democratization. The Union of Democratic Forces (*Demokratik Güçler Birliği*) was established in February 2013 as the first umbrella platform organization of its kind, bringing 18 different organizations together—not only Alevis and Kurds, but also Armenians, Assyrians, and Yezidis, around the demand for democratization.

It is interesting to note that this new initiative in Europe has very recently called on its members and supporters to vote for the HDP in the general elections of 2015. The HDP was established by the Kurdish movement as part of a new political strategy to reach out to non-Kurdish voters in Turkey. The party challenged a three-decade-old 10% electoral threshold. Considering the historical distance between Turkish- and Kurdish-speaking Alevis and Sunni Kurds, it seems to me that another threshold, which was wider and deeper, had already been crossed with this initiative. The short-lived results, due to the repeated elections in November 2015, were very promising: the HDP won 20.28% of overseas votes and gained 13% of the

votes in Turkey to become the second most successful political party among overseas voters after the ruling AKP party. It is also important to note that three representatives of the Alevi movement were nominated and elected to parliament as a
result of this collaboration. I should mention that these three names are not the only
Alevis nominated by the party. Some other well-known Alevi candidates ran in this
election, but presented themselves through the vector of their adherence to various
political agendas, not their Alevism. In other words, they are candidates with an
Alevi background, but do not run on platforms that represent Alevi demands.

This level of nuance is critical for understanding the historical significance of
this collaboration. For decades, Alevis strongly supported the Kemalist secularist
party, the CHP. This political affinity was established in the wake of the 1960
military coup in opposition to the rise of political Islamism. In this sense, Alevis
used to perceive the CHP as the only channel through which they could participate
in parliamentary politics in Turkey. Following the general elections in 2002, certain
representatives of the Alevi movement in both Turkey and Europe tried to establish
an organic link with the CHP. Their logic was very simple: if Alevis are the main
supporters of the CHP, and if they are the representatives of Alevis, then the party
should allocate a quota for the Alevi movement. None of their attempts were
successful; while Alevi areas remained the natural backyard of the party, Alevi
representatives were not nominated from electable polling districts. This was the
main political dilemma for Alevis. They even attempted to establish a new umbrella
political party, the Equality and Democracy Party (*Eşitlik ve Demokrasi Partisi*), in
2010 to avoid getting stuck with the CHP. This project also failed but left a very
critical legacy behind, especially if you consider similarities between the Equality
and Democracy Party and the HDP's party emblems. In this sense, I consider HDP
as a strategic political collaboration designed to overcome another historical hurdle,
between Kurds and Alevis, in Turkey.

What are ideological, institutional, and doctrinal differences between various Alevi communities and Alevist organizations?

Alevis began organizing around basic social needs when they first migrated to cities
starting from the 1950s. Associations established on the basis of home-village
social networks were the main organizational form in this period. These initial
associations functioned as a bridge between newly emerging Alevi neighborhoods
in the cities and Alevi villages in Anatolia, and thus were the carriers of Alevism as
a culture in the cities. As an example, let's say I am an Alevi immigrant in a large
city like Istanbul. To solve my accommodation problem, I need to squat on a piece
of public land at the urban periphery due to the housing shortage. To be able to this,
I need to keep company with my fellow villagers because this is the only asset that I
can mobilize. So, now I have a safe haven in this strange and possibly hostile urban
landscape, and as a community, we can start bringing in some more people from
our village. When we organize marriage ceremonies, communal gatherings such as
picnics, or cultural events to celebrate our common village identity, we perform
Alevism as a culture. If there is need, we can invite our spiritual leaders from our

village to conduct rituals in our neighborhood. If we lose a community member, we can cover certain expenses for the family, such as sending the funeral back to the village through mutual aid already institutionalized in the form of a funeral fund. In other words, these neighborhoods spontaneously became something like Alevi parishes. It is also important to note that these neighborhoods in Ankara, Istanbul, and Izmir were the main locations of the Gezi Park protests in 2013.

We need to understand variations in organizational forms on two main levels. First, the form and scope of organization, whether it is at the level of a home-village, a particular region (Dersim or Kızılırmak), a specific locality (saintly tombs), or on a national scale (Pir Sultan Abdal Cultural association) or umbrella organizations (the Alevi Bektashi Federation). Second, the orientation of the organization, namely how they understand Alevism and what they do to advocate Alevi demands. This is a bit of a complex issue. Let me try to explain.

The Council of Alevi Bektashi Representatives (*Alevi Bektaşi Temsilciler Meclisi*) was established as an umbrella organization to coordinate between different forms of Alevi organizations which mushroomed in the wake of the Sivas massacre of 1993, when 35 participants at an Alevi festival were killed by a mob. Later, the council became the Alevi Bektashi Federation (*Alevi Bektaşi Federasyonu*), representing nearly 200 Alevi organizations across Turkey, including nearly all forms of the organizations mentioned above. However, this does not mean that all member organizations share a similar understanding of Alevism, particularly in reference to its definition. What brings them under the same roof is the very basic demand for the "official recognition of Alevism," which we will discuss in a moment.

Another main organizational body is the Cem Foundation, which was established on the basis of the personal charisma of İzzettin Doğan in 1995. Mr. Doğan comes from a *dede* family, meaning he is a spiritual leader although he is not an active *dede*. He is a professor of law, which means that he has a secular charisma as well. His position within the Alevi movement has always been controversial, because according to the Alevi Bektashi Federation, his understanding of Alevism is in line with that of the Turkish state, and since the early 1990s he has not shied away from cooperating, both overtly and covertly, with various governments. Even the name of this organization, Cem, actually does not stand for the Alevi ceremony of cem, but is an acronym for the Republican Educational and Cultural Center (*Cumhuriyetçi Eğitim ve Kültür Merkezi*), indicating his conformist stance.

What can you tell us about Alevis' relationship to their Sunni compatriots, civil society, political parties, and state agencies? The AKP has attempted an "Alevi Opening" with no substantial policy outcomes regarding Alevi claims for recognition and equal citizenship rights. What are the most urgent demands by Alevi groups of the government?

These are not easy questions to answer, because any possible answer depends on whose point of view you adopt. First, on the question of how Alevis define *Sunnis*: is it a homogenous category with clear-cut boundaries? This is probably true, especially for Alevis coming from rural areas where their we-group identity has been historically and traumatically shaped by a sharp dichotomy against Sunnism. This is also true for Sunnis. However, Alevis, who socialize in urban settings, do not understand *Sunnism* as a homogenous category. *Their Sunnis* are those who engage with rightist, conservative, Islamist politics, and hold discriminatory attitudes toward Alevis. But they also know that there are *other Sunnis*, those who do not come from an Alevi background but at the same time do not share the same worldview with conservatively politicized Sunnis. A set of concepts including those of *intellectual, democrat, modern* have been employed to differentiate non-conservative Sunnis from right-wing Islamist Sunnis. This is a kind of buffer zone between Alevism and Sunnism that I have come to understand during my field research. I do not come from an Alevi background and whenever I was asked, "Where do you come from," I knew that this was a key question that would inevitably reveal my Sunni-ness. This was not something I tried to conceal, yet it was also not a category I employed to define myself. In this sense, I preferred to define my researcher-self in the field as *non-Alevi*, and leave the rest to my respondents. I think this brief portrayal of my personal difficulty can be generalized as a response to your question. Alevis and Sunnis share an historically rooted hesitation toward contact with one another, and since Sunnis are the predominant group, Alevis have become obliged to take this sectarian distance.

It should also be mentioned that this distance has become narrower with the establishment of *cemevis*, either as places of worship or cultural centers. A new form of relationship between Alevis and Sunnis has developed, both in Turkey and abroad, in the context of migration. Cultural events like concerts, panel discussions, and rituals organized in these new institutions are open to anyone who wishes to participate, and Alevis are willing to host Sunnis who want to learn about Alevism. Through Alevi revival, Alevis have become visible in public life with their particular culture of belief, but this visibility is still contained within the framework of an ambiguous tolerance, and not that of official recognition.

There is a very critical paradox behind this deadlock. But before coming to this, I need to clarify the goal Alevis have been struggling toward. In my analysis of 22 key documents issued by the Alevi movement from 1990 to 2010, I have located six main demands: (1) the abolition of the *Diyanet* (Directorate of Religious Affairs), the state institution constitutionally tasked with providing religious guidance and services for the entire nation, yet which in practice only serves Sunni Muslims; (2) the abolition of compulsory religion courses at schools, which only cover Sunni Islam; (3) the official recognition of cemevis as places of worship; (4) the conversion of the Madımak Hotel, the site of the major Alevi massacre of 1993, into a museum; (5) a halt to construction of mosques in Alevi villages; and (6) the restitution of convents and lodges taken from Alevi and Bektaşi communities in 1925. I think that the recognition of cemevis as places of worship is the most critical of all these demands since it would bring about the official recognition of Alevism as a particular culture of belief. All the other demands could be achieved once this demand is met.

For this very reason, this demand is the most difficult one for the AKP government to deal with. As you mentioned, the AKP government initiated a new political process in 2007, known as *açılım* (opening), with a strong promise to open the Pandora's box of Turkey. The pretext for this restructuring was to establish reconciliation between disadvantaged communities and the Turkish political system. The Alevi and Kurdish questions, the most deep-seated problems, came to the fore during this process. The AKP commissioned Faruk Çelik, the minister of state and Dr. Necdet Subaşı, a coordinator, to organize seven key meetings to formalize the Alevi Opening. These meetings, which have come to be known as the Alevi Workshops, were important because the Turkish government for the first time officially engaged the question of Alevism. However, Alevi organizations were dissatisfied with the process and publicized their critiques on various platforms. Such criticisms were based on a perception that the government had taken it upon itself to define Alevism with a sweeping gesture, but without having been attentive to the specific Alevi demands.

What was the source of this distrust? I think it is related to the paradox I mentioned above. The openings were stillborn for several reasons. First of all, the AKP attempted to play a taboo-breaking role in the wake of the 2002 general election. This was partly a genuine attempt to cement emerging social and political coalitions around the demand for democratization, which was believed to be represented by the AKP. This coalition was critical for the AKP to secure its position against the military tutelage. However, we gradually realized that this taboo-breaking call for democratization had its limitations. The AKP began enjoying the comfort of having won a majority under the strong leadership of Recep Tayyip Erdoğan, who began emphasizing his "50%" electoral support as the only legitimate ground for his actions. In other words, the promise for democratic pluralism turned into a pure authoritarian majoritarianism. Second, the AKP presented each of these taboo issues as though they were peculiar to specific disadvantaged communities, not as part of a general problem of democratization, and attempted to solve by providing community-specific privileges. For instance, as part of the Kurdish Opening, they did not hesitate to establish the *TRT Kurdi*, a new Kurdish channel established under the national public broadcasting agency, but turned a deaf ear to Alevis who have been demanding equal access to the public broadcasting service. Third, the AKP preferred not to cooperate with disadvantaged communities in defining the key issues of this opening process. This approach inevitably created another, not military, but rather patronizing form of tutelage: "I know what is best for you and I will solve your problems without paying attention to how you define them." Finally, its conservative Islamic background naturally limited the AKP's stance in the case of Alevism. Just to explain this briefly, it is commonly believed by conservative Sunnis that Shi'ism, which is affiliated with Alevism, was born as a Jewish conspiracy to divide the *ummah*. From this perspective, as a similar "heretical" interpretation of Islam, Alevism can be seen as another manifestation of this historical conspiracy. In this sense, recognizing cemevis as places of worship is seen as something blasphemous that would create a schism within Islam. That is why during the Alevi Workshop meetings the meta-issue dominating all other issues was the question of definition. When he was explaining the scope of those meetings, the coordinator, Dr. Necdet Subaşı, said, "No one has asked these people [Alevis], 'Who are you?' for a thousand years." I think this was a very critical slip of the tongue explaining why the Alevi Opening concluded as another "Clopening." If you read the final report of these meetings, you immediately understand who it addresses. It is interesting to hear a kind of voice-over trying to persuade a theoretical "Sunni public" for whom the opening was actually being carried out.

What is the impact of Alevi diasporas on Alevis and Alevist struggles in Turkey?

Alevis started organizing in the context of migration as from the late 1960s, but I am hesitant to employ the concept of *diaspora* to portray Alevis in Europe until the beginning of the 2000s. This is because I understand their activities as having been much more about establishing and maintaining familial and communal networks in order to keep Alevism alive. Alevis did not even use the category of *Alevism* publicly until the late 1980s. Then, especially in the wake of the Sivas Massacre in 1993, they began organizing funding and awareness-raising campaigns in Europe. This situation has gradually changed, though. For instance, Alevis were recognized as a "non-Sunni Muslim minority" in the European Commission progress report on Turkey (EC, 2004, p. 44). Yes, this description was rescinded by EC reporters due to the reaction of the Turkish government and of Alevis in Turkey. Yet through this incident we realized that Alevis are very well organized in Europe, and their organization could be influential beyond national borders through the agency of national and supranational political institutions.

The Turkish state is not able, as a matter of fact, to restrain and monitor political activities in this newly emerging sociopolitical space. For this reason, an interesting discourse stigmatizing Alevis in Europe as a *diaspora* has developed so as to confine their possible influence over *domestic* Alevi issues. In Turkish, the term *diaspora* evokes negative and reactionary thoughts, simply because this concept has been associated with Armenian political and/or other violent anti-Turkish activities abroad since the early 1970s. For instance, at the very beginning of the Alevi Opening process, Reha Çamuroğlu, an historian and writer of Alevi background, and a member of parliament from the AKP overtly criticized the "Alevi diaspora" as malevolent because of their Marxist background. This was not an incidental label, and additional examples portraying Alevis in Europe as the poltergeist of the opening process were commonplace during this process.

This new discourse indicates that the AKP government understands the Alevi movement in Europe primarily as an issue of national security. One of the latest examples of this mentality became apparent during an official visit by Joachim Gauck, the President of Germany, to Turkey in April 2014. In his immediate and fiery response to Gauck's comment on the question of democracy in Turkey, Erdoğan accused the German president of backing a political plot against the unity of Turkey by supporting Alevis in Europe.[6]

This reaction undoubtedly sounds quite incomprehensible to those unfamiliar with the issue, and I think this incident is related to your question. When Alevis began to mobilize in Europe in the late 1980s, they immediately realized that the first thing to do was to define Alevism for new audiences—European societies—in a completely new context—European multiculturalism. In other words, Alevism's difference compared to Sunni Islam took on new meaning, especially when considered against the backdrop of the historical and modern reservations about Islam in Europe. It seems reasonable to argue that Alevis were motivated in this process to define Alevism as a culture of belief different to that of Islam. For instance, when they were preparing their application for the right to provide religion classes in public schools in Berlin, in order to make an effective claim, Alevis had to define Alevism as a religious system other than Islam. For this reason, the AKP considers this incident in Germany as malevolent simply because it has led to the definition of Alevism as a separate religion. In accordance with this understanding, the AKP government claims that there should be only one place of worship for all Muslims —the mosque— and if Alevis consider themselves Muslims, they should attend mosques. For the AKP, there is thus no need to recognize cemevis as places of worship for Alevis. But this is absurd, because historically most Alevis did not attend mosques.

In summary, by institutionalizing their organizations in the form of a transnational social movement, Alevis in Europe could achieve two important interrelated objectives. First, they could make themselves visible by defining Alevism as a particular culture of belief. Second, in so doing, they could become more sociopolitically influential in the context of Europe. By using this new context through the agency of the EU and the European Court of Human Rights, they could possibly transplant and support Alevi demands in Turkey.

References

European Commission (1999). Rapport regulier de la commission sur les progres accomplis par la Turquie sur la voie de l'adhesion [Regular report on Turkey's progress toward accession]. http://eur-lex.europa.eu/legal-content/FR/TXT/PDF/?uri=CELEX:51998DC0711&from=FR. Accessed 19 Nov 2017.

European Commission (2004). Regular report on Turkey's progress toward accession. http://www.europarl.europa.eu/meetdocs/2004_2009/documents/sec/com_sec(2004)1201_/com_sec(2004)1201_en.pdf. Accessed 19 Nov 2017.

Besim Can Zırh is an assistant professor in sociology at the Middle East Technical University, Ankara, where he also graduated with a B.A. in sociology in 2002 and an M.Sc. in political science in 2015. He received his Ph.D. in social anthropology from the University College London in 2012. His dissertation focused on the migration experiences and transnational networks of Alevis in the context of funerary practices. His multisite ethnographic fieldwork focused on Alevi organizations in Berlin, Cologne, London, and Oslo. His research interests include diaspora politics and home-town associations.

Murat Es is an assistant professor in geography and resource management at the Chinese University of Hong Kong. In 2012, he obtained his Ph.D. at the Department of Geography at the University of North Carolina, Chapel Hill. He also has a B.A. in history and an M.A. in sociology from Boğaziçi University.

Part VI
Human Rights

A Brief Overview of the Legal System in Turkey

İbrahim Kaboğlu and interviewed by Gaye Özpınar

Abstract A big part of rights violations arise from the neglect (omission) and/or intentional actions of government officials. Rights violations happen within the chain of command of the hierarchical administrative-political structure. Preparation and active investigation of cases are suspended; the hierarchical superiors protect their juniors with rhetoric and action; legal organs do not make clear decisions, and so on. In terms of the legal process, its glacial pace, the absence of legal enforcement organizations, outside pressure casting shadows of doubt on judicial independence, tendencies and practice that undermine judicial impartiality should be pointed out. Legal practitioners sometimes let nationalistic or moralistic judgments seep into their legal decisions over the central universality of human rights, which make these decisions more political rather than legal or judicial.

Keywords Turkey · Legal system · Justice

I would like to start with the concept of justice in Turkey. Two of the biggest centrist parties in history of Turkey have been the Justice Party (AP) and the Justice and Development Party (AKP), the latter having been in power for the past 15 years. The word justice ("adalet") is even a somewhat common first name for many people. At every demonstration we demand justice; it is the quintessential slogan. What is the justice issue for society in Turkey?

First of all, we need to question whether AKP is a centerist party. In European democratic standards, AKP is not a centerist party, and that fact has become quite clear recently. In fact, it could even be questioned whether AP was a centerist party. Its leader, during his tenure as Prime Minister in the 1970s, was quoted as saying:

İ. Kaboğlu (✉)
Faculty of Law, Marmara University, Istanbul, Turkey
e-mail: ibrahimkaboglu@yahoo.fr

G. Özpınar
Boston, MA, USA
e-mail: gaye.ozpinar@gmail.com

© Springer International Publishing AG, part of Springer Nature 2019 191
E. Özyürek et al. (eds.), *Authoritarianism and Resistance in Turkey*,
https://doi.org/10.1007/978-3-319-76705-5_19

"You can't make me say the rightwingers and nationalists are killing people"[1] and "the ban on communist parties is not a deficiency of democracy." We need to be cautious to call a party centrist when its leader made such statements. Moreover, a rhetoric built on such a political mentality would block justice from being carried out. AKP is built on a mentality that takes a narrow, sect-oriented view to shape society and thus can be qualified neither centrist nor democratic. Thus, the use of the word justice in its name is deceiving for us.

The name "adalet," meaning justice, is given as a personal name to both men and women in our society. Exploring the relationship this might have with the quest for justice might be interesting... But the fact is justice, whether used by a real person or a corporate person, these names do not suffice to bridge the void in Turkey. The society is one that is tired of searching for justice.

The lack of justice could be handled in two realms: the general one in terms of freedom and equality dialectic; and the other one the more official and institutional meaning of the rule of law and judicial independence. Regarding the first realm, in Turkey's society "understanding of freedom and equality" is attenuated and so the dialectic between the two is easily overlooked. Therefore, equality of opportunity and equality before the law fall by the wayside. Regarding the second realm, if independence is a status, then impartiality is a virtue. This general framework is secured by the Article 138 of the Constitution; but in actuality it is routinely ignored by the executive branch.

It is crucial to pay attention to the actions taken towards politicizing the judicial branch: with the opening of more and more law schools, quantity has overtaken quality when it comes to cultivating lawyers and legal scholars. (By the way, the proliferation of law schools in private colleges has prioritized the profitability of a legal education over the goal of becoming a legal practicioner in search for justice.) On top of that, it can't exactly be said that judges and prosecutors are being selected from the most competent and brightest lawyers. Initiation into the profession has become more a matter of political connection than of competency. The tendency of the administration to form ad hoc courts also undermines the faith in the legal system. The biased outcomes, as well as the delayed process are also factors that contribute to the public distrust in the judiciary. We could also point out the hardships when trying to organize members of the legal profession. Lastly, we could touch on the problems surrounding the relationship between law and democracy: the role of the judiciary as an actor, factor, and trainer in democracy has been dispensed with ever since the 17 and 25 December 2013 operations and the

---

[1]Süleyman Demirel served as Prime Minister for seven times and was the President of Turkey from 1993 to 2000. His infamous and insensitive quotes have become a part of the collective memory.

political decision makers have successfully acted on their will to shrink the judiciary into a mere mechanism to settle disputes between individuals.[2]

Briefly, what structural legal reforms have been implemented from the Ottoman era to modern Turkey? What model was implemented in Turkey?

The Tanzimat (Reform) era, is deemed as the formation period of the judicial system. The organ that would later become the Council of State (Danıştay), the Council of Government (Şura-yı Devlet) being formed could be seen as the first step towards a two-pronged, judicial and administrative legal system. During the Republican period structural legal reform was undertaken with the 1961 constitution. There are three main novelties of the justice system in the 1961 constitution: (1) establishment of the Constitutional Court, (2) foresight of judicial independence guarantees, and (3) securing the order and functioning of the separation of powers in light of the principle of rule of law.

The constitutional change in 1971 aimed to reduce the guarantees of the judicial system, but the main step backwards came with the 1982 constitution. The judiciary was made into an organ under the guidance of the executive. The State Security Courts (DGM) were also established. Though there were partial improvements to the judicial system with the constitutional changes of 2001, 2004, and 2010, these were insufficient and have brought several inconsistencies. For example, in 2004, the State Security Courts were abolished. However, they were replaced with the "specially authorized courts." These courts were then dismantled when it became obvious that they damaged the judicial system even more than the State Security Courts. In turn, they were replaced with the Peace Criminal Courts, often criticized for their partisan decisions. On the other hand, the Regional Judiciary Courts, whose formation laws were passed in 2004, have not been activated. In European countries, such courts play an indispensable role. The delay in our country has increased the caseload at the High Court of Appeals and pushed that court out of its role as an arbiter of appellate decisions. In recent years, the increase in the branches and members of that court is more due to political calculations than to staffing needs.

Is it common legal practice in Turkey for human rights violations and massacres perpetrated by the government to go unpunished? How does that mechanism work?

A big part of right violations arises from neglect (omission) and/or intentional acts of government officials. In that process, the point that should be considered is that the actions that lead to violations happen within the chain of command of the hierarchical administrative-political structure. When that is the case, the

---

[2]The 2013 scandal refers to the criminal investigation of corruption and bribery charges against sons of three cabinet members and several others. This scandal was the apogee of a heated feud between the AKP government and the Islamist Gülen movement. https://www.theguardian.com/world/2013/dec/17/turkish-ministers-sons-arrested-corruption-investigation.

government officials involved in violations take steps with a preventive attitude towards the preparation and active investigation of cases. The hierarchical superiors protecting their juniors with rhetoric and action, blocking investigations, legal organs not making clear decisions, and so on. In terms of the legal process, its glacial pace, the absence of legal enforcement organizations, outside pressure casting shadows of doubt on judicial independence, tendencies and practice that undermine judicial impartiality can be pointed out. Legal practitioners at times allow nationalistic or moralistic judgments seep into their legal decisions over the central universality of human rights, which makes these decisions more political than legal. Thus, the laws concerning the preservation of essential rights and liberties, article 40, get generally ignored and not put into practice. Moreover, in some cases people who commit rights violations get rewarded by the State; even get nominated to become judges for the European Court of Human Rights.

The rights violations witnessed during the Gezi protests and resistance can be viewed as resulting from violations going unpunished.[3] Instead of public officials being punished for rights and liberty violations—just like after Gezi—there was a concerted political and administrative effort to punish the people whose rights were violated and human rights defenders by way of individual or mass lawsuits. Most recently in July 2017, ten Amnesty International activists were arrested and accused of "membership of a terrorist organization."

What did the legal "reforms" AKP implemented in the last 15 years and the 2010 Constitutional Referendum in Turkey mean for the judicial system? In that context, what was the goal of the maneuvers in the legal front of the battle between the Fetullah Gulen Community and the AKP before July 15 coup attempt?

To answer the first part of your question, a significant portion of the AKP legal reforms was actually a continuation of the European harmonization laws that were being implemented after the 2001 constitutional changes. Thus, the first three harmonization packages were issued under Prime Minister Ecevit when he oversaw the triple coalition government, and the six packages following those were issued under AKP governments. The 2007 legislative election could be seen as a turning point for the reform process. For example, the increase in powers of law enforcement officials could be seen as a marker for that change. The package that came into effect in March 2015, dubbed the domestic security package, could be seen as a continuation of the 2007 changes. On the other hand, AKP reforms have sometimes been exaggerated, and at other times misattributed. For example, the pronouncement "We got rid of the State of Emergency" is false; it was removed from Tunceli province in November 2002, as planned by the previous government. Initial substantive steps on the teaching of non-Turkish languages and minority rights were taken with the third harmonization package in August 2002.

---

[3]For more detailed information see *Gezi Report* (Turkey on the Pendulum Between Democracy and Totalitarianism), Prepared by: Gezi Legal Pursuit Group, 30 December 2014.

The 2010 constitutional change and referendum, waged under the slogan "removing judicial tutelage," which included some improvements to rights and liberties though mainly aimed to put the High Council of Judges and Prosecutors (HSYK) and the Constitutional Court (AYM) under "AKP tutelage," could be seen as a process that achieved those aims. In short, "freedoms and democract" was used to cement the AKP hold on power. To come to your second question, shortly, the imam-hatip (religious state school) mindset (an Islamic order or sect-oriented style) worked to shape a legal system that serves its goal of reshaping society through a guise of national will fetishism. In doing so, to create its own judiciary, the law became a means for the party and its leaders to get their way.

4 workers die from workplace deaths in Turkey every day. Could the Soma mining disaster, where 301 workers died and the ensuing legal process act as a mirror for the neoliberal effect on the labor laws and right to life in Turkey over the last 12 years? What is the legal basis for contracting out, creating insecure work and futures, and deunionization?

The people running the coal mines in Soma are subjects of "the freedom to work" and the miners/laborers of the mines are subjects of "the right to work." There are two unequal sides here and the miners are in a position with much higher risk of rights violation. The main responsibility of the government is to "organize, monitor, and punish;" from the miner's perspective ensuring workplace safety and health through "organizing and monitoring" falls with the government and the employer. These responsibilities aim to protect the "right to life." The employer is directly responsible for the life of the miners.

The government's responsibility starts with the process of privatization, the contract auction, and licensing; and continues with the establishment of the workplace and work activities. This chain of responsibilities is summed up in the legal trifecta of "organize, monitor, and punish." In terms of actors, the onus is on all three of legislative, executive, and judicial branches. Deficiencies in these areas, the government not fulfilling its positive responsibilities leads to the loss of life and violation of the right to life. In our country, the number of mine search licenses are in the thousands (2500–3000); just as the number of hydroelectric power plants. The identity of the beneficiaries of these licenses should be investigated in the framework of clientalist relationships. Frankly, hydroelectric plants and mine searches, in Turkey, both above and below ground, are disrupters and destroyers.

In these matters, decision-making powers previously accorded to local governments and independent units have been taken over by centralized and political power centers, while judicial oversight has been minimized at the same time. The pre-Soma landscape actually came into view with the Soma massacre. In that process, we saw that all parts of the "organize, monitor, and punish" mantra were broken.

The main burden here is on the relevant government organs. This fact of course does not lift the criminal burden off the executives of Soma Holding. However, if we do not question the system and practice of responsibility, the deadly force of savage capitalism will continue to be seen as the inescapable fate of workers. We shouldn't simply blame this on neoliberalism and be done with it. Because, liberalism acts under these two auspices in our time: (1) Economic liberalism: the organize, monitor, and punish" mantra, (2) Political liberalism: freedoms of though, demonstration, and organization to be used as means to create a popular opposition front.

In the case of Turkey: economic liberalism,–even in a social state with a strong constitutional backing—can bring savage and lethal practices. Laid back organizing and monitoring, lack of punishment and order lead to mass deaths. On the other hand, under political liberalism, even established guarantees on freedoms can be scrapped; public officials can fill the streets with police tanks and officers to stop the people from exercising their freedoms and rights. This process is seen with the convergence of conglomerate bosses and public officials (police chiefs, mayors, ministers) on a path to "zero out" the lives of civilians: the state going as far as killing people in squares across the country to prevent the exercise of freedoms (above ground), can allow for corporate bosses to lead workers to death in mines (below ground) for the greed for more money. Thus, it is necessary to see the political-constitutional and judicial system and practice in Turkey as a monolith and question it as such. There are two sacred values in this system: money and power. Religion and national will; these two are two agents used to legitimize the real values. Democracy, law, and human life are values that are left behind...[4] All this that I have noted also goes towards answering your second question: the multi-level failure of the "organize-monitor and punish" chain...The consequence: "Turkey came first in Europe in 2003 and 2011 for worker deaths."[5] The number of worker deaths in the years from 2003 to 2014 due to workplace accidents and occupational health hazards: 14,587.

Is the practice of torture over and done with in Turkey? Could you share the number of rights violations in the AKP era and the current standing of Turkey at the European Court of Justice?

Connected to this question on the first years of AKP governments the "Reports of the Advisory Council of Human Rights" could provide an idea. Per law 4643, the Advisory Council of Human Rights (IHDK)[6] was formed under the Office of the Prime Minister and produced three reports in 2003 and 2004:[7] "Report on the Prevention of Mistreatment and Torture" (October 2003); "Human Right in Turkey Report 2004" and "Cultural and Minority Rights in Turkey" (October 2004). The government, let alone abide by the necessities of these reports; opened criminal

---

[4]See İbrahim Ö. Kaboğlu, "Organize-Montior and Punish," BirGün, 22 May 2014.

[5]See Aziz Çelik, "Here are the statistics Honorable Minister," Birgün, 13 March 2015.

[6]The formation of the council satisfied the outlines laid out in the Paris Principles, in the framework of Human Rights Nurturing Institutions.

[7]For full text of the reports see Advisory Council of Human Rights, (Prepared by: İ.Ö. Kaboğlu/K. Akkurt), İmge, Ankara 2006.

lawsuits against the heads of the council and tried to disband the council, which it never called on to meet.[8] Turkey has started to show the image of a "violent society" since 2005; the variety of rights violations has gone up ever since. Between July 2015 and December 2016 there have been massive rights violations in southeast Turkey.[9] Practice of torture and mistreatment, previously confined to police stations and prisons, has become common practice in broad daylight. When discussing the violations of rights and freedoms during the AKP era we usually look at the annual progress reports of the European Union Commission, though it is also important to take the European Council data as well. The magnitude of human rights violations in Turkey can be seen from the annual reports of the Human Rights Court of Europe. Based on the number of complaint cases, Turkey is number for with 13.6% of all cases, behind Ukraine (%19.5), Italy (%14.4), and Russia (% 14.3). Moreover, the rights violated in the cases brought against Turkey fall mainly under the Right to Personal Freedom and Security—article 5 (45), Right to a Fair Trial—article 6 (31), and Freedom of Expression—article 10 (24).

There are currently over 3 million refugees in Turkey. How do you evaluate this situation in the context of international human rights and migration law?

The core of international refugee law is formed by the "Geneva Convention Concerning the Legal Status of Refugees" (1951) and the "Protocol Regarding the Legal Status of Refugees" (1967). The 1967 Protocol universalized the structural definition of refugee, as established by the 1951 Geneva Convention. Due to the increase in refugee mobility and the overarching idea that people who need international protection should be under guaranteed protection regardless of history or geographical limitations, the 1967 protocol aimed to make the refugee definition of the 1951 Geneva Convention be applicable in the context of global refugee movements. The legal status of asylum seekers in Turkey rests on the provisions of the legal status of refugees as established by the 1951 convention.[10] Turkey is party to the protocol on this matter.[11] However, Turkey limited the application of the 1951 Refugee Convention and the 1967 convention to European refugees only. A 2013 law established a system of international protection for non-European asylum seekers that brings Turkish domestic refugee law somewhat closer to international legal standards. Nonetheless, Turkey still lacks the holistic monitoring mechanism necessary to oversee the asylum process in line with international law

---

[8]On the criminal lawsuits brought against the Council President and Reporter on Cultural and Minority Rights see İbrahim Ö. Kaboğlu, What Human Rights? (Editor: Perihan Özcan), Imge, Ankara 2013.

[9]UN report details massive destruction and serious rights violations since July 2015 in southeast Turkey.   http://www.ohchr.org/EN/NewsEvents/Pages/DisplayNews.aspx?NewsID= 21342&LangID=E.

[10]Law of Acceptance: 26.08.1961-359; State News: 05.09.1961-10898.

[11]01/07/1976 dated decision of the Council of; State News: 05/081968-12968.

or determine the outcome of aylum application judiciously.[12] The provision of the law 6458 merely moves the practice of dealing with these issues from the Foreigners Division of the Police to the civilian General Office on the Management of Migration. The increase in hate crimes and hate rhetoric targeting refugees, aylum seekers, and migrants have seen a marked increase and the exclusionary and "othering" tone in the media has brought further provocation of hateful rhetoric and hate-filled attitudes.

Can you explain the period between 1982 and 2017 in terms of constitutional changes in Turkey?

We should take note that the 1982 constitution was changed almost 20 times in the quarter of a century between 1987 and 2010. Initial observations of these changes show that every legislative assembly formed after free elections (1983, 1987, 1991, 1995, 1999, 2002, 2007) used its legislative power to change the constitution. The changes can be grouped into three categories: (1) changes progressing rights and freedoms; (2) changes altering the power and responsibility of constitutional institutions; and (3) changes deepening the spirit of 1982. We can state that the 1982 constitution was no longer in use as it was originally intended. In fact, we could even talk about a metamorphosis of the 1982 text. For example, Article 13 which was rewritten in 2001, added provisions that met, and even exceeded, the European standards of the rights and liberties regime on paper. Rights and liberties as laid out in the constitution were only to be restricted by law, under conditions specified in the constitution. These conditions were not to be in contradiction with the needs of a democratic society a secular republic; they were not to violate the principle of proportinality or weaken the essence of the granted right. Indeed, the constitutional law of freedoms can only be understood in the context of constitutional law of institutions. Article 13 of the Constitution, the cornerstone of the metamorphosis, constitutes positive obligations for all public authorities, from the Parliament to the law enforcement officers. The legislative power must first take into consideration the implications of each criterion set out in Article 13: democratic society, secular republic, proportionality and the essence of freedom. These criteria must also be applied by the judge in a direct manner. They are also valid for the executive and the administration: the law enforcement officers are bound to respect above all the principle of proportionality and the essence of freedom. In practice laws in clear violation of Article 13 have been put in place. Especially after 2007 there was a deepening of the 1982 spirit. In 2014, Tayyip Erdogan became the first president directly elected by the public. This in and of itself can be interpreted as a constitutional coup. Erdogan took a political stance against the constitution at that time and created a de facto presidential system prior to creating the necessary legal framework, which would come later with the 2017 referendum.

---

[12]See Human Rights Watch Report "EU: Don't Send Syrians Back to Turkey" published on June 20, 2016. https://www.hrw.org/news/2016/06/20/eu-dont-send-syrians-back-turkey.

After the failed coup attempt of July 15, 2016 a state of emergency was declared which was then extended several times and is still in effect as of November 2017 (the time of our interview). A series of oppressive and antidemocratic decrees passed since then. Yet despite all this chaos a constitutional referendum was held on April 16, 2017. It passed with a slim majority leaving millions of people still questioning its legitimacy. What do we make of all this? Where is Turkey headed in light of this constitutional amendment?

The country in fact needed a return to constitutional order after the failed coup attempt, but the ruling Justice and Development Party (AKP) chose just the opposite: by taking advantage of the exceptional circumstances, it changed the Constitution, a change that risks putting the constitutional achievements in jeopardy (or that even annihilates them altogether). Let us first explain this structural change from a parliamentary system to a presidential one. In terms of political regime, since the period of the constitutional monarchy under the Ottoman Empire, Turkey has adopted the parliamentary regime as in most European states. But with the election of Tayyip Erdoğan by direct popular vote, the presidential powers have already been strengthened or put in place by institutional practice. The advocates of the constitutional amendment introduced the idea of "a government of the Presidency of the Republic." In other words, the executive power is incarnated in the personality of the President of the Republic and the constitutional law assigns to the head of state the entire executive power. The post of Prime Minister will be abolished officially in 2019 and his prerogatives will be transferred to the President, who will appoint and dismiss his ministers who will no longer be accountable to the Parliament. In accordance with his new powers, the President will be able to appoint one or more vice-presidents to replace him when he is traveling abroad or removed from office. The head of state will be able to determine national security policies unilaterally and will also have the power to issue executive orders to appoint senior officials. He will have power to declare a state of emergency in the event of an "uprising against the motherland" or "an action that puts the nation in danger of dividing up", and issue the decree-laws under the state of emergency. The head of state will also keep his post as the leader of a political party. The presidential term will be for five years, renewable once. In short, one person will hold three presidencies: the party, the government and the state. The Parliament will lose its powers on two levels: normative and control over the executive. In terms of control, since the executive power will be no more responsible before the Parliament, the motion of censure and the vote of confidence will be abolished. As for the normative power, the president can also bypass the parliament by governing by decree-laws in the–broad–sphere of his competences. The new parliament, de facto deprived of its powers for the benefit of the head of state, will still go from 550 to 600 deputies and term of service will be extended to 5 years. The Grand National Assembly of Turkey may be dissolved by the President of the Republic, without being obliged to respect the conditions which regulate in the first place the parliament's establishment as per the Constitution in force. The next elections - presidential and legislative at the same time- will take place on 3 November 2019. The simultaneous presidential and legislative elections could thus offer the President of the Republic the possibility of having his majority in the parliament since he will be the leader of the political party. The President, previously obliged to observe a political neutrality, can henceforth preserve the links with his political party and even manage it. Finally, the President will appoint twelve of the fifteen members of the Constitutional Court, as well as six of the thirteen members of the Supreme Board of Judges and Prosecutors, the institution responsible for selecting judicial staff. The contradiction is clear: the management of "impartial" justice will be ensured under the high supervision of a "partial" president. Now turning our focus back on the state of emergency was declared on 20 July 2016 on a constitutional basis (in order to restore public order disturbed by the failed coup attempt), its implementation through decree-laws far exceeded the Constitutional and Conventional framework. Even though the decree-law is a regulatory act, most of these texts are appended lists with names of thousands of people to be sanctioned. The exclusion from the civil service of tens of thousands of people for no reason and with a general mention such as a so-called liaison with a terrorist organization is a measure having no concern with the general principles of law and the Constitution even in exceptional circumstances. Consequently, the legal nullity of decree-laws can be substantiated both by procedural and substantive arguments. Most of the measures taken with the decree-laws are unconstitutional and unconventional. These are, in most cases, massive and widespread sanctions. To the public purge, which has affected the public sectors almost entirely, we must add the discharges and forced resignations in private educational institutions (schools, colleges, universities), in the businesses (…), the press and the media, in sports federations. Could we expect a constitutional democracy in Turkey under these circumstances? Yes, to the extent that the dialectic between democracy and the Constitution is assured. The narrow gap between the "yes" and "no" votes in the referendum can be conceived as a source of hope. Why so? Because, assuming that the results announced by the Supreme Electoral Board reflect the reality, in spite of the political and official mobilization and the pressure exerted on the supporters of the "no" campaign, the score of the "yes" remains very low. Therefore, the "yes" votes won as per law with the decision of the Supreme Electoral Board, but the "no" votes prevailed democratically. In fact, the only way to avoid political- constitutional chaos and to open the way to constitutional democracy is through the organization of democratic hope. The referendum on 16 April 2017 was also the occasion to create a "constitutional sensitivity" in civil society. From present day to 2019, the society now has to prove itself in terms of democracy to prevent personalized power from turning into absolute totalitarianism.

Author Biographies

İbrahim Kaboğlu is an internationally renowned jurist and a constitutional law expert. After obtaining his bachelor's and master's degrees in law from Ankara University, he completed his doctoral degree in public law at Limoges University. In 1994 he became a full Professor of Constitutional Law at Marmara University and served as the Chair of the Department of Constitutional Law at that same institution for several years. He was a visiting professor at several European universities, particularly in France. Between 1998 and 2001 he served as the President of the Human Rights Center of the Istanbul Bar Association. Between 2003 and 2005, he was the President of the Human Rights Advisory Board of Turkey. He has published numerous books and articles on constitutional law, human rights and political science. He is a columnist at Birgün, a national daily newspaper. On February 7, 2017 he was dismissed from his position at Marmara University by decree n°686 for having signed a peace petition. The petition by Academics for Peace had condemned the Turkish government's security operations and the egregious human rights violations in southeast Turkey.

Gaye Özpınar is an immigration and human rights lawyer, born and raised in Turkey. After completing her undergraduate degree in politics at Brandeis University, she obtained a law degree (J.D.) from Suffolk University Law School. For the past decade she has exclusively worked in the field of immigration law, representing many individuals before the US Citizenship and Immigration Services and the Immigration Court. Through the Political Asylum and Immigration Reform (PAIR) Project she worked with many torture survivors. She has given interviews with Turkish dailies such as *Agos*, *T24*, and *BirGün* on human rights issues. She is a member of the American Immigration Lawyers Association. For the past three years she has been selected as a Rising Star and a Top Female Attorney in Massachusetts by *Super Lawyers* magazine.

Human Rights Activism

Şebnem Korur Fincancı and interviewed by Aylin Tekiner

Abstract Human rights in Turkey that were the result of many years' struggle have been suspended since the failed coup attempt of July 15, 2016. Torture in police custody and prisons has escalated. No opposition is tolerated. People are arrested on a daily basis whenever and wherever they protest. More than 150,000 civil servants have been dismissed, some 7000 of them academics. Around 500 of these academics are peace petitioners, which contradicts statements made by the government that the dismissals are of those affiliated with the Gülen movement. Dismissals through decrees are used as means of opponent purge. All opposition media and NGOs have been shut down. Some 150 journalists are now in jail, members of parliament and mayors from the third opposition party have been jailed. The prison population in Turkey now exceeds 220,000.

Keywords Human rights · Turkey

Could you talk briefly about the history of human rights activism in Turkey? What were the main factors that paved the way for institutionalization of the movement?

The institutionalization of human rights activism in Turkey began during the aftermath of the 1980 military coup. Throughout Turkey's modern history the state has carried out human rights violations and torture. But the violations initiated with the 1980 coup swept across the whole of the country on an unprecedented scale. Within the first days of the coup, some 650,000 people, mostly leftists, were taken into custody. Detentions lasting up to 90 days meant being subjected to torture.

Ş. K. Fincancı (✉)
IU Istanbul Faculty of Medicine, Department of Forensic Medicine, Capa, Istanbul University, Istanbul, Turkey
e-mail: sebnemkf@gmail.com

A. Tekiner
Columbia University, New York, USA
e-mail: aylintekiner78@gmail.com

© Springer International Publishing AG, part of Springer Nature 2019
E. Özyürek et al. (eds.), *Authoritarianism and Resistance in Turkey*,
https://doi.org/10.1007/978-3-319-76705-5_20

After these initial detentions, more than 40,000 people were arrested and remained in prisons without trial for many years. Inside the prisons, detainees experienced many human rights violations, forced to live in a space that was under constant state control.

These developments necessitated public investigation into and redress of human rights violations in Turkey. Civic and grassroots human rights organizations were established and people from all walks of life were brought into the struggle to bring human rights abuses to light. We had colleagues in the medical profession in the prisons who were members of our organization, the Turkish Medical Association. They witnessed firsthand and were themselves victims of unimaginable abuses. Other colleagues within the association were even made to play a part in the abuses. As cover-up, prison doctors were tasked with developing new ways of falsifying reports. As the Turkish Medical Association, we began to ponder how best to counter these violations. The association already had a decadelong tradition of activism and a socialist medicine approach. As reports of torture increased both during and after the military coup, a human rights branch was established within the association.

There was also a need to establish a much broader organization in which prison torture, repressive junta activities, and extrajudicial killings could be discussed, publicly declared, brought into the international arena. In 1986, a group of 98 people—among whom were Didar Şensoy, one of the pioneers of the human rights activism in Turkey, Nusret Fişek from the Turkish Medical Association, Gençay Gürsoy, and other writers and intellectuals—founded the Human Rights Association of Turkey. The association began its work by staging sensational protests against prisons and torture. Over time, we began to see that those released from the prisons had very serious health problems due to torture, abuse, and the meagre living conditions in the prisons. Because they had been imprisoned, they did not have any social security and many of them were therefore unable to obtain healthcare services. At the time, there were no organizations in Turkey specializing in these social issues. In 1990, 32 human rights activists from the Human Rights Association and the Turkish Medical Association came together to establish the Human Rights Foundation of Turkey. Thus began our organizational and financial journey to find a way to ensure that people released from prisons would be able to receive the healthcare services from which they had been barred. A number of human rights organizations with different approaches and specialties, such as Mazlumder, were established afterwards.

Could you describe the most urgent human rights violations in Turkey today? Which violations are at the top of the list?

The list varies from year to year. In the 1990s, violations against the right to life, particularly in terms of extrajudicial executions, were prevalent. During that period, there were many mysterious deaths and unsolved political murders perpetrated, we now know, by the Turkish state. At the same time, we also faced the problem of the use of excessive methods of torture.

Today, looking at those areas where human rights violations predominate, we can say that there is an attenuation of the right to peaceful demonstration and to freedom of expression. People are unable to express themselves and their opinions freely today. If they become involved in political organizations, their involvement is criminalized by the government. If they demand their rights through peaceful demonstrations, their participation in those demonstrations is considered a serious crime. Each and every dissident voice is being suppressed through state violence. If we look at the years 2013–2014, we see that, according to Turkish Medical Association data (https://www.medikalakademi.com.tr/ttb-biber-gazi-kimyasal-silah-yasak-gezi-parki/, 2017), more than 10,000 people were affected by state use of chemicals during the now-symbolic Gezi protests. The protests began after hundreds of thousands of ordinary people opposing the demolition of Gezi Park at the center of Istanbul were suppressed by police forces. Eight people died, dozens of young people lost their eyes, and many people were injured as a result of police attacks where protesters were targeted with canisters of tear gas and plastic bullets. In 2014, police violence continued to escalate (Turkish Medical Association 2013). On October 6–7, during the Kobanê protests, the police carried out extreme and disproportionate attacks, assaults on the streets and in public spaces, and used torture. We still see widespread human rights violations in prisons and detentions of course, but the most visible form of human rights abuse at the moment involve violent police interventions in the streets resulting in fatalities.

There is a widespread problem of police violence in Turkey. Since the 2007 amendment to the Police Duties and Powers Law, there has been a significant increase in extrajudicial executions by the police.[1] According to research conducted by the Human Rights Foundation of Turkey (2009), the total number of torture cases in 2006 was 190; this number increased to 266 in 2007, an increase of 40%. Between July 2007 and July 2009, a total of 3605 people faced human rights violations, 416 people were tortured, and 53 people lost their lives due to police violence. Within one and a half months of passing the new legislation on police duties and powers, the police tortured 36 people (Human Rights Foundation of Turkey 2017).

Where do we stand now with regard to police violence after the Gezi protests?

There is a possibility of the expansion of the authorization of police use of firearms and the reemergence of the concept "reasonable doubt."[2] But all these things, of course, are not new. In 2006, the police staged an march with the slogan "Down

---

[1]http://www.tuerkeiforum.net/docs/tr/tihv2009raporu.pdf (pp. 279–283).

[2]The Regulation of Judicial and Preventive Search (2005) defines reasonable doubt as following: "Reasonable doubt is a doubt that usually occurs due to concrete events in the face of life's flow. Reasonable doubt is determined through taking certain factors into consideration such as venue and time of the event, attitudes and behaviors of people accompanying the defendant, nature of goods that the law enforcement officers suspected as being carried. In the case of reasonable doubt, there needs to be signs supporting the denunciation and claims. The doubt must be based on concrete facts in the case of mentioned factors. There needs to be concrete facts that would foresee finding of a certain thing or catching a specific person at the end of the search."

with human rights." This March occurred after the regulations of 2005 were set in place with provisions protecting "reasonable suspects"—detention periods were limited, interrogation and detention methods were regulated, and having an attorney during the interrogation became obligatory. As a result, the police went out to protest, claiming they would be unable to avoid committing crimes under those conditions and chanting "Down with human rights." This was of course an extremely tragic situation. Some of these regulations were withdrawn in 2007, and another set of regulations authorizing police use of firearms was reinstated, thus reversing reforms made in 2005. During the one-year period after the 2005 reforms, there had been a significant decrease in extrajudicial executions on the streets, a violation of the right to life. With the reversal of those reforms in 2007, we saw an increase in violations of the right to life.

Today, the government's attitude also paves the way for human rights abuses. During the Gezi protests, the then prime minister Recep Tayyip Erdoğan said that he himself gave the orders to the police to fire on protesters. In the context of Turkey's record, if the prime minister says that the conduct of the police was in accordance with his executive orders, it is highly likely that any human rights violations perpetrated by the police will go unpunished. In another example at a mass gathering called by the AKP during the Gezi protests, Erdoğan had the masses chant taunts about the mother of a fourteen-year-old, Berkin Elvan, labeling her as a terrorist; the boy had been hit in the head by a police tear gas cannister while going out to buy bread and later died of his injuries. Each of these instances communicates to the police that they are free to use violence and to violate human rights, and that the government will guarantee their protection regardless.

We are now facing a situation in which police violence has increased under the encouragement and protection of the government. Our Human Rights Foundation of Turkey reports reflect this situation well. Applications to our organization have increased two—and threefold over the last two years. Although our annual application prediction was 350 in 2012, we received 900 applications in 2013 and 726 during the first 11 months of 2014.

Let's talk about the culture of impunity. The examples that come to mind are the cases of Hrant Dink, the Roboski massacre, the Rojava conflict in Syria, Gezi, and Soma. In each of these cases, we face the serious problem of injustice where the rule of law ceases to function. How can the deepening problem of impunity be solved?

Unfortunately, impunity is not a recent issue. The history of Turkey is built on state violence and on the invisibility of this violence. There are very few cases in which an officer in charge is criminally tried, and the rate of conviction and punishment in such trials is exceptionally low. The Turkish Ministry of Justice and the Ministry of the Interior regularly publish statistics on such cases. Of these cases, 30% were trials initiated with a proceeding for alleged torture. Less than 1% of these trials results in a penalty for the accused officer. The Turkish Economic and Social Studies Foundation (TESEV) conducted a very valuable study (2007) (TESEV 2007) that found that three-quarters of high judges in Turkey believe that the very concept of human rights threatens the integrity of the Republic of Turkey. When such a perception exists at that level and the reflex of the judiciary is to protect the state, there is no other alternative than that human rights becomes a problem for the legal system.

This is not a problem specific to Turkey. People eventually rebel against impunity. Even so, the issue of impunity is much more visible in Turkey. According to our statistics, we encounter impunity in almost all human rights violation lawsuits. People often go to the public prosecutor's office with complaints of police brutality and torture. The public prosecutor's office dismisses most of these complaints and the cases are closed and do not even go to court. Law enforcement officers run a process we call "twin lawsuits," filing a "resisting an officer" report against people who have gone to the public prosecutor with an accusation of police brutality. The case goes to the public prosecutor's office, which then prosecutes the individual who was brutalized. The effect of such cases is that even when people have concrete evidence regarding police violence, they are reluctant to put up a legal fight due to intimidation. As a result, the public is not even aware of many of these instance of police brutality. Events that do go to court, either end with the acquittal of the police or result in tragic consequences as in the assassination of the editor-in-chief of an Armenian periodical, Hrant Dink.[3] Nothing is concrete in that case yet, but in July 2014, the supreme court ruled that the investigation had been flawed, paving the way for trials of police officials and other public authorities. Today we had the hearing of Ali İsmail Korkmaz, who was killed during the Gezi protests.[4] The policeman said with great satisfaction that he carried out his duty and had not overstepped his authority. He could not have said it more genuinely, because the state indeed gives him such authority and duties. The state promises to protect its police force and to make legal arrangements, if necessary, for their protection. Three out of four justices in the supreme court already believe that the idea of *human rights* damages the integrity of the state. The state is always prioritized over the public in Turkey.

When we look at unsolved political murders in Turkey, we see that the notion of *state secrets* is the biggest obstacle to the establishment of research commissions and the thorough investigation of murders. It is obvious that these murders have been committed by the state, yet on the basis of *continuity of the state* they are not investigated, and the documents are hidden away. According to the Human Rights Association's figures (Human Rights Association of

---

[3]The court rendered verdicts for 19 defendants in the case concerning the killing of *Agos* newspaper editor-in-chief Hrant Dink on January 19, 2007. Yasin Hayal, who had been jailed pending trial, was sentenced to aggravated life imprisonment for "instigating the murder." The defendant Erhan Tuncel was not punished. The court decided that the case was not a mafia murder.

[4]The defendants, policemen and tradesmen, were charged with the murder of college student Ali İsmail Korkmaz during the Gezi protests in Eskişehir. Police officers Hüseyin Engin and Saban Gökpınar were acquitted.

Turkey 2014)**, the number of these murders exceeds 17,000. What steps have human rights groups taken in regard to this issue?**

The work being carried out in this matter aims primarily at strengthening the families. These families have lost their loved ones and cannot retrieve the bodies for the funeral. This is deeply traumatic because the mourning process is never-ending, leading to what is called complicated trauma. As a Human Rights Foundation, our duty is to ensure that these people heal in a holistic way. By healing, I am not referring solely to biological wellbeing or mental health. We also need to ensure social wellbeing. We thus work to improve the families' social conditions, provide a social environment conducive to healing, create opportunities for education when necessary. We offer therapy services, but we also fight against human rights violations. Thus, we have to be on the streets alongside the Human Rights Association, attend the weekly sit-ins with the Saturday Mothers,[5] and participate in public awareness campaigns that highlight the health problems and living conditions in prisons. We highlight abuses on the streets and legislative shortcomings. Although we are a health-based organization, not a lawyers' organization, wellbeing requires both a fight for justice and support for such a fight. We therefore provide limited legal support. We work on extending the prosecution of cases through appeals, activating international law mechanisms when domestic legal processes have been exhausted, documenting human rights violations through the publication of annual reports, compiling the reports of individuals who experience human rights violations. When someone has been exposed to torture, murdered via torture, or died via extrajudicial killing, we get a second opinion on the case.

Impunity is not an easy problem to deal with, but we do make positive steps forward from time to time. There was a very important supreme court decision handed down in August 2015, the first in Turkey of its kind, where the local courts had penalized the police for torture of a young man severely beaten by police on the street. Defining an incident that occurred on the street as torture and punishing the act is a first for a local court. In August, the supreme court approved the decision at the appeal. This decision is very significant. Little by little, through the work of organizations such as ours, we can change impunity in Turkey. People exposed to state violence need to be empowered so that they may fight for their rights.

It is crucial that we let the public know that there is a problem, and the problem is the violation of human rights. Because we know that the mainstream media will never report on these violations, we know that most people will not even be aware of them. For example, in 1993–1994, 13 Kurdish villagers were killed in the Derik district of Mardin, and the murder remained unsolved. If the Saturday Mothers did not publicize this incident at Galatasaray Square, no one would know that Brigadier General Musa Çitil, who is still the gendarmerie regional commander of Ankara, is on trial for responsibility in those murders. Nor we anyone be aware of what the

---

[5]Saturday Mothers is a group of relatives of victims of state-forced disappearances who are under police custody and of unsolved political murders. They have been organizing sit-ins at Galatasaray Square every Saturday since May 27, 1995, as a testament to their search for their relatives.

Cizre district gendarmerie company commander Cemal Temizöz did. Between 1993–1995, Temizöz allegedly established a civilian interrogation and execution task force. With this task force, he interrogated, forcibly disappeared, or killed 22 people in the name of counterterrorism, people whom he thought were helping the PKK or whom he detained for private reasons. If the Saturday Mothers had not been gathering at Galatasaray Square for the past 500-plus weeks since 1995 holding the photographs of their missing family members in their hands, demanding "Tell us where our children are" and "At least give us our children's bones," no one in Turkey would know about these murders. The Saturday Mothers prompt the people passing by to think: why are these people standing there on the street corner and whose photographs are those that they are holding? Many of the passersby have never taken an interest in such issues. Establishing justice essentially depends on other people seeing and acknowledging the injury, the massacre, the annihilation that you have experienced—more so than on punishing someone.

In this sense, the perpetrators of these crimes are made visible and receive the necessary punishment in our conscience. This is how justice is established. Society now knows that the relatives of these people were kidnapped and never returned home, that they were burnt in acid wells, shot with a single bullet in the neck, left to rot at the edge of a wall under three pieces of stone. Having people know the facts is important to the families' sense of justice. The ultimate goal is of course to expose those who were responsible and to censure them in the eyes of society. Because the people responsible continue on with their daily lives, participate in public events, attend the October 29 Republic Day balls. We must know that those people are murderers. Veli Saçılık, a friend of ours who lost his arm in Buca Prison,[6] ran across the justice minister Hikmet Sami Turk in the market one day and shouted, "Murderer! What are you doing here? You cut off my arm and fed it to the dogs." The minister's guard replied, "Mister Veli, you are a public officer, you shouldn't say such things." To which Veli responded, "Is telling the murderer that he is a murderer an offense?" You see, I think we will have overcome this problem when we tell the murderer that he is a murderer. In other words, the important thing is not sending

---

[6]A gendarmerie operation was launched in Burdur Prison on July 5, 2000, after 11 detainees started riots and hunger strikes against poor prison conditions and a court decision to forcibly take them to a court hearing. On the day of the operation, the gendarmerie demolished the prison walls using bulldozers so as to reach the area wherein the detainees were residing. The right arm of the political prisoner Veli Saçılık was torn off by bulldozer blows during the demolition. The arm, thrown into the trash, was found in the mouth of a stray dog. After his release, Saçılık applied to the European Convention on Human Rights, which found Turkey guilty of violating "prohibition of torture and maltreatment" and sentenced the country to pay compensation to Veli Saçılık (European Court of Human Rights 2011). Later, the Turkish Council of State reversed the ECHR decision and found Saçılık guilty of damaging the state with a prison rebellion. The council asked him to pay the indemnity of 150,000 TL that he received from the state several years back, with interest of approximately 725,000 TL. It was decided that the money would be collected as deductions from Saçılık's salary. Saçılık applied again to the ECHR, reporting the newest developments. The ECHR gave its final verdict in 2015, stating that Turkey cannot require Saçılık to return the indemnity paid to him and warning Turkey to take its verdicts seriously (European 2015).

these people to jail for 20 years. I think it is more important that Kenan Evren, the key suspect in the 1980 coup and Chief of the General Staff (Meclis Araştırması Komisyonu 2012) at the time, is acknowledged as the murderer by all of us.

Turkish society has learned the truth of mass graves as a result of the Saturday Mothers. As a forensic expert, can you talk about the problems related to the excavation of mass graves?

As of today, the excavation of mass graves in Turkey does not take place in accordance with the scientific principles and methods of forensics. In recent years, there have been some changes made as a result of certain restrictions. One of the positive developments of 2005 was the amendment to the Criminal Procedure Law requiring the presence of an expert observer at the scene during autopsies or excavation of mass graves. This is in my opinion a very significant change. In Turkey, it is the Forensic Medicine Institution connected to the Ministry of Justice that carries out both the excavation of mass graves and the analysis of the remains removed from those graves. This is completely unacceptable, because you're talking about a crime possibly committed by the state, yet you vest the responsibility for the investigation in an institution linked to the state. Fortunately, with the change to the law, it is now possible to have an expert observer during excavation of graves. This change also ensures that graves will no longer be excavated with the use of outdated methods. There are now rules for mass grave excavations, you need to have an archaeologist or anthropologist, and teamwork needs to be carried out.

Last year, Hüsnü Yıldız, one of the members the Saturday Mothers, went on a hunger strike demanding that the grave of his brother Ali Yıldız be found.[7] Until that time, suspected mass graves used to be entered with earth diggers, scattering the soil and crushing the bones. Once the bones were shattered and broken into pieces, it was impossible to uncover trace evidence or make identifications. The first excavation that could be considered a proper excavation happened in Çemişgezek in 2011.[8]. The bones could be identified because they were found intact. It was possible to assess how the event happened by looking at the locations of the damage on the bones and the trauma characteristics. Unfortunately, not all excavations have been carried out in this way.

The point is not to open mass graves and expose the evidence before proper teams can be assembled. We need to train up and establish teams who have the requisite experience and knowledge with which to manage the difficult teamwork. Forensic archaeology and forensic anthropology have not yet been established as disciplines in Turkey. Although there has been some work on the issue, there is still a very limited number of experienced people in Turkey. In a country where mass

---

[7]The body of Ali Yıldız, who was killed in April 1997 in the Çemişkezek district of Tunceli along with 19 other people, was found in a mass grave in Çemişkezek after his brother Hüsnü Yıldız had continued his hunger strike in Tunceli for 66 days.

[8]Hüsnü Yıldız'ın Açlık Grevi Sona Erdi (2011), http://www.radikal.com.tr/turkiye/husnu-yildizin-aclik-grevi-sona-erdi-1059944/, Accessed 25 December 2017.

graves are so common, where many unsolved murders take place, where the soil is filled with bones, we need a number of experienced teams. I am not so sure that the public is ready to face these issues. For example, we heard for many years in the mainstream press that Abdullah Öcalan, the leader of the Kurdish political movement and of the PKK, was a baby killer. But then we learned that persecutors of most of these massacres—including the iconic Pınarcık massacre, which was frequently displayed in the news under the title of "Baby Killer" with photos of bullet-riddle babies—were in fact not the PKK, but the Gendarmerie for Intelligence and Anti-Terrorism. We heard this for the first time when Ayhan Çarkın, a special operations officer who had become known by the public in Susurluk case, made a number of confessions. The leading killer actually turned out to be the state itself. But how Turkish society will be able to face these facts is another question altogether, because the strong state society has always sided with will have suddenly to turn into a killer state. This will take quite some time. While it is not easy to shed light on these incidents, it is perhaps harder for society to face the truths.

Since our interview above, you were placed in custody. Can you tell about this?

With the elections of June 2015 hope had emerged, but was then immediately dashed with Suruç bombing and escalating violence. The situation with Rojava and the declaration of autonomy in the Kurdish settlements triggered violence. Round-the-clock curfews were put in place in August 2015. A pro-Kurdish newspaper came under attack, and the editors were facing multiple courts cases when it was decided to attempt a solidarity campaign. Volunteers would act as guest editor for one day. I was one of them. The prosecutors invited us to give our testimonies, and we visited the courthouse in groups every day. On June 20, 2016, seven of the guest editors were at the courthouse, and three of us were suddenly indicted and sent to jail. It was an unexpected but important experience for us. When I, Erol Önderoğlu, a journalist and representative of Reporters Without Borders, and another journalist, Ahmet Nesin were sent to jail, it caused a huge stir and created an environment of solidarity not only in the country but all over the world. Guest editors suddenly increased in number, which also helped to increase the visibility of the freedom of speech violations. The government could not continue for long and had to release us within only 10 days. Unfortunately, the coup attempt of July 15, only a few weeks later, has changed the climate and those detained since have not been so lucky.

When the war with the Kurds started up again after the June 6, 2015 elections, you observed the destruction in Kurdish cities. Can you share your observations with us?

Round-the-clock curfews began in August 2016, planned at first for a few weeks but extended to months for many towns and cities. One of these towns was Cizre, where there were allegations of civilians being killed. The whole of Turkey heard on their TV screens the cries for help from basements in Cizre where the government claimed armed terrorists were clashing with law enforcement. It was announced that the operation against terrorists would end in mid-February 2016, but the curfew was extended through to March 2, and as an organization, we didn't know what had occurred during the intervening weeks. We decided to visit Cizre immediately and were there on March 3 with the president of the Human Rights Association, Öztürk Türkdoğan. People led us urgently toward basements, saying that there had been no crime scene investigations and that the bodies collected from the basements were all burnt to charcoal. We entered the first and only basement open, and I found the lower jawbone of a child of around 10–12 years old, contradicting the government story about these basement being occupied by terrorists clashing with police. Buildings were severely damaged, and the distinctive stench of burnt flesh was all over the town. Our colleagues visited the town sometime after our visit, and one preliminary and one full report on human rights violations in Cizre were issued, making the authorities nervous. This was followed by my detention and human rights organizations being put on trial.

How would you describe human rights under the state of emergency since the failed coup of July 15, 2016?

Human rights in Turkey that were the result of many years' struggle have been suspended, though the government denies this. Torture in police custody and prisons has escalated. No opposition is tolerated. People are arrested on a daily basis whenever and wherever they protest. More than 150,000 civil servants have been dismissed, some 7000 of them academics. Around 500 of these academics are peace petitioners, which contradicts statements made by the government that the dismissals are of those affiliated with the Gülen movement. Dismissals through decrees are used as means of opponent purge. All opposition media and NGOs have been shut down. Some 150 journalists are now in jail, members of parliament and mayors from the third opposition party have been jailed. The prison population in Turkey now exceeds 220,000.

References

Meclis Araştırması Komisyonu. (2012). Ülkemizde Demokrasiye Müdahale Eden Tüm Darbe ve Muhtıralar İle Demokrasiyi İşlevsiz Kılan Diğer Bütün Girişim ve Süreçlerin Tüm Boyutları İle Araştırılarak Alınması Gereken Önlemlerin Belirlenmesi Amacıyla Kurulan Meclis Araştırması Komisyonu Raporu [Parliamentary Research Commission (2012) The Report of the Parliamentary Research Commission that was established towards determining the measures to prevent them, to elaborate all the process and attempts that leave the democracy dysfunctional and all the coups and memorandums that intervenes in democracy] Vol 1. No 37, Ankara: Türkiye Büyük Millet Meclisi. Retrieved November 10, 2017, from http://www.tbmm. gov.tr/sirasayi/donem24/yil01/ss376_Cilt1.pdf.

European Court of Human Rights. (2011). Case of Saçilik and others v. Turkey (Applications nos. 43044/05 and 45001/05). Retrieved December 2, 2017, from http://hudoc.echr.coe.int/eng?i= 001–105499.

European Court of Human Rights. (2015). CASE OF SAÇILIK AND OTHERS v. TURKEY (Applications nos. 43044/05 and 45001/05). Retrieved December 2, 2017, from http://hudoc. echr.coe.int/eng?i=001–153764.

Human Rights Association of Turkey. (2014). 348 Toplu Mezar, 4 Bin 201 Ceset. Retrieved December 25, 2017, from http://www.cumhuriyet.com.tr/haber/turkiye/163719/348_toplu_mezar__4_bin_201_ceset.html.

Human Rights Foundation of Turkey. (2017). Türkiye İnsan Hakları Raporu 2009. Retrieved December 25, 2017, from http://www.tuerkeiforum.net/docs/tr/tihv2009raporu.pdf.

Hüsnü Yıldız'ın Açlık Grevi Sona Erdi. (2011). Retrieved December 25, 2017, from http://www. radikal.com.tr/turkiye/husnu-yildizin-aclik-grevi-sona-erdi-1059944/.

Regulation of Judicial and Preventive Search. (2015). Law number, Turkish XX Law, 1st June 2015. Retrieved December 25, 2017, from https://www.tbmm.gov.tr/komisyon/insanhaklari/belge/um_adliveonlemearamalari.pdf.

Secretary-General of the United Nations Sub-Commission on the Promotion and Protection of Human Rights. (20XX). Title. Retrieved December XX, 2017, from http://URL.

Turkish Economic and Social Studies Foundation (TESEV). (2007). Mithat Sancar, Eylem Ümit, "Yargıda Algı ve Zihniyet Kalıpları," İnsan Hakları Savunucuları. Retrieved December 27, 2017, from http://www.insanhaklarisavunuculari.org/dokumantasyon/items/show/583.

Turkish Medical Association. (2013). TTB: Biber gazı kimyasal silah olarak kabul edilmeli ve yasaklanmalı. Retrieved December 27, 2017, from https://www.medikalakademi.com.tr/ttb-biber-gazi-kimyasal-silah-yasak-gezi-parki/.

Author Biographies

Şebnem Korur Fincancı is a forensic medical doctor specializing in torture and rehabilitation. She is a member of Istanbul University's Department of Forensic Medicine and is one of the founders of the Human Rights Foundation of Turkey. On June 20, 2016, she was detained for having served for one day as the editor-in-chief of the Turkish daily, *Özgür Gündem* (Free Agenda) as an act of solidarity. She was released 10 days later.

Aylin Tekiner is a New York- and Istanbul-based artist and activist. She received her B.A. and M. A. in fine arts and sculpture at Hacettepe University, Ankara. In 2008, she received her Ph.D. in education from Ankara University. Her book, *Atatürk Heykelleri: Kült, Estetik, Siyaset* (Atatürk Statues: Cult, Esthetics, and Politics, İletişim Yayınları, 2010), evolved from her PhD thesis. She has had numerous solo and group exhibitions of her art both in Turkey and abroad. In 2013, she taught the course "New Media, Art, and Activism" at Long Island University, New York. In 2015-2016, she was awarded a postdoctoral fellowship at Yale University's School of Drama. Act 1 of her shadow play, *Do All Daddies Have Gray Suits*, was shown at the Yale University's Satellite Cabaret Festival in 2016, and she is presently working on Act 2 and 3. She is a member of the Collective Memory Platform, a forum for the families of 28 victims of political murders in Turkey, the Research Institute on Turkey, and the Çocuklarız Bir Aradayız (We are children and together) initiative focusing on the 1980 coup d'état.

Freedom of Expression and the Press in Turkey

Fikret İlkiz and interviewed by Defne Över

Abstract There are three historical milestones in the evolution of the rights to freedom of expression and of the press in Turkey: (1) the process after ratification of the Constitution of 1961; (2) the continuity in the limitations placed upon fundamental rights and liberties; and (3) the acceptance of rights in the context of such limitations. Turkey has not yet experienced a process that would lead to an enduring acceptance of fundamental rights and liberties or their protection and development. Instead, the order institutionalized thus far is predicated upon the acceptance of fundamental rights and liberties together with the limitations upon them. In other words, limitations upon fundamental rights and liberties have thus far been accepted as the rule, while their protection has been accepted as the exception. This understanding must be challenged. Rights and liberties are essential. Only where there is a "social rule of law" where society has internalized the need for these rights as essential, can a country have a democratic and secular state. It is only under this kind of social order that the juridical, legislative, and executive bodies can function in balance, independent of one another and in impartiality, thus leading to the emergence of a democratic order.

Keywords Freedom of speech · Freedom of expression · Turkey

What are the milestones in the historical evolution of the right to freedom of expression and of the press in Turkey that we need to know in order to understand the current state of the media and of freedom of speech in Turkey?

We must begin with the approval of the Turkish Constitution of 1961. This is the single most important legal document that opened the doors of enlightenment, and

F. İlkiz (✉)
Istanbul Bar Assocation, Istanbul, Turkey
e-mail: fikret.ilkiz@gmail.com

D. Över
Goettingen Institute for Advanced Study, Göttingen, Germany
e-mail: doever@uni-goettingen.de

© Springer International Publishing AG, part of Springer Nature 2019   215
E. Özyürek et al. (eds.), *Authoritarianism and Resistance in Turkey*,
https://doi.org/10.1007/978-3-319-76705-5_21

secured constitutional guarantees of fundamental rights and liberties in Turkey. When you review the period that follows the approval of the Constitution of 1961, we see that it continues through to 1991. Between 1961 and 1991, Turkey experienced two military coup d'états, one on March 12, 1971 and another on September 12, 1980. In 1991, Turkey is said to have given the impression of reinstitutionalizing democracy and resecuring the rights to freedom of expression and of the press. Yet 1991 is also the year in which the Anti-Terror Law[1] was ratified in Turkey. When we scrutinize the process between 1961 and 1991, we see that the two intervening military coups resulted in the establishment of exceptionally repressive regimes where fundamental rights and liberties were either suspended or restricted for uninterrupted periods of time via martial law or state of exception. Thus, in the years following 1991, the earlier periods of exceptional repression were internalized and normalized. Seen from this perspective, the right to freedom of expression in Turkey has been repressed for many years, and this pressure directly affects the media. As you are well aware, people are able to remain informed and knowledgeable about the world through the work of journalists. If you block journalists' access to information and current events via administrative or legal means, or by passing judicial decisions, then democracy and pluralism will never develop in your country—just as it does not develop in any other country where the means to reporting on the news is blocked.

The thirty-year interval between 1961 and 1991 must thus be understood as one of the most repressive periods in Turkish history, a time when democracy, pluralism, and the rights to freedom of speech and of the press were brutally suppressed. We can comprehend this by looking at the Turkish Constitution of 1982. If you examine carefully this constitution, you will notice a paradox. At first glance, it appears to include the fundamental rights and liberties enshrined in the European Convention on Human Rights (Council 1950). But it also has a key measure of restriction. Accordingly, all fundamental rights and liberties can be restricted on certain grounds, for example, on the basis of the indivisibility of the state with its nation and territory, the protection of public order, or the protection of national security. This means that we live in a country where there is a key measure of restricting all fundamental rights and liberties. In other words, our exercise of the right to freedom of the press, our exercise of the right to science and the arts, our exercise of the right to freedom of expression are all dependent on this principle measure of restriction.

In 2001, this key measure of restriction on all fundamental rights and liberties was removed by the passing of an important amendment to Article 13 of the Constitution of 1982. This amendment set forth that fundamental rights and liberties

---

[1]The Anti-Terror Law was ratified on April 12, 1991. Law 3713 on the fight against terrorism has since been subject to multiple amendments and partial annulments by the constitutional court. The latest major amendment was introduced in 2006. It changed the definition of terrorist and terrorism-related offenses, and introduced new investigative measures regarding the prosecution of suspected terrorists. According to this law, punishment for terrorist offenses and offenses committed with terrorist aims shall be aggravated, and special procedural and executional rules apply.

can only be restricted in conformity with the rationales outlined in the relevant articles of the constitution without infringing upon their essence. It is only after this amendment that fundamental rights and liberties in Turkey—freedom of expression (Article 26), the freedom to science and the arts (Article 27), the freedom of the press (Article 28), all of which directly concern the media—achieved a little more of their essence and function. In that sense, the amendment was a key step.

When we review this history and the period in which we live today, we observe that because they hold power, governments draw the limits of our fundamental rights and liberties. One can think, express oneself, and publish your opinions only within these bounds. Those who hold power decide whether you can go beyond these limits. In this context, the rights to freedom of expression and of the press are often used in Turkey by those who hold political power—or by certain self-interested criminal or mafia-type organizations—as a means of exerting power or achieving their own goals. Article 20 of the International Covenant on Civil and Political Rights, adopted by the United Nations General Assembly in 1966 (United Nations 1966), prohibits the exercise of the right to freedom of expression, enshrined in the Article 19, for the purposes of war propaganda and for advocacy of national, racial, or religious hatred inciting discrimination, hostility, or violence. These exercise of speech and the press are not considered as practices of freedom of expression. Accordingly, as one of the most important actors in the public exercise of freedom of expression, journalists are expected to act impartially. Correspondingly, other actors are expected to avoid presenting journalists as biased and to avoid inciting hostility through the work of journalists. In Turkey, there are multiple examples of such incitement to hostility, and in fact this is what suppresses freedom of expression in Turkey.

Here one also needs to note that the struggles of Turkish journalists and intellectuals have been successful in cracking open the door to democracy and moving the country toward institutionalization of the right to freedom of expression. Despite penal proceedings faced at exceptional military courts, state security courts, and specialized heavy penal courts since the early 1980s,[2] many journalists and intellectuals have organized against repression. Their struggles have centered around the nature of the rights to freedom of expression and of the press in Turkey, how limitations on these rights can be diminished, and how to better inform the public of the facts. These struggles have enabled the start and spread of public discussion on how the rights to freedom of expression and of the press can be

---

[2]State security courts were established under the 1982 Constitution to try cases involving crimes against the security of the state. They began to function in 1984 as a replacement to the military courts that had been in operation under martial law. In April 1991, when the Law to Fight Terrorism (law 3713) entered into force, cases involving crimes against the security of the state began to be punished under it. The state security courts' panel of three judges included a military judge. In June 1999, in acquiescence to criticism by the European Union and the European Court of Human Rights, the Turkish government removed the military judge from the panel. In the context of a package of reforms to the constitution passed in June 2004, the state security courts were formally abolished, and their functions were transferred to specialized heavy penal courts.

protected. It is through this process of struggle that the public has gradually come to understand that they have a right to know the facts. As we look at the period that begins with public recognition of their own right to know the truth, we see that the more the freedom of expression and of the press are limited, the more pressure is brought to bear on fundamental rights and liberties, the more popular resistance there is against such suppression. We see that legal battles in the courts have extended the rights to freedom of expression, and that news of penal proceedings against journalists has changed the public's perspective on things. We now have a public that realizes the importance of the work and of the working conditions of journalists, and that understands what the dismissal of journalists actually means. In point of fact, all this repression has given birth to some positive consequences in Turkey.

So when you ask me to identify the historical milestones in the evolution of the rights to freedom of expression and of the press in Turkey, I can point to three main pillars of our framework: (1) the process after ratification of the Constitution of 1961; (2) the continuity in the limitations placed upon fundamental rights and liberties; and (3) the acceptance of rights in the context of such limitations. Turkey has not yet experienced a process that would lead to an enduring acceptance of fundamental rights and liberties or their protection and development. Instead, the order institutionalized thus far is predicated upon the acceptance of fundamental rights and liberties together with the limitations upon them. In other words, limitations upon fundamental rights and liberties have thus far been accepted as the rule, while their protection has been accepted as the exception. This understanding must be challenged. Rights and liberties are essential. Only where society has internalized the need for these rights as essential can a country have a democratic and secular state with social rule of law. It is only under this kind of social order that the juridical, legislative, and executive bodies can function in balance, independent of one another and in impartiality, thus leading to the emergence of a democratic order.

Can you provide us with more detail on the legal amendments introduced in the 2000s? How did Turkey end up, after a decade of legal change undertaken during the EU accession negotiations, becoming the country with the highest number of incarcerated journalists in the world in 2012 and 2013?

For this we need to take a closer look at Turkey's international relations. In particular, the European Convention on Human Rights, ratified on November 4, 1950, and the decisions taken by the European Court of Human Rights (ECHR), established in 1953 in accordance with the convention, directly affected Turkey's domestic laws. In 1987, Turkey accepted the right to apply individually to the ECHR, a provision which allows individuals to complain to the ECHR about states. Turkey recognized the compulsory jurisdiction of the ECHR in 1990. The 1990s are thus marked by the start of implementation of ECHR decisions in Turkey, and by the direct effects of these decisions on Turkey's domestic law. The most positive aspect of these effects is the fact that fundamental laws have been changed to protect fundamental rights and liberties. In particular, with a change introduced to the Constitution in 2004, the place of international treaties relating to human rights was defined, and, albeit in an imperfect manner, procedures were restored to meet a constitutional norm. Accordingly, in the case of a contradiction between the provisions of the duly ratified international agreements on fundamental rights and freedoms and the provisions of domestic laws, the international provision prevail. The judiciary must consequently refer to the provisions of international agreements directly and must ignore those of domestic laws. The provisions of international treaties were coded into Turkish domestic law and began to be implemented. This had a beneficial effect on the realization of democracy, media freedom, freedom of expression, and other fundamental rights and liberties in Turkey. Beginning in 1998 and 1999, Turkey's status vis-à-vis its relations with the EU and the Council of Europe turned into a matter of discussion.

The key issue here was this: were we going to amend our domestic laws in accordance with the European Convention on Human Rights and the decisions made by the ECHR, or not? The European Commission laid out Turkey's response to this question in its yearly progress reports on accession to the European Union as a member. The progress reports included information on the state of the media and the right to freedom of expression, including journalist deaths, criminal charges brought against them, how the right to the freedom of expression and of the press were suppressed. In 2001, Turkey composed a national report claiming to commit to the resolution of the problems identified in the progress reports Türkiye Cumhuriyeti Avrupa Birliği Bakanlığı (2001). In the national report Turkey enumerated actions to be undertaken in the short-, mid-, and long-term of the EU harmonization of law process. In a sense, it established its own roadmap. In 2003, the national report was reviewed, and it was observed that actions undertaken thus far were inadequate. In order for the EU harmonization process to continue, a third national report was accepted by the Turkish Council of Ministers. If you examine this decision, you see that, once again, the right to freedom of expression was positioned above all other fundamental rights and liberties, and amendments to existing laws, including the essential criminal laws, were made accordingly. Yet, when it came to the implementation of these amendments, Turkey once again experienced difficulties.

The goal of harmonization laws[3] is to minimize key measures of restriction and to introduce protections to fundamental rights and liberties. In this context, one of the intentions is to put a stop to the continual criminal proceedings directed against journalists. The legal, administrative, and political reasons behind such proceedings would have to be addressed and the situations remedied. Seen from this perspective, harmonization laws can be interpreted as efforts made by governments to correct existing problems. For example, crimes defined by Article 141 (communist organization) and Article 142 (communist propaganda) of the Turkish Criminal Code had to be removed. In 1991, these crimes were removed from the criminal code and

---

[3]*Harmonization laws* is a term used to refer to laws adopted by countries aiming to join the EU, a process required in order to achieve uniformity in the laws of EU member states.

were replaced by the Articles 6, 7, and 8 of the Anti-Terror Law, in other words, with crimes such as propagandizing for terrorist organizations or disclosing the names of those fighting against terrorist organizations. Removing Article 141 and Article 142 has therefore not helped in solving the essential problem. In another example, exceptional military courts were abolished only to be replaced by state security courts. In 2004, intellectuals and journalists were primarily put on trial at state security courts. Similarly, harmonization laws amended the Turkish Penal Code. Article 312 of Turkish Penal Code, "Incitement of Hatred and Enmity by Differentiating between People on the Basis of Class, Race, Religion, Sect, or Region," was commonly used in criminal proceedings. The EU progress reports stated that such proceedings created problems, so the government changed Article 312 and accepted criteria such as the existence of "explicit and imminent danger." Then all of a sudden, Article 312 came to be implemented less frequently, and the number of cases based on Article 169 of the penal code, aiding and abetting a terrorist organization, increased. Any kind of writing, any kind of expression, anything written in a book, could be grounds for being charged with aiding and abetting a terrorist organization. When these cases came to be recognized as a problem by the EU, Article 169 was amended, Article 301 was discovered, and criminal proceedings based on Article 301 increased. Article 301 was primarily enforced in cases filed against Armenians, Greeks, and Kurds. It hence came to be widely associated with the charge of "insulting Turkishness." The article is intended to protect constitutional organizations—for example, law enforcement officers, the Turkish parliament, and the ministries. In 2008, Article 301 was also amended, making it obligatory to get the approval of the Minister of Justice in filing charges under this article. Consequently, the number of cases filed under Article 301 diminished. Turkey presented this decrease in number as a symptom of transition to democracy. Yet, when you review the progress reports from 2004, 2010, 2012, and 2013, the European Council's Commission on Human Rights concluded that the statistical decrease in the number of cases filed under Article 301 in no ways shows that Turkey is a democratic state where rule of law prevails. In other words, the commission indicated that Turkey should be protecting and defending fundamental rights and liberties instead of pleading their case on the basis of statistics. When you look into the details of the current method of filing cases in Turkey, you see that Article 299 (insulting the president), Article 300 (insulting the symbols of state sovereignty), and Article 301 (insulting Turkishness, the republic, and the organs or institutions of the state) of the Turkish Penal Code stand out. Overall, this tells us that the Turkish Criminal Code and the system of law in general are still structured to provide the means to strengthen, utilize, and implement key measures of restriction. What needs to be emphasized when disclaiming this legal structure is the issue of implementation. The key question here is, "Why are you amending laws if you are not going to implement them?"

In Turkey, every new law, every amendment to the law, has resulted in new problems. The amendments introduced to solve problems end up creating new ones. Generally speaking, this situation is a consequence of the normalization and internalization of the thirty-year period between 1961 and 1991, such that its mentality has been accepted and embraced as normal. Time and again, amendments to laws have been introduced in order to overcome problems. We have to accept that these amendments were good, in the sense that there is no going back. As new laws are made to protect and improve the right to freedom of expression, restrictions must be kept to a minimum. But if you keep on implementing exceptions as if they are the rule, changing laws will not do any good. The problems will not decrease, but will instead pile up. Laws themselves are not sufficient for the creation of pluralism and a democratic social order. You need a change in mentality. This whole process has shown that Turkey is not yet ready for a change in mentality. It has to be accepted that if you make changes to the law, you must then implement those changes. In the 2000s, the main issue in Turkey has been about correcting problems in the law, and we are still struggling with this issue today.

You mentioned earlier that positive changes in the exercise of the right to freedom of expression can be understood by looking at the struggles of intellectuals and journalists. Could you present some examples of struggles that have resulted in changes to legal restrictions, or to the exercise and public embrace of the right to freedom of expression?

The ratification of the Constitution of 1982 after the fascist coup d'état of 1980 is defined in Turkish history as a (relative) return to democracy. The Constitution of 1982 was approved primarily in order to do away with martial law and to transition out of a two-year period of repression. With its ratification, Kenan Evren, one of the five generals who had carried out the coup, assumed the title of president. In this process, one of the main turning points was the case of the "Petition of Intellectuals." During Evren's presidency, intellectuals signed a petition, had it notarized, and, by conveying it to the office of the presidency, expressed their opinions and wishes on what must be done regarding the state of democracy in Turkey. This petition, which started as the initiative of 52 intellectuals, ended up with more than a thousand signatures. It turned into a movement in Turkey, and was ultimately accepted as an act of shaking off, a step toward the adoption of democracy. It was widely embraced. Seen from this perspective, we can accept the "Petition of Intellectuals" as an act of resistance that emerged at the tail end of the period of repression when its legal order, an order institutionalized by the fascist coup of September 12, 1980, still prevailed. The "Petition of Intellectuals" became a symbol of resistance and signified the attitude of intellectuals against the coup's military rulers. It was meant as a request for democracy, for the right to freedom of expression, and for the right to freedom of the press. In the end, every one of its signatories was put on trial.

The resistance of intellectuals and journalists of today comes out of that tradition. They are embodiments of the desire to resist. Being a dissident in Turkey is not for nothing. In Turkey, being in the opposition is a conscious and rational act. In this context, the role of intellectuals and journalists is particularly important. For example, if we were to compare the aftermath of the 1980 coup d'état with the period of 2000–2013, we must begin with an examination of a number of famous criminal proceedings at the specialized heavy penal courts, forms of exceptional courts that have been normalized into our times. As you are well aware, the Ergenekon trial, the Balyoz trial, and the military spy ring trial, caused quite a domestic and international stir.[4] Everyone talks about them. In these trials, one wing of Turkish politicians took on the role of the defense while the other took on the role of the prosecution. An arrest warrant was issued for two journalists— Nedim Şener and Ahmet Şık.[5] Upon their arrest, a group of journalists formed the Friends of Ahmet and Nedim, unconnected to any existing organization, and protested their arrest. At the precise moment that this group was drawing attention to the wrongful arrests of Şener and Şık on the grounds of their journalistic activities, the then prime minister Erdoğan gave a speech at the Council of Europe in which he compared Şener and Şık's books to "bombs." In response to this speech, journalists and intellectuals took to the streets in protest. In their view, the baseless arrests were unlawful and violated fundamental human rights and liberties. This protest in support of journalists was later reflected in the protests against bans on Twitter and internet usage, with people taking to the streets shouting, "Don't touch my journalists. Don't touch my Twitter." Seen from this perspective, the Gezi Park

---

[4]The Ergenekon trial, which started in 2008, consists of a series of high-profile trials in which hundreds of military officers, journalists and opposition lawmakers were accused of plotting against the AKP government. The trials resulted in lengthy prison sentences for the majority of the accused, including the former chief of the general staff. In the Balyoz ("sledgehammer") trial, begun in 2010, the courts sentenced 322 serving and retired military army officers to prison terms ranging from 6 to 20 years for conspiring to overthrow the AKP government; 34 were acquitted. In the military spy ring trial, begun in 2011, the courts accused 56 military officials of leaking documents thereby risking the security of the state. These three trials were widely viewed as tainted by dubious evidence and were seen as part of an act of revenge carried out by Turkey's Islamists against their former oppressors in the military, bureaucracy, and media. The trials also raised concerns about freedom of speech and the media, the independence of the judiciary, and the government's use of its parliamentary majority to pass laws without engaging in public debate. After 2014, the Supreme Court of Appeals and the Constitutional Court have issued rulings calling for retrials of all three. Following the July 15, 2016 coup attempt, the three retrials were merged with a trial accusing alleged coup plotters, on the grounds that the three previous trials had prepared the setting for the coup.

[5]Ahmet Şık and Nedim Şener were arrested for their alleged links to a purportedly clandestine, secular Ergenekon organization in the framework of the OdaTV trial in which mostly journalists and writers were accused of acting as the alleged organization's media wing. OdaTV was a Turkish news website whose offices were raided in 2011 by the police. Şık and Şener, neither of whom worked for OdaTV, were detained a month later on the basis of digital documents allegedly found during the OdaTV raid. It is commonly thought that Şener and Şık's arrests were linked to their investigative work on the Gülen movement. While Şener (2010) suggested that the movement holds undue influence in the Ergenekon investigation, Şık's book, *The Imam's Army* (2012), argued for an affiliation between the Gülen movement and the Turkish police force. The draft of Şık's then unpublished book was seized and banned upon his detention. Here we should note that after a year in jail, both Şık and Şener were released in 2012, remaining to this day under indictment in the OdaTV retrial. Şık, who continued to fiercely criticize the wrongdoings of both the Gülen movement and the AKP government after his release, was again arrested after he criticized the AKP government in his tweets in December 2016, this time for allegedly disseminating propaganda on behalf of FETÖ and the PKK (Coşkun 2016).

protests[6] developed in the aftermath of these trials. Journalists and intellectuals joined the public in these protests. In essence, these actions were the people's defense of their right to express themselves. The law on the meetings and demonstrations needs to be understood in this context as well; it was an act of civil disobedience in Turkey, and indication that people are far more aware of the need to protect their rights. They act rationally and willfully. This must bring about a more democratic order.

Thus far we have discussed the legal, international, and social aspects of the right to freedom of expression in Turkey. What can you tell us about the effects of labor relations on freedom of expression in Turkey? In particular, what is the structure of ownership of media outlets? How does this structure affect the working conditions of journalists and relations between journalists, management, and owners?

Law number 5953, the Press Labor Law, concerns the working conditions and work-related rights and obligations of journalists. Passed in 1952, it was originally called the "Law Concerning the Relationship between Workers and Employers at Presses." It underwent some changes with the passing of law number 212, the Press Labor Law, after the coup d'état of 1960. Press Labor Law 212 grants certain rights to journalists and is one of the most important laws guaranteeing job security to journalists. But because employing journalists under this law costs more, employers have resisted it since its inception, claiming that they cannot afford it.

In the past, the structure called Bab-i Ali[7] consisted of newspapers run by journalists. In other words, the owners of the newspapers used to be journalists themselves. A good example is Nadir Nadi and the *Cumhuriyet* newspaper. Another example is Erol Simavi and the ownership structure in newspapers like *Hürriyet* and *Milliyet*. At those times, the structure of ownership in the press matched the properties of the journalistic profession. Journalists therefore embraced the structure. Over time, circumstances changed in such a way that employers were no longer former journalists, and this remains the case today. In the new structure, employers and bosses have moved away from the old understanding of journalism. The new approach is that the newspaper is a business organization, and the work objectives are profit-making, running ads, and running their business. The moment that this new understanding—which we can characterize as "minding your own

---

[6]The Gezi protests were arguably the largest wave of protests in recent Turkish history wherein hundreds of thousands took to the streets to contest the proposed demolition of Gezi Park located at the heart of Istanbul's Taksim Square. A small sit-in against the construction of a shopping mall at the park area escalated by the end of May 2013 into a large-scale demonstration. The protests were interpreted as an expression of the tension between conservatives and a wide variety of groups in Turkey in the battle over public space, resistance to authoritarian tendencies of the AKP government, and minority group struggles.

[7]Bab-i Ali is a district in Istanbul where the Ottoman government and virtually all of the Turkish newspapers and publishers used to be located at. Until the 1990s, Bab-i Ali was used as a synonym for Turkish press.

business"—came to fore, the structure of journalism began to change. Newspapers were no longer dominated by concerns about journalism and producing the news, but rather about profit and loss.

This new structure was brought about by conditions created by the global economy. Under the new structure, those with the capacity to make editorial decisions have turned into a kind of managerial class. The moment they became managers, they were given such extensive rights, authority, salaries, and other benefits, that they could not refuse. For example, they were authorized to dismiss journalists they disliked. Importantly, this new structure gave rise to deunionization. With the support of employers, journalist unions were countered. The power of unions was further reduced by journalists resigning from their union membership; in other words, when journalists gave up being organized. The moment you give up your organizational ties, your work conditions come under the absolute domination of the employer. In this vein, relationships between employers and the government began to affect journalists' understanding of journalism and the publishing of newspapers in general.

Overall, journalists remained silent when other journalists were dismissed. Obviously, there are exceptions, but these are in the minority. Most journalists internalized and accepted dismissals. In this context, a reporter losing his/her job was no longer remarkable as far as a manager was concerned. Journalistic unemployment lost all meaning. In a sense, journalists took the first negative step by cutting their organizational ties. Although it's easy to criticize, one should not be judgmental. We must also take into consideration the working conditions of journalists. It's not an easy task to stand up to the pressures of employers. But after this step backwards, journalists slowly moved away from the old points of resistance such as holding regular assemblies, creating an organized work force, or collectively opposing the unwarranted dismissal of journalists. In the absences of an organizational force—be it in the form of a union or another self-organized structure—the presence of a law that ensured job security made no difference. In other words, the existing laws protecting journalists became de facto ineffective. Employers began to employ journalists with contracts designed not according to the Press Labor Law number 212, but according to the general labor law to which all other workers are subject. In this context, the pool of journalists employed in accordance with law 212 was made as small as possible. This is how problems created by globalization affected the field of Turkish journalism. Media outlets and press organizations were turned into mere business organizations.

The solution to this transformation is the ephemeral "editorial independence." Even though editorial independence is difficult to achieve anywhere in the world, it can be realized, even in Turkey. But you need journalists and employers who believe in the existence of editorial independence. Journalists need to remember the concept of editorial independence and the ethical code of journalism. In this sense, we need to protect the profession. There are many forces arrayed against journalists —those holding political power, laws, the administrative structure makes the job of journalists harder, journalists are pressured by their employers. We must nonetheless remain hopeful. The existing dissident press in Turkey is a breath of fresh air for those who want to find the truth and exercise their right to information. Journalists in these press organizations have not lost their courage. Despite all the problems, the threat of joblessness, all the pressures they face, they continue doing journalism. These rights-based journalists prove to us that another type of media can exist, a media based in rights-based journalism.

Finally, when you compare the kind of pressures brought to bear upon the exercise of free speech and the media in the past to those we experience now, how do you interpret the state of freedom of expression today?

We have never experienced a time like this before. When we compare the situation with the past, this is the darkest period, due to the mind-set of politicians at the highest level and people that surround them. What they are doing now will not be remembered well. In fact, this is true not only for Turkey, but also for other parts of the world. We are being subjected to the worst kind of state governance at a time when everyone is in contact with one another under the aegis of a global economic system.

Those in government will always try to protect themselves from the press; this is true of any time in history. Politicians obviously have personal rights that need to be protected by laws. In Turkey, laws guarantee such protection. But politicians cannot act as though journalists are the enemy, they cannot nurture enmity toward journalists in such a way as to affect their working conditions. They cannot act as if they are at war with journalist. That is not public administration. Those who govern— politicians and public administrators—have to be tolerant in the face of criticism and news. They have to be models for the public in terms of open-mindedness, debate, and toleration. In Turkey, politicians do otherwise. A person may be judged on the grounds of his action. Yet, every human being, including journalists, has a right to a fair trial. This is a universal principle. If one believes in this principle, one accepts that no head of state should use public addresses to put pressure on a journalist. In Turkey, journalists have been publicly identified and vilified, causing them to become the target of public enmity. This has never happened in Turkey before. During former periods of exceptional or martial law, there was enormous pressure placed on journalists, but those targeted were well-known and it was clear why they became targets. In the current period, it's worse because it's hard to predict what might happen or when. This is the creation of an empire of fear in the presence of democracy.

People do not feel safe. In an atmosphere where people are constantly in a state of fear, where there are no legal guarantees on what may happen, there is no law, no security, no justice. In a place where there is no justice, the government can do anything they want with law, including arbitrary governance. These are the kind of methods being used today. They make laws, the laws come to be enforced, but none of them lead to justice. When you ask them, they say that their actions are in accordance with the law. Yet all their actions are unjust. Justice prohibits discrimination. Where there is discrimination, there is no justice. In order to ensure justice, you have to abolish discrimination. In this context, no journalist in Turkey should be portrayed as the enemy of a politician. One cannot protect the rule of law by intensifying polarization and then assume that those who disagree are enemies. In short, no enemy criminal law[8] should be created. People who do not think like you, who do not agree with you, who oppose your views, are exercising their right to freedom of expression. Everyone has a right to freedom of expression. Democracy and the principles of rule of law can function in so far as the freedom of expression of those who oppose the government and the system are protected. The reverse is an authoritarian regime.[9]

References

Çarkoğlu, A., Baruh, L., & Yıldırım, K. (2013). Press-Party parallelism and polarization of news media during an election campaign: The case of the 2011 Turkish elections. *The International Journal of Press/Politics, 19*(3), 295–317.

Coşkun, C. (2016). FETÖ'nün ipliğini pazara çıkaran Ahmet Şık "*FETÖ propagandası*" iddiasiyla tutuklandi. Cumhuriyet Gazetesi. December 30, 2016.

Council of Europe. (1950). *Convention for the protection of human rights and fundamental freedoms*. Strasbourg: Council of Europe. Retrieved November 23, 2017 from http://www.echr.coe.int/pages/home.aspx?p=basictexts.

Jakobs, G. (1985). Kriminalisierung im Vorfeld einer Rechtsgutsverletzung. *Zeitschrift für die gesamte Strafrechtswissenschaft, 97*(4), 751–785.

---

[8]Enemy criminal law, known in German as *Feindstrafrecht*, is a theory set out by Gunther Jakobs (1985 and 2006) in which there is a distinction between the criminal law of the citizen and the criminal law of the enemy. In the criminal law of the enemy, people identified as enemies do not deserve the protections of the criminal law of the citizen. Certain laws may be suspended based on the idea that society or the state must be protected from the danger of the enemy. Overall, criminal law of the enemy tends to punish prospectively in order to prevent future harms. It imposes disproportionate sanctions in the name of security and departs from conventional procedural protections.

[9]By the time Fikret Ilkiz gave this interview in 2014, freedom of expression, freedom of the press and politics were already in a poor state in Turkey. According to the World Press Freedom Index, the country had dropped from a mediocre 99th position in 2007 to 154th in 2013. One after the other, established, mainstream media outlets were confiscated and over 30% of the newspaper circulation was transferred to groups closely affiliated with the ruling party (Çarkoğlu et al. 2013). Thousands of journalists were dismissed on political grounds. Broadcast and internet bans had turned into business as usual. The number of libel suits opened against citizens for their critical tweets skyrocketed, and an increasing number of journalists were charged with terror-related crimes. Since the interview, the situation has gone from bad to worse. Phone calls were leaked as evidence of corruption by the party and the Erdogan family. Turkey became further embroiled in the war in Syria. Violence against the Kurds in the southeast of Turkey escalated. Most recently, in July 2016, a coup d'état was attempted and failed, leading to the declaration of a state of emergency and a massive purge of civil servants. As a consequence of these developments, journalists who had exposed Turkey's involvement in the Syrian civil war and the corruption of the AKP, academics who had signed a peace petition against violence against Kurds, and many other critical parties including Kurdish MPs, civil society activists, artists, and random citizens, were arrested on terror charges, fired, or left with no other choice but to live in exile.

Jakobs, G. (2006). Feindstrafrecht? Eine Untersuchung zu den Bedingungen von Rechtlichkeit. Höchstrichterliche Rechtsprechung Strafrecht–HHRS, (8/9), 289–297.

Şener, N. (2010). *Ergenekon Belgelerinde Fethullah Gülen ve Cemaat.* Istanbul: Destek Yayinlari.

Şık, A. (2012). *Imamın Ordusu.* [The Imam's army]. Retrieved November 15, 2017, from http://xeberler.files.wordpress.com/2011/04/51984426-dokunan-yanar.pdf.

Türkiye Cumhuriyet Avrupa Birliği Bakanlığı. (2001). AB Müktesebatının Üstlenilmesine İlişkin Türkiye Ulusal Programı. https://www.ab.gov.tr/195.html.

United Nations. (1966). International covenant on civil and political rights. New York: United Nations. Retrieved November 23, 2017 from https://treaties.un.org/pages/ViewDetails.aspx?src=IND&mtdsg_no=IV-4&chapter=4&lang=en.

Fikret İlkiz is a lawyer registered at Istanbul Bar Association. He worked as lawyer, legal consultant and editor at the daily Cumhuriyet, as legal consultant and deputy secretary general at Press Council, and as department head at Istanbul Bar Association where he also was a member of the editorial board of the Association's Journal. İlkiz established the Center for Internship and Education at Istanbul Bar Association, and was a member of the executive committee at Turkish Bars Association's Human Rights Research and Application Center. He still is the editor of the Journal of Contemporary Law, an honorary member of Turkish Journalists Association, and a member of the board of directors of Umut Foundation and Turkish Penal Law Foundation. He holds the Press Freedom Award of Turkish Journalists Association (1998) and the Freedom of Expression Honorary Award of Turkish Publishers Association (2013).

Defne Över is an early career fellow at the Göttingen Institute for Advanced Study, Lichtenberg Kolleg, Göttingen University, Germany. She received her Ph.D. in Sociology from Cornell University, USA, her M.A. from Humboldt University, Germany, and her B.A from Boğaziçi University, Turkey. Her work centers on the study of human rights, political repression, institutional change, and social movements. In her dissertation "Political Destabilization in Turkey: The Case of Journalism, 1980–2013" she explored the making of a new field of journalism under political repression in Turkey. Her studies on complex histories, national identities, social movements and research methods appeared in Qualitative Sociology, Research in Social Movements, Conflicts and Change, and Sage Research Method Cases. Defne also holds Cornell University's Sidney Tarrow Paper Award for best paper written in the field of European Politics and Sakıp Sabancı International Research Award's Honorable Mention for her M.A. thesis on collective action in Turkey.

State and Civilian Violence Against "Dangerous" Others

Tanıl Bora and interviewed by Deniz Yonucu

Abstract The lynch regime in Turkey is an instance where lynches and vigilantism form two parts of a single mechanism, where they almost complete each other hand in hand with state terror. The perpetrators are not prosecuted according to the law because the people being attacked are described as traitors, enemies, and provocateurs by both state representatives and within the dominant nationalistic discourse. In incidents of lynching or assassination, the perpetrators are portrayed as sensitive citizens acting from righteous motivations who have somehow been provoked. In this depiction, provocation is as inevitable as are natural disasters. When treated like this, the lynching is not scandalized but normalized. I speak of a lynch regime because of the systematic, institutionalized use of this lynching discourse.

Keywords Turkey · Lynch regime · Violence

If we look at the violent history of Turkey, which groups or populations have historically been targeted by the government? Which populations have been seen by the ruling elite as "enemies within"?

To put it cynically, we might say that the ruling elite sees the whole of society as the enemy, or at least dangerous. The second president of Turkey, Mustafa İsmet İnönü, once said in a speech he gave to a group of military officers during the War of Independence, "The sultan is our enemy. Everyone is our enemy. No one should hear this, but the nation is our enemy." Although I am being cynical, this cynicism should not prevent us from noting that Turkey's ruling elites have an entrenched fear of the masses and of the people in general. During the authoritarian single-party

T. Bora (✉)
Institute of Social and Cultural Anthropology, Ludwig-Maximilian
University of Munich, Munich, Germany
e-mail: tbora@iletisim.com.tr

D. Yonucu
Iletisim Publishing, Istanbul, Turkey

© Springer International Publishing AG, part of Springer Nature 2019   229
E. Özyürek et al. (eds.), *Authoritarianism and Resistance in Turkey*,
https://doi.org/10.1007/978-3-319-76705-5_22

era of 1923 to 1950, the street was not even used for pro-regime demonstrations. Mass demonstrations played a marginal role in the propaganda repertoire of the single-party state. The founding Kemalist republican leaders held an elitist tutelary view of society. This ruling elite carried the myth of the Ottoman *Devlet-i Aliyye*— the Great Ottoman State, the Ottoman Empire—which it claimed to leave behind into the creation of the Turkish nation. They did this by transforming it.

The nationalist conservative political elite and the developing bourgeoisie continued this antidemocratic animosity toward the masses by criminalizing communism. From the 1960s onwards, the perception of threat from the street and from those below crystallized and took on a distinct class character, strengthened by the ideology of security. Having embarked on the project of nation-building on the basis of Turkish national identity, non-Turkish group became potential internal enemies. Muslim non-Turks were considered to be predisposed to assimilation, with the exception of Kurds, who were seen as particularly resistant to assimilation and dangerous due to their large numbers and concentration in one contiguous region.

After independence, the Kurdish elite who had played a founding role in the creation of the Turkish republic and who had taken part in the war felt that they had been betrayed and so organized a popular resistance movement. During the early republican period, they became the target of widespread and persistent violence. The structural and symbolic violence aimed at repressing Kurdish identity was a constant and chronic element in everyday life. So much so that this structural and symbolic violence is said to have only intermittently erupted into physical, police, or military violence. Over the last 30 years, violence has been measured out in different doses.

Following the armed struggle launched by the PKK in the 1980s, there was a transition to low-intensity warfare in the 1990s. Brutal clandestine operations were carried out on a mass scale. Disproportionate use of violence against the Kurdish movement in the cities has continued even when the peace process was formally in force.

As with the Muslim minorities, non-Muslim minorities were required by the constitution to identify as Turks. But because of their religious difference, rather than assimilation, there was a strong tendency for exclusion and dissimilation. No matter how small their numbers, Greeks, Jews, and Armenians were viewed by Turkish nationalists as microbes threatening the purity of the nation. There were pogroms in Thrace in 1934 and attacks in Istanbul with in 1955. In 2007, the assassination of the Armenian journalist Hrant Dink in relation to his public television coverage of the Armenian Genocide was a tragic indication that the violence had again erupted beyond the structural and symbolic.

During the Cold War, the anticommunism that marked the political culture of that era was made to do heavy lifting. Turkey deployed the perception of the communist threat as a geostrategic resource in order to take seat at the free world table and enter the NATO bloc. From the second half of the 1940s to the 1960s, a handful of members in the clandestine communist party were used to demonize all the opposition movements. With the rise of labor and socialist movements in the 1960s, anticommunism was mobilized against the working classes. By the 1970s, in a symbiotic relationship with the unconventional warfare of the state, anticommunist nationalism was transformed into a paramilitary configuration of violence.

Without delving into the ideological and political details, hate speech vis-à-vis every faction on the left still reigns supreme in Turkey. The psychological tropes inherited from anticommunism pigeonhole those who are seen to be cosmopolitan, elitist, or snobbish as alien to the nation; they have lost their Turkish essence by becoming ultramodern.

In the 1960s, we saw another enemy crystallizing: Alevis. Again, Cold War anticommunist rhetoric marshalled to demonize the left-leaning Alevis. The reasons for the Alevi lean to the left were both sociological and teleological. Generally poor and dispossessed, Alevis were to a large extent excluded from the clientelist networks of the nationalist conservative movement. Their faith in messianic salvation and the Alevi discourse of victimhood melded easily with socialist revolutionary discourses. For the state, identifying Alevis with communism facilitated demonization of both. The heresy of the Alevi heterodox deviancy, interwoven with grotesque exaggerations, concretized the moral degeneracy attributed to communists.

Branding Alevism as being linked to communism legitimized the established prejudices of Sunni conservatism and reiterated them into new instances of that prejudice. Socioeconomic concerns played a significant role in the incitement to violence. The rapid urbanization and upward mobility of Alevis—a people who had lived in remote rural areas for centuries and were now seen to be quickly ascending to white-collar employment—stoked the fears of Sunnis. In an environment where capitalism was expanding especially in countryside, many worried about downward mobility. In the politically polarized setting of the 1960s and 1970s, the nationalist-fascist movement used this social irritation unsparingly in their provocation campaigns. The Maraş massacre of 1978 where some 150 people were slaughtered in the state's use of unconventional warfare is the most violent event of this period.

There are two unforgettable events from the 1990s. An even more important one was the Sivas massacre where 33 people were killed. This incident began when the socialist, Crimean Tatar writer Aziz Nesin was targeted and branded as Satan by Sunni Islamists for having defended Salman Rushdie's right to freedom of speech. When Nesin attended an Alevi festival in Sivas, Islamist protesters turned into a lynching mob, chased after the so-called atheists, and set the hotel on fire. The second unforgettable event was the 1995 simultaneous anonymous automatic rifle shootings at several coffeehouses in the Gazi neighborhood of Istanbul, an area populated by Alevis. During the riots that ensured, 23 people were killed and some 1,400 injured.

With the war in the Kurdish regions and nationalist mobilization in support of the war, there were assassination attempts against the Kurds throughout the 1990s. These especially targeted those living in the Aegean and Mediterranean parts of Turkey, Kurds who had been compelled to leave their villages as a result of the state's forced displacement policies. Class rivalry was evident in these attacks: Kurdish migrants represented a competitively cheap labor force and Kurds who became microentrepreneurs vied with local tradesmen for business. These kinds of economic frustrations could easily be translated into racism.

In your works (Bora 2008, 2016), you refer to a *lynch regime* in Turkey as well as a form of *right-wing vigilantism*. At what points does right-wing vigilantism in Turkey resemble or differ from its counterparts across the globe?

The lynch regime in Turkey is an instance where lynches and vigilantism form two parts of a single mechanism, where they almost complete each other hand in hand with state terror. The perpetrators are not prosecuted according to the law because the people being attacked are described as traitors, enemies, and provocateurs by both state representatives and within the dominant nationalistic discourse. In incidents of lynching or assassination, the perpetrators are portrayed as sensitive citizens acting from righteous motivations who have somehow been provoked. In this depiction, provocation is as inevitable as are natural disasters. When treated like this, the lynching is not scandalized but normalized. I speak of a lynch regime because of the systematic, institutionalized use of this lynching discourse.

Unfortunately, we should note that this discourse is not limited to right-wing circles. While proportionally few in number, in some very specific instances, groups that are being attacked—leftists, Alevis, Kurds—can be seen to be sympathetic toward certain instances of lynching as forms of extralegal justice meted out in the absence of a functioning justice system. The reasons behind this are without a doubt linked to a deep distrust of the Turkish judicial system, which systematically victimizes them. But let me once more emphasize that I think this has to do with normalizing instead of scandalizing lynching—the core tenet of the lynch regime.

This lynch regime operate in particular in Istanbul and the cities along the Aegean and Mediterranean coasts, where attacks against Kurdish migrant groups and pro-Kurdish political party members are frequent. Alongside spontaneous developments, in some incidents we can see that groups that are politically inclined to these attacks encounter new doors being opened for them, and may easily find a way to attack. Not only do they rely on the certainty that their actions will be overlooked, by they are also made to feel by the powers that be—the state, the police—that they must take action because of the national sensitivities they should be defending. That is to say, in addition to spontaneous lynchings, there are also incidents where nationalist and fascist groups are mobilized. In incidents such as these, it is easier to talk about a lynch regime.

I do not have enough information to be able to compare it with other examples worldwide. Although my framework for analogy is that of Nazi Germany, this does not mean that we should draw ahistorical comparisons between Nazi Germany and Turkey. I do think that Nazi Germany's practice of harnessing the potential of the crowd to turn into a lynch mob is a model that can be applied to many modern nation-states. The Nazis turned the German masses against the Jewish people, then legitimized lynchings by praising the perpetrators as having been motivated by a natural, all but to be expected, nationalist anger. These attacks were predominantly carried out and controlled by the party, but in the countryside especially they were often spontaneous. The next phase was to legitimize the lynchings through the introduction of legislative regulations designed to expel the Jewish people from the body of the citizenry. These regulations also served to mollify the public's "natural" national anger. Modern states can now refer to the Nazis' barbaric use of lynching as a crisis management tool. The more a state resorts to such a lynching regime, the more barbaric the state becomes. I think that in Turkey a significant predisposition to such barbarity already exists.

Your words remind me of Walter Benjamin's thesis on history: "There is no document of civilization which is not at the same time a document of barbarism" (2007, p. 256). Benjamin is talking about a violence that is inherent to modernity. Are you at least in part using the term *barbarism* as Benjamin does. Or are you talking about a barbarism particular to Turkey. Why does such a significant predisposition to barbarity already exist?

Yes, Benjamin said that barbarism is inherent to modern culture. There is a stream of thought in political anthropology that suggests that civilization and barbarism are not in a state of a polarization, but rather in a state of dialectical tension. Some scholars have examined Benjamin's notion of "positive barbarism" (Boletsi 2013). Barbarism already exists. In all civilizations, it is established again and again by a civilization's cultural notions and opportunities. This is what Benjamin meant here. Nazism, which caused Benjamin's death and reached its maturity after his death, realized a barbarism made possible only through the use of the modern tools. In Turkey, the nation-state reanimates this kind of barbarism by equipping itself with modern civilization's tools of violence. Why is this predisposition to barbarism already significant? This excessive dose we are talking about is not only applicable to Turkey. It is also endemic to the Balkans and the Middle East, regions that were latecomers to nationalism, where nation-states were formed within the context of existential fears of extinction, and where the ruling classes now continue to live in fear of the consequences of that delay and threat. All those in power, even the most "civilized" of Westerners, will resort to barbarism when survival is the prime concern. Look at the West after the September 11 attacks. For Turkish nationalism, the trauma of losing the empire and the existential threat that accompanied it—a trauma whose very existence was thoroughly suppressed and bottled up during the foundational years of the republic—exploded during the period we are living in today. The complex sense of threat and existential anxiety keeps a strong potential for barbarism alive.

Kemalism came into being with the claim of making a radical departure from empire, envisaging itself as the force that rescued a nation about to be devoured by Western imperialists. As such, it presented a fictionalized image of the empire as having been a subjugated anti-imperialist power, rather than an oppressive imperial power. This sublimation of the imperialist past can be seen in the pronouncement of the AKP government. Followers of Kemalism, the dominant AKP narrative portrays the party both as an exception to empire

and as empire's continuation. In your opinion, does this new narrative refer to a new era in Turkey's history of violence?

The dominant AKP narrative is about both continuity and discontinuity. What we have discussed thus far is continuity, the notion that all conservatives, including Kemalists, cherish centralized statism. The discontinuity you mentioned is a renewed imperialist appetite, a desire to become a regional power, a major player in the great game of international geopolitics. This is quite different from Kemalism in terms of its orientation. Kemalism focuses on a foreign policy aimed at maintaining the status quo. It is autarchic, motivated by a strong a desire to maintain economic self-sufficiency and independence. If you ask me, this new keenness for empire increases the state's willingness to resort to violence by feeding the libido of the "powerful state." A state that desires to be powerful outside, also desires to be powerful inside. Also, this imperialist appetite expands as it ramps up the discourse on ethno-religious nationalism. This means that the atmospheric pressure suitable for incitement to lynching is on the rise.

In Turkey, both civilians and policemen taking part in lynching. During the Gezi protests, Ali İsmail Korkmaz, a college student, lost his life as a result of a violent attack by police and right-wing groups. How can we make sense of lynchings conducted by the police and right-wing nationalist groups?

We need to consider the paramilitarization of the police force as part of a global trend, not one specific to Turkey, although it is highly common here. We owe this conceptualization to Bourdieusian researchers of the police and policing, such as Loic Wacquant (2009). These researchers attract our attention to the transformation of police forces into army-like organizations. They demonstrate in their studies on France that both the police equipment and their operational abilities seem as though they are designed for war waged in cities. At the same time, the term *paramilitarization* refers to the kind of radical ideological motivation that one sees in militia organizations. In this sense, the paramilitarization of the police pushes policing well beyond the prevention of crime or the securing of civil order; in this new sense, the police appear to wage war against those they consider to be enemies. This attitude is not at all new, but it intensified after the Gezi protests. The police act in a paramilitaristic way against those whom they consider as the enemies of the state, particularly against leftists and Kurds. With emotions of cruel hatred stoked to the point where the individual is ready to beyond legal bounds, it is not difficult for police violence to transform into lynching and essentially unrecorded, unpunished forms of violence. When this is the case, it becomes much easier for militant groups to punish protesters and civilian groups alongside the police. With this occurs, the grey zone of vigilantism is enlarged and begins to coincide more and more often with police violence.

In 2016, a number of Kurdish towns and neighborhoods were demolished and months-long round-the-clock curfews were imposed in Kurdish towns such as Silopi, Cizre, Nusaybin, Gever. What can you tell us about this kind of large-scale violence?

The operations carried out in Turkey's Kurdistan by special forces between 2015 and 2016 wherein residential areas were bombed during the curfews at intervals over the course of months are a perfect example of the ideological aspect of paramilitarization. As was reflected in the coverage in the media and on social media, the special forces officers wrote racist and sexists slogans and insults on the walls of ruined buildings, even on bedrooms, and made videos celebrating their victory. This is unique to paramilitary structures where groups are specifically ideologically incited to cruelty and are authorized to act outside legal and ethical rules.

Finally, would you like to reflect on the attacks against Syrians in Turkey?

There were several large mob attacks against Syrian refuges in Gaziantep and Ankara, as well as several small-scale discrete attacks that weren't covered by the media. The crucial point about the lynching dynamics where Syrians are targeted is the potential to provoke those at the bottom. The poor, those who are subjected to precarization and treated as the lowest strata, see Syrians as competitors who want to steal their bread. They can be easily incited to see Syrians as permissible targets, because of their status as foreigners. Here I must add that it is mostly the educated middle classes who hold racist and Orientalist prejudices against Arabs. Two years ago, there was a tweet during the mob attacks against Syrians in Kahramanmaraş that read, "What was done is wrong. But no one should forget that Syrians may burn as easily as the Alevis did. This is Kahramanmaraş!" Referring to the 1978 Kahramanmaraş massacre in order to point out the threat against Syrians is an embarrassing example of the normalization of lynching as a tradition in Turkey.

References

Benjamin, W. (2007). *Illuminations*. (H. Zohn, Trans.). New York: Schocken Books.
Bora, T. (2008, 2016). Türkiye'nin Linç Rejimi [Turkey's Lynch Regime]. Istanbul: İletişim Yayınları.
Boletsi, M., & Press, Stanford University. (2013). *Barbarism and its discontents*. Stanford, California: Stanford University Press.
Wacquant, Loic. (2009). *Punishing the poor: neoliberal government of social insecurity*. Durham: Duke University Press.

Part VII
Culture and Society

On Intellectuals and Intellectualism

Pınar Selek and interviewed by Meral Akbaş

Abstract Intellectualism necessitates the ability to reflect upon and ask questions about this accumulated knowledge, a questioning that goes beyond the paradigms of daily life and politics. In order to take this further step towards the abstract, one needs to know the relevant concepts. That is to say, not everyone who asks questions is an intellectual; one definitely needs knowledge and concepts. I mean this to emphasize that what matters is not merely the amount of knowledge. The knowledge must be questioned, imbibed with experience, the content from the experience must return to experience as a questioning.

Keywords Turkey · Intellectuals · Intellectualism

Shall we begin with the question of what "intellectual" means from your point of view?

I have asked myself this question many times, Meral... For a while, I have been thinking along these lines: Intellectualism and being an intellectual necessitate certain erudition, an accumulation of knowledge. This knowledge may also be acquired from life. On the other hand, intellectualism necessitates the ability to reflect upon and ask questions about this accumulated knowledge, a questioning that goes beyond the paradigms of daily life and politics. In order to take this further step towards the abstract, one needs to know the relevant concepts. That is to say, not everyone who asks questions is an intellectual; one definitely needs knowledge and concepts. I mean this to emphasize that what matters is not merely the amount of knowledge. The knowledge must be questioned, imbibed with experience, the content from the experience must return to experience as a questioning.

P. Selek
Université Nice Sophia Antipolis in Political Science, Nice, France

M. Akbaş (✉)
Middle East Technical University, Ankara, Turkey
e-mail: meral_akbas@yahoo.com

© Springer International Publishing AG, part of Springer Nature 2019   239
E. Özyürek et al. (eds.), *Authoritarianism and Resistance in Turkey*,
https://doi.org/10.1007/978-3-319-76705-5_23

I do not wish to discriminate between people who are educated and those who did not go to school. Because in neighbourhoods, in villages, up on mountains and in many other places you see the intellectuals of that region, the people who ponder on social experience from an outside vantage point.

Being an intellectual entails conceptual knowledge as well as the ability to employ this knowledge in a quest to understand society or everyday practice. When you keep asking questions about yourself, your social situation, politics and everyday life, you do not become an intellectual; you come to possess an intellectual stance. In fact, intellectuality is an action, it is an action! Since it is an action, you may act one day or perhaps a few years, but then you might always change your stance. Therefore, it is difficult to describe a constantly occupied, fixed position as if saying "I am an intellectual!"

Here in France people often ask me: "You write novels. On the other hand, you are both a sociologist and a militant. How do you put these together?" I give them a very simple response: I cannot separate them from one another! Yes, one studies sociology or political science to understand and explain society, so you study science. However, sometimes you are overcome with a desire to express yourself, to exclaim, to rebel at what you go through. Because merely explaining is not enough! You must be in awe, you must express your sense of awe. At that point you turn to art: You paint, you write novels. Injustice prevails right in front of your eyes, you struggle against the injustice, and so you become militant. I find it funny to even consider all of these separately.

Being an intellectual entails constantly asking questions about the society, the world, everything, everything that lies outside one's self while also seeing oneself as part of this questioning; being an intellectual entails the ability to sustain this questioning.

Your words remind me of one of your books: Ülker Street: A Place of Marginalization.[1] The opening sentence of your book is a question: "What was I looking for in that street, in that dark street?" May I ask you to re-answer your question now, today? Yes, Ülker Sokak is dark but what makes that street dark is not the dearth of light or abandonment. It is a forbidden space for many people who live in Turkey. What were you doing in an outcast space, in a forbidden street?

Darkness means a place that I cannot see. I myself might be dark for a moment. I mean, it is impossible to read that place or see it with my received codes. Furthermore, that place is not even illuminated, it is a closed out space. I cannot see

---

[1]Pınar Selek, *Maskeler Süvariler Gacılar Ülker Sokak: Bir Alt Kültürün Dışlanma Mekânı* [Masks, Cavaliers, Gacis—Ülker Street: A Place of Marginalization], Ankara: Ayizi, 2011. In this study, Pınar Selek writes about the brutality against the transsexuals of Ülker Street in Taksim, İstanbul in 1996. Selek zooms in on the struggle that the transsexual residents of the street lead against the police, media, and fascist organizations as Grey Wolves who aimed at displacing them by using communal violence.

that place for I stand under the neon lights, or my eyes are not used to the lighting of that place. Therefore, it was the need to understand that first drew me out. I found myself out on the street before learning sociology. If I lived in the olden times, I would love to be a traveler. But I could not go that far. On the other hand, one so often does not even see right outside her own door. There is no need to go far away, you can be a traveler in your own city.

To me, sociology is to understand what I live through. Since my childhood, I grew up at the gates of September 12 prisons,[2] in a house like a collective, witnessed all the discussions. I lived through all the changes in Turkey before and after September 12 as a child, and perhaps found the stories out on the street. I was highly curious, and very lucky. I came from an intellectual family; it was an environment full of discussions. There were many things about socialist thought which I did not understand, which did not make complete sense to me. But I wanted freedom, I wanted love, equality. How would that come about? I realized I did not understand the dynamics of this society: A gigantic world, in which I am a teeny, tiny something. I marched on, without falling prey to the feeling of weakness. And when you begin to see, to see what is different, you start to question yourself what you held to be true up until then.

On another note, there is yet another dimension to the question of what I am looking for in the street. Curiosity comes with certain dangers. Fine, I want to understand myself and my society, but that does not mean I have a right to everything. I want to walk into people's lives to learn about them, but those people have defense mechanisms that they developed to protect themselves against the oppressive mechanisms of the society. Deciphering the people I establish contact with means that the information now becomes relevant to the dominant system. For this reason, I must ask who could use the information I attain. The question of "Why am I doing this here?" is key, at every single step.

Shall we talk about an issue that you mention in an article, the issue of "research turning into action"?

Not every research project has to turn into action. However it is important to think about who you take information from, what you will do with the information once you gather it, and how you will make it public. It is also important to think about these questions sincerely and seriously. Of course, there is no single way to this attitude. For example, we worked on masculinity.[3] That study was a work of oral

---

[2]After the military intervention of the year 1980, the people joining the street action and protests were restricted including the acts of the imprisonment and repression of intellectuals and political groups by the regime of the military administration. It can be stated that the military coup of 1980 as a landmark silenced all mass opposition almost overnight. Needless to say, it means the arrests, trials, tortures and convictions of many people who participated in politics prior to the coup.

[3]Pınar Selek, *Sürüne Sürüne Erkek Olmak* [To Become a Man Through Misery], İstanbul: İletişim, 2010. This study focuses on the experience of military service of many men from different sectors of society. The book discusses how the compulsory military service in Turkey contributed to building and reproducing masculinity as an identity.

history where we spoke to men, hence the dominant ones. It is always said of me that I work on minorities, on the subaltern. I correct that and say that I work on domination and hegemony. So; nationalism, militarism, patriarchy: The Armenians, Kurds, women, queer people. "Ülker Sokak" is not a work on transsexuals, it is a story of exclusion. My calling is domination. How are relations of domination established, and how is it possible to resist against domination? Looking back, my project on masculinity too has a certain perspective. Beyond the stories of oppression that the men told, that book tells the story of how the category of "the dominant gender" is produced. Men are not objects in this story, they are subjects. Because they are subjects, they endure any suffering because they think "it's worth this!", they endure thinking "I will be doing this one step further". Because they are not mere objects, they live through all, thinking "I will be hitting, too!"

There was not much I could give them. We sent them back their narratives, and then the book. In this way, everyone placed one another in the greater picture and saw how I read their narratives.

On the other hand, there is a different responsibility to working with the oppressed and the excluded. It is not the same thing as working with men. When I did my fieldwork in Ülker Sokak, people were under real gunfire every single day. Yet they opened their hearts and colors to me, generously and at length. Sometimes my interviews took as long as five-six days.

People I conduct interviews with think on the stories they tell me, especially through the questions I ask them. If I leave it at that, it becomes a problem. Because the person continues to feel pain. And then I will take that information to write a thesis, that does not sound right.

I wanted this dialogue to turn into a discussion. I established small groups, the discussion continued within these groups. Before the study on Ülker Sokak, I had established a workshop together with the children and youth who lived on the street. A few transsexuals and transvestites used to visit our workshop. After I completed the study, we tried to continue the discussion within the workshop to collectivize the idea. We wanted to talk altogether, and go beyond merely talking to truly expressing ourselves. Art was the path to such expression. Therefore I did not merely complete my study and leave the place. To begin with, I was not there merely for research. I was there but not really as an insider, I knew some of the transsexuals but I was not close to being inside. I went into establish solidarity with the violence they were subjected to. Then I began to understand, and write my graduate thesis. But I did not consider the thesis to be enough.

At one point there was no one, no one could go in for some nationalist groups blocked entrance. The girls could not go out and buy cigarettes or bread. So I used to go in and out like a courier, and I stayed there at nighttime so that I could later testify. We lived such horrid things there! And we read the papers the next day, they write completely false news. How are we to express what really happened? Somebody asked me: "Aren't you a sociologist?" I was not actually there for the sake of research.

That is a strange inversion, is it not? The place you went to, and the people there reminding you of what you could do as a sociologist...

Yes... But as I have said, when I was out on the street I did not cling to being a sociologist as an identity. I knew sociology, I could practice sociology. I mean, I could do sociological work but it needed improvement. But at least I could ask questions, identify some concepts, I could bring these concepts together to carry out an analysis and read them. But I realized something on the streets: People were very afraid of journalists and university people. When I figured out that children on the street did not want to be written, I promised them not to write and kept my promise. When a party does not want to be written down, one has to know that that is a point to stop. It is also important to understand who does not want to be written. When it is the oppressed, I will naturally continue to work on the state of oppression yet I do not have to reveal the experience of the oppressed and their strategies of resistance. I may reveal dominance.

On the other hand, let us assume that I conduct research on tortures by the police and they object to this study. I will not abandon the study just because they do not approve. I will conduct that study! Because in this case the disposition of the mechanisms of domination does not matter. But the oppressed, the excluded, the victim of violence already endures violence. That is to say, we are not entitled to go everywhere and write everything. Curiosity is a good thing, but not altogether innocent. Curiosity does not make everything legitimate.

There was a situation you complained about after you were released from the jail. You talked about how they tried to present you as a victim and said that you were looking for ways to dodge this. What were you able to do about this situation? Have you been able to overcome this attempt at labeling you?

The intellectual attitude is about the ability to ask anything and to pursue questions. It is the capacity to ask questions or rather to question. Not just to ask questions, but to systematically question! Because questioning is also an action, it is a transformative action. But it's not easy, especially within the particular conditions I am in. On the other hand the trial goes on, on the other hand I want to continue to question. I do continue, but I have to be taking into account many things at once. Sometimes I wish I did not have to consider them.

I question myself much; I try to be an individual who questions herself yet continues to think collectively at the same time. Therefore I do not limit myself with the academia, the structure of which is already horrific. France is no different than Turkey in this respect. A researcher can only find funding for her project if she sells the project well. This system, this mechanism molds everyone within its structures. If you try to develop collective thinking from within the academia, you find yourself within a situation where people are in constant rivalry with you. Surely you may establish a different space within the university, but you certainly have to retain a tie with the outside world. You must work towards creating other collectivities outside the given mechanisms. That is no easy feat!

What is it that makes a work of social science critical? We talked about the streets; a street is a narrow space but we are able to produce knowledge that has much broader implications just by looking at one street. Narrow spaces do not delimit us, in a way.

You have to analyze the connection between that street and the whole. When feminists said "The personal is political", they knew of the concept of hegemony, knew of the concept "political", and they were able to put forward the political nature of the personal through discussing with these concepts. Therefore, we too must be able to establish the relationship between patriarchy and nationalism, capitalism in order to successfully analyze the politics of private space. Only then would it become possible to understand any experience under people's roofs.

It is so complicated! On one hand you connect a narrow space with wider relationships and try to capture the connections, continuities and discontinuities between them. On the other hand, you have to question yourself as a researcher and to accept the fact that you cannot know or capture everything, perhaps you reprehend yourself. Because the distance is impossible to bridge entirely. Perhaps you must first accept that the distance will never be bridged entirely, and only when you accept this you are able to question yourself.

In addition, the person I interact with comes from a different background. I do not have to say what he says. I will come up with my own words, speak from a different perspective and develop a sociological analysis. I think the most important matter is to see that what is sociological is complicated, dynamic, and is multi-factored and then to be able to delve into these multiple factors. The communalization of the production of knowledge has occupied my thoughts for a very long time; I have believed that we were unable to produce knowledge about our own lives since my undergraduate years. Some people walk in, produce knowledge about our lives, then comes in the politicians who change our lives. It is a horrid thing that "being a politician" is an occupation. Similarly, it is horrid that the universities are so disconnected from the society. That is of course not to say that anyone can produce knowledge, that everyone can develop a theory with a few concepts. But there has to be critical thinking, and the knowledge based on such critical thinking has to be open to the society.

What are your opinions regarding objectivity, neutrality, distancing oneself?

There is no such thing as being neutral. It is dangerous to claim that there is! For instance, at a certain period science took the place of religion in becoming a mechanism of domination, and announced homosexuals sick in a claim to "neutrality". Therefore scientific knowledge is liable to questioning, and it is of outmost importance to question who produces scientific knowledge. The person who produces knowledge is a part of the society. The researcher is in a constant state of interaction, he is affected by what he sees or experiences and might well be writing accordingly. That is to say, you are never fully aware of where exactly you stand, which theories influence you, the method you use, your own questions, prejudices, the transformation you go through during a research. You only become objective when you can account for all of these factors. So there is no such thing as being neutral, you will begin by acknowledging that. But when you can account for where and how you stand, what you see and from which vantage point, which framework you adopt, then you become objective. Then you provide objective knowledge, by objectifying yourself. It is necessary to objectify yourself.

What is to be done so that studies on the outcasts or invisible members of the society, those that are not spoken or written about, do not turn into "victimization studies"? What kind of language should one adopt?

One must first ask "Why do I work with the oppressed? What exactly will I do, talk about their pain? What kind of a sociological analysis can come out of the description of pains and troubles?" Therefore, sociological thinking comes with considering oppression within mechanisms of domination. So, it means for instance to try to decipher how the mechanism of domination works.

To be able to place the question within a network of social relations...

Right, to evaluate the question with reference to all the relevant agents, and to place all those different subjects within a network of domination. Only then the end result is not merely a single group. One has to explain oppression while also questioning it, but of course it's difficult to question oppression.

As far as I can understand, what distinguishes a study from a "victimization narrative" is to take interest in how people resist and survive...

Sometimes resistance can be very obvious. But sometimes, for instance a woman develops her own peculiar method of resistance. She keeps falling ill, for instance. That resistance too is worthy of note. Therefore one must see the complicated nature of not only oppression but also resistance. And I will tell you something about this: Sometimes it is necessary to *not* make resistance known.

True, and a researcher might have to abstain from speaking or writing about difference methods of resistance when she finds out about them!

Within the systems of domination that we live in, the oppressed develop small tactics under difficult conditions and they do not want these tactics to be widely known. Because the moment this knowledge becomes public, the powers come up with new medicine against them. This is the reason why the question of who will benefit from my study becomes even more important.

On the other hand, it is a difficult task in itself to describe resistance. To make the invisible resistance visible is difficult but can be a good thing at times. Because the subject might be unaware that he is showing resistance. He might be performing some sort of resistance which has no organized secrecy. For instance the children on the street had secret codes, had information that the police would not understand.

When you learn about these secrets, you have to keep them from getting out. And I kept them! But there is an organized system there. In certain cases, women develop different methods to resist. It might serve these women well to tell them that their methods are methods of resistance.

If I were to ask the one thing that a social scientist cannot reach...

She cannot attain the truth. There is no such thing as truth, or a single truth to be more precise.

If she were to find something, to capture one thing, she misses another one!

Since truth is multi-dimensional and dynamic, and since it changes depending on which angle you take, it is impossible to claim to have attained truth. But you can reach the light, you can reach some source of illumination. An analysis can open a way, become a light for people. What can a researcher not attain? I will not say she cannot attain happiness, because there are some who have attained happiness. For example, me!

As you too have expressed, women have a different, a distinct way of writing. Can we talk about the relationship women build with the act of writing, and their different approaches to writing?

As we talked before, there is no such thing as neutrality. You develop your ways of thinking and expression under the influence of your social experience. Your vantage point, the experience that shapes you is crucial. People create a manner of thinking and acting through their experiences. People's manners of forging solidarity, of taking action, forming communities and communication differ. The language differs. Regarding women, it is to their advantage to not be on the dominant camp. Because that enriches their language. Of course since being a woman is not a homogenous experience, that is since there are many forms of hierarchy within the world of women, there is no single state of being a woman. That is why, I admire the language that the feminists have developed. I also admire the language developed through questioning gender relations.

This seems related to what you have named "acrobatic feminism"...

Acrobatic feminism means to me the practice of analyzing the complicated nature of all relations of domination, acquiring perspective and taking a stance against all of these. It means the ability to at least develop a perspective on all of these even when fighting all of them is not possible, to read the world from this perspective.

When you succeed in establishing connections between distinct struggles and open doors between them, an intellectual journey between them begins. The spheres of struggle transform each other. It is important to see domination, the connections between nationalism and heterosexism, and with capitalism, but this is a difficult task to achieve! That is why I call it "acrobatics". Being an intellectual demands a certain amount of acrobatics, in the sense of a constant creativity and flexibility. That is tough!

As I prepared my questions for you, I realized once again that the social changes of the 1990s have impacted your life in significant ways: Feminist struggle, Kurdish movement, journalism within the Kurdish movement, the early phases of the transsexual movement, prisons with all the organized resistance and the interventions taking place there. Your story is, in a way, the story of Turkey in the 90s. Keeping in mind the idea that is often heard nowadays that Turkey has left behind a whole sociological period and has become "new Turkey", I would like to ask: What is it that remains from the 90s to our present day?

What remains? Sociological dynamics are very strong in Turkey, which creates a constant transformation. This transformation has its counterpart in the field of social struggle. But it is not right to expect this transformation to come to fruition within a couple of decades. The Turkish nation-state has been built as a result of a process which involves large scale massacres and genocides. There is an incredible cycle of violence, and a very flawed system. A terrible, obsolete, vicious structure! The Justice and Development Party of today bring together a new structure and all the old state tradition and mechanisms. It is not easy to transform this structure.

But if you ask me what has changed since the 90s, I can answer that a good repertoire has been developed in terms of social struggle. This repertoire which actually goes back to the 80s has grown with the contributions of feminism, the LGBTI movement, anti-militarism, ecological movements, and many autonomous groups. For Turkey, the 90s meant resistance and awakening. Particularly the feminists have developed a unique opposition using multiple means.

The 90s meant the beginning of a very dynamic resistance. This applies not only to the Kurds, but also to leftist and feminist movements. The LGBTI movement is newly developing. AGOS[4] is established in 1996. The new repertoire that I am talking about takes root within these movements. I look forward to observing how this repertoire unfolds in the near future. On the other hand, the older repertoire persists, the crude mechanisms of the state are still in place. These two repertoires are not independent from each other! Because of the presence of state violence in Turkey, diverse groups are in a constant state of solidarity. That means, they keep open to each other, which nurtures the strength to resist even further.

---

[4]From the web-site of AGOS: "*Agos was founded in 1996 by Hrant Dink and a group of his friends, in order to report the problems of the Armenians of Turkey to the public. It is the first newspaper in the Republican period to be published in Turkish and Armenian. Agos's editorial policy focuses on issues such as democratization, minority rights, coming to terms with the past, the protection and development of pluralism in Turkey... As independent journalism and freedom of expression face increasing restriction in Turkey, Agos also acts as an independent platform for debate*"; see http://www.agos.com.tr/en/home [March 30, 2016].

Author Biographies

Pınar Selek was born in Istanbul in 1971. From early on in her life, she has been involved in the feminist, antimilitarist and peace movements. After completing her bachelor's and master's degrees in sociology at Mimar Sinan University, she was taken into police custody in 1998 for doing research on the Kurdish movement. While in police custody she was tortured for not naming the individuals she had interviewed as part of her research project. Her research papers and documents were confiscated and she was arrested due to terrorism related charges. Pınar Selek was acquitted five times as there was no evidence to substantiate the allegations of the prosecution, but the Court of Cassation (known as "Yargitay") reversed the lower court's decision each time, resulting in a 19-year legal battle that finally forced Pınar Selek to immigrate to France in 2009. In 2014 she completed her doctoral degree in political science. She is a lecturer on political science at Nice Sophia Antipolis University and continues her research at The Migrations and Society Research Unit (URMIS) on migration, transnational spaces and social movements.

Meral Akbaş is a PhD candidate in Department of Sociology at Middle East Technical University, Ankara, Turkey. She holds two MA degrees in Sociology from Middle East Technical University and in Anthropology from Hacettepe University. Her master's thesis about the memories of female political prisoners who were arrested at Mamak Military Prison after 1980 Military Coup in Turkey was published as Mamak Kitabı: Biz Bir Orduya Kafa Tuttuk Arkadaş [The Book of Mamak: We Challenged an Army My Friend!], as a separate book in Turkish. Meral Akbaş is now preparing her doctoral dissertation on memories of state violence in Batman, in Southeastern Turkey. She writes extensively about gender, social memory, state violence and feminist literature studies in Turkey.

Psychology and Social Identity

Cem Kaptanoğlu and interviewed by Bilal Ersoy

Abstract Turkish society was formed from the remnants of a disintegrating empire, the body of a sick man. The Kemalists intended to bind together the disparate elements of society that were divided by ethnic, religious, and sectarian differences, as well as, and to a lesser degree, by class. It was no coincidence that, in the name of social integration, the Kemalists invested radically in the corporatist ideology—the idea of society as a body with organs that require one another. The vision of society as a body with harmoniously functioning organs was the opposite of the image of the sick body, and it became the transcendental object of the republican ideology. For the official ideology, anything outside of "the inseparability of the state from its land and its nation" was insufficient. Society was formed —or rather deformed—as the object of a corporatist-fascist ideology's fantasy, the motto of which was "a unified mass with no class or concessions." This was a fetish for unity and integrity. In its work of holding together the disparate parts of society, the corporatist ideology identifies those elements that are detrimental to social organization and produces new enemies and enmities.

Keywords Turkey · Psychology · Social identity · Kemalism

To understand an individual, we inquire into the details of their personal history. That is why I would like to start our conversation with the history of the Republic of Turkey. How does historical truth affect our collective mental state? How are we as a nation doing in terms of negotiating our imperial heritage, the legacy of the founding father figure, and our official ideology?

Turkish society has been held together by the vision of a *corporatist society* for almost a century. This is unsurprising for this society. It is, after all, a site of struggle for incontrovertible differences of class, ethnicity, religion, and sect. The organs that fail to perform the functions expected of them are pushed outside the

C. Kaptanoğlu (✉) · B. Ersoy
Eskişehir Osmangazi Medical School, Eskişehir, Turkey
e-mail: cemkaptanoglu@ahoo.com

© Springer International Publishing AG, part of Springer Nature 2019   249
E. Özyürek et al. (eds.), *Authoritarianism and Resistance in Turkey*,
https://doi.org/10.1007/978-3-319-76705-5_24

corpus, demonized, suppressed via military or policing operations, disciplined, banished, deported. Turkish society was formed from the remnants of a disintegrating empire, the body of a sick man. The Kemalists intended to bind together the disparate elements of society that were divided by ethnic, religious, and sectarian differences, as well as, and to a lesser degree, by class. It was no coincidence that, in the name of social integration, the Kemalists invested radically in the corporatist ideology—the idea of society as a body with organs that require one another. The vision of society as a body with harmoniously functioning organs was the opposite of the image of the sick body, and it became the transcendental object of the republican ideology. For the official ideology, anything outside of "the inseparability of the state from its land and its nation" was insufficient. Society was formed —or rather deformed—as the object of a corporatist-fascist ideology's fantasy, the motto of which was "a unified mass with no class or concessions." This was a fetish for unity and integrity. In its work of holding together the disparate parts of society, the corporatist ideology identifies those elements that are detrimental to social organization and produces new enemies and enmities.

It is in this way that Turkish society has always had its own internal enemies whose very existence is made possible through their production. Social schisms such as left versus right, Alevi versus Sunni, secular versus anti-secular, Turkish versus Kurdish, Muslim versus non-Muslim, were provoked to the point of becoming blood feuds. Divided along identity lines, society was turned into a conglomerate of isolated communities. Christian minorities were marginalized at the earliest possible opportunity because they were thought to pose a potential threat to the project of holding society together by corporatist-fascist means. Those social groups that remain in Turkey today have now become hostile toward one another. Their main expectation from the state at this point is not to live collectively in this geographic locale, but merely to survive without falling victim to the wrath of other groups or the state. The state, in turn, exploiting the context of hostility among different groups, has assumed the role of protector and savior. In this context, it is not surprising that the most trusted institution in Turkey remains the armed forces, or that there is a common belief in the need for a bully to manage the country. Turkish society is committed to Leviathan—the idea that civil peace is best achieved by a sovereign power who is granted absolute authority to ensure the common defense—not because of some universal social chaos or state of nature, as Thomas Hobbes had argued (1981/1651), but because of a state-produced, artificial historical chaos.

In *Group Psychology and the Analysis of the Ego* (1990/1921), Sigmund Freud defines the emotional state of groups that coalesce around a leader as groups of individuals who replace identification with the self with identification with the same ideal object, and hence identify with each other as a self. The object that takes the place of the ideal self here is the leader, the role model. In this respect, we can say that as a leader Atatürk has not attained this status, whereby his ideal selfhood would enable a symbolic social unity. To the contrary, a holy Atatürk figure, whose potentially deleterious aspects were meticulously purged by the bureaucracy of the republic, was difficult for the masses to identify with. In the same book, Freud also argues that the figure of the leader—the ideal self—could be replaced by an idea or ideology. Kemalism has claimed to take this ideological place, but was never able to do so. What Kemalism was able to do was to suppress other ideologies that could replace the leader figure by demonizing them and claiming that they are foreign. Kemalism thus did not become the ideology of Turkish society. Instead, because of the predominance of the Kemalist bureaucracy, it became the prevailing ideology of the state.

Atatürk—or, as you call him, the *founding father* of the republic—did not become the father that the majority within society identified as the ideal self. Instead, Atatürk as the *overbearing father* prevented chaos and maintained public order by forcefully implementing his rules and restrictions. This instilled in society deep emotional dichotomies, including those of love/hate and obedience/resistance. There is a similarity between the founding father of the Turkish republic and the *violent primal father* in the myth that Freud relates in *Totem and Taboo* (1990/ 1913). As the protector of society's rules and restrictions, the father incites anger and rebellion—more so if his rules and restrictions are irrational. According to the myth of the democratization of the primitive tribe recounted in *Totem and Taboo*, the brothers who are banished from the tribe get together one day, kill their father, eat him, and put an end to the tribal organization. It is their unity that gives them the courage to realize what individually they cannot. On the other hand, the violent primal father is a fearsome and enviable model for the brothers.

Between 2002 and 2010, the AKP used its politics of hegemony to unite the brothers—Sunni Muslims, ethno-religious minorities, liberals, socialists—who had suffered under the founding father and Kemalism. This unification process was completed by the constitutional referendum of 2010, by which time the brothers had gathered the courage to realize what individually they could not and had killed the founding father. The fear and anger elicited in the face of the possibility that one of the brothers might replace the violent primal father, the Leviathan, determine the prevalent current social mental state in Turkey. In Freud's myth, the process that prevents the collapse of the primal tribe in the aftermath of the father's murder is this: although united in their will to overcome their father, the brothers nevertheless remain rivals in relation to women. I think we can read this by replacing the *women* here with *their ideological and class-related dreams*. Much like their father, the brothers wish to claim all the women. Or, according to my reading, they desire to be the ruler, the *one man*. Thus, the new organizational system is doomed to fail in the war to come, because neither of the brothers possess the power to successfully replace the father. And so, if the brothers—who I think can be read as *the citizens*— want to live together, they have no other choice than to adopt a prohibition on incest that will require them to give up women altogether. It is possible to read *incest* as *the adoption of the rule of the democratic constitutional state*.

Turkish society is worried that the slain founding father may be replaced not by universal values such as equality, freedom, or justice, but by the arbitrary rules and restrictions of a dictatorship. In other words, Turkey is gripped by the fear that the law of brotherhood that did not take hold in the Old Turkey will also not be established in the New Turkey.

Both our recent and distant past is full of bitter traumas. We are very inexperienced when it comes to facing, negotiating with, and mourning our traumas. I would like to ask you about the effects of state-produced social traumas that bean in the Ottoman period and continued throughout the republican period.

Turkey is a country of multiple generations of unfinished mourning—unfinished due to a state ban on mourning. It has always had its enemy others who were forbidden from publicly mourning or being mourned. The state forbade the others that it had traumatized from remembering, let alone mourning, because the practice of social mourning and collective memory—the practice of confronting and negotiating a traumatic past and its current reverberations—involves political struggle. Many who were left in horror, terror, and despair by state-inflicted social trauma were antagonized to such a degree that they had to suffer their losses silently in their private spheres, not in public. Those who wanted to mourn their lost loved ones openly, without hiding, could not find witnesses *sufficiently good-willed* to acknowledge the traumatic truth. The victims were even subjected to new state violence, which caused them new sufferings, and so their mourning and memory was left unfinished. The state banned public mourning of many social traumas—the Armenian Genocide, the 1980 coup d'état, the Roboski massacre, the state murders during the Gezi protests—thus preventing these sufferings from being recorded in the collective memory as part of the past.

Based on your observations, can we say that there are similarities between individual and social trauma? Are the processes of experiencing, confronting, and overcoming trauma similar on the individual and social level?

There are similarities, especially in terms of the reactions to traumatic events and the coping mechanisms therewith. Traumatic events, accompanied by violent emotions such as fear, horror, despair, and anger, resist the efforts of those who survive or witness these events to turn them into symbols or stories. Traces of traumatic events, although unwelcome, do find their way into consciousness to harass it. Fragile and subtle connections that evoke these traumatic traces suffice for them to invade consciousness.

Members of a society that have been traumatized en masse may appear to have buried their social trauma in the past, but their everyday attitude and behavior, as well as deficiencies or excesses in their way of relating to their environment, are symptomatic. The mental effects of the trauma, with its implicit and explicit traces on the community, are then passed onto younger generations. Communal identity is formed around the communal trauma and becomes isolated within its bounds. Inside these bounds, the communal identity keeps alive its key element, the shared trauma, and in turn solidifies itself.

Thus, those who are outside of the community are turned into others deemed incapable of understanding the community's pain. In countries where large groups are traumatized, reconciliation should not be understood as the reconciliation between the victim and the perpetrator. Reconciliation, as it is understood in such contexts, is the recognition of the victim's pain—an offering of a sympathetic testimony—by a witness who had previously failed to be a *good-willed witness* and had thus been a silent partner in the collective crime. The victim reconciles primarily with themselves through the beneficent testimony of the good witness. In other words, the victim recovers from the introversion caused by the trauma by *opening up* to others. Forgiveness or letting bygones be bygones is the ultimate stage of a social mourning or collective memory effort and is not always possible to achieve.

The first, and foremost, condition for forgiveness is the perpetrator's confession of their crime before the witnesses. The one seeking forgiveness should be prepared for rejection. Confession erases all of the doubts about the veracity of the evil that was done to the victim. The truth which was once denied is revealed directly in the mouth of the perpetrator. The helpless, passive victim of the traumatic event attains the ability to reverse their position vis-à-vis the perpetrator, though not necessarily to the point of a revenge fantasy. In the presence of the witnesses, the victim regains the power against the perpetrator that they had lost.

The second condition for forgiveness is that the accused perpetrator should make an apology. Through admission, the perpetrator expresses shame and repentance for their hostile behavior.

The third and last condition is that the perpetrator make an effort to repair materially and mentally the pain of the victim. Forgiveness should be considered a private matter, a process separate from legal or punitive processes. Victims can only forgive if processes of jurisprudence are in place. Forgiveness thus liberates the victim from their mental preoccupation with the perpetrator. The victim is freed from the burden of the past that did not pass. Imagination of the future supplants the uncontrollable images of the trauma. The victim gains the capability to freely write their own story with references to the collective story. In short, the future is reclaimed. It is important to differentiate between these processes and other symptomatic processes of forgiveness that serve as means of avoiding the memory and reevaluation of the trauma. In a process of forgiveness that satisfies the necessary conditions, the fact that society grants the victim the right to make a decision as to whether or not to forgive becomes, in and of itself, a curative. Whether individuals or communities, victims internalize the awareness that nothing—neither fantasies of revenge nor visions of justice—will bring back what they have lost; their loss is irreplaceable. Thus, they are empowered to claim their sorrow and complete their mourning process.

Where in this process of mourning are we as a society?

It can be said that we are stuck in the early stages of this process due to the lack of a safe environment, an imperative for mourning or memory work. Traumatized communities have begun, albeit with reservation and fear, speaking out publicly about their wounds and suffering. Although the society as a whole has not yet begun a collective memory work as such, the process that the AKP government has termed the *democratic initiative* can be considered progress or a very early stage of collective memory building. This initiative made possible the telling and, to a certain extent, the public reception of social narratives of trauma. I should also stress, however, that this process of telling and reception is utterly dispersed, disorganized, and uncertain. Erdoğan's reluctant apology for the massacre in Dersim, where he stated that he would "apologize if that is the convention" and offered his "condolences" to the descendants of those Armenians slaughtered in 1915, does not fulfill the necessary criteria seen in exemplary apologies that were part of successful collective memory processes. To the contrary, social wounds were reopened insensitively, only to be concealed hastily by a half-hearted discourse of negotiation. Not only does Erdoğan's way of remembering fail to soothe the social memory of trauma, but it also causes memory obsession and retraumatization, thus adding insult to injury. Memories of traumatic events that are forever reminded and recalled incautiously in the absence of good-willed and earnest witnesses can only traumatize communities again and deepen existing social wounds.

What effect does the "evil spirit of the 1980 coup" have on our social psyche? Are there still groups that summon that spirit?

The spirit of the coup of 1980 is fueled by a corporatist-fascist ideology which claims that in order for society to function as a wholesome body, each group/organ should know its place and do its job, or else be disciplined. The tail wagging the dog is the worst nightmare of corporatism. This ideology, which is called Kemalism in Turkey, determines the world view of both the oligarchy of military bureaucracy and a significant section of the generation that witnessed the emergence of the republic.

Elitist sections of society who see themselves as the owners of Old Turkey are, in fact, soul mates to the AKP in terms of the kind of relationship they envisage between state and society. Motivated by their fear of being driven into the sea, these groups watch the AKP as it takes over state institutions, public life, and even bodies —their eating, drinking, and reproductive habits—one step at a time. State power that had enabled them to feel as sovereign subjects is now in the hands of others. They urgently need to learn how to mourn their loss. They, as the privileged heirs of the founding father, had been entrusted with the sacred heritage of the state and society, but the brothers conspired against the father and murdered him. In order for the former privileged heirs to mourn their loss, they need first to accept that the father is dead and that he cannot return in the guise of a savior or a military coup.

But the Kemalists must also face the fact that they have joined their other brothers in being orphaned. Kemalists had long feared a second republic, and now it has toppled their most trusted paper tigers and has established itself on the debris of the old power structure. Yet they ignored the fact that the AKP's identity politics were successful due to the profound discontent of large sections of society who had been violently traumatized by the old regime. Now, as the new regime rapidly becomes fascistic, Kemalists respond to calls of democratic solidarity with a resentful "We told you so." Not only do they speak out against the AKP's fascism, they also make public calls for solidarity with the old regime, despite the fact that, with its sordid record, that regime was not any less fascist than the AKP. If they continue close their eyes to the dark side of the old regime—that is to say, if they refuse to mourn its loss—they are bound withdraw further from the truth.

We know that it is impossible to mourn the loss of a hyperidealized and deified father figure. The first and most important condition of any mourning or memory work is the remembrance of bot the good and bad sides of those who have been lost. The kind of mourning process that awaits the Kemalists obliges them to negotiate with and reject certain parts of the ancestral heritage that they have held sacred. If Kemalists can fulfill this principal duty, they will then inescapably renegotiate their relationship to past social traumas—the Armenian Genocide, the Dersim massacre, the 1980 coup—as well as the role of the deified father and his ideology in these traumas. It can be said that the current tensions within the CHP are, to a large extent, dictated by this impending negotiation.

Are there privileged heirs and favorite citizens in New Turkey, as there were in the old one? If so, can you describe their psyches?

The requisite for attaining the status of privileged heir in New Turkey, whose state ideology was revised as *Islamic corporatism*, is the Sunni Muslim identity. And yet, this identity, although still requisite, has become somehow insufficient since the falling out between the Gülen movement and the AKP in the wake of the 2013 corruption scandal. Now it is necessary to be a non-Gülen-affiliated Sunni Muslim.

Most Muslims in New Turkey appear to be uneasy. The main reason for their unease is their ambivalent feeling toward integrating into a global capitalist and consumerist lifestyle and ideology. Muslims oscillate between the inner voice that says, "Thou shalt not indulge" and the voice that says, "Worldly possession is your right; claim it!" This oscillation was happening with increasing intensity when, with the 2013 leaks and police stings, the government's corruption and greed came to light. The corruption scandal turned Muslims' inner unease into a full-blown identity crisis.

That is why the conflict between the AKP and the Gülen movement is not solely an affirmation of a division within the government, but also an event that has deepened the crisis within the Sunni Muslim identity, the privileged heir of New Turkey. Erdoğan's efforts to make a demonized "other" out of the Gülen movement is but a last stand against the disintegration of this Muslim identity. The most tragicomic manifestation of this is the fact that Prime Minister Davutoğlu look like a comedian even when making lofty, pious, or solemn statements. Because underneath the *pious* discourse he tries to establish, the stubborn, messy facts are jarringly evident: "There is a thief in the house!" "Murderer!" Sooner or later, Muslims will realize that the push to cover up the mess with piousness also messes up the "pious." If they use their privileged-heir status to achieve the status of the privileged class, and then to entrench themselves within that class, they will no longer feel uneasy about exploiting anything venerable, if such exploitation serves their class interests.

Is it possible to read the Gezi protests as a reaction to the killing of the father, or as a rebellion against an Erdoğan who unjustly attempted to fulfill the role of the father? What kind of a mindset does the *Gezi spirit* reflect?

The Gezi spirit refers both to a feeling and to an identity. This spirit consists of the feelings and mentality that is bound up with advocating collectively for certain shared values and resisting a common enemy that insults these values. Throughout the solidarity, sharing, cooperation, and intimacy that comes with collective resistance, shared identifications brought the Gezi spirit into presence as a shared popular sense of identity. Those who want to sustain and develop this spirit continue the struggle, as they say, at public forums that they organize in parks, on the streets, and in the squares.

In terms of group psychology, two contradictory elements produce a *common spirit* among different social groups that share the same side or the same mental state. The first element is a feeling and a concomitant demand shared in common by the subjects in a group. The second element is the incommensurable difference that exists among the members of the group. The contradiction between *commonality* and *difference* determines the internal dynamics of a group; groups are founded precisely upon this immutable tension between difference and commonality.

For every communal demand made by a social group or a subject, there will also be the irritating difference of the other. A singular social demand can only become common and equitable by joining the demands of others. To put it differently, in order for mass movements not to break down, there need to be demands and accompanying feelings that cut across different groups. The Gezi spirit, the Gezi identity, was brought into being by the incorporation of an array of problems suffered by different groups into a single signifier with a core narrative able to produce a common affect in public space—that of Gezi Park and its trees on the brink of demolition. Different subgroups that comprise the resistance saw the trees in Gezi Park as substitutes or symbols of their assorted democratic demands. The most essential dynamic of the Gezi spirit is self-identification with the higher value of protecting the trees and unification against those who wanted to rip the meaning of those trees out from under them.

Even those in power acknowledged and expressed great surprise at the diversity of the groups that converged around the Gezi protests. This eclectic unity could only unite because they were able to articulate their considerable differences into an even greater commonality by means of a discourse that aroused shared feelings in every one of them. This articulatory discourse was produced by means of a libertarian, critical, humorous political language, which was produced first on social media online, but soon went offline and on to walls, squares, and parks. The political language of the Gezi spirit defined what it was against, but it was flexible, ambiguous, and open to appropriation by different parties through their participation. To the extent that it remained open, this specific kind of language was successful in cutting across the eclectic unity to produce a Gezi spirit.

The common mental state of protesters with a common language caused a stir that reverberated throughout the government. It also created its enemy, because it made the government feel like an Other. The others of the Gezi spirit are not limited to the AKP, but include all other authoritarian, totalitarian, militaristic, sexist, discriminatory, and antidemocratic political ideologies and attitudes. With its language, discourse, and spirit, Gezi established itself as a movement against authoritarianism, despotism, all manner of discrimination, neoliberal pillage, and the ruling AKP.

In our country of never-ending corruption, poverty, income inequality, and unemployment, right-wing parties have ruled almost since the establishment of the multiple-party system. What elements intrinsic to the left prevent it from pulling itself together?

Since the time of pioneers like Mustafa Suphi, socialists in Turkey have been struggling for basic rights and freedoms, including freedom of speech, freedom to publish, the right to life, to organize, to demonstrate, to strike. In short, socialists have been responsible for defending what should be the political and ideological duty of the bourgeoisie to defend. The despotism of the Turkish state has turned the socialists' struggle for basic rights and liberties into a veritable struggle for life or death. It is practically impossible to imagine a socialist alternative and to share this alternative with the masses when one is on the verge of death; anything beyond survival is a mere pipe dream. The biggest risk in such violent struggles to the death is that one starts acting more and more like a true enemy. A significant section of the Turkish left has ended up behaving like the very state they struggle against, adopting the same state methods for asserting power—hierarchy, discipline, violence, puissance. The belief that governance should be the main goal of a socialist struggle and that the establishment of a revolutionary subject will follow upon the socialist takeover of government—that democracy is only a means for taking over power—is the expression of a power fetish, a resemblance to those already in power. The left gave into totalitarianism, which they called *democratic centrism*, when they were supposed to work toward a radical democratization of all power relations.

In reality, the state that the socialist ideal aims to take over is a non-state, and its political organization must first be built. The building process can be put into action today simultaneous with policies of socialist hegemony. Put in Gramscian terms, when the necessary political organization is in place, the people become the state, rather than take it over.

The left in Turkey has overidentified the working classes with industrial workers in an attitude that attributes too much to class. It has been widely accepted on the left that other proletarian groups, including white-collar workers who constitute a significant portion of the population, were suffering from a petit-bourgeois disorder that needed to be treated. Many of the legitimate democratic demands of such groups have been diagnosed and "exposed" as symptoms of petit-bourgeois pathology. It was thought that only that party, class, or leadership that pursued an "objective analysis" of "objective conditions" using "scientific methods" would hold the only keys to "absolute knowledge." Leftists who considered themselves the sole beholders of the truth were able to rid their mental world of ambiguity. And their language became more definitive and rigid. This self-aggrandizing language of socialists in Turkey did not lend itself to communicating with the people, especially in the context of political defeat in the wake of the 1980 coup and the disintegration of the Soviet Union. The left became an in-group, talking among themselves and not with the people.

For this reason, most leftist thinkers today agree on the need for a new language for the left. The new leftist subject should internalize the fact that, like any language, their language too is imperfect. For leftists to be open to understanding and learning other languages, it is necessary that they first acknowledge the castration of their own language. Only then can they become aware of and keep in check the self-aggrandizement and the thirst for power hidden in their language, which strives to hide its own deficiencies. Only a nondogmatic language that embraces ambiguity and reflects the inconsistency of life can penetrate and express real life. Such a language will make possible a dialogue with the other, as well as the possibility for others to speak from within the new language by incorporating other languages. The principled yet flexible language of plurality of the Gezi movement did just that by incorporating difference into its ambiguous language. Let us hope that the people will be receptive to this language of multiplicity, despite its slippages and glitches.

Author Biographies

Cem Kaptanoğlu graduated from Istanbul Medical School. He has been a faculty member in the Department of Psychiatry at Eskişehir Osmangazi Medical School in Istanbul since 1992. His professional interests are in mental trauma, supportive psychotherapy, and psychoanalysis and culture.

Bilal Ersoy is a psychiatrist and psychoanalytic psychotherapist. He graduated in 2002 from Ege University Medical School in İzmir. His interests include literature, performance art, cinema, and psychoanalysis.

Turkish Literature

Jale Parla, interviewed by Mehmet Fatih Uslu and Özge Ertem

Abstract My basic thesis about the cultural and epistemological significance of the theme of the fathers and sons has not changed over the years. The quest for a father as absolute authority continued to inform Turkish thought and literature, with only a few exceptional interludes as with the novels of the 1970s. It is, I feel, a mind-numbingly uninteresting phenomenon. Why? Because it has been the same for centuries—the quest for a father, the readiness to escape from freedom, the insecurity when faced with the possibility of a fatherless vacuum, and the need to fill it at all costs. In my subsequent work, I rethought and revisited the Tanzimat (Reorganization) period of 1839–1876, and I came to realize that certain themes that persist in the literary and cultural spheres—modernization, Westernization, issues concerning language reform—were taken up and debated much more judiciously and liberally back then, particularly when compared to the sectarian, prejudiced, and hostile debates of later periods. In this respect, I draw the line with the *Servet-i Fünun* (Wealth of Knowledge) period of 1891–1901, during which cultural and literary quarrels became harsher and were carried into the partisan disputes of the Republican era.

Keywords Turkish literature · Figure of the father · Trends in literature

J. Parla (✉)
Istanbul Bilgi University, Istanbul, Turkey
e-mail: jale.parla@bilgi.edu.tr

M. F. Uslu
Istanbul Şehir University, Istanbul, Turkey
e-mail: mfatihuslu@sehir.edu.tr

Ö. Ertem
Koç University, Istanbul, Turkey
e-mail: ertemozge@gmail.com

© Springer International Publishing AG, part of Springer Nature 2019
E. Özyürek et al. (eds.), *Authoritarianism and Resistance in Turkey*,
https://doi.org/10.1007/978-3-319-76705-5_25

Your book, *Fathers and Sons: The Epistemological Foundations of Tanzimat Novel* **(1990), has become a classic and a textbook. In this work, you claim that although early examples of the Turkish novel demonstrate the confrontation between Western and Eastern epistemologies, they were in fact strictly informed by an Oriental-Islamic episteme. Almost 30 years later, have your ideas about this period changed at all?**

My basic thesis about the cultural and epistemological significance of the theme of the fathers and sons has not changed over the years—I wish it had. As a matter of fact, my readings in more recent historical periods have only served to confirm it. The quest for a father as absolute authority continued to inform Turkish thought and literature, with only a few exceptional interludes as with the novels of the 1970s. It is, I feel, a mind-numbingly uninteresting phenomenon. Why? Because it has been the same for centuries—the quest for a father, the willingness to escape from freedom, the insecurity when faced with the possibility of a fatherless vacuum, and the need to fill it at all costs. In my subsequent work, I rethought and revisited the Tanzimat (Reorganization) period of 1839–1876, and I came to realize that certain themes that persist in the literary and cultural spheres—modernization, Westernization, issues concerning language reform—were taken up and debated much more judiciously and liberally back then, particularly when compared to the sectarian, prejudiced, and hostile debates of later periods. In this respect, I draw the line with the *Servet-i Fünun* (Wealth of Knowledge) period of 1891–1901, during which cultural and literary quarrels became harsher and were carried into the partisan disputes of the republican era.

Literature in general and the Turkish novel in particular have had close ties with politics. Not only have political actors attempted to manipulate the literary field, but also some authors deliberately chose to use the novel as a political tool. What is your understanding of the relationship between the Turkish novel and politics?

Indeed, political content—that is to say, message, background, doctrine—has been a distinctive characteristic of the Turkish novel, particularly in the republican period beginning in the 1920s through to the 1990s. With the 1990s, we can speak of a generalized depoliticization of the intellectual sphere, in which the novel partook. Actually, the political novel can be viewed within distinct categories, so strong is its presence in and impact on novelistic practice. We begin with the so-called national struggle novels (*Milli Mücadele romanları*), move on to village novels (*köy romanları*), and from there to the novels of the two juntas after the coups of 1971 and 1980. That brings us to the 1990s. The political novels have been criticized by literary scholars such as Berna Moran and Murat Belge for their uniform structure and cliché characterizations. Overall, I agree with these assessments, albeit certainly with a few exceptions say, like, Kemal Tahir's *The Law of the Wolf* (*Kurt Kanunu*) (1969), and Latife Tekin's *Night Lessons* (*Gece Dersleri*) (1986). The problem with the political novel—a problem that is inherent to the genre in general—is that it fails to recognize that "the personal is political" in the way that Stendhal recognized it in *The Red and the Black* (1830), or Joseph Conrad in the *Heart of Darkness* (1899) and *The Secret Agent* (1907), or Albert Camus in his short story "The Guest" (1957), or as in the unforgettable Ettore Scola movie *A Special Day* (Ponti and Scola 1977). I must add that the most recent Turkish novels, such as those written by young novelists like Emrah Serbes and Ayhan Geçgin, are cynically political. They do underscore the effect of politics on individual lives, but at the same time they undermine its impact through indifference, irony, paradox, *mise en abyme*, and the avoidance of choice-making. This, of course, is quite a personal impression and needs to be grounded in more research and closer readings.

Since the social realist novels of 1960s—especially the works of writers such as Orhan Kemal and Fakir Baykurt—what do you think about the role of class in Turkish novels? What changes and continuities can we observe today in literary engagement with class?

This question is related to your previous question. Perhaps I can better answer this as an elaboration of the question of politics in the Turkish novel. Again, there is an intense preoccupation with class. Its literary renderings, however, have remained schematic. Unfortunately, this is a predicament that novels based on class suffer from more generally. Except for Dickens, the English novel, for example, was not able to produce great works about class in the nineteenth century. Or then again, maybe not. I might also mention here Samuel Butler's *The Way of All Flesh* (1903) and Thomas Hardy's *Jude the Obscure* (1895) as fine novels based on class. In the Turkish novel, class is depicted as an exposition on unjust income distribution or dire poverty, but hardly ever as a tension that not only cuts through the layers of society, but also penetrates into the bones and skins of the protagonist, as we see in Balzac or Dickens. Novels dealing with poverty are not necessarily novels that deal with class. The latter must be panoramic, must span from "great expectations" to "lost illusions," must have numerous characters, not just a few representatives, that make up the classes; they must create a whole society as in Balzac's *Human Comedy* (1829–1847) or Zola's *Les Rougon-Macquart* (1871–1893). Political novels may be based on a single theme or idea—usually that of dilemma and choice —and may focus on a single protagonist—such as in Joseph Conrad's *Lord Jim* (1899–1900); but not so the class novel. In this sense, the Turkish novel has not produced class novels, although it has produced fine "poverty" novels like those of Kemal (1954) and Tekin (1983, 1986). One narrative that in my opinion can be considered a class novel is Hikmet's 1966 *Human Landscapes from My Country* (*Memleketimden İnsan Manzaraları*), for its panoramic depiction of class in two trains that make a parallel journey on the same railroad but remain absolutely divergent in all other directions of being.

Nevertheless, there are three novelists that I think have successfully combined the political and the personal. These are Orhan Kemal, Yaşar Kemal, and Kemal Tahir. In his classic 1954 novel, *On the Fertile Soils* (*Bereketli Topraklar Üzerinde*), Orhan Kemal exposes the ruthless exploitation of the poor by the rich.

His ironic use of the word *fertile* refers both to the country and the city; the land, the factories, buildings are fertile only for the owners; they are the "fertile soils" for the exploitation and abuse of the needy. These soils nourish instinct, survival at all costs, sickness, betrayal, and corruption. Orhan Kemal is also an impressive novelist of the socio-economic change from artisanship to factory production and its impact on familial relations. Yaşar Kemal shares quite a few topoi with Orhan Kemal's work, including the exploitation of the poor, the impact of socio-economic change on collective morals and values, as well as on individual lives. Hence, the two Kemals are the icons of a social realism presented in mythological, romantic, and naturalistic terms, all at the same time. Yaşar Kemal, however, is also a creator of myths and archetypes, and the poetic language that suits those. His accounts of dissident folk heroes—as in the 1955 novel *Mehmed, My Hawk* (*İnce Memed*) or the story of seasonal migration of mountain villagers to the cotton fields and back in the 1960 trilogy *The Wind from the Plain* (*Dağın Öte Yüzü*) (2015/1960)—introduced the technique of magical realism and the fantastic to the Turkish novel that was emulated by later novelists such as Latife Tekin. Yaşar Kemal's contribution to the novelistic tradition in Turkey was not only his narratives of dissidence or the fantastic; he also managed to weave into these narratives a subtle insight into psychological realism through the eccentric characters upon which he built his narrative strategies.

When speaking of the novels of social realism, the third name that cannot be forgotten is Kemal Tahir. That makes three Kemals. Among them, they have managed to add a new twist to the Turkish novelistic tradition. Kemal Tahir's work may be roughly classified under the rubric of the historiographic novel. Tahir approached the genre from a Marxist angle that underscored the differences in the modes of production between the development of Turkish and Western capitalisms. He is the novelist of dramatic historical moments as they reflect on individual dramas, as Berna Moran has analyzed in his seminal work of literary criticism, *A Critical Approach to the Turkish Novel* (*Türk Romanına Eleştirel Bir Bakış*) (1983–1994).

After the 1960s, we began to witness the growing presence of female novelists. The number of women writers increased and they became more influential in the field of Turkish literature. What do you think about the role of women novelists such as Fatma Aliye, Leyla Erbil, or Aslı Erdoğan in Turkish literature?

The Turkish novel has been terribly gendered from its very beginnings in the late nineteenth century. If one has to give a very general definition of the gendering of the novel in Turkey, one could justifiably argue that everything—religion, nationalism, morality, creativity, good, evil—has been argued over figurations of the female by representing female characters as embodiments of the pros and cons of any controversy that male inclination chose to take up. Consciousness of gender, however, is a 20th-century phenomena that began with the feminist movements of the 1970s, during which time we witnessed a remarkable eruption of female novelists into the Turkish novelistic arena. What I have noticed, personally, as the distinguishing trait of that emergence is this: practically all of the major women writers—Sevgi Soysal, Adalet Ağaoğlu, Peride Celal, Leyla Erbil, Latife Tekin, Firüzan, Halime Toros, Aslı Erdoğan—have foregrounded the theme and structure of *Bildung*, of self-cultivation and education, in at least one, but often more than one, of their novels. Thus, their major concerns have been with the development of the self, with personal histories, how to cope with and resist gender imprisonment, how to meet the challenge of taking their lives into their own hands. My thesis is that *Bildungsromane* have been written by women in Turkey, not by men. In this sense, women writers have made a greater claim to individualism, freedom, and autonomy, and they have explored the conditions of possibility for the realization of these things more intensely than have male writers.

If freedom (or shall we say liberation?) from prejudice, societal norms and values, early childhood trauma or guilt—whether successfully achieved or not—is one major theme of the **Bildungsroman**, the other is hope and aspiration. The topos to be liberated from is the house. The confinement to the house is a moral and spiritual confinement, as well as a physical one: it is slavery, it is sickness, it is degeneration, it is death. A surprising number of bildungsroman novels written by women have the house, the sickroom, and the sickbed as their setting, in which a whole past that extends to two and sometimes to three generations is conjured up. In all of these novels, the protagonist nurses a sick member of the family—usually it is the mother, sometimes a sibling. And it is in this setting that the great revelation takes place. And what is the revelation? Usually, it is the awareness that an unwritten, unacknowledged history exists, a fate that somehow pushes the women into confinement, into enclosed space. This space is sick space. It is beset by guilt, by dreams deferred and hopes frustrated. And every woman has to find her own way out. To kick herself free of sickness and death often invites a breakdown, a collapse. Sometimes they burn the house, or have fantasies of burning it. They emerge from these rooms mentally and physically wounded. But before they do, or at the same time that they do, they break free through cracks they generate by their writing. Writing is the remedy, the resistance, the one activity women have to help them cope with the nightmare of history. The most pathetic of these, from Erbil's 1985 novel, *The Day of the Darkness* (*Karanlığın Günü*), is the half-written journal the mother leaves in her room before being confined to the mental institution. My favorite is the page that breaks free from the confinement of the house in Tekin's 1983 book, *Dear Shameless Death* (*Sevgili Arsız Ölüm*). It is a page of writing that flies from the rooftop of the house where the protagonist Dirmit is confined and sails all over the city.

The most important development in the Turkish novel over the last years was arguably the awarding of the Nobel Prize to Orhan Pamuk. How has this influenced Turkish literature? How do you evaluate the public reception of the prize in Turkey? What do you think about Pamuk's place in Turkish and world literature?

You cannot expect me to be impartial in my response to this question; I am a great admirer of Orhan Pamuk's novels. All I can do, then, is to enumerate my reasons and call upon my colleagues to analyze them for their judiciousness.

Pamuk likes to use a particular structure in virtually all of his novels: he sets up the local themes of the *father*, the *house*, *history* as *memory* and *identity*, *writing*, and the *writer*, and then he casts them all along the grand axis of the *quest*. This is a clever strategy for combining the local and the universal. However, Pamuk does not seize upon this formula as an easy way out. He works hard on the theme of *quest* and charges it with his own worldview. His questers—practically all writers, poets, or *artistes manqués*—are problematic characters, neurotic and opportunistic. We are now approaching the Lukacsian definition of the novel as a *modern epic*. The quest these characters engage in is debased by their own shortcomings, as well as by other forms of corruption and stupidity, such as cravings after social and personal power, silly partisanships, failed projects, and absurd obstacles planted on their path. This quest, to borrow another term from György Lukács' 1920 book, *Theory of the Novel*, takes place in a *transcendental homelessness* which can never be realized because, (a) the questors are problematic, (b) the quest has been debased, and (c) the transcendence that is sought is possible in art only, but the artist-protagonists are *artistes manqués*. The seemingly simple structural formula I spoke of above thus becomes deeply complicated by the ironies and paradoxes that Pamuk heaps one on top of the other, and by a comedic, mocking voice that displays a sophisticated use of humor.

If Pamuk has alienated some of his readers—which seems to be the case—that is because of these many layered ironies that, in the final analysis, add up to a cruelly indifferent gaze at society and the individual. I think it takes courage to meet this gaze.

Although Pamuk veils his narrative voice behind a cool and indifferent tone, he is a writer of atonement, another paradox that pervades his narrative structures and voice. In this culture, there is a huge stock of deeds and issues that require reparation. He tries to meet that need in the only way he knows: by writing. For Pamuk, atonement can only be achieved through writing; hence his meticulous effort at enriching his narratives with numerous stories of expiation, and with storytellers who reach out for restitution.

As for the Nobel Prize, you can guess that my personal opinion on that topic is that it was more than deserved, for reasons I have explained above. What is the Nobel Prize compared to all the studies dedicated to Pamuk's novels? There is not a single discussion that does not refer to Orhan Pamuk's presence on the scene of world literature. This kind of recognition I value more than a Nobel Prize win.

Over the last one or two decades, thanks to new research and an increasing number of translated works—especially from Armenian and Greek into Turkish—readers in Turkey have found more opportunities to appreciate the lost literary heritage of the Ottoman Empire, whose diverse multilingual sources are rooted in a shared geography. What kind of impact have non-Muslim writers had on Turkish literature, in both canonical and non-canonical senses?

Over the last two decades we have indeed witnessed a remarkable rise in scholarly interest in the translation and study of hitherto neglected works in the Armenian, Kurdish, and Greek languages. I might even venture to call the period beginning in the 1990s a *renaissance* in the study of these languages and literatures. Not only has it opened up new vistas of intertextuality in Turkish literature, it has also inspired a remarkable number of academic activities and studies, ranging from panels, symposiums, and graduate theses written in comparative literature and cultural studies programs, to the publication of anthologies and book series. Writers such as Zabel Yesayan, for example, that who had remained unknown outside a small circle of specialists have now become the focus of such theses. Your translations and your work on plays in the Armenian language, *Conflict and Negotiation: Turkish and Armenian Dramatic Literature in the Ottoman Empire* (Uslu 2015), are among the best scholarly output of this era. Literary periodicals in Greek and Armenian published in the late 19th and early 20th centuries that had been omitted from official histories of Turkish literature are now included in recent literary histories (Uslu and Altuğ 2014). Moreover, intertextual exchange among Kurdish, Armenian, and Greek works that are set in Turkey have contributed to the growing interest in elegiac and mnemonic modes, such as can be seen in Leyla Erbil's last novel from 2011, *Kalan* (*The Remaining*). These modes are more about what was lost than about what has been preserved. The loss may be summarized as that of a heterogeneous community of modest people—Greeks, Armenians, and Muslims— who lived more or less in harmony in Istanbul until the atrocities of September 6–7, 1955. The novel is an effort at remembrance. The technique is evocation through sound; the associational, repetitive, and formulaic employment of phrases, echoes, and meaningless fragments as a mnemonics that marks the protagonist Lahzen's evanescent reminiscences. This technique is accompanied by a series of metamorphoses that involve the transformation of the human into animate and inanimate nature—stone, statues, and especially stone ruins. It is a novel that makes use of affective memory, which, I think, became a technique employed after the publication of the testimonial narratives, such as those of the September 6–7 massacres and the 1915 genocide. These, of course, are all exciting, enriching developments. What troubles me, however, is the question of whether or not this acceleration over the last two decades will continue, given the recent dismissals of academics from their universities by the state of emergency decrees of 2016–2017.

References

de Balzac, H. (1829–1847). *La Comédie humaine* [*The Human comedy*]. Paris: Madame Béchet, Charpentier, Furne.

Butler, S. (1903). *The way of all flesh*. London: Grant Richards.

Camus, A. (1957). "L'Hôte" [The Guest]. In *L'Exil et le royaume* [*Exile and the kingdom*]. Paris: Gallimard.

Conrad, J. (1899). Heart of darkness. *Blackwood's Magazine, 165*.

Conrad, J. (1899–1890). Lord Jim. *Blackwood's Magazine, 166–167*.

Conrad, J. (1907). *The secret agent: A simple tale*. Cambridge: Cambridge University Press.

Erbil, L. (1985). *Karanlığın Günü* [*The day of darkness*]. Istanbul: Adam Yayınları.

Hardy, T. (1895). *Jude the obscure*. London: Osgood, McIlvaine & Co.

Hikmet, N. (1966). *Memleketimden İnsan Manzaraları* [*Human landscapes from my country*]. Istanbul: De Yayınları.

Kemal, O. (1954). *Bereketli Topraklar Üzerinde* [*On fertile soils*]. Istanbul: Remzi.

Kemal, Y. (1955). *İnce Memed* [*Memed, my hawk*]. Istanbul: Çağlayan Yayınevi.

Kemal, Y. (2015). *Dağın Öte Yüzü* [*The Wind from the plain*]. Istanbul: Yapı Kredi Yayınları (Original published in 1960).

Lukács, G. (1971). *The theory of the novel: A historico-philosophical essay on the forms of great epic literature*. Cambridge, MA: MIT Press (Original work published 1916).

Moran, B. (1983–1994). *Türk Romanına Eleştirel Bir Bakış* [A critical approach to the Turkish novel] (Vols. 1, 2, 3). Istanbul: İletişim Yayınları.

Parla, J. (1990). *Babalar ve Oğullar: Tanzimat Romanının Epistemolojik Temelleri* [*Fathers and sons: The Epistemological foundations of the Tanzimat novel*]. Istanbul: İletişim Yayınları.

Parla, J. (2011). *Türk Romanında Yazar ve Başkalaşım* [*Author and metamorphosis in the Turkish novel*]. Istanbul: İletişim Yayınları.

Ponti, C. & Scola, E. 1977. *Una giornata particolare* [A special day] Compagnia Cinomatografica ChampionItaly.

Stendhal (1831). *Le Rouge et Le Noir* [*The Red and the black*] Hilsum Paris.

Tahir, K. (1969). *Kurt Kanunu* [*The Law of the wolf*]. Istanbul: Bilgi Yayınevi.

Tekin, L. (1983). *Sevgili Arsız Ölüm* [*Dear shameless death*]. Istanbul: Adam Yayınları.

Tekin, L. (1986). *Gece Dersleri* [*Night lessons*]. Istanbul: Adam Yayınları.

Uslu, M. F. (2015). *Çatışma ve Müzakere: Osmanlı'da Türkçe ve Ermenice Dramatik Edebiyat* [*Conflict and negotiation: Turkish and Armenian dramatic literature in the Ottoman Empire*]. Istanbul: İletişim Yayınları.

Uslu, M. F., & Altuğ, F. (Eds.). (2014). *Tanzimat ve Edebiyat: Osmanlı Istanbulu'nda Modern Edebi Kültür* [*The Tanzimat and literature: Modern literary culture in Ottoman Istanbul*]. Istanbul: İş Bankası Kültür Yayınları.

Zola, É. (1871–1893). *Les Rougon-Macquart* [The Rougon-Macquart family]. Series of novels.

Author Biographies

Jale Parla is professor of English and comparative literature in the Department of Comparative Literature, at Istanbul Bilgi University. After completing her BA in comparative literature at Robert College in 1968, she obtained her PhD in English, French, and German literatures at Harvard University in 1978. She became a professor in 1988. She taught in the Department of Western Languages and Literature, Boğaziçi University from 1976 to 2000. She is the author of Efendilik, Şarkiyatçılık ve Kölelik (Masters, Slaves and Orientalism, 1985), Babalar ve Oğullar: Tanzimat Romanının Epistemolojik Temelleri (Fathers and Sons: The Epistemology Foundations of the Literature of the Tanzimat Era, 1990), Türk Romanında Yazar ve Başkalaşım (Writer and Metamorphosis in Turkish Literature, 2011), Don Kişot'tan Bugüne Roman (From Don Quixote to the Present-Day Novel, 2000), Don Kişot: Yorum Bağlam, Kuram, and Orhan Pamuk'ta Yazıyla Kefaret. She is coeditor with Sibel Irzık of Kadınlar Dile Düşünce (Gender and Literature, 2004) and with Murat Belge of the English-language volume, Balkan Literatures in the Era of Nationalism (2008).

Mehmet Fatih Uslu is assistant professor of Turkish Language and Literature at Istanbul Şehir University. He is the author of Çatışma ve Müzakere: Osmanlı'da Ermenice ve Türkçe Dramatik Edebiyat (Conflict and Negotiation: Armenian and Turkish Dramatic Literature in the Ottoman Empire" (2014). He is also the co-editor of the volume Tanzimat ve Edebiyat: Osmanlı İstanbul'unda Modern Edebi Kültür (Tanzimat and Literature: Modern Literary Culture in the Ottoman Istanbul), with Fatih Altuğ (2014). He has translated numerous works of literature and humanities from English, Italian, and Armenian into Turkish. He continues to translate from Armenian, with a special focus on the works of Ottoman Armenian writer Zabel Yesayan.

Özge Ertem is currently editor at Koç University's Research Center for Anatolian Civilizations (ANAMED) in Istanbul. She studied political science and international relations at Marmara University, Istanbul, before pursuing graduate studies in the field of history. She received her MA in 2005 from Boğaziçi University's Atatürk Institute and her PhD in 2012 from the Department of History and Civilization at the European University Institute, Florence. Her research focuses on the social and cultural history of famines in the late nineteenth century. She taught classes on world history; history of the Ottoman Empire and Turkey, and worked as a librarian. She is a member of the theater collective buluTiyatro.

Turkish Cinema

Ahsen Deniz Morva Kablamacı and interviewed by Kıvanç Sezer

Abstract The purpose of this chapter is to outline the history of the cinema in Turkey from the late Ottoman period to the present day. Questions provide to look at the history of Turkish cinema within the framework of the political, economic and social changes. For the readers not familiar with development in Turkey, are seen how the historical and social changes in Turkey affects Turkish cinema industry. This chapter underlines the important turning points. The Ottoman and Republic period, after the transition period from a single-party to a democratic system which led to a decadelong right-wing DP government, the 1980 coup d'état etc.- and also social movements—feminist, Kurdish, leftist, and Islamist movements. Not only historical and social changes, but also the reflection of these changes in films are also discussed. The reflections of political transformations in the Turkish cinema are handled within the framework of films that characterize the period.

Keywords Turkish cinema · Film industry · Yeşilçam (green pine)

Cinema was officially born on December 28, 1895 in the Grand Café on Capucines Boulevard, Paris, with the Lumière brothers' first-ever public showing of 10 short films. Between that moment and Fuat Uzkınay's 1914 documentary footage of the demolition of the Russian monument at Ayastefanos (present-day Yeşilköy, Istanbul), a number of films were made, beginning with the screenings at Abdulhamit II's Yıldız Palace. How would you define this period through to the end of World War I in terms of cinematography?

Eugène (Alexandre) Promio was a cinematographer for the Lumière brothers who came to Istanbul in 1896 to shot footage around the city. He filmed scenes on the Bosphorus and the Golden Horn and is reported to have said, "As for my trip to the

A. D. M. Kablamacı (✉) · K. Sezer
Istanbul, Turkey
e-mail: dmorva@gmail.com

© Springer International Publishing AG, part of Springer Nature 2019
E. Özyürek et al. (eds.), *Authoritarianism and Resistance in Turkey*,
https://doi.org/10.1007/978-3-319-76705-5_26

Ottoman Empire, in no other country have I encountered such difficulty in intro-
ducing a camera." I find this signification for two reasons. First, the cinematographer came to this land shortly after the beginning of the cinema. Second, censorship
is as old as the history of cinema.

The first film screening in the Ottoman Empire was right after the discovery of
cinematography. It was held in Yıldız Palace in 1896. This screening was for the
palace only. The first public screenings took place in the Pera district of Istanbul at
the end of 1896, organized by Sigmund Weinberg, a Romanian citizen of
Polish-Jewish descent who was the representative of the French company Société
Pathé Frères. He also opened the first permanent cinema house, Pathé, in the
Tepebaşı district of Istanbul. The first screenings on the Anatolian side were at the
Feyziye Coffeehouse in the Şehzadebaşı district. This district was famous for
hosting traditional Karagöz shadow plays during the month of Ramadan. On March
19, 1914, the brothers Cevat and Murat Boyer converted the Feyziye Coffeehouse
into the *Milli* (National) cinema theater, the first built-in cinema theater on the
Anatolian side.

Another controversial issue concerns the first Turkish movie. The government
destruction of the Russian monument to their victory over the Ottoman Empire in
the Ottoman-Russian War had been planned. For this purpose, an agreement was
made with the allied Austro-Hungarian film company Sascha-Messter Film. It was
decided that a demolition of the monument should be made by a Turk. The event
was filmed by Reserve Officer Fuat Uzkınay. There are so many questions about
this film. What happened to this film is unknown. Actually, we do not even know
whether it was actually made or not. Despite all these question marks, the historical
narrative of the beginnings of Turkish cinema has been constructed around this
film, *Ayastefanos'taki Rus Abidesi'nin Yıkılışı* (The Destruction of Russian
Monument at San Stefano). But the acceptance of the beginning of Turkish cinema
with this film ignores previous films made by Ottoman minority groups such as the
Greeks and the Armenians. For example, while another film about Sultan Reşat's
visit to Salonica and Manastır still survives. It was shot by the Macedonian brothers
Yanaki and Milton Manaki and is dated much earlier than the Uzkınay footage. It
should be added that during and after World War I, military and semi-military
establishments such as the Central Military Office of Cinema, the Society of
National Defense, and the Society of Disabled Veterans were the first cinematic
establishments in Turkey. Their first films were *Pençe* (The Claw, 1917) and *Casus*
(The Spy, 1917). These films were directed by Sedat Simavi who later founded
Hürriyet Daily Newspaper, and were promoted by the Society of National Defense.
Mürebbiye (The Governess, 1919) and *Binnaz* (1919) both produced by Ahmet
Fehim, were two other films made in support of the Society of Disabled Veterans,
which also brought the first Turkish comedy film to the screen with *Bican Efendi
Vekil Harç* (Bican Efendi, The Butler, 1921). To summarize, the introduction of
cinematography to this Turkey happened not long after the creation of cine-
matography; the first impressions, the first shots, were made by non-Muslims.

The development of cinema as a form of art dates back to end of 1940s. Very important directors like Ömer Lütfi Akad, Atif Yilmaz, and Metin Erksan produced films that, unlike their predecessors, distinguish between the cinema and the theater. This was also a transition period from a single-party to a democratic system which led to a decadelong right-wing DP government. How would you characterize the indirect and direct effects of the structure of capital on the films produced in those years?

The answer to this question is related to the political and economic changes in Turkey at that time. The films produced by the first companies were limited. Through the tax reduction act of 1948, the number of film production companies increased. Film production in Turkey became more profitable than the importation of films from abroad. This financial situation led the filmmakers, who are importers and businessmen, to produce domestic films.

The most significant era in the history of Turkish cinema began in the late 1950s. Turkey joined NATO in 1952, turning its face to the Western world. The populist policies of the DP significantly shaped our cinema industry. Mechanization, the rapid increase of the population, immigration to the cities, the facilitation of public transportation, the spread of electricity all affected the Turkish cinema. The number of movie theaters increased across the country. Devaluation in 1958 had a huge impact on cinema. Crude film costs rose rapidly and the cost of imported films increased. Quotas for film imports were implemented, leading to an increase in local productions; before 1950, film production companies had made money from film imports.

Although production became cheap and population growth resulted in an increase in demand, the film sector faced significant economic problems due to a lack of capital necessary to meet demand. Because of this, producers who did not want to take production risks made films fit to the expectations of their audience. Reflected in the production policies of the producers was a Turkish audience only recently migrated from rural areas to the cities. This audience, which had grown up in relatively closed cultures, was not yet detached from traditional social structures and was under the influence of the populist policies of the Democratic Party. It was a profitable job to make a film, but the technical infrastructure and provision of trained staff were inadequate. There was no state support. Because cinema developed in Turkey in the context of these practical possibilities and dynamics, films were produced to fit the expectations of the masses. Since there was no accumulation of capital, it caused the formation of a PR spin industry, which found its source of income in the audience. Despite this, a number of new and valuable filmmakers such as Ömer Lütfi Akad, Atıf Yılmaz, Metin Erksan, and Memduh Ün entered the industry. Importantly, we can point to the establishment of numerous filmmaking organizations: the Association of Turkish Filmmakers, Cinematographers and Technicians Cooperative (1955), the Local Filmmakers Association (1956), the Filmmakers and Turkish Film Producers Association (1958), and the Local Filmmakers Association (1959).

During the same period, Turkish cinema began to progress technically and to become more open to world cinema festivals and films other than blockbusters. This has been called the Yeşilçam era. Looking back, how would you describe the Yeşilçam era?

Yeşilçam (green pine) is a street in Istanbul's Beyoğlu district where many film studios were located. It is a sobriquet for the Turkish film industry. When the film industry first became a profitmaking business, a large number of film production companies opened on Yeşilçam street. In the early 1960s, Anatolia was divided into distribution regions. Regional distributors focused only on the region they were located in, and this localism began to influence the types of films that were made. They told producers what types of stories were in demand by their audience and provided the producers with minimum ticket-sale guarantees, which then financed the film production. This system became the general working principle. But a solid cinema industry was never built. Yeşilçam is thus the name for work in which commercial relations dictated the films that were produced, films that followed a specific narrative structure whereby temporary solutions to problems were found.

Ömer Lütfi Akad, a unique filmmaker who influenced Yılmaz Güney and other later directors, made social realist films. He thought a lot about the form of cinema and educated himself during those years. Is it possible to understand Turkey politically, historically, and socially through his films? If so, what are the distinguishing features of Akad and Güney's social realist films?

If actor and director Muhsin Ertuğrul can be seen as the one-man "founder" of the Turkish cinema industry, it would not be wrong to say that Ömer Lütfi Akad is the first important director in Turkey to make films with the language of cinema. He entered the cinema industry with the production of his first film, *Vurun Kahpeye* (Strike the Whore, 1949). Following in Akad's footsteps, Metin Erksan made his first film in 1952, Atıf Yılmaz in 1957, and Memduh Ün in 1958.

Soon thereafter in the socially progressive atmosphere of the 1960s, another very important period in the history of Turkey began with the production of notable examples of social realist cinema. These directors were all politically sensitive and wanted to tell stories based on the everyday lives of ordinary people. Club Cinema 7 (1962) and the Turkish Cinematheque Association (1965) were both established during these years. There was a sharp increase in the number of film periodicals being published and in filmmakers who think about the nature of cinema and publicly discuss the type of cinema that should be made. These years were thus socially, culturally and politically very fertile years for cinema. Ertem Göreç's *Karanlıkta Uyananlar* (Those Awakening in the Dark, 1964) was the first film to explore workers' strikes; Halit Refiğ's *Gurbet Kuşları* (Birds of Exiles, 1962) looked at rural to urban migration; Metin Erksan's *Yılanların Öcü* (Revenge of the Snakes, 1962) and *Susuz Yaz* (A Dry Summer, 1963) focused on the situation in rural Anatolia. Through Lütfi Akad's films, you can understand the socioeconomic structure of Turkey and its influence on people. You can analyze Turkish society through his films on the city, his migration trilogy, his Anatolian trilogy, his documentaries and films made with the Turkish Radio and Television Corporation. Lütfi Akad's cinema asks questions but does not give answers. He diagnoses the illness, but does not offer a prescription for the treatment.

In 1970, Yılmaz Güney made his film *Umut* (Hope) and it was almost like a revolution in Turkish cinema. How do you describe this film and its importance?

With *Umut*, Yılmaz Güney stood squarely against Yeşilçam's established order, its star system, studio system, cliché narrative structure aimed at box office success. Yılmaz Güney's way of looking and seeing was radical because it stands against the deformation of our way of seeing class difference. It reveals class distinction without resorting to agitation. For him, every discipline of art is a vehicle for conveying thought to the masses. Art takes its place with great care in the struggle to change the world. The artist must be considerate of the function of art in this struggle. Filmmakers convey what they want to say through cinema. Güney's cinema tells society of difference, of the lives of people from different classes. His cinema is a tool for the emancipation of the working class. In *Umut*, Güney tells the story of waiting. He wants to tell the story of a deceptive hope that does not offer a solution. He used "hope" as a symbol of disorganization here, to show the life of someone who dreams of hopeless things. And he deliberately does not show a way out; had the film shown a way out, it would not be a film. He believes that revolutionary films does not show the way out. *Umut*, was a revolution for our cinema. Güney said that we should look at, grasp, and reflect upon the reality that surrounds us in the streets we hurry through every day. With *Umut*, he defied the Yeşilçam tradition. Yılmaz Güney hit a nerve in this country. Because of him, whatever the circumstances, filmmakers will find a way to make movies and find a way to break down traditions. Not only in terms of the content of a film, but also the possibility of making a movie that says, "another world is possible" outside prevailing conditions.

Coming to the 1980s, the production of sex films increased and many actors and film crew members began to earn their living from these films. What was the need behind this development and how long did these films continue to be produced?

In his book, *Işıkla karanlık arasında* (Between light and dark, 2004), Lütfi Akad says that 1975 was a very difficult year. This was the year that something in Turkish cinema began to change. Akad decided to retire when there was no hope anywhere. The year he retired marked a period roughly between 1974 and 1979 when a large number of productions were what we call "sex films." The major producers were cautious and watchful; they could survive and continued to make their usual run of melodramas, comedies, adventure and historical films. But the minor producers were constantly making films. The subjects of these films were not directly pornographic, but the themes tended to be sexual in nature. These minor producers survived by targeting another mass of spectators. Some producers, directors, and actors, and were drawn from that sex film sector, but it also attracted new actors to the movie industry. Some people saw sex films as an alternative. The aim was to create a sector of the film industry based only these sexual themes, and it eventually led to the development of the porn film industry.

The downturn in Turkish cinema is a result of problems that have accumulated over the ensuing years. By 1974, there was a kind of movie inflation in the sector. In 1972, the Turkish film industry was the fourth most productive in the world, turning out 298 films that year. Low-budget "B" films dominated. Interestingly, at the time, there was heavy censorship of political films, but both imported and Turkish-produced sex films were not subject to censorship. The corruption of economic exploitation and politics is always reflected in the cultural sphere, and the effects on cinema and art generally were deliberately ignored by the government. At a time when political struggle was on the rise, the right-of-center Justice Party, in coalition with two extremist right-wing parties, tolerated the sex film industry. The masses, who were not interested in any art that reflected the streets, was able to keep Turkish cinema alive only through their consumption of these kind of films.

During the 1980s the cinema industry abandoned its blockbusters and avoided meddling in politics. Individual despair and the artist's depression became prominent themes. How did society and politics change filmmakers, and then how did society continue to relate to movies?

Following the 1980 the coup d'état parties and unions were shut down, books and films burned and banned, people tortured and imprisoned without trial. This was a crucial breaking point politically, sociologically, and economically. It was a time when people lost their belief that it was possible to change the world. At the same time, it was also a period of opportunity and promise.

The September 12, 1980 military coup also deeply affected the cinema industry. Due to censorship and the detention of certain filmmakers, film production decreased, and audiences almost preferred not to go to the theaters. The mood of the 1980s was also reflected in film content. In the second half of the 1980s, films addressed the themes of prison conditions, prohibitions, repression, torture, the death penalty, and freedom.

Turkish cinema survived the crises of the 1980s by finding appropriate solutions. The only funding source for Turkish cinema at the time was the Turkish audience. Meanwhile, the sector failed to modernize and remake itself in order to compete with the rise of television. The decrease in the number of theater-goers had a negative effect on the regional distributors. For a time, videos came to the rescue, but this posed serious problems for movie theater owners. The showing of videos both in coffeehouses and in tea gardens posed a danger that the already diminished audience would be completely lost.

In this period, a self-reflexive cinema emerged from a younger generation of filmmakers, posing a new challenge for an audience used to Hollywood or Yeşilçam cinema. When you look at the filmmaking style and the content of the films of this period, the diversity is striking. The advent of new media in the 1980s and the diminished financial resources of Turkish cinema led to drastic changes. Cinema lost its old audiences and venues at the same time that a new mass of spectators was born. While the family was watching television and videos at home, a new generation of young audiences began to watch high-quality festival films. Despite all the adverse conditions, Turkish directors were internationally successful in that period. There were films about the lives of urban women who seemed happy with their choices. With the development of feminism in Turkish society, films began to break some of the social taboos. Women characters were no longer portrayed as "poor but happy," or as an elderly grandmother or housewife, but we began to see women as *women*. This enormous change in social structure transformed commercial cinema into making what is known as the *arabesque film*. Films were made about the internal affairs of the individual, alienation, social transformation, criticism of new values.

In the 1990s, Hollywood productions dominated the theaters, but some new Turkish blockbusters were also produced. What are the important films of this period, and what happened to the Turkish film industry in 1990s?

In the 1990s, different production models existed simultaneously. Because producers didn't want to invest in films at the time, directors became the producers of their own films. At the same time, films began to be produced under the influence of private television broadcasting. When private TV broadcasting companies began filling in their timeslots with Turkish films, film production was then turned over to the television companies. This was the first of two effects. The revenue from the sales of these films to the television channels was not transferred back to the sector for new film production. Television channels supported the production of films in the preproduction phase only, which meant that they purchased television rights to movies. But this led to a second effect: instead of going to cinemas and watching movies, audiences preferred to watch the same films over and over again in their homes. Television channels also preferred to screen old movies rather than supporting the production of new films. This interaction led the cinema industry to begin producing television series for the channels.

Founded by the Council of Europe in 1989, Eurimages became a new production facility for Turkish cinema. At the same time, major American film production companies began to enter the country. Warner Bros-Turkey was founded, United International Pictures opened a branch in Turkey. While entering the market, these American majors also invested in renovating movie theaters, and they began to release their new films in Turkey in concert with the rest of the world. Turkish films could hardly find a movie theater that would screen them. With Hollywood domination, private channel broadcasting, and the low cinematic standard of domestic film production, only a few Turkish films made it to the screen. During this period, a new genre called "white cinema" made by production companies owned by Islamic capital began to appear. Another group of films of this period is the result of the developing advertising industry; companies transferred money earned from commercial advertising films to the making of motion picture films. Reductions in the taxation of domestic films during this period also had an effect. With the making of films like Yavuz Turgul's *Eşkıya* (The Bandit, 1996) and Gani Müjde's *Kahpe Bizans* (Perfidious Byzantium, 1999) the domestic film audience increased to more than 1 million. It's important to note that these films were watched by more filmgoers than were the first two films in the *Lord of the Rings* trilogy in Turkey.

What about the generation of Turkish filmmakers who began to produce films in the mid-1990s? Nuri Bilge Ceylan is the most famous director of this generation who was awarded Palme d'Or at the Cannes Film Festival, the only Turkish filmmaker other than Yılmaz Güney to win the award. Other important directors of this generation are Zeki Demirkubuz, Yeşim Ustaoğlu, and Derviş Zaim. What are the similarities and differences between these directors who all continue to make films?

In the 1990s, we see both positive and negative developments in Turkish cinema. Diversification of the resources required for filmmaking and the genres now in demand have led directors to make films in different styles. 1996 was a turning point for the country's film industry for many reasons. More than 2.5 million people watched Yavuz Turgul's *Eşkıya*. Derviş Zaim's *Tabutta Rövaşata* (Somersault in a Coffin, 1996), an ultralow-budget art house picture, won four awards at the Antalya International Film Festival, the oldest national cinema industry event. Then Nuri Bilge Ceylan's first feature film, *Kasaba* (The Small Town, 1997) premiered in Berlin. In the same year as *Kasaba*, Ferzan Özpetek's *Hamam* (The Turkish Bath, 1997) and Zeki Demirkubuz's *Masumiyet* (Innocence, 1997) were made. Özpetek became a leading figure in transnational cinema and Demirkubuz became one of the key figures in low-budget filmmaking in Turkey. In the late 1990s, every filmmaker from this younger generation had a new vitality. Even though they had been raised on our own culture and history, they spoke to a universal language of cinema. The preceding generation had devoted itself to making political films. After the 1990s, certain Turkish directors began to come to terms with the past regarding minority communities. New identity-related questions about feminism, environmentalism, homosexuality, ethnicity, religion, and class became the new subject of cinema. Since the second half of the 1990s, the new problems of the working class such as privatization, subcontracting, unionization, and the extension of flexible work have been major topics.

Coming to the 2000s, the AKP has become the ruling party and taboos on the Kurdish question have been broken. Kurdish filmmakers such as Kazım Öz, Hüseyin Karabey, Orhan Eskiköy produced films about Kurdish culture, language, and presence. This triggered a discussion of the relevance of the terms "Turkish cinema" and "cinema of Turkey." How would you describe this period and its films on identity?

Over the last years, Kurdish cinema has emerged as one of the most important areas in Turkey's film industry. Kurdish films and Kurdish filmmakers have been increasingly present at national and international film festivals. An increasing number of publications have worked to advance the cause of Kurdish cinema. This is also the effect of film theory seminars, film production workshops, and an accumulation of short films produced in the mid-1990s by the cinema unit of the Mesopotamian Cultural Center. As a field of artistic discourse, Kurdish cinema has created its own cinema industry, which has always been transnational due to the absence of an official Kurdish state. In this period, the films that addressed the Kurdish question were of particular significance because they required presenting the past through the use of unofficial records. These directors were in essence constructing a countermemory despite the fact that there was no official or formal process in Turkey designed to come to terms with the past. These films can also be read as a ground of struggle that depicts the dynamism of survival, existence, and resistance. In this context, a domestic and international debate on Kurdish cinema, informed by Kurdish filmmakers from Turkey and other countries, began for the first time, and theses, articles, books, began to address Kurdish cinema.

Reference

Akad, L.Ö. (2004). *Işıkla karanlık arasında* [Between light and dark]. Türkiye İş Bankası Kültür Yayınları.

Author Biographies

Ahsen Deniz Morva Kablamacı worked as an associate professor of film studies until she was dismissed during the state of emergency academic purges after the attempted coup of July 2016. In 2015–2016 she was a guest lecturer at Tufts University, where she conducted comparative research on post-dictatorship cinema in Latin America and Turkey. Her research interests include Turkish cinema, collective memory and cinema, trauma and cinema, and political cinema in Turkey. She directed the feature film *Breakage* (2009) and the full-length documentary *Smile and Re'as'sist* (2016) and together with Ilkay Nişancı co-directed a short film entitled *Çengelli İğne* (Safety Pin, 2002). From 2003 to 2007, she was a regular contributor to *New Man New Cinema magazine*.

Kıvanç Sezer studied editing in Cineteca di Bologna for two years. In 2009 he returned to Turkey and worked in several documentaries and TV programmes as an editor. He wrote and directed two short films and a feature length documentary. His debut My Father's Wings was premiered in 51. Karlovy Vary Main Competition and received more than 20 awards. He participated to Berlinale Talents Script Station with his next Project The Little Things and at the moment is developing the project in Nipkow Programme, Berlin. He is awarded residency at the Villa Kult Programme.

Art Production in Turkey from 1980s to Today

Hale Tenger Interviewed and by Isin Önol

Abstract This interview focuses on the impacts of the political developments in Turkey from the 1980 military coup d'etat up until today on freedom of expression in the field of visual arts. It primarily deals with political expression in contemporary art starting from the personal experiences of Hale Tenger, looks at singular examples.

Keywords Contemporary art · Visual culture · Freedom of expression
Osman Kavala

The following interview was first conducted in 2014, a year after the Gezi Protests. It was completed and updated first in July 2015, then in November 2017. However, to be able to compare and contrast the political landscape of today and of two years ago, we deliberately decided to keep some of the responses from 2015.

Işın Önol: We started this interview back in 2014, ended in June 2015 and now in 2017, it is very difficult to update the issues that were discussed here, under the shadow of the events that took place during the past two years. Although we had experienced the Gezi Park Protests and its primary consequences back then, no one would have expected these drastic changes in the country. Over the past years, we have been terrified to see the extent of state violence, bitterly iterating the history from the eighties. You have been an artist since the early nineties and witnessed the obstruction of freedom of expression first-hand. 1980 was the year

H. Tenger (✉)
Galeri Nev Istanbul, Istanbul, Turkey
e-mail: haletenger@gmail.com

H. Tenger
Green Art Gallery, Dubai, UAE

I. Önol
University of Applied Arts, Vienna, Austria
e-mail: isinonol@gmail.com

© Springer International Publishing AG, part of Springer Nature 2019   279
E. Özyürek et al. (eds.), *Authoritarianism and Resistance in Turkey*,
https://doi.org/10.1007/978-3-319-76705-5_27

of the military coup d'état, where thousands of people were killed, detained, or had to flee. Since then, each decade had its own suppression primarily perse-cuting left-wing thinkers of the country. Now we are back to an era where anyone can be detained unlawfully. I would like to start with your experiences from the earlier years: As an art practitioner, you always had a critical voice and dared using bold and strong political images. You faced some undesired consequences of using these images. Then these experiences became symbolic cases in the recent history of art production in Turkey. Could you elaborate more on these cases? What have you done and what have you encountered?

Hale Tenger: I was taken to court because of the work titled *I Know People Like This II,* which I installed at the 3rd Istanbul Biennial in 1992. The first lawsuit was for insulting the Turkish flag. Since there was no real Turkish flag in the piece, that case was dropped and a new one was opened; this time I was charged with insulting 'Turkishness' by using emblems of the nation. It all began with a right wing columnist's article targeting me directly, causing a reader to call and file a com-plaint with the Prosecution Office. They filed a legal case against me in a lower Civil Court of Peace. That court dismissed the case on grounds that it lacked jurisdiction, and the case was re-opened in a Criminal Court of General Jurisdiction. My lawyer and I declared in our plea that the theme of the art piece had nothing to do with Turkey specifically, but was rather about the universal oppression of women by men. Subsequently, I was acquitted. If I had told that it was about the repressive politics of Turkey, the state violence, or in particular about the Kurdish problem, I would have directly ended up in jail. The '90s were years of brutal state violence, political assassinations, unidentified murders, burning of Kurdish villages, forced evacuations of thousands from southeastern Turkey. Overall, the legal case filed against me took almost a year to be resolved.

Isin Önol: In that work, you composed the star and crescent of the Turkish flag together with the Greek deity Priapos, known for his erected penis, and the popular image of 'the three monkeys'. What did the installation include, what were your motivations, and what happened to the work at the end?

Hale Tenger: *I Know People Like This II* was a wall installation composed of the three wise-monkeys (don't see/don't hear/don't speak) and those of Priapos. They were all ready-made figurines, bought from the souvenir shops in the Grand Bazaar of İstanbul. The figurines of the three monkeys formed the background of the compo-sition, and those of Priapos formed several stars and a crescent. Regarding the original Priapos figure exhibited in the Selçuk Archeological Museum of Ephesus, an ancient fertility deity, not only its phallus is bigger than the rest of his body, but also its head is comparably very large. However, in the touristic souvenir versions, the head had shrunk and this was particularly perfect for me to use it as a symbol not only of excessive power but also to underline the feeblemindedness. What had motivated me to create this piece in the first place was the urgency to say something about the atrocities going on in the '90s and the male-dominated politics in Turkey. The Priapos figurines narrated what I wanted to express in that sense and the three monkeys obviously symbolized the repressed and silenced society. The piece was exhibited throughout the Biennial. Then at the end of the Biennial, after a female reader made the complaint over the phone to the prosecutor, the police prohibited the removal of the installation from the wall as part of the procedure of gathering evidence. So it stayed on the wall even after all the artworks were gone and the building was emptied.

Isin Önol: Could you tell us more about the court decision and your experiences after that? For example, did you feel unsafe during that period? Did you have any support from the art community?

Hale Tenger: Facing a criminal charge was a great source of stress for me, and it was my first such experience. Before producing the work, I had consulted some acquaintances about the possible legal outcomes. I was warned by most of them that I would be directly taken to the State Security Court. Under the 1982 Constitution State Security Courts (*Devlet Güvenlik Mahkemeleri*, DGM) were established by the then military government. The panel of three judges included a military judge in each State Security Court. In 1999 military judges were removed from the bench and in 2004 State Security Courts were formally abolished. Since I trusted the opinions of the people I spoke with, I decided to change the composition of the piece and added more stars. It helped me in the end; if it were only one star and one crescent, who knows which court I would have ended up at. It was not possible for me to stand before the court and say that it was a work criticising the state politics, especially against left wing people and Kurds unless I wanted to be jailed. In terms of solidarity, I got legal support from the IKSV (Istanbul Foundation for Culture and Arts), especially from the late committee member Onat Kutlar. They helped a lot in issues such as finding a lawyer suitable for this specific case and determining a strategy during the court process. I was advised by them not to go public, which I already had by giving interviews to the media during the Biennial. Their idea was to keep it as quiet as possible, not to draw further media interest. Some rightwing newspapers had reported the court case and I was receiving threatening phone calls at my house. Apart from legal support, my family proudly stood by my side, my father even came with me to the courthouse when the prosecutor wanted to take my statement. Vasıf Kortun, the curator of the exhibition came to the courthouse on the first day of trial. I still felt lonely though; during that year only my close friends supported me. But then there was no social media, no mobile phones etc. and my feeling of being isolated was perhaps related to my semi-distant personality in social surroundings.

Isin Önol: How did this judicial process affect your subsequent artistic production? How did your critical use of language and symbolism evolve after that? Could you tell us about your strategy on censorship and threats regarding your art production?

Hale Tenger: When I was invited to the 4th Istanbul Biennale in 1995, I directly came up with a reactionary piece. It was sort of my response to the court case. René Block the curator of the biennial, took me and some other artists to see the exhibition space, and I came across an old wooden guardhouse. Its windows and walls from inside were all covered with printed images from the nature as if whoever used this guardhouse didn't want to see the outside, although it was on the second floor of the abandoned old customs building overlooking the Bosphorus. I made my decision at that moment and told René I was going to use it in my installation. I surrounded it with barbed wire fence and added a few objects inside and installed a radio playing Turkish folk songs. The title of the piece was *We didn't go outside; we were always on the outside/We didn't go inside; we were always on the inside* a quotation from a poem by Edip Cansever. Once again, I said whatever I wanted to say but I used a strategy so that a court case was not triggered. I even used the star and crescent in the form of a brooch inside the guardhouse. It was a work questioning the boundaries between being in the inside/in jail and being on the outside/not being in jail, when there is no freedom of speech to begin with. In short, I developed a method, which enabled me to express whatever I wanted to express through different means.

In 2013, I made a new work for the exhibition *Envy, Enmity, Embarrassment* at Arter, Istanbul. It was an installation titled *I Know People Like This III*, consisting of a labyrinth of hundreds of images of political violence, mostly state violence, which I gathered from media photo archives. The images transformed to look like radiograms were printed on x-ray films and were presented on giant negatoscopes. The display started at the storefront of Arter building in Beyoglu with the images of the most recent street clashes in the southeast towns of Turkey, which were not covered in the main stream media. About nine hundred images ended with the *Events of September of 1955 (the Istanbul Pogrom)*. We were in a way concerned about whether showing such images would cause a negative reaction or not, but nothing happened.

Isin Önol: Looking from today's perspective in 2017, I see that some kind of legal system existed back then, that you could dance around it a little. Today, after all these incidents, we lost our trust in the judicial system completely. Academics, artists, human right activists, journalists, writers are imprisoned one by one. The circle is becoming smaller; any critical voice is under a great danger, and the country itself has become an "empire of fear". Today, I am not supposed to ask any of these questions to you, and you are not supposed to respond to them. May be we are not taken aback for the current atrocities and unlawfulness, because we have already experienced the '80s, but how can we trust and have faith in law in today? Were we too naïve?

Hale Tenger: I don't claim that we ever had a democratic, libertarian government in the past and we don't have one now either. Turkey has always been a country ruled by a central state power, whether governmental or military. There have been restraints on the media before as well, but the level and the means of oppression is unprecedented. The oppression is not only on the media, it's everywhere, on social life itself, on individuals, on institutions, associations, businesses etc. We have also seen unlawfulness previously but, at the present time the judiciary is directly controlled by one man and it is carried out in the open. Most court cases are initiated after the president's accusations are made live through the media and I think this is deliberately and systematically done. Most of these practices are against the law but we're living under an eviscerated system of law and order. It's not going to be easy if there'll ever be a chance to fix things up.

Isin Önol: You had been contending with taboos long before all those incidents. For example, your work named The School of "Sikimden Aşşa Kasımpaşa" (not to give a fuck) is one that might be much riskier to display today: A cauldron filled with blood, that would overflow as soon as the ablution taps are opened or when one of the over-hanging swords drops. What reactions did that work receive? What reactions would it receive today in 2017 as Ottomanism is very popular?

Hale Tenger: That work was first put together and exhibited in 1990 and faced no intervention or reaction whatsoever. When it was displayed in 2011 at Istanbul Modern, there was again no hindrance. A columnist in a pro-government newspaper published an article that tried to target the work, claiming that it was insulting Islam, which was of course baseless and nothing happened. But I was a bit nervous for a while wondering if I would find myself in a legal battle again. The piece actually came out as a consequence of two tragic events in 1990 that distressed me immensely. First, was an article I read in the Cumhuriyet newspaper, reporting the horrific case of an accountant who died after being imprisoned for 70 days, when one of his clients filed a claim against him in court. Although he was in an unconscious state for a long time, his family was informed only four days prior to his release. When his family could finally take him to the hospital he had bloodstain on his pants and his last words were "enough, don't you see I cracked." He then stopped talking and eating. There was no physical diagnosis of a sickness. He died shortly afterwards. His family thought he was raped, tortured. On the same day I read that article, Bahriye Üçok was assassinated by a mail bomb at her house (a female Turkish professor of theology, women's rights activist, left-wing politician). I deliberately used three types of swords, Western type, Ottoman type and a toy sized type for children. Along with political connotations gender issues are also involved in it. I'd prefer not to show it in Turkey nowadays because we're going through a hysterical period and no one can guess what is going to happen about anything.

Isin Önol: And then comes your work Down Up, through which you displace Ankara and move it into the Southeast Anatolia. If you had expressed your views therein within a written text rather than in the form of an artwork, that publi-cation would, without a doubt, have been banned and pulled off the shelves. We are talking about 1992, a time where it required immense courage for one to talk about "the responsibility of Ankara" —i.e. the Turkish State, in the Kurdish struggle. Nothing has changed as of today.[1] Ankara still uses the same force

---

[1]The question of "today" and the answer here dates back to June 2015, before the elections that first generated a lot of hope for a change in Kurdish issue. We have decided to keep it as it is to be able to contrast the political landscape of two years ago from today.

around the region. And still, the "Aşağı Tükürsem Sakal, Yukarı Tükürsem Bıyık" (Between the devil and deep sea) perspective, which you referred to in your work, is alive. The next election is coming up very soon. We do not know whether the only party to represent Kurds would pass the 10% barrier or not, needles to say that the said barrier was put in action during the '90s against Kurdish parties. What is your take on this today (in June 2015)?

Hale Tenger: We moved from "Kurds do not exist" of the '90s to "Kurds do exist"; however, repression of Kurds in the region still continues. "Peace process" is on the table; but I have doubts about its progression when the government that leads the peace talks declares, just before the elections, that HDP (the party representing Kurds) would create great problems if it passes the barrier and enters the parliament. I at least believe that the process would not go backwards, and I think that the debates would continue eventually, although there is now a pause due to the approaching elections. Majority doesn't want any clashes anymore.

Isin Önol: Coming to another 'today', to November 2017, number of improbable incidents happened that we wouldn't be able to imagine at the time we conducted the interview in 2015. If I try to summarise: The pro-Kurdish party HDP entered the Parliament, passing the %10 barrier, but a coalition government could not be founded. A snap election took place in November 2015. Between the two elections, there were bomb explosions at many peace demonstrations. You were very right about your doubts in relation to the government's declaration that HDP entering into parliament would create great problems, it truly did. However, you also believed that the peace process would not go backwards. Today, we are not able to talk about peace anymore. During the conflicts between Kurdish forces and Turkish military forces many people died or were injured. Last summer, we had another military coup attempt. The leaders and the majority of the members of the HDP are in prison. As of last week, Osman Kavala a left-wing businessman, human rights activist and founder of Anadolu Kültür, an active non-profit institution that runs art and culture projects and fights against fascism and discrimination, is in prison. We are back to the days where "Kurds do not –or must not- exist". From today's perspective what can you say about the Kurdish issue and its place in the field of art?

Hale Tenger: As you say, I was right about my doubts and concerns on the government side but unfortunately thinking that things won't go backwards as of clashes and violence was a naive and wishful thinking on my part. So many catastrophic things happened since we talked back in June 2015. We are now living under the rule of State of Emergency since July 2016, consecutively for 16 months. When HDP won 13% of the votes, AKP remained at 41% and could not form a government by itself as a single party, and this lit the fuse. After 15 July 2016 coup attempt came the extensive arrests and purges that turned into a counter-coup, a crackdown on whatever dissent is left in Turkey. With each new step the government takes, we think the unthinkable is happening. It is beyond our limits of comprehension. After the arrest of human rights advocates holding an open door training workshop at a hotel in Büyükada (they were released last week but charges and court case continues), now Osman Kavala is arrested. The charges that they are accused of are simply absurd. It is not a judicial process we are witnessing, it is a pathetic parody. In almost all court cases now, it became a standard issue that the indictment accuses defendants of being member of all terror organizations at once (FETÖ/PDY–PKK/KCK–DHKPC, MLKP). On top of that Kavala is also accused of being an organizer and overseer of the Gezi incidents. As Prof. Ayşe Buğra commented on Anadolu Kultur's public release after Kavala's arrest, "Moreover this also means that Osman Kavala was involved in the attempted coup along with the members of the organization who collected the evidence which led to Kavala's arrest, which is tragicomic beyond being unlawful." Coming to your question, not only the Kurdish issue, everything is at a halt right now, nothing is normal. We all try to carry on with our lives, continue working, doing the best of what we can do, but it is like living in an aquarium, loaded with unhappiness, tension, guilt feelings for not being able to be of much help in defending democratic rights. Arts and all are in this aquarium, in a state of limbo.

Isin Önol: Could you compare the participation of the artists in political resistance during the Gezi protests and today? How does the politics of fear affect the field of visual arts? Do you see any form of unification, alliance, collectiveness among the people working in the field of art and culture?

Hale Tenger: I would prefer to talk about it not only by focusing on arts and artists since the crackdowns are massive, in every field, everywhere. A professor, a civil servant, a student or a housewife is amongst all in an endless list of citizens being targeted, either by signing a petition as in the case of "Academicians for Peace" or by a social media post. Gezi events came out as a reaction, there were people from various backgrounds; the common ground was that everyone was fed up with the way things have been going on politically. Huge crowds gathered in Taksim Square for many days and just as well in many other cities all around Turkey. Masses were out on the streets simply as exasperated citizens. Gezi opened up new forms of getting together, standing together, public discussion platforms for people from non-homogeneous backgrounds. It was a truly peaceful and inspiring experience and brought optimism that was not in our reach for a long time. Nowadays it is just the opposite, there is extreme pressure from the government for silencing every aspect of our lives. Even delivering a message on social media makes one think of whether you might be targeted next. I have seen the '80s, '90s but what we are experiencing now is different, wondering whether your family members can also be targeted, witnessing a wife or husband being taken into custody or arrested as a retaliation to their partner, that a whole family's assets can and are being seized. This is the end of law. Only a very small minority is still vocal and the rest is in a vacuum.

Isin Önol: Back in 1997 Halil Altındere constructed a work with national ID cards within the Dance with Taboos series for the İstanbul Biennial. The work, which was tackling identity, faced a similar interrogation process as yours. Altındere covered the face of Atatürk on the 1.000.000 banknote with his own "Kurdish" hands. The court questioned whether a crime of "insulting Atatürk and the Turkish Lira" was committed. Then in 2005, the catalogue of the exhibition Free Kick within the 2005 Biennial was puled off for violating the Turkish Criminal Code Nr. 301. One could argue that the visibility of the biennials renders them more susceptible to censorship than regular contemporary art activities. Do you think that things have changed in this regard in today's Turkey (2015–2017) compared to the '80s and the '90s? What are the taboos today?

Hale Tenger: (2015) Nothing has changed for example regarding exhibiting my work *I Know People Like This II.* Although the peace talks are in progress and the ban on the Kurdish language has ended, it could still be said that the sensitivities about national symbols has not lessened, if not increased. We see this clearly, considering the countless lawsuits filed by even the most senior government officials against ordinary people, based on claims of insult where there is none. Yes, there have been some changes, but it is a pretty discretionary system that determines when, where, and for whom these changes would create an area of freedom. This discretion blurs everything. One of the biggest problems of Turkey is the uncertainty created by this discretion in the practice of law.

(2017) I now would say that sensitivities about national symbols of Turkishness are much more prevalent with the support of governmental policies. The civil servants are under extreme pressure if they are not pro-government. Taboos are widespread and differ depending on where you stand. Even conversations with a taxi driver, or a shopkeeper are constrained these days, as political cleavages are even sharper.

Isin Önol: Do you think that, in spite of all that discretion, freedom of speech in artistic production has improved or conserved in Turkey since the '80s? (2015)

Hale Tenger: Visual arts scene is still a rather obscure field in Turkey and therefore accommodates more freedom. On the other hand, more popular exhibitions like biennials or art fairs can attract attention in a negative sense, and reactionary interventions might occur leading to censorship. So, we never know what will happen, if an artwork might face censorship or backlash. The imprudence in the practice of law also plays its role in arts. There is a constant repression caused by uncertainty. For example back in 2007 there was going to be a group exhibition presenting highlights from the previous Istanbul Biennials at Istanbul Modern, and although I was acquitted from the previous lawsuit, the lawyers I consulted informed me that a similar lawsuit can be filed if the work will be exhibited again. Therefore I prefer not to exhibit *I Know People Like This II* in Turkey. Despite progress on the political front, and improvements since the oppression of Kurds in the '90s to peace debates of today, lack of freedom of speech still persists.

Isin Önol: How would you answer this question today, in 2017?

Hale Tenger: It is much more rigid nowadays. First because of State of Emergency and second because of the atmosphere created by so-called protests at exhibitions, which look pretty organized. Recently an organized attack occurred at the exhibition of Ömer Koç's collection at Abdülmecit Efendi Palace, twice in one day. The groups attacked the guards and shouted, "Is this secularism? This country is in this condition because of you. These works cannot be exhibited". Also last year, at the opening of Istanbul Contemporary art fair a group attacked and claimed a sculpture to be removed as they found it offensive. People involved in such incidents are set free immediately after being taken to the police station and are usually not charged.

Isin Önol: Although artists actively participated in the Gezi resistance, a lot of them declared their concerns about displaying works about it. You have displayed only one piece, in Germany, that tackled this process. Could you elaborate on that?

Hale Tenger: A day before the Gezi events, on May 30th, I had a meeting with René Block to discuss which work to present at an exhibition he was curating in Berlin. At that time *Swinging on the Stars*, a video installation of mine was being presented at Galeri Nev in Istanbul. The video consists of many three wise-monkeys, a re-occurring motif in my works, dancing in outer space, depicted in a slightly ghostly way similar to that of x-ray images. The lyrics of the popular song (titled Swinging on a Star) featured in the video includes parts such as "if you don't do your homework, you will turn into a mule, if you don't do this and that you will turn into a fish, pig" etc. The monkeys only opened their eyes, ears and mouth when such threats in lyrics were heard. We agreed to show this video in Berlin and René went back next morning. The next day the Gezi events started and I had my first experience of being pepper sprayed. That day it occurred to me that it would be unfair to show the video we had agreed upon, after all I had witnessed huge crowds on the streets. Afterwards I wrote to René explaining that I could not show that work, asking him to forgive me. He proposed to include my long letter as a manifesto in the exhibition and I replied that I would think about it. As time passed by, the turmoil cooled down; I had the idea of making a new version of the video and presenting both in a loop during the exhibition. In the new version, the three monkeys were wearing a gas mask each, with eyes and ears open, raising their fists in the air and singing along the famous song "Fire! We'll see!" (a popular political chant based on police spraying pepper or tear gas). This video was titled *¿HOPE?* and was my first work right after the Gezi events. In 2014, I made an artist's book with the same title. It was composed of selection of photographs and stills from videos I had taken during Gezi. The book was presented at Gezi-themed exhibition *Stay With Me* at the Apartment Project in Berlin, together with many other artists' books.

Isin Önol: We observe in that particular work that by placing question marks before and after the title, you question whether the Gezi period could be a source of hope, or at least you hoped that it would. Two years forward, what do you think of hope today? (2015)

Hale Tenger: Gezi events and the forums surrounding them were platforms of claiming and defending rights, with a measure of extent and attendance we've never seen before. This course of events gave hope to those who had lived under coups d'états and oppressive regimes for decades. Unfortunately, neither the laws of security that followed, nor the government's continuing oppressive politics promise any hope. However, if there will be a weakening of this oppressive authority it might be because of the corruption they are surrounded with and the conflicts within the ruling party. Hope appears only at this point. This party who had come into power ten years ago with promises of more freedom and less military tutelage became a tool of a centrist and oppressive regime itself. And that is the irony.

Isin Önol: I have to repeat my question here: How would you answer this question today, in 2017?

Hale Tenger: I was perhaps too hopeful again back in 2015, neither the corruption nor the economic distress has led to any positive changes. The government is even more authoritarian and oppressive. Actually, it is hard to call it a government; hardly any power is left of the parliament. It is a one-man regime. Nothing lasts forever, all oppressive regimes come to an end, and if that counts as of having hope I still have it.

Isin Önol: In September 2013, after Gezi, while the streets were still full of pepper gas and upside down with the protests, the Istanbul Biennial took place. Its conceptual frame had been built on public space, tackling urban issues that also lead to the start of Gezi events. However, that time the biennial could not take place on public space due to the ongoing violence on the streets. This was probably the most realistic and safe option due to high number of participants. However, it was criticized by various communities. For some, the biennial should have stayed in the public domain and should have continued as part of the battle for using public spaces freely. For others, the withdrawal of the biennial from public space in and of itself was a political statement. At the end of the day, it was not ethical to enable the use of public space by collaborating with local authorities who had been invading the public space in an oppressive manner, and it was not safe to use it unauthorized. What was your view and stance about this issue?

Hale Tenger: I think it was the correct decision; it would not have been reasonable for the Biennial organizers to request permission from local authorities that were in accord with the government's position.

Isin Önol: We are getting near to April 2015, where the hundredth year commemoration of the genocide will take place. When this piece is published, the related activities will be long over. One of them is a Wish Tree Project of yours; could you tell us about that one?

Hale Tenger: It was mentioned that the members of the Armenian diaspora who will join the hundredth year commemoration of the genocide would like to experience a ritual of tying up pieces of clothes with wishes on a tree in Taksim. The idea was of Nancy Kricorian and the *Wish Tree* proposal was from Osman Kavala. I accepted the proposal with pleasure as it is a ritual practiced in Anatolia as well and I had an earlier work titled *Wishing Tree* dating back to 1990. The metal tree sculpture that I built, reflecting this worldwide popular tradition formed a symbolic yet intensely sentimental space for the Armenians who came to Istanbul to commemorate their lost ones. In a short time, the branches of the tree were covered with pieces of clothes and ribbons with the names of the lost ones and wishes written on them. The *Wish Tree* will be displayed at Depo for some time after the Commemoration.

Isin Önol: It is very ironic that two years ago, we finished this interview with Depo, and its founder Osman Kavala. He was shockingly detained ten days ago, and although we all thought he would be released immediately, he was arrested after a quick court case. We don't know how long he will be imprisoned for. He is one of the strongest voices in arts and culture in Turkey, creating platforms for discussions about untouchable subjects such as Kurdistan, forced disappearances, Armenian Genocide… Now, together with him, all our hope for freedom of expression is imprisoned. Now it is November 2017. Where do we go from here?

Hale Tenger: I had a dream in which Özlem (Dalkıran, from Citizenship Association, former Helsinki Citizens Association, Istanbul, one of the arrested human rights advocates in Istanbul) was approaching me with a big smile on her face, and I was asking her how come she was there, the trial was due next week and with a cute hush gesture she was saying they released her early. I woke up so happy. On that same day I learned of Osman Kavala's detention, and was shocked that it had come to this. The following week all human rights advocates were released, but then Kavala was arrested. I am sure Kavala will be released as well, but they are stealing days from peoples' lives. It has become too absurd and I'm worried about how this unlawfulness will be remedied. Besides Turkey, the whole Middle East is again on the verge of new developments. While Syria is still unresolved, now hot news are coming from Saudi Arabia and Lebanon. We had thought the cold war had ended, but it actually never did. Turkey is in the middle of it too just like the rest of the Middle East.

Hale Tenger In her wide range of production Hale Tenger creates three dimensional narratives inspired by diverse historical, political and psychosocial references. Built by an unconventional use of materials, audio and video, her installations focus on presence and experience, a pivotal element in her practice.

By operating with the qualities of mood, sound, texture and affect, her installations, whether creating an uncanny atmosphere or a meditative one, trace out the relationship between presence and absence, material and intelligible. Tenger's narratives often oscillate between sameness and alterity, between fragility and persistence. The signs of oppression and repression therefore are recuperated by the signs of resistance and transition for healing and change.

Selected recent solo exhibitions include: Protocinema, NY (2015); Galeri Nev, Istanbul (2013); Smithsonian Institute, Washington (2011); Green Art Gallery, Dubai (2011).

She has participated in numerous biennials including: Venice (2017), Kwangju (2000), São Paulo (1994), Manifesta (1996), Istanbul (1992 and 1995), Havana (2003), Johannesburg (1998).

Her work has been featured in institutions including: Centre Pompidou, Espace Culturel Louis Vuitton, Paris; ARTER, SALT, Istanbul Modern, Istanbul; Museum Boijmans Van Beuningen, Rotterdam; NBK, Martin-Gropius-Bau, Berlin; tba21, Vienna; Palais des Beaux Arts de Lille; Carré d'Art Museum, Nimes; Museum Arnhem; The New Museum, New York.

Isin Önol (1977, Turkey) is a writer and curator based in Vienna and New York. She is a member of Center for the Study of Social Difference at Columbia University, New York. She works as a guest critic at the Arts & Design MFA program at Montclair University, New Jersey and as a visiting curator at the Social Design—Art as Urban Innovation MA Program at University of Applied Arts, Vienna. Since 2009, she has been working as an independent curator in Vienna and abroad. Before that, she leaded the Elgiz Museum of Contemporary Art as its director and curator in Istanbul for three years.

Önol is a Ph.D. Candidate at the Department of Cultural Studies, University of Applied Arts, Vienna, Austria. She has completed her Master of Advance Studies on Curating at ZHdK, Zürcher Hochschule der Kunst, Zürich, Switzerland (2009–2011). She participated to Ecole du Magasin, International Curatorial Training Programme, Centre National d'Art Contemporain, Grenoble, France and Gwangju Biennale International Curator Course, Gwangju, South Korea (2009). She received her MFA in Visual Arts and Visual Communication Design from Sabanci University (2003), and her BA in Art Education from Marmara University (2000), Istanbul, Turkey.